Authority and Speech

Authority and Speech

■ **Language, Society, and Self in the American Novel**

Louise K. Barnett

The University of Georgia Press

Athens and London

© 1993 by the University of Georgia Press
Athens, Georgia 30602
All rights reserved
Designed by Betty Palmer McDaniel
Set in ten on thirteen Linotype Walbaum
by Tseng Information Systems, Inc.

The paper in this book meets the guidelines for
permanence and durability of the Committee on
Production Guidelines for Book Longevity of the
Council on Library Resources.

Printed in the United States of America
97 96 95 94 93   C   5 4 3 2 1

Library of Congress Cataloging in Publication Data
Barnett, Louise K.
    Authority and speech : language, society, and self in the
    American novel / Louise K. Barnett.
        p. cm.
    Includes bibliographical references and index.
    ISBN 0-8203-1520-6 (alk. paper)
        1. American fiction—History and criticism.   2. Speech in
literature.   3. English language—Spoken English—United States.
4. Literature and society—United States.   5. Language and
culture—United States.   6. Authority in literature.   7. Self in
literature.
I. Title.
PS374.S735B36   1993
813.009—dc20   92-31434
                                     CIP

British Library Cataloging in Publication Data available

For Rob and Greg

Verbal discourse is a social phenomenon—social throughout its entire range and in each and every of its factors, from the sound image to the furthest reaches of abstract meaning.

M. M. BAKHTIN,
The Dialogic Imagination

We are in a position to understand why social facts can strike people as things—their being socially real is sufficient for that.

KENT BACH AND ROBERT M. HARNISH,
Linguistic Communication and Speech Acts

Contents

Acknowledgments

■ In a profession where we all have enough to read and write, it's a pleasure to acknowledge colleagues who generously assume additional burdens. I am grateful to Gillian Brown, Uli Knoepflmacher, Janet Larson, David Leverenz, and Alan Nadel for reading some part of this book and giving me valuable suggestions. To Janet Gabler-Hover I am especially indebted for a rigorous reading of the entire manuscript. As always, my husband, Robert J. Barnett, Jr., was the last word on matters of style. Researchers can have no better friends than librarians: in their respective libraries Evelyn Lyons and Joan Lewis were most helpful to me. I also wish to thank Karen Orchard, my editor at the University of Georgia Press, and Jean Ross, my copyeditor. Jill Millerand and Jean Mecka were endlessly patient in formatting and producing the various drafts of my manuscript. Needless to say, none of the above is responsible for those occasions when I didn't follow their good advice.

Portions of some chapters have been previously published in different form in the following places: chapter one, *ESQ*, 29 (1983), 16–24; *Studies in American Fiction*, 11 (1983), 139–51; and *Desert, Garden, Margin, Range: Literature on the American Frontier* (New York: G. K. Hall, 1992); chapter two, *Papers on Language and Literature*, 25 (1989), 59–77; chapter three, *College Literature*, 6 (1979), 221–31; chapter four, *Novel*, 16 (1983), 215–29; *Connecticut Review*, 11 (1989), 54–63; chapter five, *University of Mississippi Studies in English*, 8 (1990), 168–84; and chapter six, *The Centennial Review*, 30 (1986), 400–414.

Note on Editions Cited

■ Quotations from the primary texts listed below will be followed by page numbers in parentheses.

Barthelme, Donald. *Snow White*. New York: Atheneum, 1967.

Clemens, Samuel L. *Adventures of Huckleberry Finn*. Ed. Walter Blair and Victor Fischer. *The Works of Mark Twain*. Vol. 8. Berkeley: University of California Press, 1988.

Cooper, James Fenimore. *The Deerslayer, or The First War-Path*. *The Writings of James Fenimore Cooper*. Ed. James Franklin Beard. Albany: State University of New York Press, 1987.

Faulkner, William. *The Hamlet*. New York: Random House, 1956.

Fitzgerald, F. Scott. *The Great Gatsby*. New York: Charles Scribner's Sons, 1925.

Hawthorne, Nathaniel. *The Scarlet Letter*. *Centenary Edition of the Works of Nathaniel Hawthorne*. Ed. William Charvat et al. Vol. 1. Columbus: Ohio State University Press, 1962.

Hemingway, Ernest. *The Sun Also Rises*. New York: Charles Scribner's Sons, 1970.

Hurston, Zora Neale. *Their Eyes Were Watching God*. New York: Harper & Row, 1990.

James, Henry. *The Ambassadors*. Vols. 21, 22. *The Novels and Tales of Henry James*. New York Edition. 24 vols. New York: Charles Scribner's Sons, 1909.

Melville, Herman. *Billy Budd, Sailor (An Inside Narrative)*. Ed. Harrison Hayford and Merton M. Sealts, Jr. Chicago: University of Chicago Press, 1962.

———. *The Confidence-Man: His Masquerade*. Vol. 10 in *The Writings of Herman Melville*. Ed. Harrison Hayford et al. 15 vols. Evanston and Chicago: Northwestern University Press and the Newberry Library, 1984.

———. *Moby-Dick or The Whale*. Vol. 6 in *The Writings of Herman Melville*. Ed. Harrison Hayford, et al. 15 vols. Evanston and Chicago: Northwestern University Press and the Newberry Library, 1988.

———. *The Piazza Tales and Other Prose Pieces, 1839–1860*. Vol. 9 in *The Writings of Herman Melville*. Ed. Harrison Hayford et al. 15 vols. Evanston and Chicago: Northwestern University Press and the Newberry Library, 1970.

———. *Pierre: or, The Ambiguities*. Ed. Harrison Hayford et al. *The Writings of Herman Melville*. Vol. 7. Evanston and Chicago: Northwestern University Press and the Newberry Library, 1971.

Pynchon, Thomas. *The Crying of Lot 49*. Philadelphia: J. B. Lippincott, 1966.

Stowe, Harriet Beecher. *Uncle Tom's Cabin or Life Among The Lowly*. New York: Viking Penguin, 1981.

Vonnegut, Kurt. *Breakfast of Champions*. New York: Delacorte Press, 1973.

West, Nathanael. *The Complete Works of Nathanael West*. New York: Farrar, Straus and Giroux, 1957.

Wharton, Edith. *The House of Mirth*. New York: Charles Scribner's Sons, 1905.

Authority and Speech

Introduction

The longer I continue, the more it seems to me that the formation of discourses and the genealogy of knowledge needs to be analysed, not in terms of types of consciousness, modes of perception and forms of ideology, but in terms of tactics and strategies of power.
MICHEL FOUCAULT, *Power/Knowledge*

■ This is a book about the changing relationship of personal and social expression in the direct discourse of fictive speakers in the American novel. Like all forms of language, speech—including fictive speech—is a field on which opposing forces of social and personal intentionality struggle for dominance. Much of our speech can be broken down into an unembellished statement of individual desire, a simple model on the order of wanting or not wanting ———, and the veneer of language that makes it socially acceptable: "Please sir, may I have some more" versus "Gimme food." The theoretical dichotomy between naked and clothed desire does not, of course, reflect the complexities and subtleties of real language practice in which a speaker has been so acculturated into verbal decorum that it becomes an unthinking part of individual intention in speaking, as it may be in other kinds of behavior. Under ordinary circumstances, if I want you to get out of my way I won't even consider pushing you aside, much less actually do so; nor will I yell, "Get outta my way." I will automatically choose a polite form of communication such as a gentle tap or a "Please excuse me." In this case social and individual intentions converge since society and I both prefer such encounters to be harmonious.

The focus of my study is instead that portion of the terrain where these intentions diverge, where individual—in this case fictive—speakers and society are open antagonists, or where ideological premises that the speaker is unaware of constrain or manipulate his or her intentions. Apart from the considerable question of individual linguistic facility, a number of social determinants shape spoken and written utterances: grammatical and syntactical rules, conventions of discourse, the amount of "linguistic capital" available to the speaker/

writer, and the hidden agendas of a myriad of competing ideologies in the public domain.[1] Direct expressions of pure and unironic individual intentionality are rare and generally unacceptable in ordinary social discourse.[2]

To explore this contested field of discourse I intend to rely primarily upon two related theoretical bases: speech-act theory, which seeks to assess the authority of utterances by determining their relationship to constitutive rules, and sociolinguistics, which approaches the same issue of authority from the perspective of social requirements. Both kinds of "rules" are socially determined, that is, are based upon conventions of behavior within a particular sociolinguistic community, and they furnish conventional norms for fictive as well as actual speech.

In providing "an account of the conditions of intelligibility, of what it means to mean in a community, of the procedures which must be instituted before one can even be said to be understood,"[3] speech-act theory offers a framework for analyzing speech as meaningful communication, as an act that expresses intentions and leads to consequences. Its first formulations as a theory are associated with J. L. Austin, the originator who, like Ferdinand de Saussure, bequeathed to his followers more ideas than published texts. Continuing Austin's work, John R. Searle has systematized speech-act theory in a number of publications, the most important of which are *Speech Acts* (1969) and *Expression and Meaning: Studies in the Theory of Speech Acts* (1979). Throughout this study I use Searle's classification of speech acts into five types: assertives, directives, commissives, expressives, and declarations. As he describes these categories in a summary statement, "We tell people how things are, we try to get them to do things, we commit ourselves to doing things, we express our feelings and attitudes and we bring about changes through our utterances."[4] By rigorously analyzing the constitutive rules for utterances and by insisting upon speech as a form of action—that is, collapsing the traditional distinction between saying and doing—speech-act theory establishes the conditions necessary for successful performance and makes it possible to assess the success or failure of speech as communication.

Searle continues his taxonomy by identifying the conditions for performing a given speech act. Requirements for giving an order, for example, are as follows: "The preparatory conditions include that the speaker should be in a position of authority over the hearer, the sincerity condition is that the speaker wants the ordered act done, and the essential condition has to do with the fact that the speaker intends the utterance as an attempt to get the hearer to do the act."[5] (In other words, Starbuck would not fulfill the most significant preparatory condition for giving an order to Captain Ahab—unless he set aside the conventional basis for such authority by, for instance, waving a gun at his captain, a move he fleetingly contemplates.) Further, a speech act that expressed insincerity—"I don't mean what I'm saying"—or violated the essential condition—"I don't care if you obey my order or not"—would be defective as a speech act, although we can always imagine circumstances that would in fact override any speech-act condition. Speech-act theory assumes that intention precedes expression, but at the same time it assumes that intention is accessible only *in* expression.

Searle also lists twelve "significant dimensions of variation in which illocutionary acts differ from one another," of which the most useful is the direction of fit, whether the utterance attempts to get words to conform to the world—as do assertions, descriptions, and explanations—or instead seeks the world's conformity to words—as do orders, requests, and promises.[6] Declarations are unique in moving in both directions: they bring about and also describe a state of being, as when someone in authority tells you "you're hired"—or fired. Often the most serious verbal clashes spring from confusion of the direction of fit. Zora Neale Hurston's Jody Starks verbally orders his wife to behave as he prefers, in reality coercing her to tailor her actions to his words while he maintains the fantasy that his words merely describe rather than manipulate.

Two other terms are necessary to complete the speech-act vocabulary: illocutionary act and perlocutionary effect.[7] Following Austin, Searle describes an utterance with intentional meaning and conventional force as an illocutionary act (as opposed to uttering a series of sounds without meaning). A speaker says "hello," to use Searle's example, in order to perform the act of greeting, an act recognized as such by a hearer because within that linguistic community "hello" is a conventional form of address. If the speaker used "hello" to mean "good-bye," the hearer could not be expected to get the illocutionary point of the utterance as intended by the speaker unless a private agreement obtained between speaker and hearer to use "hello" with this contrary meaning. Without the complicity of a hearer, such a condition of intentional meaning but unconventional force characterizes much of Jay Gatsby's speech. As a result, it seldom rings true.

The perlocutionary effect of an utterance, as opposed to its illocutionary force or point, is a result or consequence that the speaker expects to achieve by means of the illocutionary act. As Searle explains, "the meaning of the sentence 'Get out' ties it to a particular intended perlocutionary effect, namely getting the hearer to leave. The meanings of 'Hello' and 'I promise' do not."[8] For Searle, when a speaker says "hello," a hearer's *recognition* of being greeted is all that the speaker's intention encompasses in speech-act terms. I would suggest, rather, that few utterances made in the hearing of others are limited to such a purely illocutionary intention: even the simple "hello" expects the perlocutionary effect of acknowledgment in some form or other. Such expected consequences make more of a difference than Searle recognizes in his example of the speaker who speaks merely out of a sense of duty without caring whether the hearer believes him or not. The response to a promise may be quite different if the hearer does not believe the speaker or does not believe that the speaker can carry it out, regardless of intention. Many legal contracts are formalized written promises the terms of which, Searle might argue, the recipient need not care if the promiser understands or intends to honor: the hearer/ lender can repossess the promiser/borrower's goods regardless. If we consider the recent savings and loan debacle, however, it becomes apparent that such a cavalier disregard for the promiser's intentions or ability to make the promised payments ultimately leads to disaster.[9]

In short, perlocutionary effects are everywhere, and Austin's remark that "language can never be forearmed against all possible cases that may arise"[10] can also be applied to speech-act theory. Critics such as Mary Louise Pratt have noted that in spite of its concern with the reality of performance, speech-act theory seems actually to describe an ideal competence. She writes that "people always speak from and in a socially constituted position, a position that is, moreover, constantly shifting, and defined in a speech situation by the intersection of many different forces."[11] What is "systematically missing," she finds, are "affective relations, power relations, and the question of shared goals."[12] This kind of grounding must supplement speech-act analysis in order to fully understand an utterance, for useful as speech-act theory is in revealing the structure of utterances and some of the conditions that make them successful or unsuccessful, sociolinguistics offers equally helpful paradigms for discovering and evaluating the social dimensions of speaking. Here a convenient point of entry and general premise is Pierre Bourdieu's description of the difference between a sociological and a linguistic critique:

In place of grammaticalness it [the sociological critique] puts the notion of acceptability, or, to put it another way, in place of "the" language (*langue*), the notion of the legitimate language. In place of relations of communication (or symbolic interaction) it puts relations of symbolic power, and so replaces the question of the meaning of speech with the question of the value and power of speech. Lastly, in place of specifically linguistic competence, it puts symbolic capital, which is inseparable from the speaker's position in the social structure.[13]

Bourdieu's perspective deemphasizes the purely linguistic competence that philosophers of language invoke in favor of a socially derived legitimacy or authority. Talk exchange, like other forms of social interaction, is an arena of power as well as an economic transaction between a producer and a consumer; it cannot be divorced from a speaker's entire "capital of authority."[14] (A character who is verbally impotent, like Tom Buchanan in *The Great Gatsby*, or silent, like Flem Snopes in *The Hamlet*, can nevertheless exert power because his capital of authority is based on other things: Tom's enormous wealth, Flem's unbeatable financial acumen.)

The requirement of authority links sociolinguistics to speech-act theory, for the conditions that make utterances effective are socially determined. A speaker must have extralinguistic authority to perform in words—to pronounce people married, divorced, or dead—to give an order, or to report on an event. In short, speakers must have socially recognized credentials—or the facsimile thereof—to perform speech acts felicitously.[15]

Sociolinguists such as Bourdieu provide valuable analyses of real language use. M. M. Bakhtin is more directly relevant to my enterprise because he brings the perspective of descriptive sociolinguistics into literary criticism. For Bakhtin, in the words of Allon White, language is "the concrete and ceaseless flow of *utterance* produced in dialogues between speakers in specific social and historical contexts."[16] This emphasis on the social dimension distinguishes my focus from that of deconstruction, which treats texts "not as specific performances within a social discourse, but as abstract repertoires of competence."[17] Bakhtin, on the other hand, repeatedly calls attention to the conflict operating in and through language between the individual speaker and society, insisting that "language is not a neutral medium that passes freely and easily into the private property of the speaker's intentions. . . . Expropriating it, forcing it to submit to one's own intentions and accents, is a difficult and complicated process." [18] Sharing the condition of actual speech, fictive speech inescapably embodies this struggle. [19]

■ During the last hundred years the confident speech of mid-nineteenth century novels has devolved into a contemporary lack of articulation bordering on silence, a process that has increasingly shifted authority from the pole of individual expression to that of society and its attendant ideologies. This phenomenon appears to be strongly linked to a growing distrust of all forms of "public language," Basil Bernstein's useful term for that language which emphasizes "a powerful sense of allegiance and loyalty to the group, its forms and its aspiration." [20] The line between language and public language is difficult to draw since language as a system is always both social and coercive. What I refer to as public language is that language whose appeal to uniformity of perception, as well as thought, is particularly blatant, a discourse that eschews a total or unbiased view and functions prescriptively to maintain the values and attitudes of some collective entity. The vision of the world inculcated by public language is inevitably some sort of official or authorized version.

The group Bernstein refers to may be any definable collective entity that asserts some sort of authority over the individual; in my discussion of literary texts society, with all of its usual meanings, will best designate this authority: society as nation, as other people, as institution, as behavioral norm, as value system, as class structure, as political system, as—above all—ideology. In short, society is the man-made context of the individual life, and as such, a presence in any given novel although different texts formulate it differently. Moreover, as Elizabeth Langland writes in *Society in the Novel,* "there are a number of behavioral taboos that form the deep structure of Western society and need no justification or explanation at all." [21] Reader, writer, and character share a multitude of such assumptions that need not be made explicit in the text, and they include positive prescriptions and descriptive data as well as taboos.

Until a fairly recent period of literary history, the novel was identified as the genre that expressed in fiction the dynamic of the individual and society. According to their differing ideologies, angles of vision, and modes of presentation, novelists thought of their texts as representations of an external world whose existence was unquestioned. In Ian

Watt's standard definition, the novel is "a full and authentic report of human experience, and is therefore under an obligation to satisfy its reader with such details of the story as the individuality of the actors concerned, the particulars of the times and places of their actions, details which are presented through a more largely referential use of language than is common in other literary forms." [22] This commitment to an elaborate authenticity entails certain assumptions about the nature of the world. According to Murray Baumgarten, "Realistic prose assumes the natural attitude, posits the world's existence, predicates the notion of cause-and-effect, values foreground over and against background, and turns into a positivist instrument for the description (if not the control) of the world. . . . The novel thus comes into being as an artistic mode of exploring the world, thus complementing the bourgeois mode of commerce and science." [23] Both Watt and Baumgarten define the novel as a genre whose rationalistic principles describe a world that is not only real but knowable—knowable, it might be added, in the orderly categories and detailed specificity that are well suited to a middle-class Western worldview.

As the novel moved into the twentieth century, it gradually abandoned the assumption of knowability and concentrated upon forms of private experience subjectively portrayed and increasingly removed from social significance. While novelistic protagonists had always been in some sense socially problematic—i.e., not readily assimilated by society—it had been the business of the novel to punish such individuals or change them in some way that would effect their integration into the group. Society was often criticized in this process, but not from a nihilistic perspective; even deeply flawed, it remained the source of authority and necessary context for individual experience. "In the nineteenth century," Leo Bersani observes, "realistic novelists usually judge their society with great severity. But the critical judgments are qualified by a form which provides this society with a reassuring myth about itself. Their fiction gives us an image of social fragmentation contained within the order of significant form, and it thereby suggests that the chaotic fragments are somehow viable and morally redeemable." [24] The modern novel instead supported its protagonists in their antisocial stances and no longer required their commerce with a collective entity viewed more and more as too inimical for any reconciliation. The energy of the genre reversed its flow from centrifugal to centripetal; rather than bringing the individual into conformity with society, the novel asserted the validity of its avoidance and finally its irrelevance.[25] Loss of confidence in social goals and institutions ultimately entails a loss of confidence in the language that traditionally connected fictive and real worlds and the replacement of conventional ordering processes in the novel with modernist techniques: the flux of stream-of-consciousness, indeterminacy, and the uncommitted stance of impersonal narration. The postmodern novel questions all forms of literary and social institutionality, frequently through a mocking lack of seriousness. Deemphasized as a legitimate concern of the individual, society is nevertheless a palpable presence in the modern novel; in the postmodern era it exists only as a parodic version of itself.

The literary process which at first glance exalts consciousness as the only significant arena of experience, and then as the sole arbiter of what constitutes reality, ends by reducing the individual to inconsequentiality in much the same way that it first diminished the public world. Just as the twentieth-century novel moves away from the idea of society as the source and instrument of humanistic values and positive forms of order, it similarly abandons belief in the individual as capable of ordering life and creating value.

The reversal of traditional background and foreground gestalten underlies many of the literary developments associated with the breakdown of character as a coherent entity in the modern novel.[26] Qualities formerly attributed to people, such as stability and knowability, are now preempted by things. Consequently, an increasingly independent world of objects and forces now claims centers of novelistic energy and attention once occupied by characters. Joel Weinsheimer states that "under the aegis of semiotic criticism, characters lose their privilege, their central status, and their definition. . . . As segments of a closed text, characters at most are patterns of recurrence, motifs which are continually recontextualized in other motifs."[27] Weinsheimer's ahistorical semiotic argument differs from my own sociolinguistic explanation, which envisions this situation as a twentieth-century phenomenon. Moreover, unlike Weinsheimer and Shlomith Rimmon-Kenan, whose division of character under the rubrics of story and text is a happy reconciliation of the demands of mimesis and semiotics, my interest is in the speech of characters rather than in character construction.[28]

But more compelling than this redistribution of power in terms of content is the diminution of *all* content and the more insistent claims of technique. Although language had never been a transparent medium for conveying plot, character, and other novelistic elements, before the twentieth century writers generally behaved as if it were. In the post-modern period, a genre that once metaphorically or metonymically recreated an external world and often went to great lengths to conceal its status as fiction evolved into one which turned from referentiality to flaunt and celebrate its fictive nature.

Inevitably, the modern loss of confidence in public language in particular has contributed to the establishment of a self-creating and self-reflexive linguistic universe freed from mimesis and referentiality much as the development of photography freed painting. Society and the individual, life and literature, all fragment and dissolve into uncertainty under the diverse pressures and complexities of the modern world; the world moving from the nineteenth to the twentieth century simply became too complicated to be explained by any mono-mythic system. Scientific relativity; the capitalistic economic system with its cycles of recession and inflation; consumerism; megabureaucracy; technology; and the intellectual paradigms of Darwin, Marx, Einstein, and Freud all challenge cherished human assumptions and values both individually and collectively. As a result, they have undermined our social institutions, including language.

But given the nature of language as a social institution whose conventions are, if artificial, long established, what Roland Barthes calls "the most momentous of all breaks—that from the language of society" —may involve little less than a break with language itself.[29] While there is something paradoxical in a writer's falling silent as a strategy of self-expression or renouncing writing because it can be done only with words, a number of writers have envisioned silence as the only uncompromised response to the tarnished mediacy of words.[30] This sense of language as an inherently inadequate medium is a philosophical concept, a universal property of Language (*langue*), while what we encounter in life and literature is always *parole,* the product of a particular time and place—in short, historical discourse.[31] "Language" is a hypothetical construct: what we speak and write is never divorced from the specifics of time, place, and culture or, for that matter, from personal circumstance. Just as writers must accept the constraints of a particular rhyme scheme in order to write a sonnet, so they must accept the given of philosophical limitation in order to write at all. These are the demands of the medium, the chosen art form. Similarly, sociolinguistic perspectives such as Bourdieu's premise that all spoken words are impregnated with the speaker's social class and Bakhtin's assertion that the word is "an always shifting, always changing means of social communication" do not necessarily lead to a blanket condemnation of public language.[32] Rather than proceeding inevitably from the nature of language or literature, the repudiation of public language because it has become dysfunctional—lying, inflexible, oppressive, or merely worn out—grows out of a specific historical and cultural matrix in which actual abuses have become widespread and blatant.

Perhaps the most obvious way that twentieth-century novelists have initiated a dialogue with silence is through the attenuation of social discourse, a natural corollary of the devaluation of character and of public language. As Pratt remarks, "At the level of the fictional speaker's text, we find in many twentieth-century novels a tendency to increase the limitations on the fictional speaker's ability to fulfill his communicative purpose."[33] The author can transform his novelistic world into a self-contained verbal space; characters, however, are part of the world transformed rather than agents of transformation, and their declining power of speech itself protests the social corruption of language. Indeed, while twentieth-century writers go on writing, enlarging their own privileged domain, their characters literally fall silent, reduced to onlookers in a genre that once gave them major speaking parts.

■ Since the novel is both a written form of discourse and an artwork, we conventionally assume that it is both a stable text and a finished product, revised and refined before publication to be a meaningful communication. The degree will vary not only among individual texts but among genres. I have no wish to attempt a definition of literature, but surely one of the properties we commonly attribute to literature is the kind of meticulous craftsmanship produced by revision. The actual relation of the text to such a process is not germane: Shakespeare supposedly blotted few lines, but we experience his poetry as highly wrought.[34] "Art," Roland Barthes writes, "does not acknowledge the existence of noise (in the informational sense of the word). This is precisely what distinguishes it from 'life,' which offers only a 'blurred' communication."[35] One specific form of life which might readily be substituted in Barthes's statement is speech, which may be garbled, inaudible, drowned out by other sounds, inappropriate to the occasion, hasty, interrupted, wandering, or otherwise "blurred"; its recipient may be inattentive, uncomprehending, or unable to hear. We can imagine circumstances that would interfere with the process of reading a novel, some of which are the same as those which can disrupt oral communication; but since the written text is complete and permanent, an object, its reading may be postponed until more favorable conditions obtain or may be repeated for increased comprehension. Because a novel is the product of a demanding prepublication process, it is not likely to suffer from those hazards of communication attributable to the speaker rather than to transmission or reception.

By virtue of its incorporation into the novel, fictive—i.e., represented—speech escapes the varieties of noise which can blur an oral communication, but it also lacks many of the aspects which enhance the communicability of natural speech or reveal personal speech idiosyncracies: vocal features such as tone, volume, stress, and quality of articulation; facial expressions; accompanying body language; actions simultaneous with speech; and mannerisms such as those listed by Norman Page: "hesitations, false starts, repetitions, corrections, contradictions and changes of direction."[36] All of these elements may be represented, the nonverbal ones translated into a supporting linguistic context, but the abstraction characteristic of all representations of experience in language will be particularly felt here; even indicating who is speaking in an extended passage of dialogue can be a problem. As Mark Twain observed, "The moment 'talk' is put into print you recognize that it is not what it was when you heard it; you perceive that an immense something has disappeared from it."[37]

As a written utterance and as a representation, fictive speech is doubly removed from 'talk,' no longer perishable and no longer utilitarian because it is not an historical speech event. As part of the language of fiction it operates according to conventions of diminished responsibility which, in Searle's words, "enable the speaker to use words with their literal meanings without undertaking the commitments that are normally required by those meanings," the commitments which relate illocutionary acts to the world.[38] But Searle's formulation is too dismissive. It must also be said that within and to the world of fiction, language can be as fully (or as imperfectly) committed as it is in the world of actuality. In the real world there are real consequences to speech; in the world of the novel there are fictive consequences that *represent* those of the real world. Should the radio and the narrator of *A Farewell to Arms* both report that rain is falling in Milan, we classify the information as belonging to different orders of being, historical reality and fiction, although fiction is a general and imprecise category in this regard and must be subdivided at least into mimetic and nonmimetic. Each utterance functions according to the conditions of its context. If I go out on the streets of Milan after hearing the broadcast, I assume that I may get wet, whereas if I simply read that it is raining in Milan in *A Farewell to Arms*, I have no expectations about the weather in that city. I do expect that, given the kind of novel *A Farewell to Arms* is, if Frederic Henry and Catherine Barkley go out into fictive Milan after Frederic's announcement, they will encounter rain.

Since they function in different worlds, the assertions of meteorologists and characters in novels are more readily differentiated than those of authors and characters, both fictive voices within the novel regardless of what kind of narrative persona the author chooses to assume.[39] At its most extreme, the difference is between a divine omniscience and human fallibility, but even when the authorial voice appears to relinquish some of its powers, its utterances are potentially more authoritative, and always less restricted, than any character's voice. The authorial voice creates and controls not only the text as a whole but the specific contexts in which the characters' voices are inscribed. It speaks at great length, and it commonly projects an aura of greater reliability, not only because it is not under the pressures of social interaction which can distort a character's utterance, but because its responsibility for the entire fiction automatically privileges it. We ordinarily endow this voice with the same good faith that we impute to other speakers.[40]

Narrator and character may be the same person—Frederic Henry, narrator of *A Farewell to Arms*; and Frederic Henry, a character speaking to other characters within the narrative—yet the two voices will be distinguishable, not necessarily as verbal structures but insofar as the requirements of different audiences and different contexts shape them. The narrator's audience is the reader; the fictive speaker's audience is at least two-tiered, the recipient or recipients of speech within the novel and the reader outside it, to which may be added an intruding author. As a character involved in a conversation, Frederic Henry tells Catherine Barkley that he loves her; as the narrator of the novel he tells the reader the contrary: "I knew I did not love Catherine Barkley nor had any idea of loving her. This was a game, like bridge, in which you said things instead of playing cards."[41] The reader's understanding of the conversational situation in effect when Frederic's lie occurs supports the direct statement of the narrator:

> She looked at me. "And you do love me?"
>
> "Yes."
>
> "You did say you loved me. didn't you?"
>
> "Yes," I lied. "I love you." I had not said it before. (31)

In order to continue their relationship, as he wishes, Frederic must answer Catherine's repeated questions in the affirmative, but as narrator addressing the reader he has no reason to conceal his true feelings. Within the traditional novel atypical narrators readily come to mind: madmen, children, and those who might be lumped together as no better than they should be as narrators because they reveal themselves to be biased, quirky, self-deceived, unintelligent, or insensitive—in short, unreliable. The list of such possibilities is long, but we initially assume that the narrator is reliable just as we initially expect that any novelistic world will conform to some plausible model of the real world.[42]

If the authorial voice has powerful advantages, fictive speech has the dramatic immediacy that characterizes the dynamic and competitive process of conversational interaction. Compared to the pronouncements of the authorial voice, its unmediated nature has experiential validity for the reader, the impact of showing rather than telling. A longer passage of the dialogue between Frederic Henry and Catherine Barkley will most cogently demonstrate the difference:

> She looked at me, "And you do love me?"
>
> "Yes."
>
> "You did say you loved me, didn't you?"
>
> "Yes," I lied. "I love you." I had not said it before.
>
> "And you call me Catherine?"
>
> "Catherine." We walked on a way and were stopped under a tree.
>
> "Say, 'I've come back to Catherine in the night.' "
>
> "I've come back to Catherine in the night."
>
> "Oh, darling, you have come back, haven't you?"
>
> "Yes."
>
> "I love you so and it's been awful. You won't go away?"
>
> "No. I'll always come back."
>
> "Oh. I love you so. Please put your hand there again."
>
> "It's not been away." I turned her so I could see her face when I kissed her and I saw that her eyes were shut. I kissed both her shut eyes. (31)

With the exception of line four, where Frederic indicates that he has lied, that he had not yet said that he loved Catherine, the only authorial telling which supplements the dialogue fleshes out the context with accompanying physical movements of the characters. Even the assertion of line four is descriptive rather than evaluative. It simply puts on record that Frederic had not yet said "I love you" to Catherine—a revelation of Catherine's anxiety more than Frederic's feelings toward her. Catherine's insistence, and her assertiveness in a matter in which her role would ordinarily be that of the recipient, are signs of deviant rather than normative speech. Instead of the standard "Please call me Catherine" or "Will you call me Catherine?" she says, "And you call me Catherine?"—a statement masquerading as a question that erroneously suggests the confirmation of a condition already in effect. Along with her imagining that Frederic has already said that he loves her, and her emphasis on his return to her, this is part of a fantasy that an intimate relationship is in progress instead of a brief acquaintance. Although Catherine actively initiates and directs, formally playing the dominant role in the conversation, the syntax and substance of her utterances exemplify insecurity. Frederic, who passively acquiesces to all of her demands, actually has more power, the power to give or withhold the reassurance she pleads for. He gives that reassurance minimally, when she asks, "Oh, darling, you have come back, haven't you?" and he responds, "Yes" (31). In addition to direction, all of the conversational energy is Catherine's; Frederic mechanically follows where she leads, but with no evident enthusiasm.[43] After the completion of the exchange, the narrative voice explains his position:

> I thought she was probably a little crazy. It was all right if she was. I did not care what I was getting into. This was better than going every evening to the house for officers where the girls climbed all over you and put your cap on backward as a sign of affection between their trips upstairs with brother officers. I knew I did not love Catherine Barkley nor had any idea of loving her. This was a game, like bridge, in which you said things instead of playing cards. (31)

Much of what Frederic tells the reader directly could be readily deduced from his conversation with Catherine: his lack of enthusiasm suggests that he does not love her; the brief and mechanical responses extracted by her promptings ritualize the talk so that it seems more like a game than an ordinary conversation; and Frederic's willingness to say what is expected of him indicates a readily imagined motive for continuing the relationship. What the passage of narrative telling does supply by confirming the reader's speculation is certainty, a momentary resolution that is one of the satisfactions of aesthetic experience.[44] When resolution and certainty are absent, as they often are in postmodernist texts, the reader accustomed to traditional novels is apt to be uneasy, prey to a deepseated conviction that since the literary construct *can* provide order and significance to an extent that life cannot, it ought to do so.

Fictive speech and authorial telling, in whatever form, work in this complementary fashion to create the traditional novel. The first represents natural speech in writing, and as such it provides unmediated data and character interaction; the second represents a written form of discourse, removed from the give and take of talk exchange and therefore more studied and authoritative. But what is most significant in distinguishing the two kinds of fictive voice is the difference between the freedom conferred by the literary context versus the restrictions of the speech situation. The authorial voice can speak when it pleases; characters can speak only when spoken to, as it were, or only when the authorial voice chooses to be silent and allow them to speak. Moreover, it has almost unlimited freedom to say what it pleases, and in whatever manner: to include newspaper headlines, popular songs, mathematical formulae, and other exotic materials; to chat, ruminate, meditate, pontificate, moralize, digress—all this and much more.

Fictive speech is capable of all of these modes and subjects as well, but not as easily, and thus in practice it seldom has the range and flexibility of the authorial voice. Beyond the conventions and rules which govern all language use, it is doubly responsible: it must observe the conditions of an encounter which is both linguistic and social. As Bakhtin writes, "The immediate social situation and its immediate social participants determine the 'occasional' form and style of an utterance. The deeper layers of its structure are determined by more sustained and more basic social connections with which the speaker is in contact."[45] The unwritten rules of social discourse apply to fictive speakers, not their authors, along with such extralinguistic factors as the "capital of authority" that each speaker commands and the type of social occasion which furnishes the context for their talk. For these reasons,

the role of language as a social instrument is more directly apparent in
fictive speech than in authorial utterance.

■ The chapters that follow will look at the American
novel chronologically, beginning with the major antebellum romantic writers who use public language successfully and unselfconsciously:
Cooper, Hawthorne, Stowe, and, at first, Melville. As he experienced
more and more commercial difficulty, Melville moved from the verbal
confidence of his early work, culminating in the extraordinary richness
of *Moby-Dick*, to various forms of linguistic withdrawal: the silence
of Bartleby, the corruption of the word in *The Confidence-Man*, the
tragic failure of communication in *Billy Budd*. Yet the striking moder-
nity of Melville's increasingly obscure texts was neither realized nor
assimilated by the literary tradition of his time, and accordingly, it is
Adventures of Huckleberry Finn (1884), the book that begins the modern novel in so many respects, that marks a turn away from the ability
of characters to use language with confidence within the mainstream
of American literature. From serving as the cooperative vehicle of
speakers in dealing with ethical and epistemological issues, language
becomes conspicuous as a problem in its own right, a barrier to, rather
than a means of, communication and self-expression. From *Huckleberry Finn* to postmodernist texts, a continuum of positions stretches
between the extremes of fluency and virtual silence; my examination
of a variety of these seeks to demonstrate the widespread occurrence of
an increasingly self-conscious verbal skepticism which has contributed
to the radical alteration of the novel.

A large number of texts could be adduced in support of this view,
but I have chosen to concentrate on a group of novels which, I believe,
will continue to be valued as major achievements of American literature while the canon expands to include previously neglected works.[46]
(Moreover, even were they to lose favored novel status tomorrow, the
long history that most have had as privileged texts would justify such an
examination.) These particular novels also repay the analysis of their
direct discourse: more than simply containing a certain amount of talk,
they are in some meaningful and distinguishing way *about* speech acts.
All illuminate from different perspectives the central issue of authority
in fictive speech. My last principle of selection is the most idiosyncratic.
Although these texts all exemplify my thesis and reveal other kinds

of intertextuality, they do not replicate each other. Each renders the struggle for authority on the field of speech in a distinctive voice.

■ In her book *The Body in Pain* Elaine Scarry writes about the euphemistic names given to various forms of torture, words whose original meanings are innocuous: "To attach any name, any word to the willful infliction of this bodily agony is to make language and civilization participate in their own destruction; the specific names chosen merely make this subversion more overt."[47] Revisited in our own time, this is the already familiar ground of George Orwell's "Politics and the English Language" and other texts that offer extreme examples of public language malpractice. At this end of the spectrum public language is corrupt and corrupting, while at its positive end this shared discourse makes it possible for people to act together and to enjoy the security of belonging to groups at all levels of social organization. If my study focuses on the abuses or inadequacies of public language in spite of these positive aspects, it does so because protagonists in the American novel tend to be at odds with society in some form and to some extent, and therefore their linguistic aims diverge from those of whatever group they are defined against. The subject of my inquiry, that fictive space where the desire for self-expression encounters a collective will, is necessarily a place of conflict, one in which competing voices seek to wield authority over the word.

Part One

From Confidence to Skepticism in the Nineteenth-Century Novel

Prologue

■ In spite of the "numerous demands for an independent literature" which Benjamin Spencer documents in *The Quest for Nationality*, the rapport of the American author with society was tenuous from the start.[1] Unlike his counterpart in England, who "on the whole enjoyed a stable relationship with his class, his audience, and his genre,"[2] the nineteenth-century American novelist felt some degree of uncertainty in all three areas. As Alexis de Tocqueville wrote in 1835, the American literary marketplace was in a state of flux:

> Here, there is a motley multitude with intellectual wants to be supplied. These new votaries of the pleasure of the mind have not all had the same education; they are not guided by the same lights, do not resemble their own fathers; and they themselves are changing every moment with changing places of residence, feelings, and fortune. So there are no traditions, or common habits, to forge links between their minds, and they have neither the power nor the wish nor the time to come to a common understanding.[3]

Poe and Melville are painful cases of writers who expended themselves to exhaustion and desperation in attempts to identify an audience among the "motley multitude," but they are simply the most prominent illustrations of a paradigmatic situation for the American writer: "The problem faced by many American writers of that time [was] a reading audience so mixed that it was difficult to predict public reactions to deviations from common beliefs and accepted standards of decorum. . . . The stratification which gives writers a degree of freedom in our time did not begin in America until well after 1850."[4] The novelists' uneasy relationship with a heterogeneous audience mirrored their relation to their social class. Like most American writers they were social anomalies who either derived status or livelihood from some other area, as Cooper and Irving did, or lived in semi-isolation like Hawthorne and Melville. The pattern continues in the latter half of the century. James became an expatriate; Howells made a living through literary journalism; and Twain found an audience, but like the early Melville, not the right audience for a serious novelist. In terms of genre there was a similar lack of stability. Novelists complained of the dominance of British writers in their own country and the absence of manners, traditions, history—in short, the cultural matrix needed to produce literature.[5] Unsurprisingly, given the writers' perception that society was unfriendly to the enterprise of serious fiction, antisocial attitudes are characteristically inscribed in the American novel.

In the major romantic novelists, the questioning of society occurs on the level of plot: Natty Bumppo's repeated withdrawal into the wilderness, Hester Prynne's expulsion from the community, the defiance of society by the opponents of slavery in *Uncle Tom's Cabin* and by Ahab in *Moby-Dick*. By assimilating images of social fragmentation, the traditional structure of the novel valorizes social authority; as an institution the novel remains conservative although, significantly, in the American novel the resolution tends to be the protagonist's death rather than social integration. *The Confidence-Man* anticipates the twentieth-century exacerbation of tensions between literature and society, but at the time of its publication it seemed to be an aberration presaging only Melville's imminent silence instead of a radical shift in the form of the novel.

Describing the American literary tradition before *Adventures of Huckleberry Finn*, Sacvan Bercovitch finds that "from Mather through Emerson, auto-American-biography served rhetorically to resolve the conflicts inherent in the very meaning of 'free-enterprise': spiritual versus material freedom, private versus corporate enterprise, the cultural ideal expressed by the country's purest minds versus the cultural fact, embodied in a vast economic-political undertaking."[6] With *Huckleberry Finn* the inherent tensions of these polarities are acknowledged: language is foregrounded as an area of conflict between collective and individual values, a beginning point in prose fiction paralleling the assertion of late-nineteenth-century poets that ordinary and poetic language are different.[7] The novel, with its more direct tie to the world, is not at first interested in establishing a separate language so much as in controlling that social rhetoric which functions ideologically to uphold vested interests at the expense of a total or unbiased or merely dissenting view. At the beginning of the modern period novelists condemn language not because of its referentiality but because it fails to refer accurately.

That language can be misused is hardly a new idea. What makes *Huckleberry Finn* notable in this respect is the scope and intensity of its indictment, its vision of a linguistic corruption which is not confined to an isolated confidence man or Machiavellian politician but is inherent in the language that everyone uses. Within society there is no escape from a language which influences thought and precludes truthful communication, regardless of the intention of the speaker. "The sign is no mere accidental cloak of the idea," Ernest Cassirer writes, "but its necessary and essential organization. It serves not merely to communicate a complete and given thought-content, but is an instrument, by means of which this content develops and fully defines itself."[8] By showing the operation of social perception upon language and the role of language in shaping thought, expression, and action, *Huckleberry Finn* places this thesis within the mainstream of the American novel.

Huckleberry Finn's indictment of public language, as well as Huck's failure to reach an accommodation with society, become familiar paradigms for the twentieth-century American novel. Perhaps the closest parallel to Huck in these respects is Holden Caulfield, who would enact Huck's literal withdrawal metaphorically by pretending to be a deaf-mute. In this way, he reasons, he "wouldn't have to have any goddam stupid useless conversations with anybody."[9] Such linguistic withdrawal takes a number of forms in modern American fiction. Characters in the very different worlds of Hemingway and Faulkner, Frederic Henry and Addie Bundren, both reject abstract words—that is, public language—because such language is not faithful to experiential reality. Listening to a soldier's patriotic slogans, Frederic feels embarrassment because the words are so remote from the reality of the experience. Thinking about words like *motherhood* and *pride*, Addie also concludes that "words don't ever fit what they are trying to say at": a word is "just a shape to fill a lack."[10] Nathanael West's Miss Lonelyhearts, faced with the inadequacy of his journalese rhetoric to the miseries of his readers, retreats into the silence of madness, while that latter-day romantic Quentin Compson commits suicide when he finds that he cannot impose a vocabulary of idealistic abstractions like *virginity* and *honor* on the chaos of modern experience. Most recently, the inarticulate and diminished protagonists of the postmodernists carry on Huck's alienation from society in linguistic terms; that is, unable to accept or dominate an authorized discourse, they withdraw from speech itself.

Chapter 1

Verbal Confidence

> All life therefore comes back to the question of our
> speech, the medium through which we communicate
> with each other; for all life comes back to the question of
> our relations with each other. These relations are made
> possible, are registered, are verily constituted, by our
> speech, and are successful . . . in proportion as our
> speech is worthy of its great human and social function;
> is developed, delicate, flexible, rich—an adequate
> accomplished fact. The more it suggests and expresses
> the more we live by it—the more it promotes and
> enhances life. Its quality, its authenticity, its security, are
> hence supremely important for the general multifold
> opportunity, for the dignity and integrity, of our
> existence.
>
> HENRY JAMES, *The Question of Our Speech*

■ In the romantic masterworks of the American novel
—*The Deerslayer, Uncle Tom's Cabin, The Scarlet Letter*, and *Moby-Dick*—language is envisioned as adequate to the needs of speakers. The assumption of these texts is that of John Locke's classic formulation: "God having designed man for a sociable creature, made him not only with an inclination, and under a fellowship with those of his own kind; but furnished him also with language, which was to be the great instrument, and common tie of society."[1] The ever-present dialectic between speech and silence is represented in these works in terms of intentionality: when characters speak, they are able to express themselves eloquently, but they may *choose* silence as the preferable course. Problems of verbalization are social in *The Deerslayer, Uncle Tom's Cabin*, and *The Scarlet Letter*, epistemological in *Moby-Dick*—never linguistic. These fictions demonstrate full confidence in the traditional ability of language to articulate accurately a world outside itself and to achieve congruity between intention and utterance and between speak-

ing and understanding—in short, a faith in the ability of characters to speak and be understood.

Given this confidence in spoken language to communicate meaning, it is hardly surprising that all four texts are speech-act dramas in which speaking or withholding speech has profound consequences for the entire fiction. *The Deerslayer* and *Moby-Dick* are both dominated by one speaker, but whereas Deerslayer's massive utterance consists of assertions that physical reality and the behavior of other characters constantly validate, that of Captain Ahab is a complex mixture of directives, declarations, and assertions whose validity is challenged by other aspects of the novel's discourse. Ahab attempts to coerce the world to fit his speech, but he cannot achieve the perfect correspondence between speaker and reality that governs *The Deerslayer*'s universe of discourse. Yet he speaks on energetically until literally deprived of breath by strangulation. *The Deerslayer* and *The Scarlet Letter* are similar in the climactic importance of a speech act: Deerslayer's promise to the Hurons to return to captivity and probable death; Dimmesdale's long-withheld confession that he is the father of Hester's child. In each case the commitment to speech is a public revelation and an ultimate test of character. *Uncle Tom's Cabin* has a similarly climactic speech act in the refusal to betray the two runaway slave women that causes Tom's death.

Compared to the texts that follow historically, these four all exhibit a commitment to language as capable of meaningful, albeit not unambiguous, communication. But each could be deconstructed to foreground problematic aspects: for Cooper, the limited possibilities of contextualizing truthful speech that restrict it to a wilderness setting; for Stowe, the powerful vested interests that manipulate language to preserve slavery. In *The Scarlet Letter* and *Moby-Dick* an almost intolerable tension between the individual and society is resolved only by isolation and death, a trajectory that becomes paradigmatic in Melville's later texts.

Speech as Ideal Discourse in *The Deerslayer*

■ Successive literary revolutions have made Cooper's ideas of novelistic praxis increasingly remote, but the Leatherstocking Tales continue to invoke a central conflict of the American experience—the tension between wilderness and settlement values which poses the more universal issue of social order versus individual freedom. Pastoral is the ideal genre for Cooper's acute sense of these polarities, and no book of his is more successful as a model of American pastoral than *The Deerslayer*, the last and "most fascinating" of the Leatherstocking Tales.[2] Cooper's wilderness is not the howling desert of the Puritan imagination, which, in their traditional imagery, must be "cultivated" and "made to bloom," but a nurturing presence whose pristine existence is superior to any other environment for man. " 'What comfort can a man look for in a clearin', that he can't find in double quantities in the forest?' " Deerslayer asks. " 'The whole 'arth is a temple of the Lord to such as have the right mind. Neither forts nor churches make people happier of themselves. Moreover, all is contradiction in the settlements, while all is concord in the woods' " (266).

But nature is the perfect place for man only insofar as he lives there according to those principles of right conduct that he has learned from other men; consequently, the mythic protagonist must be acculturated enough to have imbibed correct values without similarly acquiring the corrupt practices of existence in society.[3] That Deerslayer is "at heart, a Moravian," as Hurry Harry accuses, might reasonably be inferred from his frequent citing of the Moravian missionaries and his adherence to their teachings, yet his rejection of society is equally emphatic. Moreover, "its rich romantic, mythic, and pastoral elements notwithstanding, [*The Deerslayer*] is, in a very substantial way, about social hierarchy and class."[4] Cooper is as inflexible as Zola in predicating Judith Hutter's fate upon her mother's failure to find her proper social level, first aiming too high and bearing children out of wedlock, then marrying beneath her.[5] Deerslayer's commentary on such violations of hierarchy asserts the superiority of rigidly maintained class distinctions: "Onequal matches, like onequal fr'ndships, can't often tarminate kindly" (425). Without prior knowledge of her mother's history Judith has already repeated the first phase of it, and she makes vigorous efforts to complete the pattern by marrying Deerslayer, a man who is—whatever his virtues—socially beneath her and as removed from class affiliation as Thomas Hutter.

Neither Judith's earlier desire for the upper-class garrison officers nor her later interest in Deerslayer can give her a secure place in society, for her full identity, like that of so many characters in American fiction, eludes social definition. In spite of her remorse for the past, she is permanently limited by it, her own evolution under Deerslayer's tutelage ironically useless since she, unlike him, cannot live independently in the wilderness. Had Cooper had the same interest in his women characters as Hawthorne or James had in his, Judith's story might have rivaled Deerslayer's as a locus of textual energy. Nor does it take much effort to see this spirited and intelligent heroine, in the hands of a more sympathetic writer, as a possible Isabel Archer, innocently struggling for self-realization in terms that her world does not offer.[6] But Judith's story is delimited by the conventional, just as Isabel Archer is eventually "ground in the very mill of the conventional," and Judith's role in the novel is only that of Virginia Woolf's proverbial feminine mirror, to reflect the glory of the male protagonist.

Judith's story is simply the most dramatic encapsulation of the principle that governs *The Deerslayer*'s perfect economy: nothing is suitable that is out of character. This is the "matrix-sentence" of Deerslayer's truth, to borrow a Barthesian term, and it applies equally to the twin spheres of nature and gifts, what is inborn and what is acculturated.[7] Nature is the unalterable life stuff that each society shapes into a distinctive culture by developing the appropriate gifts.[8] For every nature, there is natural behavior, the basic core of being that cannot be modified by experience. Nothing can "alter a Mingo natur'" or "change a wolf into a squirrel," although Deerslayer tells his apt pupils, the Hutter girls, that "there's a considerable of human natur' in mankind ginirally" (256). Environment determines the acquisition of "gifts," which are built upon the foundation of nature, and certain gifts are more suited to certain natures.[9] As Deerslayer tells Judith and Hetty, " 'Stick to your gifts and your gifts will stick to you'" (216).[10] Such deterministic reasoning reveals a world organized into fixed hierarchies that unite nature and society according to the divine plan, a system in which everything is not only explicable but classifiable in language.

■ "We understand you, Deerslayer," returned Judith, hastily, "and take all that falls from your lips, as it is meant, in kindness and friendship. Would to Heaven all men had tongues as true and hearts as honest!" (383)

In spite of its token gesturing toward the plot action of frontier romance, the hackneyed staple of Indian captivity, *The Deerslayer* is a novel of speech much more than action, almost static when compared to *The Last of the Mohicans*. While the text as moral tract presents a schematization akin to a morality play, in which the familiar virtues and vices can be readily assigned to the characters, the text as romance explores the familiar issue of identity.[11] Who the characters are is finally the novel's greatest preoccupation, and it is constantly revealed first through speech and only later through some other form of behavior. Even the torture scene is a ritualized tableau in which speechifying outweighs the Indians' physical assault and Deerslayer's reaction.

Although language shares the divided nature of society, capable of ordering and corrupting, no writer has more confidence than Cooper in its power to achieve an ideal discourse. In the categorizing constantly done by Deerslayer and by the authorial voice, there is no indication that language may be anything other than a transparent medium derived from God to present an organization that inheres in the world itself. When words are used to express this order, i.e., nature, they can always be understood. " 'Such language,' Deerslayer affirms, 'is as plain in one tongue as in another; it comes from the heart, and goes to the heart, too' " (432).[12] Deerslayer's world contains no ambiguities, no complexities, no realities that stubbornly withhold their nature from language. The world is fallen, so it often swerves from the divinely appointed order; but like the Puritans, Cooper believes in a clear standard of right according to which every aspect of the creation can be measured and judged. Deerslayer professes himself to be puzzled that Providence allows such violations of hierarchy as the Hutter marriage, yet even these departures from universal decorum can be adequately labeled as aberrations and made to serve the system they flout. They are not comparable to the "sore abysses" of the Jamesian linguistic universe or the silent mysteries of the Melvillian cosmos, matters which baffle and frustrate the efforts of language to articulate them; instead, a perfect correspondence between signifier and signified governs *The Deerslayer*'s universe of discourse.

The world of *The Deerslayer* is in fact an ideal speech-act laboratory, where Deerslayer's audience, sometimes with the exception of Hurry and Hutter, responds to his utterances with unquestionable acceptance of their validity. The Hutter sisters immediately recognize Deerslayer to be a truthteller and accord him an authority based on personal merit. This perfect correspondence between signifier and signified and personal authority and speech is possible only in the wilderness; in the macrocosm of town and settlement hypocrisy, deceit, and political pressure deform language.[13]

" 'I'm glad it has no name,' Deerslayer says of the lake, 'or at least no paleface name; for their christenings always foretell waste and destruction. No doubt, however, the redskins have their modes of knowing it, and the hunters and trappers, too; they are likely to call the place by something reasonable and resembling' " (45–46).[14] But even in the wilderness language is threatened by deception and self-interest, for ultimately it is only as good as its speakers. As Deerslayer tells Hetty, "Men are deceived in other men's characters, and frequently give 'em names they by no means desarve. You can see the truth of this in the Mingo names, which, in their own tongue, signify the same thing as the Delaware names . . . and no one can say they are as honest or as upright a nation. I put no great dependence, therefore, on names" (67). Such assertions suggest that Deerslayer values nature as presence over any representations of it, but other pronouncements indicate that the enabling principle of his own discourse is that language can adequately reveal nature when the speaker is truthful and moral.

Deerslayer's own credibility as a speaker joins the text as moral tract to the text as romantic fiction, allowing him to function both as sage, the passive hero who enlightens others through speech about the nature of the world, and as potential martyr, the active hero who risks death to preserve his integrity. Thus the keyword of the novel's discourse is nature, the ultimate presence, and the keyword of its metadiscourse is truth. Even the enemy acknowledges Deerslayer's veracity by allowing him to leave captivity on "furlough." Rivenoak tells his prisoner, " 'You are honest; when you say a thing it is so' " (471–72).

Deerslayer monopolizes the novel's speech because his is the only truthful discourse in the twofold sense of conforming to nature and being spoken disinterestedly: because the behavior of other characters and physical reality constantly validate his utterances, agreement with Deerslayer is a touchstone for judging other characters. His reverse image, Hurry Harry, instructs misguidedly, expounding a system of classification that assimilates Indians to wolves and hence justifies killing and scalping them. Hetty's discourse articulates the unchanging moral imperatives of religious ideology, which frequently reminds us of the institutional nature of such supposed absolutes and the concomitant importance of context.[15] When Hetty enjoins Deerslayer to return good for evil, he replies: ' Ah Hetty, that may do among the missionaries, but 'twould make an oncertain life in the woods. . . . 'Twould have been ag'in natur' not to raise a hand in such a trial, and 'twould have done discredit to my training and gifts" (486). Other speakers lack this power to assess experience precisely because they are all marked by some barrier to truthful speech: Judith's need to conceal her past, Hurry's prejudice, Hutter's rapacity, Hetty's feeblemindedness. Deerslayer is also able to weigh the speech of others accurately because understanding as well as speaking depends upon character: "the ears of a man can tell truth from ontruth" (226). Deerslayer condemns Hurry's innuendoes about Judith as unmanly behavior, yet at the end of the novel he confesses (for once speechlessly) that they have influenced him—presumably because they are true in spite of their dubious source.

In his role of "Straight Tongue," one of his earlier Indian names, Deerslayer enlightens his error-prone associates. A "full-fledged fictional Adam," he exercises the Adamic function of naming by correcting Hurry's notions of race, reproving Judith's love of finery, admonishing the two trappers for wanting to scalp Indians, informing both whites and Indians of the differences between red and white gifts.[16] Most of the failings Deerslayer exposes are errors of classification; like Hurry's categorizing of Indians, they impose convenient but inaccurate labels to justify self-serving behavior. All of these instances conform to the novel's master paradigm of linguistic behavior, the ordering and classifying of experience. The majority of Deerslayer's illocutionary acts belong in Searle's category of assertions, "those utterances which commit the speaker to something's being the case, to the truth of the expressed proposition."[17] Such speeches tend to be long because of what Melville called "linked analogies": each subject participates in complex patterns of discourse representing relationships in the physical world. Since reason and nature are in harmony, Cooper treats these statements as self-evident truths which will be instantly recognized as such by rational listeners. Accordingly, his assertions have the perlocutionary effect of directives. When Judith hints that she might becomingly wear some fine clothing discovered in her father's chest, it is enough for Deerslayer to explain the decorum of clothes and social hierarchy to immediately change her frivolous attitude:

> "That you are as glorious in that dress as the sun when it rises or sets in a soft October day, I'm ready to allow; and that you greatly become it is a good deal more sartain than that it becomes you. . . . You are Thomas Hutter's darter, and that gownd was made for the child of some governor, or a lady of high station. . . .

"I'll take off the rubbish this instant, Deerslayer," cried the girl, springing up to leave the room; "and never do I wish to see it on any human being again." (215)

Although Judith is beginning to care for Deerslayer, and his exegesis is framed by skillful, if sincere, compliment, Cooper always shows her attachment to be rational: if she responds to his personal authority here, it is only because this authority is based upon his recognized character and expertise. Certainly this talk exchange is a model of ideal persuasive discourse, but it is a great deal more; it is also a model of discourse based upon proper personal credentials and a rational argument. This is indeed speech before the Fall, words corresponding to realities and understood as such by a receptor who requires nothing further.

"Truth is truth," Deerslayer is fond of proclaiming, an assertion that recalls Falstaff's to Prince Hal: "Is not the truth the truth?" A world of verbal sophistication separates Shakespeare's protagonist from Cooper's; Deerslayer is both naive and forthright, an innocent truth-teller whose context can only be the backwoods. Falstaff calls attention to the cleverness of his utterance and invites the larger audience to ponder the complexities of "truth." Indeed, if Falstaff's transparently outrageous story is truth, then such a concept is worthless as a means of conveying reality. It exists here as a ploy among others to be used to individual advantage.

That difficulties of communication do occur in *The Deerslayer* fails to undermine either the accepted certainty of the assertion Deerslayer makes or its content. The dialogue bristles with self-reflexive references to its own procedures, which demand plain speaking and view understanding as a process achieved through speech. At first no one comprehends Deerslayer's plan of returning to Huron captivity, but through his usual method of precise categorizing and defining he explains his position until everyone, even Hetty, understands it:

"If you are bound, with what are your hands and feet fastened?"

"With a furlough, gal; that's a thong that binds tighter than any chain. One may be broken, but the other can't. Ropes and chains allow of knives, and desait, and contrivances; but a furlough can be neither cut, slipped, nor sarcumvented."

"What sort of thing is a furlough, then, if it be stronger than hemp or iron? I never saw a furlough."

"I hope you may never feel one, gal; the tie is altogether in the

feelin's, in these matters, and therefore is to be felt and not seen.
You can understand what it is to give a promise, I dare to say, good
little Hetty?"

"Certainly. A promise is to say you will do a thing, and that binds
you to be as good as your word." (459)

The questions of *The Deerslayer*'s world always have answers, and it remains only for Deerslayer to link "furlough" with "promise" to satisfy
Hetty's puzzlement about the invisible captivity: the binding power of
language upon honorable men and women.

Failures of understanding, like those of speech itself, are governed
more by character than by language. When Hurry interrupts Judith's
account of why she refuses to marry him by insisting that he understands her, his statement expresses his own assessment of Judith's history. The Hurons are similarly unable to understand Hetty's reading of
the Bible, not because the Word is defective, but because their "gifts"
are for another sort of belief.

■ Talk exchange in *The Deerslayer*, as Mark Twain
observed in his own version of Cooper's longwindedness, is unrealisti-
cally prolix: "To believe that such talk really ever came out of people's
mouths would be to believe that there was a time when time was of
no value to a person who thought he had something to say, when it
was the custom to spread a two-minute remark out to ten, when a
man's mouth was a rolling-mill and busied itself all day long in turning
four-foot pigs of thought into thirty-foot bars of conversational railroad
iron by attenuation." [18] The novel's speech is implausibly ponderous
because Cooper's failure to differentiate the spheres of narrative and
dialogue burdens direct discourse with a number of authorial jobs that
are patently inappropriate to the speech situation. Talk habitually turns
into protracted speech making in which intrusions of authorial purpose
mix uneasily with a character's reason for speaking. When Judith ex-
horts Deerslayer, "Pull, Deerslayer . . . pull for life and death—the lake
is full of savages wading after us!" (151), her relatively brief and simple
communication is suited to the urgency of the speech situation. But
she continues: "Pull, Deerslayer, for Heaven's sake! . . . These wretches
rush into the water like hounds following their prey! Ah!—The Scow
moves! And now the water deepens to the armpits of the foremost; still
they rush forward, and will seize the ark!" (152). In Judith's second

speech the inclusion of description embellished with literary simile, material appropriate to the narrative and language at odds with the speech occasion, diminishes the drama of the escape.

What is equally striking in the speech of *The Deerslayer* is not the irrelevance Twain complained of but the absence of the irrelevance that at least occasionally characterizes any real conversation. Nothing is spoken that is truly irrelevant to the novel's single-minded display of Deerslayer's exemplary character and capabilities within the overall design of narrative cum moral tract, and it is in fact this weighty double purpose that transforms talk exchange into verbal essays of didactic generalizing. When Judith offers up her own finery to ransom Hutter from the Indians, it is germane to the action for Deerslayer to pose the question that he does: "But are you sartain, gal, you could find it in your heart to part with your own finery for such a purpose?" (203). The lengthy speech on human frailty that follows, an example of what Twain meant by irrelevance, is gratuitous to narrative progression but important to Deerslayer's role as disseminator of wisdom.

Most of Deerslayer's assertive utterances follow some recognizable version of an expository pattern: definition, comparison, contrast, exemplification. They are sermons or lectures that might easily be arranged according to topic. Cooper realizes that the awkward mesh of narrative with set pieces of exposition needs to be acknowledged, and his reference to the "unpolished sincerity, that so often made this simple-minded hunter bare his thoughts" offers a rationale for Deerslayer's sententiousness. Free from social proprieties that would restrain or deflect speech in more socialized speakers, Deerslayer simply utters a whole and unvarnished truth regardless of consequence or context. This openness of speech, a reflection of wilderness simplicity, characterizes the other white speakers as well, although in their cases disingenuous rudeness reveals character traits less admirable than Deerslayer's love of truth.[19] The insensitive and boastful Hurry Harry tells Deerslayer three times in the same conversation that he is not good-looking. Later he remarks, "I don't expect you'll prove much of a warrior" (101). Hutter's suspicions about Deerslayer, which he voices in his presence, express his own criminal asociality.[20]

While the authorial voice all too frequently intrudes in substance, speech is stylistically differentiated according to character. Hurry's rash and impulsive nature, his braggadocio; Hetty's naiveté; Hutter's taciturn and suspicious nature; Judith's settlement-influenced sophistication and natural vivacity are all embodied in their speech, in addition to the broader effects of education and social class.[21] The Indians speak a more formal and figurative language than the whites without sounding alike: speech reveals Chingachgook's stolid dignity, Rivenoak's slyness, and Hist's strong feelings.

These distinctive voices are all subordinated to that of Deerslayer, which is at times plausibly humble, at times implausibly poetic or philosophical. Shifts in level are often abrupt, as in the passage Twain singled out for particular ridicule, in which Deerslayer justifies to Judith his participation in the recovery of Hist: " 'It consarns me, as all things that touches a fri'nd consarns a fri'nd' " (139). As Twain reasonably objected, we would expect a man who speaks like this to have some difficulty in organizing the world verbally; yet in the next breath, Deerslayer responds to Judith's question about his sweetheart with a poetic speech containing no grammatical errors or deviant pronunciation:

> "She's in the forest, Judith—hanging from the boughs of the trees, in a soft rain—in the dew on the open grass—the clouds that float about in the blue heavens—the birds that sing in the woods— the sweet springs where I slake my thirst—and in the other glorious gifts that come from God's Providence!" (139)

The two utterances might be used to illustrate Coleridge's description of rustic and cultivated speech: "The rustic, from the more imperfect development of his faculties, and from the lower state of their cultivation, aims almost solely to convey insulated facts, either those of his scanty experience or his traditional belief; while the educated man chiefly seeks to discover and express those connections of things, or those relative bearings of fact to fact, from which some more or less general law is deducible."[22] Deerslayer speaks in both styles, sometimes even mixing them in the same speech; but while such obvious inconsistency is contrary to realistic expectation, Cooper's intention, as he wrote in the preface to the Leatherstocking Tales, is to encompass an ideal of character: "A leading character in a work of fiction has a fair right to the aid which can be obtained from a poetical view of the subject. It is in this view, rather than in one more strictly circumstantial, that Leatherstocking has been drawn" (7). Because Deerslayer's first response to Judith is so circumscribed, it is easily expressed within the limited resources of his frontiersman's mode of speaking. Nature, however, inspires his deepest feelings, and the elevation of his speech is Cooper's way of rendering in language what would, in a realistically conceived woodsman, remain inchoate and nonverbal. What is appropriate to Deerslayer is the feeling, which can be most effectively expressed in a language that is unsuited to this illiterate character.

In his discussion of voice in *As I Lay Dying* Stephen M. Ross observes that objections to such inconsistencies and implausibilities in a character's speech reflect "the assumption that voice must be an index of personal identity. . . . It is assumed not only that a voice belongs to some person but also that it is in crucial ways 'appropriate' to that person—to his or her socio-economic class, level of education, and so on." [23] While Deerslayer's speech does not maintain a consistent level of class and education, there is a predictability of content and attitude that makes his voice recognizable throughout the novel and creates "personal identity" although this identity is not primarily determined by the form of his speech. In terms of experience and morality, his utterances are informed by a capital of authority that always dominates the speech of others.

■ A series of speech acts, followed by corroborative actions, tests each character's identity in the novel's climactic crisis. Deprived of a selfish motive by Judith's rejection, Hurry announces that he will not remain to defend the Hutter daughters, while Chingachgook, Hist, and Judith all profess loyalty to Deerslayer. Hurry departs; the others act upon their words by attempting to free Deerslayer from the Hurons. The greatest proof of the significance of speech is of course reserved for Deerslayer himself, a coalescing of his roles as moral preceptor and active hero. Through repeated discussion, since everyone but Chingachgook and Hist requires a separate explanation, the pledge given to the Hurons comes to represent the conditions of all speech, its capacity for character revelation and for an absolute of commitment that transcends "the wants of the body" and "the cravings of the spirit." When Hurry objects that Deerslayer need not keep his word to the Indians because they "have neither souls nor names," Deerslayer replies with his most comprehensive argument:

> "If they've got neither souls nor names, you and I have both, Harry March, and one is accountable for the other. This furlough is not, as you seem to think, a matter altogether atween me and the Mingos, seeing it is a solemn bargain made atween me and God. . . . The words are said to the ears of the Almighty." (405)

The social linguistic contract merely replicates the divine, according to which the integrity of the speaker assures the invisible bond of meaning and intention. Speaking is always a moral act, and thus an index of the speaker's morality. The denigration of the Hurons here and elsewhere is deeply ironic. As John P. McWilliams, Jr., has pointed out, "*The Deerslayer* is the only frontier novel in which the frontiersman becomes an Indian, while the Indian resembles an honorable white. Rather than scalping their white captives, the Hurons honorably ransom them for chessmen. The Mingoes venerate Hetty Hutter; Hurry and Tom condescend toward her. When the Hurons declare war, they give forewarning through a bundle of bound pine knots. Harry shoots indifferently and without warning."[24]

While it seems to be a matter of course for Deerslayer to keep his word to God and man, his final conversation with Judith imposes a more difficult test of his commitment to truthful speech. If, as Judith says, the "arts and deceptions of the settlements" do not enter into their discourse, social decorum is nevertheless a powerful influence on both speakers. To avoid the insult of telling Judith outright that he does not love her, Deerslayer substitutes a curious euphemism for the honest speech of his credo: "If Father and Mother was livin', which, however, neither is—but if both was livin', I do not feel toward any woman as if I wish'd to quit 'em in order to cleave unto *her*" (543). In the presence of an explicitly sexual overture, albeit one couched in the institutional form of marriage, the protagonist retrogresses to a juvenile dependency made doubly absurd by the contrary-to-fact condition. It is Judith who puts the rejection into direct language, preempting Deerslayer's role of instructor and truthteller, and enjoining him to confirm her speech by his own silence. Cooper reinforces the image of Deerslayer's retreat from adulthood by describing him as obediently mute, "playing with the water, like a corrected schoolboy." Continuing their role reversal, Judith poses another probing question, to which Deerslayer fails to respond in words: "Truth was the Deerslayer's polar star. He ever kept it in view; and it was nearly impossible for him to avoid uttering it, even when prudence demanded silence. Judith read his answer in his countenance" (545). Ordinarily able to master the world through speech, and even impelled by personal integrity to utter the truth, Deerslayer now says nothing, a non sequitur that requires explanation.

Since Cooper tells us that Deerslayer's heart was never touched by Judith, his failure to speak is evidently motivated by a conflict between the social injunction that forbids giving offense to a woman and his personal injunction against lying. This uncharacteristic silence, upon which Cooper ends the novel, emphasizes that like other American Adams, Deerslayer eschews adult sexuality, and this, as much as his distaste for other aspects of life in society, accounts for his inability to live there permanently. In order to be understood in that world, Deerslayer's tongue would have to express the "contradictions of the settlements" rather than the "harmony of the woods," a deviation from the ideal of speech that he has espoused and exemplified.

Divinely Authorized Speech in *Uncle Tom's Cabin*

■ Little connects Harriet Beecher Stowe with the other writers discussed in this chapter: in Ellen Moers's words, "[she] was different because she was a woman writer."[25] While Cooper, Hawthorne, and Melville were all accepted as writers of "serious" literature—at the time an exclusively male occupation—Stowe, a harassed wife and mother, felt herself impelled to write by the moral issue of slavery, and she regarded her book as a religious witnessing against the chief evil of her time and as a feminine obligation.[26] Her motive was unabashedly perlocutionary, as was her success: President Lincoln's characterization of her as "the little lady who started the big war" endured. Nor did the tremendous success of *Uncle Tom's Cabin* cause her to assert a belatedly discovered art: throughout her long life she insistently disavowed literary intentions or strategies, describing the novel as "an irresistible outburst" for which she deserved no particular credit.[27]

Stowe shares with Cooper a belief in the transcendent nature of the signified and the stability of the sign because ultimately language comes from God. Referring to Scripture, she writes in *Oldtown Folks*: "Let us treasure these old words, for as of old Jehovah chose to dwell in a tabernacle in the wilderness, and between the cherubim in the temple, so now he dwells in them."[28] As Fred G. See comments, "This is the scene of her texts: theo/logical—word, speech, discourse of God; God-speaking."[29] Stowe also shares with Cooper a confidence in perlocutionary effects, but speech in *Uncle Tom's Cabin* is far more accomplished than the clumsy dialogue of *The Deerslayer*, and its context is more realistically complex. When Natty Bumppo speaks, others listen, immediately understand, and act accordingly—a simple direct relationship that the text makes clear would not obtain in those topoi of corruption, the "settlements." Cooper entertains the possibility of language's inaccurately reflecting reality when Natty speaks of the "false names" that white settlers are apt to confer, but this idea is over-shadowed by a tremendous confidence that words can communicate truth when they are spoken by the truthteller Natty Bumppo in the pristine world of nature that he prefers to inhabit. For Stowe, language functions most typically as the compromised creature of the "settle-ments," above all, of the marketplace. *Uncle Tom's Cabin* accordingly places language in its full social context as an instrument of power and possession. Where Cooper distances both power and the corruption of language from his protagonist's field, except for their inadequate rep-resentation in Hurry Harry and old Hutter, Stowe's various truthtellers are constantly embroiled in a battle of discourses posed as a contest be-tween societal power and religious morality. And in contrast to Natty's series of triumphs throughout the Leatherstocking Tales, they are often defeated.

In this dynamic, as well as in its subject matter, Stowe's novel is closer to *Adventures of Huckleberry Finn*, but slavery in the later text is simply the convenient vehicle to suggest the general principle that society always distorts and misuses language for its own (illegitimate) ends—preserving and justifying the interests of the powerful. In this intention *Huck Finn* is closer to philosophical satires such as *Candide* than to *Uncle Tom's Cabin*, whose pointed juxtaposition of the socially distorted and the morally absolute has the single-minded focus of at-tacking and overcoming a specific evil, the current practice of slavery.[30] While the novel vigorously condemns anyone involved in slavery, its chief targets are not the slave dealers and zealous slaveholders who would be unlikely to read it or be swayed by it, but rather Stowe's ver-sion of the *hypocrite lecteur*, the respectable Northerner or Southerner whose complicity is casual or unexamined.

The conflicting meanings of "humanity" in the first chapter of the novel establish the centrality of the verbal arena, where worldly power seeks to appropriate terms of moral value for morally outrageous prac-tices. In attempting to distinguish himself from the slave trader, with whom he has been forced into an uncomfortable proximity through their business dealings, Shelby styles himself a humane man—meaning that, unlike Haley, he resists separating a mother and her child. The slave trader hastens to claim the attribute of humanity for himself as well although his is an instrumental meaning of humane behavior, i.e., the treatment of slaves designed to protect their monetary value. "Humanity," he tells Shelby, "is the great pillar of my management" (8). Shelby, who maintains the illusion that his idea of humanity is superior, condescendingly laughs at this "piquant" and "original" definition, but his willingness to separate mother and child in spite of humane reservations shows his own notion of humanity to be as subservient to economic motive as the slave trader's; it has simply been protected from an engagement with necessity until this moment.[31] Shelby's every effort to distance his behavior from the slave trader's only points up their underlying congruence:

> "Circumstances, you well know, *obliged* me," said Shelby, haughtily.
> "Wal, you know, they may 'blige *me*, too," said the trader. "Howsomever . . . as to my treatin' on him bad, you needn't be a grain afeard. If there's anything that I thank the Lord for, it is that I'm never noways cruel."
> After the expositions which the trader had previously given of his humane principles, Mr. Shelby did not feel particularly reassured by these declarations; but, as they were the best comfort the case admitted of, he allowed the trader to depart in silence, and betook himself to a solitary cigar. (80)

Recapitulating Shelby's reason for discomfort may seem unnecessarily heavy-handed, but this motive must be tangibly present to make the rapid dissolve to complacency more arresting. Shelby regards Haley's "declarations"—technically, assertions—as without validity, yet he immediately accepts them as truth because it is comfortable to do so. The reader, seeing Shelby comfort himself with a cigar, must regard Shelby's own professed commitment to humanity in a similar light.

Even morally scrupulous characters like Ophelia and her sympathetically rendered cousin Augustine St. Clare can respond to the prevailing societal context by verbally dehumanizing slaves. St. Clare introduces Topsy to Ophelia as "a purchase for your department," causing Ophelia to exclaim, "What in the world have you brought that thing here for?" Topsy is then defined as a "funny specimen in the Jim Crow line" and summoned by a whistle, "as a man would . . . call the attention of a dog" (352). Although Ophelia and St. Clare have every intention of treating Topsy kindly, they refer to her as a "concern," an "image," and a being who inspires the same kind of amusement that a man might obtain from "the tricks of a parrot or a pointer." [32] Like the corresponding moment in *Adventures of Huckleberry Finn* when the benevolent Aunt Sally casually reveals her acceptance of a distinction between "human being" and "nigger," this quiet scene in a work originally subtitled "The Man that was a Thing" has profound implications. Even the authorial voice becomes complicit in the dialogue's joking terminology, announcing that "the thing struck up, in a clear shrill voice, an odd negro melody" (352). Such language on the part of such characters suggests the ease with which a socially constructed reality—the classification of one group of people as nonhuman—becomes accepted as natural. [33] In slavery, as Philip Fisher observes, the inequity of such a classification is starkly exposed: "Unlike the prisoner and the madman who are made invisible by the institutions to which they are sent so that the reality of their suffering has to be discovered by investigation and can be forgotten for the most part . . . the slave is a visible prisoner, confined within the family itself." [34]

Mrs. Shelby's passionate, despairing response to the sale of the family slaves—her refusal to be consoled—illustrates the text's marked gender differentiation between the commitment of men to the public sphere, represented as the site of pecuniary gain devoid of morality, and of women to the private sphere of Christianity and family, where genuine humanity flourishes. [35] What distinguishes the speech of such characters as Mrs. Shelby and Mrs. Bird from that of their husbands is their rejection of the institutionalized categories enshrined in labels: however much their husbands invoke the masculine abstractions of reason and legality, they will not be deflected from the brute fact of a slave's status as a human being. The text thus distinguishes between a private, feminine discourse espousing the values of Christian morality, with its attendant recognition of familial bonds, and a public, masculine discourse that privileges economic and social power. [36]

Commentators have frequently noted that Uncle Tom is an exception to the prevailing gendered discourse, a man who exemplifies Christian morality more profoundly than any other character. But as Amy Schrager Lang observes, "moral rectitude . . . is a luxury of dependence" more than an attribute of sex. [37] As a slave, Tom is feminized to the extent that, like women, he is free from decision making in the economic sphere, and as a black man who has no hope of passing for white, he has no choice of roles such as George Harris has.[38]

Mixed blood enables George to look and act like a white man;[39] he is granted the physical escape from slavery while Tom receives, indeed chooses, the spiritual. These differences are equally sharp in the speech of the two slaves. Tom, like all of the other fully black characters, speaks ungrammatically and colloquially, although not consistently and not as markedly as some of the other slaves; George Harris has both "white" speech and ambition, contextualized as natural because of his preponderance of white ancestry and possible because of his white appearance. If in Tom Stowe represents Christian goodness so close to perfection that it must be recognized, even in a black slave— and acknowledged to be superior to the Christianity of most whites— in George she makes another argument, that many persons classified as black slaves are in all respects indistinguishable from free whites. The same desire for freedom that motivates George, condemned as the most heinous crime in his society, would be recognized as "sublime heroism" on the part of a "Hungarian youth" (299).[40]

In representing Mr. Wilson's conversion to George's point of view, the text constructs a model for rational discourse, but one clearly at odds with the societal power that ordinarily shapes talk exchange. Mr. Wilson first invokes the abstraction of "the laws of your country" to the runaway slave, to which George responds with a moving personal history of suffering brought about by these laws. Throughout the conversation George's arguments reduce Mr. Wilson to ineffectual responses: the laws that he reveres are a vague general category that can no longer be embraced so wholeheartedly when they allow the violent sundering of familial ties. Much like the Hutter girls responding to one of Deerslayer's speeches demonstrating the workings of truth, Mr. Wilson accepts George's logic entirely and is therefore forced to approve his escape. But unlike the pattern discourse of *The Deerslayer*, in which assent is instantaneous and unproblematic—simply a matter of hearing truth articulated—Mr. Wilson's acquiescence is in the mode of Huck Finn abandoning his conscience: " 'I s'pose, perhaps, I an't following my judgment,—hang it, I *won't* follow my judgment!' " (188). "Judgment," like "reason" and "business," is not neutral but partisan, part of the public discourse whose values are shaped and enforced by white men. Not surprisingly, as part of his identification with the members of this ruling group, George embraces the rhetoric of possession and violence as well as that of freedom and opportunity.[41]

    ■ In one among many retrospective comments, Stowe denied to an admirer that she had "written" *Uncle Tom's Cabin*. When he asked in understandable puzzlement for the name of the real author, she replied: "God wrote it. . . . I merely did his dictation."[42] Although Stowe had a sense of mission appropriate to an enterprise of high moral seriousness, more is at work here than the conventional invocation of divine aid for a literary undertaking of magnitude. Describing the process as a literal act of transcription reflects Stowe's desire to endow the voice of her text with absolute authority, especially its direct authorial pronouncements. The authorial voice in *Uncle Tom's Cabin* belongs under Robyn Warhol's rubric of the "engaging narrator," an author-surrogate who tries "to foster sympathy for real-world sufferers."[43] Such a narrator, Warhol continues, "encourages the reader to apply to nonfictional, real life the feelings the fiction may have inspired."[44]

The text is saturated with references to and manifestations of voice, designed to place characters not in terms of the usual social categories but along a spectrum of religious belief and morality. When Legree rejoices that Tom's "mouth's shut up, at last," the authorial voice reminds us that he cannot similarly silence the voice of conscience within. Unable to respond to the genuine message of Tom's exhortations, he succumbs to Cassy's fraudulent performance, perhaps because its summoning to death and damnation in the accusatory figure of his mother accords with his deepest, unacknowledged fears. Although the reader knows that Cassy has spoken the sternly intoned directive—"Come! come! come!"—the supernatural interpretation resonates with the spiritual message of the entire text and with the added assertion of the authorial voice that this fate is Legree's just punishment. Cassy, the author, and God all convey the same message and hence God's authority extends to the other voices, just as in another conjunction Tom, the author, and God are united against Legree.

Regarding the entire text as the reported speech of a divine voice is also consonant with the climactic intrusion of this same voice directly within the text. After Tom has resisted the satanic temptations of Simon Legree by repeatedly invoking his belief in God, he has a vision in which he both sees Christ and hears him promise salvation. Later, the "savage words" of Tom's torturer, Quimbo, are drowned out by "a higher voice" instructing him to "fear not them that kill the body, and, after that, have no more that they can do" (414). This directive, pronounced within a religious vision, has absolute authority although it is spoken by a character denied full human status by language and law.

Opposed to the social, economic, and political power of slavery, all of which generate a tremendous capital of authority, Stowe invests even those characters who are powerless with a higher, unassailable power: God's speaking through them outweighs the linguistic capital of those on the side of slavery. Because of this divine affiliation, these voices—author and character alike—are empowered beyond the boundaries of the text to generalize authoritatively about the kinds of human behavior that those within the text represent.

Private and Public Speech in *The Scarlet Letter*

■ Speech fulfills the whole range of traditional functions in *The Scarlet Letter* and it does so with a clarity and a certitude markedly different from the ponderous expression of *The Deerslayer* and single-minded focus of *Uncle Tom's Cabin*. Hawthorne's preface to the *Twice-Told Tales*, a conscientious statement of intention, aptly characterizes the dialogue in *The Scarlet Letter*: "Every sentence, so far as it embodies thought and sensibility, may be understood and felt by anybody who will give himself the trouble to read it, and will take up the book in a proper mood."[45] When characters choose to speak, they can express themselves eloquently, and they have no self-conscious preoccupation about words, even of the naive sort that arises in defining the king and the duke, or man and Frenchman, in *Adventures of Huckleberry Finn*. Like other romances of the first half of the nineteenth century, *The Scarlet Letter* demonstrates a confidence in the resources of language to communicate meaning; that is, to articulate a world outside itself and to achieve congruity between intention and utterance in fictive speech.

These assertions involve my reading in a critical controversy over the referentiality of Hawthorne's language.[46] For Millicent Bell, the novel is "an essay in semiology," whose theme is "the obliquity or indeterminacy of signs."[47] Evan Carton similarly finds that "*The Scarlet Letter* insists that words and things are not fundamentally joined." In particular, "Hester's letter is openly displayed at the outset but takes on various significances and remains enigmatic to the end."[48] As the novel's titular sign, the scarlet letter has naturally preoccupied commentators, but I would argue that in spite of the absence of the word *adultery* from the novel, we, and the fictive readers within the text, are never in doubt about the letter's meaning. The revelation of Hester's sin is not dependent upon words: she is a woman apart from her husband who gives birth to a child. Later, her exemplary behavior causes some of the citizenry to say that the letter means "able." Neither this charitable reinterpretation nor ignorance of the officially prescribed meaning constitutes indeterminacy.

The "various significances" Carton refers to accrue in an orderly fashion. In the initial scaffold scene no one, it is safe to say, misconstrues the meaning of Hester's letter. When her mode of life makes an adjustment appropriate, "many people refused to intepret the scarlet A by its original signification" (161). There is no confusion or indeterminacy, however. The letter's original significance has not been forgotten; it coexists with, or is superseded by, another meaning that seems to characterize Hester more accurately at that particular time. (The letter seen in the sky is also variously interpreted, but for quite different reasons. Because its context is natural or supernatural, not human, it is open to individual contextualization by whoever sees it until some official meaning is agreed upon.)

Pearl is often regarded as another indeterminate sign, although her relationship to the scarlet letter is stable enough. She is literally the letter in another form, the agent who transformed secret sin into public shame. Pearl is not indeterminate so much as mysterious, a sign that withholds its meaning or means different things to different people in a way common to the complexity of human character. To move from such naturally occuring signs as comets and human beings to signs in the man-made sign system of language is an unwarranted leap.

Indeterminacy should also not be confused with the ambivalent attitude of the authorial voice about events in the novel. It would be a mistake to equate all of these instances with Hester's letter, a social artifact with an explicit institutional contextualization and a stable meaning, or to conclude that language is indeterminate in the novel. Hawthorne, I would suggest, has not so much lost confidence "in the sacred grounding of signs"[49] as in society's interpretation of this "sacred grounding," its reification of signs in ways that stifle the human spirit and thus force individuals into deceptive postures and untruthful speech.

Instead of indeterminacy, Fred See finds in his examination of the changing status of literary signs during the nineteenth century a Hawthorne torn between "the immense pressure of inherited forms" and the imaginative energy that leads to a reshaping of literary signs. See thus moves the clash of opposing forces of the novel to the level of the individual sign, which becomes a microcosm of the conflict between individual expression and public language.[50] He concludes, nevertheless, that Hawthorne "could not relinquish the noumenal language which in fact he shared with Mrs. Stowe and the school of domestic sentiment."[51]

While she does not focus on speech, Nina Baym is closest to my reading in posing this opposition as a conflict between "passionate, self-assertive, and self-expressive inner drives and the repressive counterforces that exist in society and are also internalized within the self."[52] In a recent powerful reading, Janet Gabler-Hover triangulates the field by adding ethics to the conflict between law—"something patriarchally or ideologically determined"—and passion. Where law and passion exist in an oppositional tension, each requiring the existence of the other, ethics provides a "process of regulating our behavior through our emotional apprehension of the common bond of humanity."[53] She sees Dimmesdale and Hester trapped in the closed dichotomy of passion and law until the novel's conclusion, when Dimmesdale exhibits ethical behavior by making a public confession, and Hester is redeemed by Pearl from a selfish reification of passion. Gabler-Hover's elegant tripartite division of forces offers an appealing structure of explanation; however, I am not entirely persuaded of the fit between it and aspects of *The Scarlet Letter*. Theoretically, a separation between law and morality creates a desirable gap for individual conscience; in reality, as Hawthorne reminds us, for the legalistic Puritans, religion takes the form of law. Dimmesdale is ineluctably bound by the Puritan belief system, so that his public admission of guilt becomes the delayed application of the law that the community wished to apply seven years earlier. Granted that he makes the choice of self-exposure: throughout the novel he is the perfect emblem of Puritan psychology in the anguish of his concealment and his belief that confession ensures his salvation. Pearl is not humanized by any action of Hester's but by her father's recognition—a final testimony to the weight of patriarchal authority in the text. We might assume that her life is salvaged because she escapes from Puritan society and inherits a fortune from Roger Chillingworth.

■ Linguistic confidence, manifested in the ability of characters to speak and be understood by others, must be qualified by the societal restraints imposed on speech. In the Puritan society of *The Scarlet Letter*, truth would be harshly consequential and so must remain unspoken. Thus the text reveals a socially constructed gap between thought or action and speech. Tension between the individual and society inhibits or deforms speech, isolating confident speakers and portending the radical disjunction between public language and the individual that quickly comes to typify the mainstream tradition of the American novel.

The novel begins with an account of the stifling experience of government employment which, from the moribund time-servers gathered at the Custom House to the dwindling of intellect induced by its stagnancy, is rendered in images of death and decay. Those who hold public office in the novel proper are more vigorous than the doddering relics who crept about the Salem Custom House during Hawthorne's tenure there, but they are also more antipathetic; in the earlier society genuine fellow feeling exists only in the interstices of the group: the young wife who has compassion for Hester, the man who admonishes some grimly judgmental women. John Wilson, foremost member of the Puritan clergy and its spokesman against Hester, had no more right than a "portrait" in old volumes of sermons "to meddle with a question of human guilt, passion, and anguish" (65). In its adjudication of such matters, however clumsy and mean-spirited, society nevertheless performs the necessary function of enforcing at least an outward accountability in human relations, an accountability that the authorial voice seems to approve and also regard as inescapable: to flee to another place under a new name, as Dimmesdale momentarily contemplates, would be an evasion of responsibility that denied the self, a symbolic suicide that would certainly put him beyond the possibility of salvation. Dimmesdale must decide between the danger of self-revelation that affirms his identity and the security of a fraudulent conformity, a choice embodying the recurrent dilemma of speakers in the American novel: whether to give their allegiance to public language, the speech of belongingness, power, and social status, or to embrace some form of verbal rebellion that asserts the primacy of self-expression over the collective vision. As I read the novel, in a society devoted to the law, to the letter as an inflexible unitary sign, there is no middle ground.

To an unusual extent the poles of speech and silence define public and private worlds and create the dynamic of *The Scarlet Letter*.[54] While the unuttered remains to some extent unthought, unformulated

by consciousness, speech has the burden of transforming reality—
often irrevocably. Such is the emphasis that Hawthorne gives to Roger
Chillingworth's revelation to Hester Prynne of the part of fiend he
has played in Arthur Dimmesdale's life, a role he can speak of to no
one else:

> The unfortunate physician, while uttering these words, lifted
> his hands with a look of horror, as if he had beheld some frightful
> shape, which he could not recognize, usurping the place of his own
> image in a glass. It was one of those moments—which sometimes
> occur only at the interval of years—when a man's moral aspect is
> faithfully revealed to his mind's eye. Not improbably, he had never
> before viewed himself as he did now. (172)

The transformed self, which Hawthorne expresses in an extended visual
image, is actually recognized only through the creation of a verbal construct: by labeling himself a fiend in speech, Chillingworth discovers
that he has become one.

Numerous commands to speak and statements about speaking further emphasize that the creation of identity within a public context also
depends upon speech:[55] all three of the protagonists are wrongly categorized by the community because their antisocial thoughts remain unspoken while their words deceptively conform to society's expectations.
Chillingworth and Dimmesdale *speak* deceptively, but Hester's silence
is equally open to misinterpretation. For the community, Hester's aloofness "might be pride, but it was so like humility that it produced all
the softening influence of the latter quality on the public mind" (162).
Charles Feidelson, Jr., observes "Beneath the measured speech and
ceremonial behavior of the Boston theocracy is a vast realm of the publicly unsaid and even unsayable—the esoteric community of Hester,
Dimmesdale, and Chillingworth."[56] Beginning with society's demand
that Hester name the father of her child and ending with the social imperative finally fulfilled by Dimmesdale, the novel's significant events
are speech acts or moments when elicited speech fails to take place. For
Dimmesdale the struggle between public and private plays itself out
solely in terms of speech: the central question of *The Scarlet Letter* is
whether or not he will perform the speech act that will change his social
classification in the community from godly minister to adulterer. The
space of the novel proper is that period when speech to the community
is deliberately withheld, not, as Feidelson would have it, "unsayable."

This absence defines *The Scarlet Letter*'s moral issue and structures its plot: shortly after its protagonists finally speak honestly—first Hester to Dimmesdale, then Dimmesdale to the community—each speaking to the audience that he or she values most, the novel ends. Until this climax, the silence of all three characters in the face of society's injunction to speak preserves the status quo: Chillingworth's assumed identity, Dimmesdale's reputation for sanctity and his position in the community, Hester's errancy and alienation from it.

Hester never repudiates her estrangement from the public values she has transgressed against. Obeying Dimmesdale's directive to join him on the scaffold "as if . . . against her strongest will" (252), she clearly has little enthusiasm for his course of action. His final rebuff of her hope in a union after death thus closes off any interest Hester might have in heaven. When she returns to the colony after an absence of years, it is to become a secular saint, promulgating her belief that "a new truth would be revealed, in order to establish the whole relation between man and woman on a surer ground of mutual happiness" (263).[57] In spite of the definitive closure of Dimmesdale's death, Hester remains committed to her passion as the truest expression of her genuine self, and in its commemoration she now *chooses* to wear the scarlet letter, acknowledging the capacity of the social penalty to endow her passion with greater significance. At novel's end Hester remains a duplicitous character, oddly recapitulating Dimmesdale's false relation to his community. Her life is outwardly selfless and austere, attracting admiration, while inwardly she continues to cherish her sinful opposition to Puritanism: the adulterous passion *and* the unpuritanical freedom of thought. Gabler-Hover condemns Hester's passion for not allowing her to move beyond itself,[58] but in my reading Hester *has* moved beyond it in her intellectual speculation, the vital product of a margin created by the combined forces of law and passion. What she cannot do, because of the rigidity of her society, is move from the margin back to the center.

■ The famous meeting in the forest between Hester Prynne and Arthur Dimmesdale crystallizes the linking of truthful speech with the private world and silence or deceptive utterance with the public.[59] The dialogue, which moves through revelation and estrangement to accord, reveals the energizing potential of a truthful discourse impossible on the terrain of society. By articulating the meeting of hearts, it makes possible the meeting of minds that concludes the encounter.

Here, as so often in *The Scarlet Letter*, speech itself becomes a subject of conversation—its difficulty, its importance, its explication—but unlike the talk exchange that takes place in public, this speaking moves beyond social constraints to achieve genuine communication:

> Hester Prynne looked into his face, but hesitated to speak. Yet, uttering his long-restrained emotions so vehemently as he did, his words here offered her the very point of circumstances in which to interpose what she came to say. She conquered her fears, and spoke.
>
> "Such a friend as thou hast even now wished for," said she, "with whom to weep over thy sin. thou hast in me, the partner of it!"— Again she hesitated, but brought out the words with an effort.— "Thou hast long had such an enemy, and dwellest with him under the same roof! . . ."
>
> "Ha! What sayest thou?" cried he. "An enemy! And under mine own roof! What mean you?" (192)

The tension between speech and silence that encompasses and almost overwhelms the dialogue's propositional content is mirrored in a similar hesitation in the authorial voice: "Such was the ruin to which she had brought the man, once,—nay, why should we not speak it?—still so passionately loved!" (193). It is a moment of articulating withheld knowledge for the authorial voice as well as for Hester, and like Hester's words, it redefines one of the novel's key relationships.

Hester, whose assertive nature ordinarily expresses itself only non-verbally in society through fanciful embellishment of the letter of communal meaning, becomes verbally aggressive here.[60] Condemned to public silence because the letter labels her to the satisfaction of the community, Hester has more invested in private speech than Dimmesdale does. She challenges the minister repeatedly, meanwhile encircling him in her arms, until he answers her question affirmatively by pronouncing forgiveness. This admission begins a train of thought for Dimmesdale which, in keeping with *his* nature, quickly becomes egocentric and self-justifying. His forgiveness of Hester leads to the hope of God's forgiveness of both sinners, and then to the comforting idea that Chillingworth is "worse than even the polluted priest." For Dimmesdale, self-definition is still in terms of his social role, even when it is qualified by the negative *polluted*. To elicit Hester's support

for his reasoning, Dimmesdale shifts back from himself alone to the
two of them:

> "We are not, Hester, the worst sinners in the world. There is one
> worse than even the polluted priest! That old man's revenge has
> been blacker than sin. He has violated, in cold blood, the sanctity
> of a human heart. Thou and I, Hester, never did so!"
> "Never, never!" whispered she. "What we did had a consecra-
> tion of its own. We felt it so! We said so to each other! Hast thou
> forgotten it?"
> "Hush, Hester!" said Arthur Dimmesdale, rising from the
> ground.
> "No; I have not forgotten!" (195)

Although confirming the minister's conclusion, Hester's response is
once more an aggressive challenge, a going beyond the sought-after
agreement. Where Dimmesdale uses a single *never*, she answers with a
double; where he expresses his idea negatively—[we] "never did so"—
she provides a positive counterpart that carries it into far different territory. "What we did had a consecration of its own" implicitly contains
the idea that what was done was *not* consecrated by the community:
the assertion opposes what is legitimately consecrated by the laws of
God and man and proclaims the power of the individual will, a view
both lovers apparently voiced at one time. The statement becomes an
index of social commitment, for Hester has persevered in heretically
misapplying *consecration* to an act that society calls adultery, just as she
has developed ideas contrary to societal values. Dimmesdale, on the
other hand, maintains a large capital of authority, a power and prestige
that he values. He is an errant creature of the group rather than a rebel.
Accordingly, he retreats from an expression of the private meaning of
consecration that he and Hester share.

As the assertive speaker and social rebel, Hester reminds Dimmesdale of their former union in three short sentences which invoke feeling, utterance, and finally, memory. Where she responds eagerly to his
signal for support, he now recoils from her more radical appeal with
the powerful response of a silencing imperative, a reminder of the politic silence associated with their encounters in society and of his greater
authority. These words are coupled with a physical action that also ends
the dialogue, but Dimmesdale modifies the abrupt character of this
response with a conciliatory closure, "I have not forgotten." The com-

munication of thoughts and feelings by both speakers then proceeds to a point of resolution and unity that does not require language: "They sat down again, side by side . . . hand clasped in hand" (195). Silence now expresses unity rather than its customary isolation.

As Quentin Anderson has written, "the scene in the wood . . . is the closest approach to the actualities of passion between grown men and women our nineteenth-century novels managed."[61] Speech carries the major burden of realizing this passion, and more. That the words spoken and the dynamics of the exchange reveal each speaker's character, and that the religious terminology is apt for both the speakers' and the novel's purposes, are literary virtues which may obscure the accomplishment of the primary social purpose of speech: to foster the mutual understanding and agreement that make society possible.[62] For the moment Dimmesdale and Hester constitute an antisociety of two, forerunners of Frederic Henry and Catherine Barkley in a withdrawal from allegiance to the greater world. Once they have verbally committed themselves to a private vision, one which does not recognize the strictures of the Puritan community, further agreement becomes possible, this time in the form of a more extreme withdrawal. "Then, all was spoken!" (198)—as it never can be in the novel's public space.

Freed from the deformations of Puritan constraints, the lovers' speech can function as it ideally should within society: a realm of feeling and action is accepted as a given which can be accurately described in language, discussed, interpreted, and mutually understood. The extent and nature of Hester's and Dimmesdale's opposition to society is registered in their speech, but public language is not itself an issue. Signifying ideas deeply rooted in the Puritan culture, the words upon which their communication turns—*forgiveness, sin, revenge*—serve according to their ordinary communal meanings. In Hester's speech the basis for *consecration* shifts from collective or institutional authority to that of the individual without requiring the term's redefinition, although its use implies a radically individualistic perspective that shocks Dimmesdale.[63] An accord is reached through private speech, although predictably it cannot be sustained in public; once out of the forest, the site of unregulated passion, Dimmesdale will repent and repudiate the plan made with Hester, his immediate sense of guilt manifesting itself in an impulse to undermine his parishioners' faith and punish himself with public exposure.[64] Subversive private speech, it seems, must inevitably lead to subversive public speech, hence the wisdom of the Puritans in calling for a rigorous discipline, even over thought.

■ That truthful speech occurs so seldom in the novel can be attributed not to the faulty instrumentality of language but to the nature of the society which language reflects. In the sermon the community finds its quintessential idiom—accusatory, judgmental, commanding, and threatening—but these qualities, as David Leverenz writes of the historical Puritans, inform all community speech: "Even the most private conversation sounds like a speech to the troops, full of repetitive cadences, melodramatic instances of God's grandeur or personal calls to arms, and emphatic gravity."[65] This coercively hortatory and didactic public language serves the dual purpose of reinforcing an orthodoxy constantly in need of support and masking socially unacceptable personal motives with official rationales. The vindictive speech of the women who observe Hester's public penance transmutes sexual jealousy into righteous indignation, just as the ritualistic exposure of Hester's sin is described as "a blessing on the righteous Colony of Massachusetts, where iniquity is dragged out into the sunshine" (56) rather than as a voyeuristic opportunity to be titillated by illicit sexuality. By means of public language, the forbidden and destructive can be renamed and redirected into respectable social behavior so that in language as in action the condemnation of Hester is a ritual of collective self-validation.

Through language alone, as the magistrates' deliberation on Pearl witnesses, the unacceptable can be incorporated into the rigid structure of Puritan orthodoxy. Pearl herself is the same unsocialized being throughout the scene, an outlandish scarlet figure who behaves capriciously and appears to have had no religious training, but her status changes according to the words used to describe her condition.[66] As it did in the initial scaffold scene, the community commands Hester to speak, yet this time the question is rhetorical: "Were it not, thinkest thou, for thy little one's temporal and eternal welfare, that she be taken out of thy charge, and clad soberly, and disciplined strictly, and instructed in the truths of heaven and earth?" (110)

There is no meeting of minds between Hester and the magistrates; her passionate utterance fails to move them just as their invitation to assent failed to evoke the expected response from her. Hester then passes on the social imperative to Dimmesdale: "Speak thou, the child's own

mother!" becomes "Speak thou for me!"—whose unspoken completion, "the child's own father," is almost palpable. Dimmesdale's appeal
is mediated by his secrecy; he speaks covertly in his unacknowledged
role as the earthly father of Pearl and officially as Hester's pastor, the
representative of the Heavenly Father filling the void of Pearl's unnamed parent.[67] Hester argues that Pearl "is the scarlet letter, only
capable of being loved, and so endowed with a million-fold the power
of retribution for my sin" (113). In a more prolix and less dramatic form
Dimmesdale's speech merely restates that argument: "It [the child]
was meant, doubtless, as the mother herself hath told us, for a retribution too; a torture, to be felt at many an unthought of moment; a
pang, a sting, an ever-recurring agony, in the midst of a troubled joy!
Hath she not expressed this thought in the garb of the poor child,
so forcibly reminding us of that red symbol which sears her bosom?"
(114). Coming from a respected member of the community, Dimmesdale's words draw upon a capital of authority that Hester's lack, but in
addition, they elaborate Hester's terse identification of Pearl with the
letter into an instructive text that multiplies the exemplary potential
of the community's original lesson. Where Hester's speech embodies
her individual passion, Dimmesdale's reflects society's values. Hester's
incorporating Pearl into the orthodox structure of signification emphasizes once again the process of turning deviant behavior to social use
through the imposition of an approved explanation, just as the privi-
leging of Dimmesdale's words points up the importance of social status
in conferring power upon speech.

Adhering to Christ's obliteration of the line between sinful thinking
and the commission of sin, the Puritan ethos seeks a total conformity
that denies the self any deviation from group mores, even in its most
private moments. By empowering the individual at the expense of the
collective definition of experience, Hester's assertion—"what we did
had a consecration of its own"—is as radical and intolerable as the
apostasy of Ann Hutchinson, although it remains a private communication, confided to Dimmesdale's unwilling ear in the depths of the
forest.[68] Ideally, public language should assimilate personal language
into general patterns of meaning that strengthen the bonds of community.[69] Thus, when Dimmesdale announces himself from the pulpit to
be the worst of sinners, his words can easily be interpreted imperson-
ally to invoke a universal rubric of human frailty rather than a personal
condition of particular transgression. The tendency of public language

to express "the normative arrangements of a group rather than the individuated experience of its members" allows Dimmesdale to speak without the danger of being understood.[70] As long as he expresses the familiar generalities of public language, categoric statements about the human condition as perceived by his society, Dimmesdale simply reinforces the stereotype of his sanctity.[71] Converting the personal and the particular into the impersonal and the general, public language transforms "the very truth . . . into the veriest falsehood" (144). Social context reinforces the traditional meanings that Dimmesdale's parishoners ascribe to his veiled confessions, for the minister appears before them in a familiar role, that of an officially sanctioned preacher of morality to those who are sinners.

Even Dimmesdale's final speech is susceptible to this process of transformation because it employs the familiar verbal formulas of ministerial address and because his conviction cannot quite sustain his courage:

> "At last!—at last!—I stand upon the spot where, seven years since, I should have stood; here, with this woman, whose arm, more than the little strength wherewith I have crept hitherward, sustains me, at this dreadful moment, from grovelling down upon my face! Lo, the scarlet letter which Hester wears! Ye have all shuddered at it!
>
> Wherever her walk hath been,—wherever, so miserably burdened, she may have hoped to find repose,—it hath cast a lurid gleam of awe and horrible repugnance round about her. But there stood one in the midst of you, at whose brand of sin and infamy ye have not shuddered!". . .
>
> "It was on him!" he continued. . . . "God's eye beheld it! The angels were forever pointing at it! The Devil knew it well, and fretted it continually with the touch of his burning finger! But he hid it cunningly from men, and walked among you with the mien of a spirit, mournful, because so pure in a sinful world!" (254–55)

As the structure of his speech reveals, Dimmesdale remains to the end a conflicted personality.[72] After the direct beginning in first person, the shift to third person is a faltering that interposes a slight but telling distance between public and private selves. The very nature of Puritan public language and ritualistic confession makes plausible the interpretations of "certain persons" (259) who experience Dimmesdale's utterance not as a deathbed confession of personal culpability but as the enactment of an emblematic tableau, a last exemplum dramatically rendered by the dying pastor for the benefit of his flock.

It is, of course, both, since Dimmesdale exists as saint and sinner entirely within public language. The antisocial impulses released by his forest meeting with Hester shape themselves into a predictable language of negation, not a new vision; for unlike Hester, who is consoled by fictions of a far different kind of society, he can imagine no other world. Dimmesdale's ground of being is not the defiance of society but the difficulty of living up to its standards; he experiences desire only as the blaming of desire, as sinful pleasure. In an extreme form Dimmesdale represents the typical Puritan syndrome of private anxiety coupled with public orthodoxy, but in his case the social mechanism of adaptive transformation, which Leverenz describes as "a reordering of feelings to orient the self toward group expression," [73] is blocked by the obstacle of deception. Iniquity must be "dragged out into the sunshine" before regeneration can begin. Dimmesdale is the most dramatic participant in this speech-act drama because he is subject to the most conflict, radically torn between equally unpalatable identities of liar and sinner, the false-speaking public man and the silent private self. Neither Hester nor Chillingworth feels guilty about presenting a public self that is seriously misleading because each responds more strongly to private imperatives: Hester to her passionate will, Chillingworth to his revenge. Dimmesdale has no such life in opposition to society's values: his private self, narcissistically absorbed in a secret drama of guilt and punishment, is weak rather than deviant.

The doubleness of Dimmesdale's character actually threatens society in a more insidiously subversive way than the defiant individualism of Ann Hutchinson. It demonstrates, as Leo Bersani writes of *Mansfield Park*, that "character is not necessary to maintain the structures of community life," [74] thus opening an abyss between appearance and reality. As a sinner, Dimmesdale appears to be a saint; at those moments when his sinfulness is closest to the surface he is most eloquent in the service of God, following his midnight scaffold vigil with "a discourse which was held to be the richest and most powerful, and the most replete with heavenly influences, that had ever proceeded from his lips" (157).

Gabler-Hover regards Dimmesdale as a dangerous influence on his flock because his eloquence "prompts passion rather than compassion." [75] The authorial voice, however, suggests that Dimmesdale's own anguish stimulates a powerful empathetic relation: "But this very burden it was, that gave him sympathies so intimate with the sinful brotherhood of mankind; so that his heart vibrated in unison with theirs, and received their pain into itself, and sent its own throb of pain through a thousand other hearts" (142). Given Hawthorne's perspective that the situation is more complicated than Puritan ideology allows for, it is fitting that the pain of Dimmesdale's sin—which tortures his psyche and wastes his body—ironically intensifies his ability to function in his social role.[76] Indeed, both Hester and Dimmesdale have been empowered by their status as sinners to reach out to others more effectively, and this challenges society's coercion of them into either/or positions.

Wherever Hawthorne furnishes a verbatim text—Dimmesdale's exhortation to Hester in the first scaffold scene, his plea on her behalf to the magistrates—the language is unremarkable. If we look at the lengthy description of Dimmesdale's Election Day sermon, his greatest public triumph preceded by his frankest confrontation with his sin, we find that Hawthorne's reference to what the minister actually says is vague. On this occasion, the authorial voice takes some pains to present the appeal of Dimmesdale's discourse as primarily nonverbal and nonintellectual.[77] Recording the performance from Hester's point of view necessarily excludes meaning since she is too far away to distinguish the words. The passage emphasizes the minister's "very peculiar voice," which "breathed passion and pathos, and emotions high or tender, in a tongue native to the human heart" (243). The weight of suffering and pathos, bypassing language to speak directly through the vocal instrument, creates the "profound and continuous undertone that gave the clergyman his most appropriate power" (244). Hawthorne's choice of *appropriate* both acknowledges the connection between the private and public selves and characterizes it as the proper source of Dimmesdale's power over his audience. In the way in which the anarchic desires of the private self fuel the contrived public performance, Dimmesdale transcends his historical context to become the Everyman of Western depth psychology, intermittently capable of shaking off repression-induced neurosis and sublimating his libidinous desires into an acceptable social role. My account partially agrees with the seminal reading of Frederick C. Crews, who writes, "If the written form of the Election Sermon *is* a great Christian document . . . this is attributable not to Dimmesdale's holiness but to his libido, which gives him creative strength and an intimate acquaintance with the reality of sin." [78] Crews and the Puritan community both insist upon an either/ or reading of Dimmesdale's character, whereas saint and sinner, like law and passion, are inextricably bound together.[79] Just as the sermon depends upon Dimmesdale's libido for the reason Crews adduces, so it also depends upon his "holiness."

Through speech Dimmesdale creates his most triumphant moment as a public figure, and through speech he creates an identity that destroys the speaker of the Election Day sermon (while saving his soul). Fittingly, the public responds to his confession with sound alone, the language of their "awe and wonder"; words would require some form of evaluation that the baffled community cannot yet make. Later, reassuring versions of what happened will be promulgated to maintain the minister's public image. Once he has spoken clearly and openly, Dimmesdale must die as a member of his society, which has no place for the self that he has verbally integrated, the man who is both an inspiring public figure and a private sinner. Those like himself, whom he once described to Chillingworth, live a dilemma admitting of no solution: "Guilty as they may be, retaining, nevertheless, a zeal for God's glory and man's welfare, they shrink from displaying themselves black and filthy in the view of men; because, thenceforward, no good can be achieved by them; no evil of the past redeemed by better service" (132). In context this is a self-serving rationalization, of course, but it also accurately describes Dimmesdale's society. Its rigid either/or classification, saint or sinner, is partial and reductive because it demands coherence, even at the expense of totality. It accepts a convenient limited perspective in place of a complex whole because indeterminacy of character eludes social classification and control. Society's belief system is upheld with the death of one sinner and the exclusion of the other, but at a cost of waste and suffering that sharply questions Puritan ideology. Yet Hawthorne never commits the authorial voice to a solution. By setting the novel proper in Puritan times, he avoids the necessity of a direct statement about his own society. When he does engage it in *The Blithedale Romance*, the conclusion is equally unsatisfactory: the destruction of valuable human potential and society unchanged.

The moral of Dimmesdale's life for Hawthorne—to "show freely to the world, if not your worst, yet some trait whereby the worst may be inferred" (260)—affirms society's right to protect itself from the private self, anarchic or merely flawed; and in this respect, as Lionel Trilling observes, Dimmesdale disappoints our ideal of the autonomous self: "Hawthorne could indeed conceive of our longed-for autonomy. But his own piety was committed elsewhere."[80] Committed, but hardly fulfilled: society as an official entity does not foster nurturing relations in any of his novels, and the tension between individual speakers and social authority in *The Scarlet Letter* has no positive dimension.

The Speech of Individual Assertion in *Moby-Dick*

■ Coming from the verbal homogeneity of *The Scarlet Letter*, the speech of *Moby-Dick* is strikingly differentiated, a part of the ambitious plenitude that informs all aspects of the novel. The elements of fiction are commensurate with the scale of its physical world, in which huge creatures (squid as well as whale) swim through vast seas and eerie flames of lightning turn the *Pequod*'s masts into gigantic candles. To render the infinitely meaningful and mysterious universe of *Moby-Dick*, Melville draws upon the languages of drama, exposition, narration, argument, exhortation, and prophecy—all of which, in the crucible of his style, are steeped in the same rhetorical intensity and embellishment.[81] This linguistic richness and exuberance match the wonders of the phenomenological world of the novel and everywhere assert the power of words to transmute the neutral stuff of reality, the passive beingness of nature, into subjective visions of meaning and order.[82] As J. L. Austin writes, "Sensa, that is things, colours, noises, and the rest . . . are dumb, and only previous experience enables *us* to identify them. If we choose to say that they 'identify themselves' . . . then it must be admitted that they share the birthright of all speakers, that of speaking unclearly and untruly."[83] This is the epistemological terrain of the novel: language, the text proposes, can provide a coherent perspective, a story that may be more or less authorized. Definitive explanation is beyond its reach, not because of its own inherent limitations but because the stuff of reality is ultimately intractable to the sense-making process of language. In Melville's words to Hawthorne, "We incline to think that God cannot explain His own secrets, and that He would like a little information upon certain points Himself."[84] Moreover, he speculates: "Perhaps, after all, there is no secret,"[85] a void of meaning that no effort of communication can overcome. This opaque

universe, mysterious even to the deity, is a polar opposite of the world
that Cooper and Stowe represent as governed by God, understandable
to reason, and communicable in language.[86] In the face of the novel's
many fictive voices and Captain Ahab's meditated assault, nature remains silent and impenetrable, a condition more frustrating and en-
raging to Ahab than what he takes to be the wilfully inflicted blows of
Moby Dick. Malignity may be understood and responded to—it is part
of a dialogue; inscrutability offers no cues for physical or verbal action.
A man of both action and eloquence, Ahab opposes an adversary whose
"great genius" is "declared in his pyramidical silence."

Society also presents serious difficulties to the ordering and expressive functions of language, but of a different sort from those in the world
of nature; its ground is ethics rather than metaphysics. As hierarchy
and institution, society is unfailingly flawed and coercive throughout
Melville's fiction, a collection of "civilized hypocrisies and bland de-
ceits"; as community, a locus of shared purpose and feeling, it is fatally
ambiguous. The same road to felicity that Ishmael extols in "A Squeeze
of the Hand" disintegrates under the feet of Pierre, and Queequeg
suspended on the monkey-rope is in equal danger from friend and
foe. Seeing his tie to Queequeg here as a symbol of the human condition, which is "a Siamese connection with a plurality of other mortals,"
Ishmael offers two further examples of dependence: "If your banker
breaks, you snap; if your apothecary by mistake sends you poison in
your pills, you die" (320). Whereas mutual affection infuses the labor
of Ishmael and Queequeg, these instances are impersonal commercial
transactions and thus susceptible to the additional hazards of performance divorced from feeling. Such a state of uncertain dependency is
the Melvillian dilemma: isolation warps the spirit, but, through lack of
caring, the collective existence can be oppressive, unjust, and unchari-
table.

Social rigidity and individual egocentricity menace necessary human
relationships, but the difficulty of distinguishing exploitative forms of
authority from those that create genuine community menace them
more. It is both a "mutual, joint-stock world, in all meridians" and a
"wicked world in all meridians" (62, 56), but these partial views, which
the noble savage Queequeg holds and harmonizes in his radically simplified worldview, become associated with Ishmael and Ahab respectively. Of the two, the sociality and cooperation that Ishmael espouses
as the ultimate good of existence and the cosmic evil that Ahab en-

visions as the ultimate truth of it, the atypical nature of most speaking in the novel encourages the negative view that would come to dominate Melville's later fiction: the view that the world is a place where communication is suspect and perhaps impossible. The self-contained soliloquy, in which speaker and hearer are the same person, especially suits Ahab, who admits no one else to his level of being; but those in some way committed to a joint-stock world—such as gregarious Stubb and conformistic Starbuck—also use it. All of these circumstances portend the linguistic impotence of speakers in Melville's later fiction yet do not diminish the vigor of speech in *Moby-Dick*—most likely because Melville's recent immersion in Shakespeare profoundly affected the novel's language, and this influence was expansive and affirmative.[87] Already in *Pierre*, only a year later, the impulse had mostly spent itself, and Melville began to lose control over the kind of long, eloquent speech that is consistently effective in *Moby-Dick*. Such rhetorically brilliant set pieces disappear after *Pierre*, as Melville's developing tendency toward verbal skepticism asserts itself in stylistic restraint, but in *Moby-Dick*, speech, especially that of Captain Ahab, is charged with a Shakespearian ebullience that challenges the problematic nature of communication.[88]

If we think for a moment of the unexceptional dialogue of the autobiographical romances preceding *Moby-Dick* and the increasing attenuation of speech in Melville's later fiction, the many voices that articulate the world of this novel are all the more remarkable. Like the Anacharsis Clootz deputation that was a favorite Melvillian image, this Bakhtinian heteroglossia consciously represents the heterogeneous collectivity of mankind.[89] This speech is individualized but seldom realistic, pervasively marked as it is by Shakespearian wit and rhetorical extravagance.

Here as elsewhere throughout *Moby-Dick* Melville replicates Ahab's heroic quest for knowledge of the universe by seeking out and testing the limits of literary structures. This exploration of the interface between what can and cannot be said creates a powerful dialectic between confident verbalization and silence. Because speech is made to bear a weight of philosophic inquiry that we would ordinarily expect to be conveyed through narrative alone, it tends to be far more declamatory than conversational. This conjoins with the importance of hierarchical relationships in the novel to produce a number of one-sided speech situations in which speaking is more likely to be some form of exhortation—sermon, order, challenge—or dramatic soliloquy than normative dialogue.[90] A large block of speech is directed to an audience that lacks full participatory status: the crew of the *Pequod* addressed by Ahab, collectively and individually; the congregation for Father Mapple's sermon; the men in the whaleboats exhorted by their officers during the chase. All of these one-way speech situations, because they are based upon the inequality of speakers, emphasize the omnipresence of a social order that reduces many would-be speakers to silence. Once the voyage is underway, the only talk exchange on the basis of equality occurs between Stubb and Flask and between Boomer and Bunger on the *Samuel Enderby*. (The latter is a noteworthy exception because, like the relationship of Ishmael and Queequeg, it instances the transcendence of social hierarchy by affection.) Pip is the most extreme example of distortion of speech by social pressure: cut off from all community when a society that places little value on his life abandons him, Pip dramatizes the connection between membership within a group and speech by his inability to speak thereafter in a recognizable idiom.

Diverse problems of communication also prevent speech from becoming successful talk exchange. Most of the *Pequod*'s encounters with other ships involve some difficulty ranging from the literal failure to hear words spoken to the divergent purposes of the interacting speech communities. Moreover, a thread of unintelligible utterance is persistently woven into the fabric of discourse. Like the speech of Pip's madness, the arcane language of prophecy that runs through the novel offers glimpses of a tantalizing world of verbal signification that eludes understanding.

■ In spite of the seeming abundance of speakers, one voice dominates the speech of *Moby-Dick*. Most of the novel's speech that is not uttered by Ahab is spoken to him or about him, or serves to characterize him indirectly. The inconsequentiality of the brief, fragmentary utterances of the sailors in the "Midnight, Forecastle" scene, Stubb's bantering, Flask's materialism, and Starbuck's traditional pieties all emphasize the single-minded commitment of Ahab's speech to high significance.

Although Melville often calls our attention to Ahab's physical appearance—the "livid brand" that marks his face, the "barbaric white leg upon which he partly stood," the "crucifixion in his face"—these vivid particulars are supporting rather than primary; above all, Ahab is a powerful voice. Silenced, he would merely be a posture of fortitude or eccentricity, or even pathos, whereas through his commanding rhetoric Ahab creates himself as the heroic protagonist as fully as he creates Moby Dick as the great antagonist he desires, endowing both roles with transcendent significance. Ahab does not imagine Moby Dick to embody all evil in the universe, however; the whale is merely the wall "shoved close," the self-aggrandizing symbol that presents itself in Ahab's own life, and the necessary focus of his quest.[91]

In a long passage claiming heroic status for Ahab, the authorial voice goes to some length to establish his speech as singular, the product of a direct encounter between exceptional individuality and nature:

> So that there are instances among them of men, who, named with Scripture names . . . and in childhood naturally imbibing the stately dramatic *thee* and *thou* of the Quaker idiom; still, from the audacious, daring, and boundless adventure of their subsequent lives, strangely blend with these unoutgrown peculiarities, a thousand bold dashes of character, not unworthy of a Scandanavian sea-king, or a poetical Pagan Roman. And when these things unite in a man of greatly superior natural force, with a globular brain and a ponderous heart; who has also by the stillness and seclusion of many long night-watches in the remotest waters, and beneath constellations never seen here at the north, been led to think untraditionally and independently; receiving all nature's sweet or savage impressions fresh from her own virgin, voluntary, and confiding breast, and thereby chiefly, but with some help from accidental advantages, to learn a bold and nervous lofty language—that many makes one in a whole nation's census—a mighty pageant creature, formed for noble tragedies. (73)

In spite of the Quaker accoutrements that give his speech an Old Testament grandeur, Ahab is represented as bypassing society in his acquisition of language and learning an idiom that blends the antisocial with the presocial. That Ahab belongs to an interpretive community of one, speaking a "bold and nervous lofty language" beyond the reach of ordinary men, accounts in part for the lack of genuine communication between him and other speakers.[92] It is always Ahab's desire, as Stanley Fish writes of Coriolanus, "to stand alone, without visible or invisible supports, as a natural force. He wants to be independent of society and of the language with which it constitutes itself and its values, seeking instead a language that is the servant of essences he alone can recognize because he alone embodies them."[93] Ahab intends his speech to be an instrument of cosmic confrontation, which explains why he prefers speaking to nature, to the "clear spirit of clear fire" that he addresses in "The Candles" or to the "vast and venerable head" of the whale. And while Ahab frequently laments the refusal of nature to speak, his preference for apostrophizing the inanimate and denying speech rights to other men suggests that he would hardly be comfortable dealing with nature as autonomous speaker.

If Ahab's language cannot succeed in opening a dialogue with nature, neither is it suited to speech with other men, especially to the other men to whom it is usually addressed, his unthinking and unknowing crew. Even those extended utterances putatively directed toward some human audience—for instance, the famous pasteboard mask speech—are like soliloquies, dialogues with self divorced from the requirements of the verbal occasion. Since other men exist for Ahab as tools of his will or limited versions of himself, his language is primarily an instrument of self-assertion and self-validation, not a means of establishing connections with other men or exploring the world.[94] His utterances are often directives, whose aim is to get "the world to conform to words," as opposed to assertives, which get "words to conform to the world."[95] Ahab regards physical reality as a "magician's glass" which "to each and every man in turn but mirrors back his own mysterious self" (359). He therefore sees himself everywhere, simultaneously imposing his image on the universe and distancing himself from its separate reality. The special status that Ahab accords Starbuck, Fedallah, and Pip correlates with his perception of them as partial or exemplary versions of himself. Starbuck's eye mirrors wife and child, a self that Ahab has put aside, while Fedallah's eye reflects the mixed nature of the quest, its promise of suprahuman knowledge and its taint of demonism. Pip, superficially the opposite of Ahab, gives back to Ahab his sense of his own cosmic victimization. Resisting more than such limited identification with other men, Ahab sees himself as a complete being in "grand and lofty things": the tower, volcano, and mountain fowl of the doubloon.

In keeping with his ideal of godlike power and self-sufficiency, Ahab projects his most complete self-image onto Moby Dick, ascribing to it an intentionality much like the aggressive malevolence that has characterized his own pursuit of whales: "The madness, the frenzy, the boiling blood and the smoking brow, with which, for a thousand lowerings old Ahab has furiously, foamingly chased his prey—more a demon than a man!" (544). And if the whale is a fatal magnet because he best embodies the inscrutability of the universe, Ahab sees himself as moved by the same force—"nameless, inscrutable, unearthly"—and is himself seen by others as inscrutable. In the confrontation with Moby Dick, Ahab seeks knowledge of himself, but the only language the two have in common is aggression, a condition that forecloses the possibility of fruitful communication. As language, Ahab's speech is unquestionably magnificent, but as utterance appropriate to a particular occasion, it often succeeds only through its extraverbal qualities. In spite of Ahab's substitution of personal for social goals, much of his effectiveness as a speaker is vested in his role as captain of the ship; he has supreme authority over the speech of his community because social hierarchy gives him the preeminent right to speak on board the *Pequod* and for the *Pequod* elsewhere, a power that, regardless of what he says or how he says it, allows him to monopolize speech and to a large extent control the speech of others.

Dialogue as ritual, in which each utterance is prescribed and the end result is to confirm a value he already holds, is Ahab's paradigm for verbal interaction. Unveiling his intention to hunt the white whale, he guides his mystified crew to seemingly innocuous verbal responses which confirm each step of his unfolding plan and intensify their feeling:

> "And what do ye next, men?"
> "Lower away, and after him!"
> "And what tune is it ye pull to, men?"
> "A dead whale or a stove boat!"
> More and more strangely and fiercely glad and approving, grew the countenance of the old man at every shout; while the mariners began to gaze curiously at each other, as if marvelling how it was that they themselves became so excited at such seemingly purposeless questions. (161)

Here Ahab builds upon his authority by manipulating the speech situation to induce an excitement that the men find baffling but which can readily be accounted for: the unification of the crew in giving Ahab the routine information he requests and the attendant satisfaction at being able to do so, the rhythm of the antiphonal chant, the suspense of a climactic progression, and Ahab's own conspicuous emotion infuse the familiar words with new significance. Given the crew's lack of sophistication, these simple techniques for enhancing speech are enough.[96]

To counter Starbuck's hesitation requires more and different verbal strategies. When Starbuck demurs at Ahab's announced goal, he is first coached to return the desired response—"Art not game for Moby Dick"? (163)—but when his rejoinder is negative, he is overwhelmed by a torrent of Ahab's words, which make a number of arguments in succession. The "little lower layer" of philosophical explanation with its prologue flattering Starbuck's intellect is followed by a casuistic apology for offending Starbuck, a reference to the crew's wholehearted support of Ahab (implying Starbuck's isolation), and an attempt to devaluate the hunt to routine ("tis but to help strike a fin") coupled with a complimentary denomination of Starbuck as "the best lance out of Nantucket." Ahab's speech is a virtuoso performance, a compendium of rhetorical appeals, but as speech act it fails: Starbuck does not obey the command to speak or acknowledge the sense of any of Ahab's arguments, and his later capitulation is brought about by an almost magical emanation of personal force rather than by language: "Something shot from my dilated nostrils, he has inhaled it in his lungs. Starbuck now is mine; cannot oppose me now, without rebellion" (164).

In all respects Ahab is an awesomely closed system that rejects outright any opposing view or converts it into sport. Fedallah's prophecy that hemp alone can kill him can only be, to Ahab's ears, a reference to the gallows, another pledge that he is invulnerable to Moby Dick. When his mates shrink from serving as cup-bearers to the harpooners, Ahab transforms his own command into an assertion of *their* intentions: "I do not order ye; ye will it" (166). In speech-act terms such a pronouncement is infelicitous because, as Austin puts it, "you can't just make statements about other people's feelings."[97] Ahab, of course, is not describing the mates' feelings but coercively regarding them as projections of his own will.

When a speaker challenges his purpose more openly, Ahab peremptorily withdraws, uninterested in further speech.[98] Verbally assaulted by Gabriel when the *Pequod* meets the *Jereboam*, "Ahab stolidly turned aside" (317). With his own subordinate Stubb, a more definite closure is called for: "Begone, or I'll clear the world of thee!" (127). For speakers of higher status, like Captain Gardiner, Ahab provides something like the expected closure of social discourse, but its mitigating phrases are surrounded and overwhelmed by what Ishmael calls the language of "unconditional and utter rejection":

> "Avast," cried Ahab—"touch not a rope-yarn;" then in a voice that prolongingly moulded every word—"Captain Gardiner, I will not do it. Even now I lose time. Good bye, good bye, God bless ye, man, and may I forgive myself, but I must go. Mr. Starbuck, look at the binnacle watch, and in three minutes from this present instant warn off all strangers: then brace forward again, and let the ship sail as before." (532–33)

Characteristically, the self-reflexiveness of Ahab's verbal style and his directive mode dominate the speech. Ahab wishes God's blessing upon Captain Gardiner and forgiveness of himself by himself, polarities that encapsulate social and individual systems of value.

Ordinarily, Ahab observes the decorum of polite conversation only to the extent that it is essential to acquire intelligence of Moby Dick; his model of discourse with the world beyond his ship is the unembellished question "Hast seen the White Whale?" and an economical answer, preferably the coordinates of Moby Dick's position. Even when information is to be had, as it is from Captain Boomer, Ahab's impatience and egotism constantly disrupt the normative process of talk exchange by breaking into the other speaker's narrative with questioning, direction, and interpretation:

> "Presently up breaches from the bottom of the sea a bouncing great whale, with a milky-white head and hump, all crows' feet and wrinkles."
>
> "It was he, it was he!" cried Ahab, suddenly letting out his suspended breath.
>
> "And harpoons sticking in near his starboard fin."
>
> "Aye, aye—they were mine—*my* irons," cried Ahab, exultingly—"but on!"
>
> "Give me a chance then," said the Englishman, good-humoredly. "Well, this old great-grandfather, with the white head and hump, runs all afoam into the pod, and goes to snapping furiously at my fast-line."
>
> "Aye, I see!—wanted to part it; free the fast-fish—an old trick—I know him." (438)[99]

Boomer's leisurely and good-humored account of his misfortune describes events without assigning meaning, whereas Ahab's staccato interruptions express the certainty of positive identification and possession: "It was he," "They were mine," "I know him." Boomer's story simply gives Ahab raw material for his own compulsive fiction in which attention is almost equally divided between himself and Moby Dick, between his action which has marked the whale—as the whale has marked him—and his understanding of its behavior. While complaining that nature refuses to speak to him, Ahab is eager to speak for it, to appropriate the whale verbally by asserting his interpretation of it.

Similarly, when he addresses the head of a dead whale, Ahab both protests its silence and asserts his own version of its experience, the usurpation of a domain for which he cannot be an authorized speaker: "Thou hast seen enough to split the planets and make an infidel of Abraham, and not one syllable is thine!" (312). His particularization of this experience is in the indicative rather than the subjunctive, a series of incidents introduced by phrases such as "thou hast been" and "thou saw'st." Austin commonsensically observes that "there are very many things which having no knowledge of, not being in a position to pronounce about, you just can't state." [100] Ahab accepts neither ordinary discourse agreements nor the limitations of his ability to speak about the world.

Ahab's denial of authority to other speakers leads him at times not only to misinterpret or disregard what is said to him but literally to fail to hear it—token of his inability to suffer any dissenting voice. Absorbed in his victory after Starbuck has succumbed to his will, "Ahab did not hear his foreboding invocation; nor yet the low laugh from the hold; nor yet the presaging vibrations of the winds in the cordage; nor yet the hollow flap of the sails against the masts" (164). As Ahab leaves the ship on the fatal third day of the chase, Pip warns of sharks and calls him back: "But Ahab heard nothing; for his own voice was high-lifted then" (566).

Predicated upon his assumption of superiority over other speakers, Ahab's speech always denies his kinship with other men, both by rejecting outright their statements and requests and by rejecting implicitly the social paradigms that their speech invokes. Immediately before the climactic encounter with Moby Dick, Ahab faces his single critic and simply talks him down, adducing from the mild weather first the serenity of untroubled life and then the hegemony of fate and death.

When Starbuck responds to Ahab's first speech by recalling Nantucket, Ahab allows himself to enter this vision, seeing "the far away home" in his eye; but when Starbuck joins the image of the boy waiting at home to the directive "let us away!"—Ahab chooses to look no longer. He begins to speak again himself, shifting his discourse to fate and death. While Ahab's words enforce his vision of reality on Starbuck, causing the mate to blanch "to a corpse's hue," the words of Starbuck and other speakers capture Ahab's acquiescence only momentarily; because he rejects the institutions they represent, they never persuade him. Captain Gardiner, who makes the unvoiced appeal of a fellow Nantucketer to Ahab, explicitly refers to their mutual fatherhood and to the Golden Rule, appeals that Starbuck also makes to Ahab. All of these pleas speak to primitive and essential kinds of relationship, as does Captain Boomer's attempt to elicit Ahab's agreement about Moby Dick on the basis of their common injury. Whereas Boomer can contemplate the loss of his arm without rancor, sustained by his friendship with Bunger, Ahab's grandiose concept of self cannot assimilate either the violation of bodily integrity or its resulting dependency.

■ For all of its testing of literary boundaries and all of Melville's dark allusions to its lack of orthodoxy, *Moby-Dick* does not finally deviate from the conventional ideology of nineteenth-century fiction: the individualistic hero is destroyed and social and even cosmic equilibrium restored at novel's end. If we apply to the language of *Moby-Dick* David L. Minter's useful idea of the interpreted design, in which a "man of design or action" is juxtaposed to a "man of interpretation,"[101] the obsessed and inflexible speech of Ahab, the character with a goal to achieve, exists within the controlling idiom of Ishmael, his narrator/interpreter. It is not so much Ahab's inevitable defeat that gives the novel its ultimate meaning but the enclosure of Ahab's story and his egocentric rhetoric within Ishmael's more inclusive vision and language. For society's economic criteria of value Ahab substitutes his personal goals, yet the society of the *Pequod* reconstituted in his own image is no less exploitative, and the view of mankind upon which it is predicated is equally dehumanized.

Ishmael, on the other hand, begins as someone who goes to sea because of impulses which make him unfit for society, but he is purged of his antisocial feelings by his commitment first to Queequeg and then, in "A Squeeze of the Hand," to humanity in general. Intellectually saved by repudiating the narrowed perspective of Ahab's quest, and physically saved by the caring of others—the search of the *Rachel* for her missing children—he is returned to a society whose common totems—"the wife, the heart, the bed, the table, the saddle, the fire-side, the country" (349)—he now willingly embraces. Ishmael tells Ahab's tale, but his own encompassing vision rebukes Ahab's restricted view as his survival rebukes Ahab's quest. Where Ahab errs, it seems clear, is in sacrificing others to his egocentric interpretation of reality. Turning his back on the values of community, he imposes the fictions of the autonomous self on his hapless crew.

Disvaluing speech with other men in his desire to have a dialogue with speechless nature, Ahab inevitably experiences the tragedy of isolation that lack of communication and lack of community entail. Where Ahab's sense of importance creates a language of self-validation that functions only in a circular fashion, Ishmael is, in Edgar A. Dryden's words, a "verbal wanderer," able to entertain and articulate numerous perspectives and correspondingly free from hierarchical prejudice.[102] Whereas Ahab constantly interposes hierarchy between himself and other speakers, creating barriers to free communication, Ishmael overcomes social barriers to achieve a dialogue with Queequeg.

Yet Ahab is not destroyed because his assumed posture does not finally correspond to the facts. The Ahabean reading of the universe is a self-fulfilling prophecy, enforceable because nature, as Melville wrote in *Pierre*, "is not so much her own ever-sweet interpreter, as the mere supplier of that cunning alphabet, whereby selecting and combining as he pleases, each man reads his own peculiar mind and mood" (342).[103] Whatever physical reality is remains elusive, and the catastrophic meeting with Moby Dick is exactly the kind of conclusion that Ahab's belief in willful malignity inscribes upon the universe, a confirmation that man cannot strike through the mask to absolute knowledge. Ishmael's description of this end—"retribution, swift vengeance, eternal malice were in his [Moby Dick's] whole aspect" (571)—valorizes Ahab's perspective.[104] The necessary criticism of Ahab's speech is not its failure to conform to "reality" but its violation of the mutuality of talk exchange. Ahab abrogates this linguistic social contract through his solipsistic indifference to the rights of other people, other speakers.

In keeping with his function as observer rather than hero, comic rather than tragic protagonist, Ishmael is both more pragmatic and more speculative than Ahab; the metaphysical uncertainties that torment Ahab are only one part of his vision of the universe. As the chapter on the whiteness of the whale especially shows, Ishmael's language accordingly reflects a holistic desire to embrace—rather than cut off—possibility. Nevertheless, the tempting equation of Ishmael's attitude to that of the text needs to be resisted, for the text proposes an integration of comic and tragic worlds in *Moby-Dick*, not a choice between them.

Chapter 2

"Truth Is Voiceless": Speech and Silence in Melville's Later Fiction

The words betray the thoughts they are supposed to
express. Even the most generalized truth begins to look
like special pleading as soon as you trap it in language.

TOM STOPPARD, *Jumpers*

■ In *Moby-Dick* Ahab rejects society's valuation of commerce and embarks upon a personal quest in direct opposition to social goals, but his rebellious individualism does not extend to language: he expresses himself vigorously and eloquently to the end, or to the penultimate moment when, not sharing a common tongue with the whale, he must attempt to strike through the mask or wall with his harpoon. But Ahab is a self-reflexive system, whose actions and language always refer back to himself. Fittingly, his death is self-generated, not brought about by actual contact with the whale but through his own rope, which claims first his power of speech and then his life: "Voicelessly as Turkish mutes bowstring their victim, he was shot out of the boat, ere the crew knew he was gone" (572).

Already in *Pierre*, Melville's only major novel set foursquarely in American society, the tragic grandeur of Ahab's inflexibility has become attenuated, and to a large extent by a new attitude of skepticism about language.[1] The protagonist is still an impassioned *isolato*, but the defiance of his final moments is curiously undercut by the wish to escape his physical self and begin anew: "Well, be it hell. I will mold a trumpet of the flames, and with my breath of flame, breathe back my defiance! But give me first another body! I long and long to die, to be rid of this dishonored cheek" (360). Pierre's Ahab-like resolve fades because, unlike Ahab, he is a divided soul, finally overcome by the ambiguities of human relationship, an aspect of life that Ahab has consciously eliminated from his consideration. Having reduced the

multiple possibilities of life to one, Ahab pursues his goal monomaniacally; reversals only confirm his sense of the magnitude and worth of
his undertaking. Lacking such certainty and single-mindedness, Pierre
comes to function out of desperation alone. Charles Feidelson, Jr., sees
Pierre as marking "an important change from . . . Melville's previous
novels." It lacks the balance between Ahab and Ishmael that characterized *Moby-Dick*, Feidelson believes, because "Melville's considerable
sympathy with his hero's passionate resentment robs him of aesthetic
balance."[2] Feidelson's well-known study convincingly establishes the
history of symbolism in American writing as "one continuous movement from the Puritan era . . . to the new philosophy of Emerson";[3]
however, since he is most interested in a philosophical examination
of the difference between logical and symbolic uses of language, he
entirely ignores its social dimension.[4] If Ahab had the power to remove himself from society, Pierre is completely enmeshed in a social
world that constantly subjects him to hostility. Whereas Ahab inadver-
tently silences himself, believing that he is engaged in a dialogue with
the universe, Pierre, doubting that his words can order or clarify his
experience, chooses to silence himself.

   The willed withdrawal into silence of Pierre becomes the rule in
Melville's later fiction, precursor of Melville's own withdrawal from
the profession of writing. As Alan Lebowitz observes, *Pierre* seems
to reflect "a last perception that the world no longer offered meaningful subjects for his fictions and that the act of writing was itself a
fruitless act."[5] Indeed, after *Moby-Dick*, the antisocial element previously articulated forthrightly in Melville's work assumes this subtler
linguistic form. Those characters strongly identified with social codes
of speaking—that is, public language—are evil or misguided, and the
diminished protagonists become linguistically impotent, unable to express their private quests in the language of society and its institutions,
winding down to silence. This developing impulse is conjoined with
Melville's setting of much of his post–*Moby-Dick* fiction in American society, for however much the earlier texts deal with sociopolitical
issues, they avoid the actual terrain of nineteenth-century America.
The various ships and exotic South Sea island communities are special worlds which replicate only certain limited aspects of macrocosmic
social existence, whereas the physical setting of American society enjoins a more direct and obtrusive social import. Pierre must contend
with numerous forms of social disapproval: the denial of the most basic

communal tie, that of kin; the deprivation of property; the opposition of the church. His living arrangements fit into no acceptable social category, and in killing his cousin he finally puts himself in total opposition to the institutions of family, church, and state. Yet it would be misleading to see this massing of social force against the individual as *Pierre*'s primary focus. As Richard H. Brodhead writes of Melville, "His vision impels him to be less interested in the actual processes of human experience, understood in its social, psychological, moral or historical aspects, than in the meaning of experience seen in its largest conceivable dimensions."[6] *Pierre*'s philosophical quest for meaning, his attempt to fathom epistemological mysteries, is the novel's chief concern—although of necessity it takes place within society and engenders a struggle with the authority of institutions whose social consequences ultimately lead to Pierre's silencing.

The Piazza Tales

■ Melville's tales bridge the period between the failure of *Moby-Dick* and *Pierre* to find an audience and the jumping-off place of *The Confidence-Man*, the last novel to be published in his lifetime.[7] While it seems clear that in turning to short fiction Melville was still trying to remain a commercially viable author, it is equally clear that once again other intentions worked against this purpose. William Charvat writes, "That he was trying to come to some sort of terms with the common reader is suggested by the subject matter of his shorter pieces: three are returns to the romantic Pacific; nine have rural settings, and seven deal with the popular subject of home and women. . . . Yet when we examine these eighteen shorter works, we find that only three do not deal with some kind of loss, poverty, loneliness, or defeat."[8]

The linguistic counterpart of these thematic concerns is the withdrawal of the Melvillian protagonist from the verbal extravagance of the earlier texts. In the *Piazza Tales*, the best known of Melville's short fiction, speech dissolves in two directions: where experience is too horrific or incomprehensible; or, where communication is impossible because of the social context or the bad faith of speakers, it moves toward silence. "Truth is voiceless." Melville had written in *Mardi*, and as he came to feel more and more the difficulties of truthful speaking, his fiction becomes dominated by deceptive speakers.

Like *Moby-Dick*'s Ahab-Ishmael pairing, in which Ishmael's flexible

narrative encloses Ahab's rigidly egocentric rhetoric,[9] the *Tales* reveal
versions of a structure in which an interpreter, who may be narrator
or character, speaks a public language inadequate to the situation he
observes. Since both language and understanding are limited in the
observer, the various protagonists suffer the frustration that failure to
communicate entails, an inability to use language that leads inexorably
to silence—often the silence of death.

■ The narrator and the crew valorize individually and
collectively the purest form of silence as a response to horrific experience, that of the Chola widow in "The Encantadas." When the unperceptive captain presses Hunilla about encounters with passing ships,
she "would not, durst not trust the weakness of her tongue" (157). The
rapport established between Hunilla and the crew is appropriately nonverbal; the sailors answer her reticence by forming a "voiceless circle"
around her and according her the "silent reverence of respect."

Whatever Hunilla did say, the narrator will not repeat: "The half here
shall remain untold. Those two unnamed events which befell Hunilla
on this isle, let them abide between her and her God. In nature, as in
law, it may be libelous to speak some truths" (157–58). For the narrator,
the violation of the heart appears to be the paramount consideration
urging restraint; for Hunilla, restraint is indicated by the inadequacy of
language to describe her ordeals. Beyond the simple and brief form her
recital takes, her words are devoted to fending off inquiry and resisting
elaboration, in striking contrast to the florid speech that the narrator
puts into her mouth when he imagines her thoughts:

> "The ship sails this day, to-day . . . this gives me certain time to stand
> on; without certainty I go mad. In loose ignorance I have hoped and
> hoped; now in firm knowledge I will but wait. Now I live and no
> longer perish in bewilderings. Holy Virgin, aid me! Thou wilt waft
> back the ship. Oh, past length of weary weeks—all to be dragged
> over—to buy the certainty of to-day, I freely give ye, though I tear
> ye from me!" (156)

Self-reflexively, the language of the entire sketch is about the limitations of language to express truth, philosophically because, as Tzvetan
Todorov writes, "to designate feelings, to verbalize thoughts, is to
change them"[10] and socially because "it may be libelous to speak some
truths." The choice is to falsify individual experience by transforming

it into the language of the community or to transgress against social
mores with forbidden speech. What remains is a narrative in which the
detailed description of place and an austere account of events continually remind us of its linguistic boundaries. The emphasis on nonspeak-
ing informs all of the sketches of "The Encantadas," for only *isolatos*
have ever populated the barren islands. What speaking is done, other
than Hunilla's, tends to be deceptive or corrupt, from the treacherous
"Light ho" of the desperadoes on Charles's Isle to the elegant fiction
of Oberlus's letter.

■ Ironically in "Benito Cereno" the language of Captain Amasa Delano is no more equal to the reality of the situation
aboard the San Dominick than it was to the contrived performance he
first takes for the truth; similarly, the archenemies Babo and Benito
Cereno are assimilated to one linguistic standard, first in deceptive
speaking and then in a lack of speech. All three characters, representing
widely different degrees of perception, are imprisoned within a public
language that categorizes behavior according to rigid social hierarchies and corresponding behavioral expectations that the events of the
narrative repudiate. The unconscious commitment to the conventional
ways of assessing experience reified in public language causes Delano
to disregard the evidence of his own eyes and to ignore the promptings
of intuition. Time and again, familiar labels reassuringly transform
his unsettling observations and nebulous anxieties into stereotypes. If
the Spanish captain behaves in an inexplicable manner, it is because
"Spaniards are all an odd set; the very word Spaniard has a curious,
conspirator, Guy-Fawkish twang to it" (79). The Negresses with their
young exemplify "naked nature . . . pure tenderness and love, thought
Captain Delano well pleased" (73).
Although Benito Cereno knows that the black stereotypes that please
Delano are an elaborate pretense, a fiction, he is himself the victim of
the same stereotypes, unable to survive the shock of their violation. It
is the reality of "the negro" that reduces Cereno to silence and death,
for there are no words in his vocabulary to square his experience on
the San Dominick with society's official doctrines of black tractability
and inferiority. The wordless gulf between signifier and signified that
the slave revolt opens up fatally envelops Cereno, but neither he nor
Delano truly explores it. Delano has no incentive to probe the comfortable stereotypes of his culture: he will surely return to that feeling for

Negroes akin to a fondness for Newfoundland dogs. For Cereno the
forced abandonment of social verities has been brutally traumatic: he
prefers to die rather than reevaluate.[11]

Babo is a prime example of speech-act infelicity: in assuming command of the ship, he contravenes J. L. Austin's condition that "the
particular persons and circumstances in a given case must be appropriate for the invocation of the particular procedure invoked."[12] His
authority is outside the institutional agreements that ordinarily validate
directives, an analogue of the force that originally gave Don Alejandro
Aranda authority over him. If Delano and Cereno wish to retain the
version of events prescribed by public language but controverted by the
black rebellion, Babo is unsuccessful from the opposite direction. He
can temporarily enact a subversive fiction, but it is one that can express itself verbally only in distorted forms of the oppressor's language:
the oath he requires of the Spaniards, the mock-servility to Cereno for
Delano's benefit, and finally, silence. Whatever the motive of Babo's
"voiceless end"—the impotence of words to create the world he wanted,
a disdain for self-justification, the power of withholding what his white
captors demand—Babo is culpable by definition; it would be futile for
him to plead the injustice of slavery to the tribunal which judges him
but will not allow him, or any black, to testify. Unlike the two captains,
Babo can face the truth: where Cereno faints rather than look upon
his adversary, even after death Babo unflinchingly looks out upon the
society he has challenged:

> The body was burned to ashes; but for many days, the head,
> that hive of subtlety, fixed on a pole in the Plaza, met, unabashed,
> the gaze of the whites; and across the Plaza looked towards St.
> Bartholomew's church, in whose vaults slept then, as now, the
> recovered bones of Aranda: and across the Rimac bridge looked
> towards the monastery, on Mount Agonia without; where, three
> months after being dismissed by the court, Benito Cereno, borne
> on the bier, did, indeed, follow his leader. (140)

In this remarkable sentence the authorial voice concludes the story
with Babo's sightless perspective, cinematically moving over the city
and dominating it from the elevation of the pole on which his head is
placed. The institutionality of the white world is strongly inscribed in
the narrative denomination of space: the Plaza—typically a gathering
place of the citizenry to witness such public acts as the exhibiting of

Babo's head—church, monastery, and court. Within this hierarchical space the image of the head emblematically inverts society's stereotype of the slave as a laboring body. Babo is, instead, a head, or leader, raised above the body politic of a white city-society. The final vision seized in his unabashed arrogation is one of his enemy's complete passivity and defeat: his former master/servant Cereno *dismissed, borne,* and *following* his leader into death, not heroically in action at sea, but abjectly on shore.

Foreshadowing *The Confidence-Man* and *Billy Budd*, Melville has constructed a fiction in which almost all language, including his own, is calculatedly deceptive or tragically inadequate.[13] In its successive interpretations of a single structure of events the narrative form is similar to the rhetorical figure of syllepsis; since the false interpretation precedes the true, the narrative misleads the reader as Delano is misled by his encounter with the San Dominick. The Deposition, society's official version of the episode, may have more validity than the account of Claggart's murder in "News from the Mediterranean," but like that account, it is merely a surface chronicle whose limitations are emphasized by the authorial voice's refusal to say more and by the subjective mode of the predictive clause: "If the Deposition have served as the key to fit into the lock of the complications which precede it, then, as a vault whose door has been flung back, the San Dominick's hull lies open to-day" (114). The apparent tidiness of this structure is so markedly undercut by irony and ambiguity that the image of the "vault whose door has been flung back" mocks the idea of resolution it symbolizes. One world of false appearance has been exploded; others endure. Moreover, the equilibrium restored is that of a notoriously corrupt slaveholding autocracy. Neither the prejudice of Captain Delano nor the coercion of the Spanish regime is a responsible alternative to the slave revolt. Since neither Cereno nor Babo speaks at the end, the authorial assertion of truthful revelation is no more than a perfunctory gesture of closure, akin to Delano's offering of platitudes to assuage Cereno's anguish.[14]

■ "Bartleby the Scrivener" shares with "Benito Cereno" the same dynamically paired figures—imperceptive observer and enigmatic protagonist—the same form of closure without genuine resolution, and the same dialectical movement between a constricting public language and silence, but it offers a more dramatic confrontation between the collective idiom and a dissenting individual voice, as well as a more meaningful connection to the two major novels preceding it. "Bartleby" develops the same pattern of defiance, isolation, and death found in *Moby-Dick* and *Pierre*, but its treatment of these structural and thematic paradigms is notably austere, its world circumscribed.[15] Where Ahab has personal power over the *Pequod* supported by his position within a recognized social hierarchy, and Pierre presides over a heterogeneous group of women without a corresponding social validation, Bartleby has neither personal charisma nor worldly authority. Where the aristocratic Pierre is a writer, the proletarian Bartleby is merely a scrivener. In the progression from Ahab to Pierre, the quest for meaning becomes increasingly less specific and the engagement with the universe less creative and active: from action, the killing of the whale; to knowledge, the secret of Isabel's parentage; to nameless malaise. In each text the world remains mysterious, but if we get no answers in *Moby-Dick* and *Pierre*, at least we get questions. As Nina Baym writes, "Ishmael has many questions, but he does not question his own activity, the activity of verbalizing."[16] In "Bartleby" even the questions are elusive.

Into the void of self that Bartleby's lack of definition creates, critics have poured any number of religious, philosophical, psychological, and aesthetic rationales, most of which are to some degree plausible if only because Bartleby's characterization is both limited and ambiguous.[17] Why he refuses to behave like an ordinary scrivener can never be known since the explicit provocation that sets Ahab and Pierre in motion is absent in his case, and he offers no explanations. Bartleby is, above all else, the man who will not explain himself.

The nebulousness of the philosophical dilemma and the protagonist's passivity play against a sharply particularized setting. If Bartleby is mysterious, the nature of his social context is not: for a menial worker like a scrivener the business world is dehumanizing, coercive, and exploitative—a portrait all the more arresting because it is ironically filtered through the unperceptive and self-satisfied narrative of the lawyer.[18]

To borrow David Leverenz's words about Franklin and Edwards, the language of the lawyer exemplifies a recurrent American desire "to appropriate the voice of respected authority as one's best self."[19] Because the lawyer's iconic figure, John Jacob Astor, is an embodiment of capitalistic ideology notorious for his exclusive devotion to moneymaking, the adoption of the capitalistic/Astorian ideology produces a complacent and self-validating verbal posture that functions as a closed system. Whatever data might challenge this politicized view of self and reality is translated into public language and then incorporated into the lawyer's controlling vision. Recounting his visit to Bartleby in prison, for example, the lawyer remarks, "I went to the Tombs, or, to speak more properly, the Halls of Justice" (42). Speaking "properly" evades reality with a misleading euphemism, but for the lawyer, social decorum outweighs an inconvenient truth. By substituting the official for the colloquial, the lawyer replaces a pejorative with a positive critique and an antisocial evaluation with a socially sanctioned one. In Bartleby's case at least the designation of tomb is more appropriate than hall of justice.

If the lawyer's commitment to the Astorian ideology of safe gain is often his theme, the form of his narrative, as opposed to his direct discourse, conveys an unintended message of conflict with this ideology—one that the lawyer cannot afford to pursue consciously. As Stephen Zelnick describes his style, "the sentences are paradigms of cautious qualification, suppressed agency, and softened assertion."[20] Such characteristics do not appear uniformly throughout the narrative but are associated almost exclusively with moments of decision in the lawyer's treatment of Bartleby, and more commonly, with those cruxes when an apparent loss must somehow be converted into a gain.[21] Since the logic of moneymaking demands that Bartleby be fired when he first refuses to carry out an order, the lawyer must find a means of rationalizing his treatment of his employee without forfeiting his claim to the prudence and method of Astorian commendation. He does so by transferring the profit from business to self-image:

Nothing so aggravates an earnest person as a passive resistance. If the individual so resisted be of a not inhumane temper, and the resisting one perfectly harmless in his passivity, then, in the better moods of the former, he will endeavor charitably to construe to his imagination what proves impossible to be solved by his judgment. Even so, for the most part, I regarded Bartleby and his ways. Poor fellow! thought I, he means no mischief; it is plain he intends no insolence; his aspect sufficiently evinces that his eccentricities are involuntary. He is useful to me. I can get along with him. If I turn him away, the chances are he will fall in with some less-indulgent

employer, and then he will be rudely treated, and perhaps driven
forth miserably to starve. Yes. Here I can cheaply purchase a de-
licious self-approval. To befriend Bartleby; to humor him in his
strange wilfulness, will cost me little or nothing, while I lay up
in my soul what will eventually prove a sweet morsel for my conscience. (23–24)

The end of the passage is arresting as an illustration of the Benthamite
calculation of spiritual value, but the steps leading up to this conclu-
sive transformation of liability into asset equally reveal the unconscious
working of ideological bias in the lawyer. At first, the ponderous and
abstract language gropes its way to a tenable position, distancing the
narrator from the situation through impersonal forms of reference: "an
earnest person," "the individual so resisted," "the resisting one." Once
resolution is achieved, the style reverts to a syntactically simpler mode
and the lawyer's more customary short, direct assertions.[22]

The lawyer hesitantly advances his tacit definition of himself as
"not inhumane" in an indirect form because of the dubious status of
humanity in the pantheon of business virtues. More significantly, he
can define Bartleby as one who is harmless in his passivity, whose
behavior is beyond his control like a physical illness rather than an
intentional offense, and therefore he can indulge him in much the
same manner as he indulges Nippers and Turkey. By being given precise, nonpolitical labels, none of the scriveners' eccentricities poses any
threat to the established order of the lawyer's financial universe. Two
statements of undisguised profit—"He is useful to me" and "I can get
along with him"—are surrounded and enveloped by two expressions
of pity for Bartleby, as unfortunately afflicted with involuntary eccentricity and as vulnerable to the abuse of an employer less kind than the
lawyer.

Rather than supporting the charitably drawn self-portrait of the narrative, the lawyer's actual speech ultimately establishes his kinship
with the "less-indulgent employer." He ordinarily speaks to Bartleby
in peremptory directives—"Bartleby! quick, I am waiting" (21)—and
abandons the imperative address only when Bartleby has ignored his
orders so consistently that its futility is palpable.[23] His new manner of
asking questions is superficially different but equally domineering in
its attempt to extract not work but information from the reluctant Bartleby. When Bartleby refuses to leave the office, the lawyer confronts

him with the traditional rights of property: " 'Do you pay any rent? Do you pay my taxes?' " (35). The reason he gives Bartleby for moving his office is a lie, and his denials of responsibility—both to others for Bartleby and to Bartleby for his imprisonment—are half-truths, his proffers of friendship and refuge merely expediential ways of dealing with the "intolerable incubus." Ironically, the extravagant fate that the lawyer imagines for Bartleby at the hands of the "less-indulgent employer" becomes Bartleby's fate at the lawyer's own hands once he perceives the scrivener to be an absolute liability.

Affirming a status quo that maintains his own capital of authority, the lawyer's language builds verbal walls which define such key words as *reasonable, human,* and *sane* in ways that exclude Bartleby.[24] Turkey and Nippers self-deceptively employ this same public language to create fantasies that obscure the severity of their proletarian lot, Turkey by styling himself his employer's "right-hand man," Nippers by emulating a lawyer in his business of prison and court. Nippers labels his seedy visitors "clients"; Turkey constructs a heroic military image of his work to emphasize his value to the lawyer: "In the morning I but marshal and deploy my columns; but in the afternoon I put myself at their head, and gallantly charge the foe, thus" (16). Like Ahab, Bartleby faces the blank wall shoved near to him, but unlike Ahab he does not articulate an inflated romantic vision of the wall in order to enlist agreement. Since he disregards basic conventions of social discourse, never initiating speech or responding more than minimally, one of his preferences appears to be silence. This reluctance to participate in verbal exchange may well be predicated upon Bartleby's realization that in his social context responsible or truthful speech is unacceptable.

"To prefer," according to the *Oxford English Dictionary*, is "to set or hold (one thing) before others in favour or esteem, to favour or esteem more, to choose or approve rather; to like better"—definitions redolent of the hierarchical nature of language.[25] Bartleby's "I would prefer not to" is "an interruption of habitual circuits of communication," as John Carlos Rowe writes,[26] but it is also more than this, an assertion of individual partiality. Its negative form is a protest rather than a program, perhaps because Bartleby knows only what is intolerable: the light entering his window reveals that there is "no view at all," a blankness or lack of meaning more horrifying than the ugly slum panorama it has replaced. As a speech act, Bartleby's utterance is indirect, an assertion masquerading as an expressive.[27] Neither is appropriate as a response to an employer's directive. For the lawyer, "prefer not to" means "refuse point blank," an insubordination that causes him to consult "Edwards on the Will" in order to elucidate Bartleby's stance. As might be expected, the lawyer has chosen the wrong text, for Bartleby asserts the primacy of feeling, not will—the radical thesis that one should do only the work he "likes better" and reject all else.[28]

In the workplace "I would prefer not to" as a complete statement is so unthinkable that when the lawyer first hears it, his frenetic motion is violently arrested.[29] The phrase must be repeated and cogitated upon before the lawyer can accept the tripartite flouting of authority: his own as employer, common usage, and common sense. As the indirect beginning testifies, his own faith in his code is fleetingly undermined until he can solicit the support of the office community, the microcosm of his financial universe.[30] The speech is typical of the "widening distance between rhetoric and existential reality" that Sanford Pinsker has observed in the lawyer's narrative.[31] In speech-act terms, the lawyer realizes the gap between perlocutionary effect and consequence in his relations with Bartleby. From the lawyer's point of view, his directives to Bartleby fulfill all the conditions for felicitous speech acts, yet the scrivener refuses to respond properly. Such a moment reveals the extent to which we rely upon linguistic conventions: Bartleby, as Stanley Fish writes of Coriolanus, "declares himself outside . . . the system of rules by which society fixes its values by refusing to submit to the (speech-act) conditions under which its business is conducted."[32] Highly charged and biased language—*browbeaten, unprecedented, violently unreasonable, stagger, faltering*—transforms Bartleby's mildly voiced pronouncement into an almost physical assault.

Here and on other crucial occasions group support reaffirms social values for the lawyer although his dependent clerks are hardly "disinterested persons." Locked into the ideology of business, which confers no value on a worker's preference and regards any manifestation of personality as counterproductive, they are equally unable to understand Bartleby. He must be insolent or *luny*, in need of being beaten or fired. Neither master nor man can afford to hear Bartleby's utterance as rational or tenable.

What first moves the lawyer to thoughts of freeing his office of Bartleby is the realization that the scrivener has "in some degree turned the tongues" both of himself and the other clerks, a dangerous subversion since public language requires that "I would prefer not to" be heard as nonsense, a sign of dementia. When the lawyer finds himself "involuntarily" using " 'prefer' upon all sorts of not exactly suitable occasions," that is, when he would ordinarily use a directive verb, he is fearful of "further and deeper aberration" (31). In unconsciously following the usage of Bartleby, the other clerks have acquired the form without the substance of Bartleby's rebellion, an indication both of their disavowal of his position and the unacknowledged identity of their interests as workers.[33]

There is a real question how much of the impossibility of communicating Bartleby's vision of reality is due to brute facts, the mysterious nature of the world, and how much to institutional facts, those socially and culturally dependent constituents of meaning.[34] When Bartleby repeatedly says that he is not particular and at the same time rejects a series of possible occupations,[35] the lawyer regards these two positions as contradictory—not because they are so in the physical world, but because, asserted together, they violate a collective view that arbitrarily excludes other possibilities of meaning. Similarly, when the lawyer urges Bartleby to be "reasonable" and Bartleby declines, what is at issue is a social norm, according to which it is "reasonable" to toil unremuneratively for long hours in a dimly lit, closed-in space. And the wall that provokes Bartleby's reveries, a wall that was shoved near rather than sought out, is itself a man-made barrier.

Bartleby's rejection of speech, the tie that binds the human community, may be for reasons of communication more than self-expression; that is, it may be possible to articulate his vision but impossible to have it understood. On the one occasion in the tale when Bartleby poses a question of his own—"Do you not see the reason for yourself" (32)—thus inviting the lawyer to answer his own question as to why Bartleby has ceased to copy, the lawyer finds an obvious and socially acceptable reason which normalizes Bartleby with the same kind of reductive physical explanation that reconciles him to the aberrations of Turkey and Nippers. Seeing the problem as internal rather than external, a product of fate rather than society, does not result in communication with Bartleby, but it does relieve the twin promptings of conscience and introspection that challenge the Astorian business ethic.

That "Bartleby" has less frequently been read as a subversive image of American society than as an emblem of individual maladjustment is due not only to the open-ended philosophical issues which preempt attention but to the textual strategies that enforce the reader's assumption of the lawyer's point of view. Reader and narrator have a common relation to Bartleby, an interest in plumbing the mystery of the hapless scrivener and a sense of frustration in being unable to do so. At the same time, the privileged entry afforded by first-person narration into the lawyer's mind—with its motives, explanations, and self-justifications, its tone of sweet reasonableness and inviting intimacy—encourages sympathy, whereas the cryptic aloofness of an externally observed Bartleby fosters distance and bafflement. Yet Melville characteristically works against the familiar responses of fictive conventions, and the dialectical movement between Bartleby's few words and the lawyer's narrative strikingly juxtaposes truthful and deceptive speech:

> "I know you," he said, without looking round—"and I want nothing to say to you."
> "It was not I that brought you here, Bartleby," said I, keenly pained at his implied suspicion. "And to you this should not be so vile a place. Nothing reproachful attaches to you by being here. And see, it is not so sad a place as one might think. Look, there is the sky, and here is the grass."
> "I know where I am," he replied. (43)

Bartleby's speech does not observe any of the usual discourse agreements that regulate communication within a linguistic community. Violating the Cooperative Principle,[36] he fails to invite continuation when he is greeted; instead, he (rudely) closes it off, emphasizing his refusal of dialogue by not turning to face the lawyer.[37] His assertions both seem truthful, one because of the likelihood that he would recognize his former employer, the other because it depends upon his own will rather than any other agent. In contrast, the lawyer's speech does not respond to truth but to the social imperative of presenting a self appropriate to the occasion, in this case a self guiltless of Bartleby's imprisonment. Smacking of the false cheer of polite condolence, the remainder of his condescending speech tries verbally to recreate the prison as a positive environment, an endeavor that is patronizing and hypocritical. Nature may be more evident in the prison yard than in Wall Street, a sad commentary on the urban world outside the Tombs, but in its artifically confined and diminished state it cannot be expected to have the revivifying powers of a pastoral setting.

In painting his optimistic picture the lawyer has carefully avoided the word *prison*, using instead *here*, *this*, and *place*. When Bartleby replies, "I know where I am," he rejects the lawyer's attempts to disguise reality. Nor does he, presumably, obey the lawyer's command to look upon the evidence of nature. that is, to make the world conform to the lawyer's words.[38] Throughout the exchange Bartleby has faced the wall, the barrier here and outside to a life that could be embraced as a preference.

The entire prison episode is an ironic reversal of fortune for Bartleby. Once he is no longer a threat to society, he can be given a measure of liberty; permitted to wander "freely" in the prison yard, he is seen outdoors for the first time. Yet Bartleby's contemplation of the viewless view had made apparent the impossibility of genuine change or escape: if the walls of prison confine less than the walls of Wall Street, they are still barriers that he chooses to face rather than ignore. Although Bartleby remains steadfastly himself here, still rejecting the lawyer's overtures, through the instrumentality of his former employer he is categorized first as a gentleman and then as a criminal in a network of association that eventually implicates the lawyer himself. Since "such gentlemen as have friends" hire the grub-man, the lawyer's payment and his designation of Bartleby as his friend establish that in the restricted public language of the prison world Bartleby can be defined as a gentleman. Bartleby's relation to the grub-man now parodies the lawyer's former relation to the scrivener: he can command the grub-man's services and receives his exaggeratedly deferential attentions. This speech is as untruthful as the lawyer's and based upon the same premises: "Your sarvant, sir, your sarvant. . . . Hope you find it pleasant here, sir; nice grounds—cool apartments" (44). Honest but penniless, Bartleby would get short shrift from the grub-man; his failure to take advantage of the erroneous classification, like his earlier deviation from common usage, is condemned by society, whose extremes of class, embodied in the grub-man and the lawyer, agree upon his derangement.[39] In paying for Bartleby's food the lawyer has once again made a gesture of friendship that costs him little, and once again he withdraws when a greater commitment seems called for. Judging by appearance that Bartleby is a "gentleman-forger," that is, a criminal from the lawyer's class and business world, the grub-man wonders if the lawyer may not have also known the notorious forger and swindler Monroe Edwards. The lawyer's denial that he was ever "socially acquainted with any forgers" and his immediate departure simultaneously register his discomfort at the implicit threat to his status and evoke the fraudulence of his relationship to Bartleby—its subterfuges, stratagems, and dishonest or incomplete communications.

After Bartleby's death, the rumor that he had worked in the Dead Letter Office provides the lawyer with a pleasingly romantic fiction to explain the scrivener's anomie, a confirmation of the reassuring thesis of Bartleby's constitutional hopelessness that the lawyer has always held. Consigning Bartleby to a predisposed and unalterable despair naturally absolves the lawyer of any need to seek the cause of Bartleby's behavior within his own office or world. Although his final exclamation—"Ah, Bartleby! Ah, humanity!" (45)—indirectly acknowledges his bond of secret likeness with Bartleby, its all-encompassing vagueness submerges the individual in the species and further precludes responsibility for his fate.[40]

Unlike Ishmael, the lawyer cannot pass beyond the artificial barriers society erects to separate men; he cherishes, rather than rejects, the distinctions which have given him preeminence and comfort, and he quickly overcomes the momentary sense of fraternity which he feels first for Turkey, who actively invokes their common age, and for Bartleby, who passively suggests "the bond of common humanity." He resists "presentiments of strange discoveries" in favor of the snug and the safe because, as Melville wrote in "The Lee Shore" chapter of *Moby-Dick*, the need to abandon the land's measured security in order to venture upon the amorphous sea of "deep earnest thinking" is a "mortally intolerable truth" (107). Bartleby is, after all, only a potential double, an example not followed. For the lawyer, the walls of custom and language that confine Bartleby, like the hierarchical society that enslaves Babo, give welcome definition and confirmation of identity.

The *Piazza Tales* move away from the copious speech of Ahab and Pierre, both at least would-be truthtellers, to the few words and silence of Bartleby, Benito Cereno, Babo, and Hunilla. Melville had always created powerful emblematic images; in the *Tales*, as protagonists fall silent in the face of the impossibility of using language to communicate, such pictures have more authority than verbal exchanges. What communication there is flows around rather than through language, as the narrator reports of Hunilla's story: "Construe the comment of her features as you might, from her mere words little would you have weened that Hunilla was herself the heroine of her tale. But not thus did she defraud us of our tears. All hearts bled that grief could be so brave" (155). In "Bartleby" it is the speech of things, the simple articles

of Bartleby's housekeeping, that produces an onrush of fraternal feeling in the lawyer, whereas talking to Bartleby simply underscores the
gulf between them. In "Benito Cereno" the tableau of Babo bending
over Cereno in the ritual of shaving provokes Captain Delano's most
valid flash of insight: "Nor, as he saw the two thus postured, could he
resist the vagary, that in the black he saw a headsman, and in the white
a man at the block" (85). Cereno's broken spirit and Babo's defiance
are revealed more forcefully by means other than speaking.

If those who might articulate mysteries—including the speaker of
the text—are silent, other speakers in the *Tales*, notably the lawyer and
Captain Delano, use a public language whose commitment to vested
interests makes their speech inadequate and falsifying. Still others, like
Babo pretending to be a solicitous servant, the lightning rod man, and
the "mechanician" Bannadonna, make use of this same language but
pervert it to their own deceptive or egoistic ends. By the time of *The
Confidence-Man* only such false speakers remain as successful participants in verbal exchange, wielding the language of social discourse
in the service of a predatory individualism that enacts the collective
values of self-interest and gain. Their victims are those who expect this
language to function according to common values of disinterested and
charitable community.

The Confidence-Man: His Masquerade

■ In "Benito Cereno" an elaborate performance
staged for the benefit of Captain Delano and the reader creates a false
appearance of normality that is exposed and replaced by genuine normality: the rebellious slaves at first pretend to be subservient to the
Spaniards; by the tale's end they have been subdued and rendered truly
subservient. From the temporary stage world of "Benito Cereno" to the
sustained masquerade of *The Confidence-Man* involves no major reassessment of the nature of reality: Melville's omission from the novel of
the tale's sham resolution, in which a familiar evil is restored to power,
is simply a more overt acknowledgment that there is no hope of ame-
lioration. In other respects *The Confidence-Man* is sui generis, a text so
puzzling that even the most basic judgments of value and classification
have been ongoing critical issues.[41] In the perspective of the twentieth
century the work now seems to be strikingly contemporary, perhaps
the first postmodernist novel. What Melville had discovered between

Moby-Dick and *The Confidence-Man* was the impossibility of communicating the truth he aspired to tell in the genre of fiction. From *Pierre* to *Bartleby*, his protagonists are frustrated by society's often intentional failure to understand their words; by the time of *The Confidence-Man* truthful speech has devolved into silence and left unopposed in the linguistic marketplace the most corrupt form of public language, one that no longer serves any community but instead masks individual fraud with an appeal to communal ideals.

In his previous fiction, for all the experimentation with conventions, Melville had retained the most basic structure of narrative, what Tzvetan Todorov has defined as "a passage from one equilibrium to another."[42] Although each episode disrupts and then restores a condition of equilibrium, *The Confidence-Man* has no such overall movement: its iterative structure posits a changeless paradigm of trickery in which the shape-shifting of the confidence man merely parodies the dynamic quality of life. As Lawrence Buell forcefully states in his seminal article on *The Confidence-Man*, "the main problems of the novel are insoluble."[43] Commenting on the "entropic structure of the book," he writes, "The reader is encouraged to infer, but not permitted to know, the motives of the solicitor and the wisdom of the solicited."[44] The fiction declines to impose traditional narrative order on these materials or to invest them with significance, almost as if, after stretching the genre to accommodate the diverse materials of *Moby-Dick* and the forbidden passions of *Pierre*, Melville is testing the boundaries of the novel from the direction of austerity, attempting to discover how much can be jettisoned and still produce a work of fiction.

We immediately miss certain hallmarks of Melville's writing: the emblematic tableaux which concentrate meaning in an arresting image, the ballast of fact, the visually compelling descriptions, the intensity of a moral passion at work on large issues. Even the walled-in and colorless Bartleby is invested with grandeur—"like the last column of some ruined temple," "a sort of innocent and transformed Marius brooding among the ruins of Carthage"—and his tale is transfused with Melville's feeling, clearly so much stronger than that of the shallow speaker.[45]

What makes *The Confidence-Man* unique in Melville's fiction is the withdrawal of this passionate sensibility and moral engagement. There is nothing of value in this world he has created, and Melville accordingly invests no feeling in or commitment to it. Foreshadowing the exitless universe of postmodernist fiction, Melville's satire is all-encompassing, embracing not only the fools and knaves of the confidence transactions but those few who are "too skeptical or cold-blooded to be victimized."[46] Like the author described by Stephen Dedalus, Melville remains distanced and indifferent, but unlike those twentieth-century writers who emulated Flaubert, for Melville this posture signifies despair over the possibilities of fiction. While he plays the same verbal games as author that his Mississippi operators do, his satisfaction is palpably less. "Although such gestures might be praised today as evidence of sophisticated awareness," Baym writes, "to Melville the breach between language and reality had no redeeming compensation."[47] While the swindlers manipulate their victims to the full extent of their powers, creating and using confidence for their own ends, in the name of truth the authorial voice just as wilfully destroys the reader's confidence.

Even temporal organization, characteristic of the most primitive form of storytelling, is essentially negated by the break in character between the successive avatars of the confidence man, a lack of definite connection which has led more than one commentator to argue that the various episodes concern different confidence men, and to question whether or not the mute of chapter one belongs to the confidence conspiracy.[48] The issue of the mute's character is not resolvable by the usual means since Melville has shrouded all of the usual means in ambiguity, but it can be clarified by reference to the text's iterative structure. Whereas the silent advocacy of confidence by an apparently innocent person might work positively in an ideal community, the controlling mode of trickery establishes that in this particular fictive space the outcome is the same whether the mute is an authentic religious figure or a fraud: victims are set up for the confidence man.[49] Similarly, the words of the confidence man would be noble if trust did not lead inevitably to victimization, if the controlling context was not predatory deception.

Although critics have devised various rationales of progression from one confidence man to the next and from one victim to another, in character as in event, this imposition of fictive convention is misdirected; such efforts are overingenious attempts to assimilate *The Confidence-Man* to traditional forms of prose fiction and thus minimize its uncomfortable singularity. What preempts attention and importance is not the individualized agent or activity but the enduring and inescapable paradigm, which constantly displays new gimmicks, new victims, and new

swindlers: "Within this unconditioned field of action individual characters are only so many interchangeable ciphers."[50] Because these are
the choices afforded by the paradigm, those who live in contact with
their fellow men are either knaves or gulls, a division replicated in the
brief stories of other times and places and confirmed by the novel's final
sentence: "Something further may follow of this Masquerade" (251).
What may follow can only be more of the same, eternally repeated.

There is a third type of character who can be identified as a twisted
remnant of the Melvillian truth teller, an *isolato* unfit for society because he refuses to play either role. He embodies total distrust, an
attitude that denies community and—equally important—flouts social
decorum. The difficulty of maintaining such a bitter misanthropy is
apparent in those *isolatos* like the Missouri bachelor who momentarily
succumb to the confidence man and in the dual existence (or split
personality) of the Indian hater, Colonel John Moredock.

■ To an unusual extent the pattern of action in *The
Confidence-Man*, the iterative structure of trickery, is articulated
through a series of speech acts. Conversation dominates both the text
and its speakers, who are predictable stereotypes of the preyed upon—
a respectable widow, an old man, a college sophomore—or barely designated versions of the swindler. This presentation of character, while
it suggests allegory, seems to indicate equally strongly the imperson-
ality and anonymity of chance encounters in an urban setting, where
appearances and speech are unverifiable and opportunities for deception are therefore multiplied. Writing about *The Confidence-Man*,
Michael Paul Rogin remarks this characteristic in terms of traditional
and modern societies: "Status, family, historically rooted relationship,
and the insignias of dress marked a person's identity in traditional,
stable societies. Modern strangers who came together to buy, to sell,
and to persuade revealed themselves by their performances."[51] The
Fidèle is an extreme illustration of the urban or modern condition, a
transient association of strangers whose shipboard confinement provides no extralinguistic means of establishing credibility.[52] In this world
speech reigns supreme, cut off from accountability, even from—given
the continuous metamorphosis of the confidence man—an internal
consistency that is more than momentary.

A dumb show that paradoxically establishes the importance of speech
in the novel to come precedes the action proper of *The Confidence-*

Man. Introducing a triangulated field of force—the precursor or first
mask of the confidence man, the crowd of potential victims, and the
inscription proclaiming no trust—this prelude contains no direct discourse but instead bristles with printed texts which offer organizing
rubrics for what is to follow. Its opposed messages, the mute's charity
versus the barber's "no trust," are written signs; while a placard offers
"a reward for the capture of a mysterious imposter, supposed to have
recently arrived from the East; quite an original genius in his vocation" (3).[53] The legendary figures evoked, notorious bandits of the past,
have been transmuted into books hawked among the crowd by ped-
dlers. Their heritors, the "Mississippi operators," accomplish their ends
through subtle verbal deceptions clothed in the official language and
values of society rather than through directly antisocial physical violence, a substitution of urban/urbane methods for those of the frontier.
The uniformly mocking and unfriendly reception of the deaf mute dramatizes the inert quality of a message bluntly disseminated without
such benefits of speech as the preparation of the audience to receive it,
verbal embellishment and explanation, and tone of voice. Limited to
his slate, the confidence man has no persuasive powers. The barber's
equally blunt message has a context, that of the business transaction,
that limits its application and renders it intelligible.

Following this prologue, the novel proper explores a failure of spoken communication brought about by the conjunction of a dishonest
speaker with the inherent elusiveness of abstract language itself—the
seemingly irresistible impulse to translate the spiritual, intangible, and
immaterial into the familiar and graspable, into *things*.[54] As an abstraction that is "symbolically blank but emotionally active,"[55] confidence lends itself to this transformation, specifically, to the efforts of
the swindler to enforce a definition that equates the affirmation of confidence with the tendering of cash. The unwary victim unsuspectingly
embraces confidence as a vague spiritual good, only to find that in
the confidence man's catechism this affirmation is made to entail the
proffering of money. Following the model of transformation employed
to convert confidence into cash, the confidence man invokes public
language to gain agreement and then uses it as a cover for his own
antisocial purpose.

Conventions of communication predispose in favor of the confidence
man since, as Austin asserts, "it is fundamental in talking (as in other
matters) that we are entitled to trust others, except in so far as there

is some concrete reason to distrust them."[56] In eliciting an admission of confidence, the confidence man has the powerful force of social and religious approbation on his side—the official injunctions to be charitable, to love one's fellow man, and even to be agreeable rather than rude, suspicious, or misanthropic: to admit lack of confidence can be an embarrassing violation of decorum, a confession of failure to subscribe to public pieties which can incur such penalties as the pummeling a clergyman administers to the wooden-legged man who maintains that "charity is one thing, and truth is another" (14). Aside from the difficulties of the immediate social situation, making the payment desired by the confidence man is less psychologically painful for those whose perceptions are rigidly institutionalized because it preserves the implicit basis of all linguistic communication: Austin's maxim that "our word is our bond."[57] To withhold confidence is to call into question not only one's credentials for belonging to a community but the very possibility of community itself.

Like words, the common forms of social discourse in *The Confidence-Man* are perverted to serve egocentric ends. In the encounters between confidence men and their victims, the operators consistently place positive constructions on words and actions, thereby preempting an idealism and generosity that are difficult to assail socially. The skeptics they encounter typically seek to change these positive terms into negatives, like the Missouri bachelor's redefinition of "Philosophical Intelligence Office" as a "swindling" concern "kept by low-born cynics" (115). When the representative offers to "accommodate" the Missourian with an apprentice, the Missourian utilizes the abstract instrumental nature of the word to counter the confidence man's positive fiction with an unfavorable fictive scenario: " 'Accommodate! Obliging word accommodate: there's accommodation notes now, where one accommodates another with a loan, and if he doesn't pay it pretty quickly, accommodates him with a chain to his foot' " (116). Language, such exchanges suggest, can be used in a predatory fashion to attract the listener with a positive meaning and then suddenly reverse direction.

In spite of his initial distrust, the Missourian ultimately falls victim as much to his own susceptibilities as to the confidence man's skill in changing tactics to exploit the weakness of individual marks. In this case, he allows the Missourian to talk at length while he listens sympathetically and patiently endures the man's insults. While the Missourian is lulled into believing himself in control of the conversation,

his diatribe reveals both his pride at being proof against victimization—("'Don't try to oil me,' he says. 'The herb-doctor tried that.'"
(117)—and the long history of victimization that establishes a propen-
sity to be cheated united with a continuing hope of changing his luck.
When the confidence man shifts the basis of argument from passion
to science, claiming the latter ground as his own, he has hooked his
victim. Having exhausted his passion in the first part of the conversation, the Missourian eventually gives in "for the sake purely of a
scientific experiment" (128). Yet the prestigious label of science only
gives him a face-saving means of reversing his position. As the confidence man has discerned, the Missourian *wants* his bleak philosophy
to be proved wrong.

Immediately recognizing that he has been gulled, the Missouri
bachelor ascribes his relaxation of a customary vigilance to "the crafty
process of sociable chat" (130), a description that is at war with itself.
The distinction between talk exchange as crafty process and as sociable
chat is obviously crucial: approached according to a frame of interaction based upon the conventions of conversation, the victim finds the
frame suddenly altered to that of an exploitative discourse that will ultimately part him from his money. The familiar rituals of socialization
are so strongly engrained, and so expertly invoked by the confidence
man, that rather than making an antisocial gesture such as refusing
point-blank or abruptly ending the conversation by walking away, the
victim will usually play the prescribed role. Having been stung once,
the Missouri bachelor is willing to make the antisocial gesture which
effectively ends the confidence man's efforts—he exposes the fraudulence of his appearance: "'You are Diogenes, Diogenes in disguise.
Diogenes masquerading as a cosmopolitan'" (138). The other alternative is to repulse the confidence man at the beginning of his speech,
as several passengers do when accosted to make a contribution to the
Widow and Orphan Asylum for the Seminoles. This is an easier remedy
to apply when the appeal is a direct solicitation for money than when
the dialogue is opened upon other terms, hence the skillful practitioner
will establish a conversation before introducing the appeal for money.

Underlying both the social response—the conventions of politeness
and of cooperative discourse—and the deeper level of social principle
is an ideal of human behavior that the confidence man taps. All but
the most hardened misanthropes fall victim to a desire to have the evidence of their reason and experience contradicted, to believe in the

gratuitous act of kindness memorialized in such compelling myths as those of Baucis and Philemon and the Good Samaritan. The cynical cripple, whose narrative is the novel's most flagrant example of injustice and misfortune, is thus instantly converted from jeering disbelief to pathetic gratitude when the herb doctor makes him the gift of a box of liniment:

> "Stay—thank'ee—but will this really do me good? Honor bright, now; will it? Don't deceive a poor fellow," with changed mien and glistening eye.
> "Try it. Good-bye."
> "Stay, stay! *Sure* it will do me good."
> "Possibly, possibly; no harm in trying. Good-bye."
> "Stay, stay; give me three more boxes, and here's the money." (99)

Since the beginning of the encounter, when the herb doctor initiated discourse and the cripple attempted to close it off with a gruffly spoken "you can't help me. . . . Go away" (94), the speakers have exchanged positions. The cripple's plea to detain the departing herb doctor is repeated nine times; he now seeks verbal assurance that the salve will help him, an assurance that the herb doctor refuses to give. Like a tightrope artist scorning the net, the confidence man refuses to provide the easy guarantee; a sympathetic ear and the unexpected gift suffice to hook the victim without the buttressing of actual deceit. The gift, of course, is a shrewd come-on. From the cripple's earlier assertion—"I ain't destitute; to-day, at least, I can pay my way" (94)—the confidence man knows that his victim will insist on paying him.

The final guise of the confidence man, the cosmopolitan "philanthropist," is the most verbal and most daring mask assumed, the confidence man as artist. Unlike his earlier identities of beggar or vendor, the Cosmopolitan associates confidence with no tangible end, and we see him gain nothing more than a shave through fraudulence. Like the authorial voice, his absorption in the multiform possibilities of verbal deception is intellectual, a detached investigation into what the traffic will bear or merely an indulgence in word play—the game for its own sake. When Mark Winsome warns him that his friend is a "Mississippi operator," the Cosmopolitan explicates the term in words which change its meaning from negative to positive. Where Winsome is presented as speaking forthrightly in order to convey information, the Cosmopolitan plays a metalinguistic game in which he establishes his own meaning within the boundaries both of Winsome's own definition and of truth. Flirting with exposure later, he makes himself his text by reading an accurate description of the confidence man to a potential gull and announcing himself to be sorely troubled by it. Told that the passage is from the apocrypha and thus "of uncertain credit," he protests that "the uncanonical part should be bound distinct," a separation of authorized and spurious that would eliminate his own vocation but which, of course, he knows to be impossible. Nor is it the position he advocates moments later when he advises the old man to throw away his Counterfeit Detector. In all of these instances the confidence man substitutes for socially committed speech a verbal manipulation that is both autotelic and solipsistic.[38]

The mutability of language is one aspect of a pervasive instability in human affairs which affects character as well as fortune and which is imaged throughout Melville's fiction by conditions in the natural world. The masquerade of the confidence man then is only a blatant example of the universal condition of flux which makes the world a dangerous and unpredictable place. But unlike the vagaries of health and wisdom, the permutations of the confidence man are consciously contrived; through his own artifice he becomes the master rather than the plaything of instability, an amoral and self-regarding artist who, like other makers of fiction, rewards the confidence he demands with nothing more substantial than words.

The literary artist, as Edgar A. Dryden asserts, "is himself a part of the empty masquerade,"[59] yet he is not to be confused with the confidence man, whose calculated misuse of language destroys community in the service of egocentric exploitation; or with the mystic, whose verbal obscurity unintentionally thwarts comprehension; or still less with the gulled passengers, whose failure to question the language they use or the social rituals they engage in leads to their victimization. While the "comedy of action" insists upon the ultimate mystery of reality and the corruption of language, the "comedy of thought" equally insists upon the uncertainty principle as the *truthful* basis for the novel: "Fiction based on fact should never be contradictory to it," the authorial voice states, "and is it not a fact, that, in real life, a consistent character is a *rara avis*?" (69) Because the writer has a responsibility to the world that is the case, Melville refuses to take the easier and more acceptable road of fiction predicated upon principles of consistency and order that do not obtain in reality: "After poring over the best novels professing to portray human nature, the studious youth will still run risk of being too often at fault upon actually entering the world; whereas, had he been furnished with a true delineation, it ought to fare with him something as with a stranger entering, map in hand, Boston town; the streets may be very crooked, he may often pause; but, thanks to his true map, he does not hopelessly lose his way" (71). The Melvillian irony here, of course, is that the "true map" of character charts a confusion that cannot be resolved.

In *The Confidence-Man* Melville's commitment to this "true delineation" leads to the representation of a world of deception and ambiguity whose reality can be imaginatively rendered but not interpreted. Difficult and unpalatable as the text is, it does not sever the connection between art and life; Melville is still a truthteller, but the bitter truth of *The Confidence-Man* is that conventions of discourse are exploited by deceptive speakers and truth is unknowable. As Gabler-Hover concludes, "For Melville, the divine authority of the *logos* could only be a confidence game perpetuated by knaves or fools either to tyrannize over and to deny or repress the realities of human experience." [60] The long period of Melville's failure as a commercial novelist which the novel's publication capped led him away from the medium of fiction to the private voice of lyric poetry.

Epilogue: *Billy Budd*

■ Melville's return to fiction after a hiatus of some thirty years is a return to the same ideas that inform *The Piazza Tales* and *The Confidence-Man*: in *Billy Budd* reality is still dangerous and unknowable, language still deceptive and inadequate to experience. Yet instead of the bleak paradigm of verbal trickery that structures *The Confidence-Man*, these ideas now produce something rich and strange, a work which encloses this fallen world within a vision that can be at peace with uncertainties and valorize the limited truth attainable.[61]

If *The Confidence-Man* anticipates postmodernism in its paradigms of verbal trickery, *Billy Budd* anticipates it in the devolution of speech. While the authorial voice assumes a carefully delimited amount of authority, speech is consistently misunderstood and inadequate—from Billy's innocent farewell to the *Rights of Man* through the Dansker's oracular warnings about Claggart to Captain Vere's deathbed utterance of Billy's name. Communication flows intuitively around rather than through speech: Billy is a stutterer who is all but inarticulate, yet everyone apprehends his rare goodness; Captain Vere immediately distrusts Claggart's polished speech; and Vere's own words to the drumhead court impress not because of the logic of their argument, which the officers fail to understand, but because of their weight of institutional authority.[62] Billy's final words—"God bless Captain Vere!"—are echoed by the crew as words of the lips only: "At that instant Billy alone must have been in their hearts, even as in their eyes" (123). Their real feelings find expression only in wordless sound, a murmur "possibly implying a sullen revocation on the men's part of their involuntary echoing of Billy's benediction" (126).

On all levels of the social hierarchy of *Billy Budd*, speech is divorced from truth. It operates coercively in this world of military discipline to preserve the traditional forms of institutional order that the authorial voice questions, for that voice does claim access to truth: it makes clear that Billy is no traitor, Claggart no patriot, and Vere no Nelson deserving of the blessing that the crew confers "without volition, as it were," as an act of homage, not to the vested authority of their captain but to the asocial and nonverbal charisma of Billy.

That the truth of *Billy Budd* can be represented in fiction is an unexpected resolution of Melville's long struggle with the genre and his abandonment of it for more than thirty years. The "inside narrative" pointedly withholds information about Claggart's hatred for Billy, Billy's last meeting with Captain Vere, and Vere's deathbed utterance of Billy's name. Its method throughout is to call attention to its limitations, the difficulties of interpreting man and nature, without allowing these limitations to overwhelm narrative design. However imperfect knowledge of the world must necessarily be, *Billy Budd* asserts that it can be imaged in fiction more successfully than in history or poetry—witness the distorted account in a naval publication, "all that hitherto has stood in human record to attest what manner of men respectively were John Claggart and Billy Budd" (131), and the equally false version preserved in the sailor's ballad.

Just as symmetry of form is unattainable in "a narrative essentially having less to do with fable than with fact" (128), so complete communication is an unrealizable ideal. According to Austin, "ordinary language breaks down in extraordinary cases. . . . words fail us."[63] Melville preferred such extraordinary cases in which truth cannot find a voice in the utterances of characters: in his last fiction all three pro-

tagonists are differently flawed in their speech. Much is left unsaid
for other reasons as well, for Melville's distrust of cognitive resources
ultimately subverts all certainty and determinacy. Nevertheless, in the
text, that space of art which refracts the imperfect social context, the
authorial voice may modestly order the claims of competing discourses,
and it may paradoxically inscribe in its fictions the assertion of *Mardi*
that "truth is voiceless."

Chapter 3

Verbal Skepticism in
Adventures of Huckleberry Finn

Labelling extends social control over the forces of
nature, reducing the anxiety of society.
                    IVAN ILLICH, *Medical Nemesis*

Knowing *what a thing is*, is, to an important extent,
knowing what the name for it, and the right name for
it, is.
                    J. L. AUSTIN, *Philosophical Papers*

How we group words into kinds will depend on the aim
of the classification—and on our own inclination.
                    LUDWIG WITTGENSTEIN,
                    Philosophical Investigations

■ The traditional novel or romance affirms social conformity by destroying the problematic individual or integrating him
or her into society. In *Adventures of Huckleberry Finn* this ideology is
challenged by the book's structure and ending: even the inappropriate
return to the comic mode in the final episode makes a conventional
resolution only partially attainable, a difficulty that must have contributed to Twain's inability to complete the novel. The distanced "Notice"
which prefaces *Huckleberry Finn* forthrightly reflects Twain's scorn of
literary critics and his desire to protect his own work from their enterprise, but its warning against finding motive, moral, and plot also reveals an implicit uneasiness about *Huckleberry Finn*'s alteration of the
relationship between the novel and society, a transformation intimately
connected with the linguistic reality Twain posits. More justly than
Melville, Twain might have proclaimed that he had written a "wicked
book," not only by presenting society satirically and challenging the
morality of "conscience," but by building into the very generic fabric
of the novel a repudiation of society, albeit one that reflects Twain's
characteristic ambivalence about unpalatable truthtelling.

Twain's linguistic achievement in *Huckleberry Finn* seems to me to have been imperfectly understood through its usual restriction to his success in recreating the vernacular in serious literature.[1] While this accomplishment does initiate the modern era of the American novel, as novelists and critics alike have widely acknowledged,[2] it is only part of a broader concern with language that has been equally significant, one suggested by the role that T. S. Eliot assigns to the author of *Huckleberry Finn*: "Twain, at least in *Huckleberry Finn*, reveals himself to be one of those writers, of whom there are not a great many in any literature, who have discovered a new way of writing, valid not only for themselves but for others. I should place him, in this respect, even with Dryden and Swift, as one of those rare writers who have brought their language up to date, and in so doing, 'purified the dialect of the tribe.'"[3] Although Eliot may simply be praising Twain's use of the vernacular, his reference to purifying the dialect of the tribe brings into focus the larger area of the novel's concern, the implications of different verbal codes for individual freedom and genuine community. What emerges from the dialectical confrontation of opposed verbal codes is the condemnation of public language, that language which inscribes special interests, like the definition of a feud as an honorable enterprise or of a human being as property, on the linguistic currency that everyone must use. For all of the physical adventures, survival in *Huckleberry Finn* is decided finally on the ground of language.

Huck's opening speech raises the issue of the novel in the form of truthtelling versus lying, linguistic representations of the experiential ethic identified with individual consciousness versus collective a priori positions that often demand a falsification of experience. This central dilemma, a social oppression that no speaker can totally avoid, engenders an attitude of verbal skepticism which defines freedom in the most universal terms. Even the truthtelling of "Mr. Mark Twain" (i.e., the author behind the narrator) is qualified: "There was things which he stretched, but mainly he told the truth" (1). Huck himself lies constantly: creating a series of identities more acceptable to society than his own enables him to survive in a verbal universe where speakers either deceive themselves or deceive others.

■ Most of the white speakers Huck encounters have a greater capital of authority than he does. Buttressed by various attributes such as physical force, fatherhood, legal or moral sanction, adults invariably place Huck in a subordinate position while peers like Tom and Buck exert leadership on the basis of their greater knowledge—knowledge which they have acquired through an acculturation process that Huck has not had. All of these figures act as Huck's linguistic mentors, manipulators of language in ways which do violence to the experiential world. In order to express himself as an individual Huck must penetrate the deceptive facade of public language and create a speech true to his own feelings and experience.[4] The problem at novel's end is whom he can speak to: society, "sivilization," insists upon the language that Huck has rejected. As Remy Kwant observes, "The individual cannot begin afresh to construct a world of meanings for himself in an entirely autonomous way. He is destined to live in a common inherited world."[5]

Much of what Huck learns from his more acculturated mentors is a matter of applying the right labels, names which are politicized because they embody a social attitude.[6] As Yuri Lotman writes, "To a culture directed towards expression that is founded on the notion of *correct* designation and, in particular, correct naming, the entire world can appear as a sort of text consisting of various kinds of signs, where content is predetermined and it is only necessary to know the language."[7] Lacking the word *grace* hampers Huck both in his ability to describe the widow's behavior before a meal and to interpret his observations: "You had to wait for the widow to tuck down her head and grumble a little over the victuals, though there warn't really anything the matter with them" (2). What is a nonsensical sequence without the organizing concept of *grace* becomes a meaningful ritual with it: the widow bows her head, and her lips move in a prayer of thanksgiving for the meal. But while a definition of the word *grace* would modify Huck's perception of the behavior observed (not *tucking down* her head but *bowing* it, not *grumbling* but *praying*), it would not necessarily confer the intended value. Huck lacks the veneration of socially prescribed labels ordinarily acquired through acculturation. In society's view he is aberrant because he sees the activity without the social meaning which an official label provides and demands that it justify itself empirically.

Unlike Huck, those characters in harmony with their society have learned the right words; more significantly, they usually accept them on authority rather than through some process of independent verification or understanding.[8] Tom contends, for example, that the authority invested in the word *ransom* is more important than the meaning and more important than the reality that stubbornly resists its implementation:

> "Ransomed? What's that?"
> "I don't know. But that's what they do. I've seen it in books; and so of course that's what we've got to do."
> "But how can we do it if we don't know what it is?"
> "Why blame it all, we've *got* to do it." (10–11)

Tom invokes literature to justify ransom, but the paradigm of authority originates in direct social sanction; "language," Roger Fowler remarks, "not only encodes power differences, but is also instrumental in enforcing them."[9] Buck Grangerford's effort to define *feud* is only slightly superior to Tom's with *ransom*, but here, too, the failure to define inhibits neither allegiance nor action. Like Tom, Buck knows what has to be done and the authority behind it. What eludes all the participants in the feud is the origin of the process whose name has governed their behavior for some thirty years.

Inflexibility and coercion necessarily follow from the prescriptive nature of public language; facts must be made to fit official definitions whenever possible. Tom's successful imposition of his romantic requirements on Huck in the final episode of the novel, in contrast to his earlier failure, is due at least in part to his ability to change real circumstances. He could not literally transform the Sunday school picnic into Arabs, but he can furnish Jim with all the accoutrements of escape which the "rules" demand and thus satisfy some of Huck's desire for verification. Where the real world proves too stubborn, Tom is willing to substitute "letting on" for actual change—letting on that picks are case knives, for example—and thus privilege the purely verbal in contradistinction to Huck's desire for perfect correspondence between language and his experience. As Lee Clark Mitchell describes the difference, "Unlike Tom, who engages language as a play of signifiers, Huck at every point looks for verification to 'reality.'"[10]

Tom's alteration of the external world to satisfy an inappropriate official definition parodies the behavior of adult victims of the Sir Walter Scott disease: the feuding Grangerfords and Shepherdsons have disregarded the pastoral-agrarian destiny of their names and the homey domesticity exemplified by the furnishings of the Grangerford house in order to conform to a definition of aristocracy totally unsuited to their milieu: "Colonel Grangerford was a gentleman, you see," Huck tells us

(142). A similar a priori concept guides Colonel Sherburn, a definition of self that precludes the possibility of suffering an insult. All of these characters succeed in making a world-to-word fit—that is, creating a reality to conform to their definitions—but the reality that fits their needs is one of violence and death.[11]

There are times, however, when the labels preferred by society demonstrably fail to apply to a perceivable reality. The scene in which Colonel Sherburn addresses the would-be lynch mob is actually a clash of labels: according to the social group, the mob, they are brave men and the colonel is a worthy candidate for lynching; according to Colonel Sherburn, he is the brave man and they are cowards. Sherburn removes the comfortably self-serving labels the mob has appropriated and substitutes a highly charged negative description which effectively dehumanizes them: " 'The pitifulest thing out is a mob; that's what an army is—a mob; they don't fight with courage that's born in them, but with courage that's borrowed from their mass, and from their officers. But a mob without any man at the head of it, is *beneath* pitifulness. Now the thing for *you* to do, is to droop your tails and go home and crawl in a hole' " (90–91). Sherburn's definitions triumph because they correspond to a reality that cannot be ignored under present circumstances: the men *are* cowards, and a courageous man is calling their bluff. Ordinarily, when not put to the test of experience, the reassuring official labels prevail. As Sherburn tells the mob, "Your newspapers call you a brave people so much that you think you *are* braver than other people" (190).[12]

The reaction of the audience at the first Royal Nonesuch performance is a similar contest of labels, this time between society and the picaresque rogues the king and the duke. Defined as fools by these knaves, the crowd is advised by an authority figure, the judge, to escape this designation by becoming knaves themselves. Through participating in the selling of the fraudulent show to their fellow townsmen, they will "all be in the same boat," a microcosm of social homogeneity based upon connivance in trickery. By revenging themselves at the show's final performance they intend to retrieve the positive label of *men*, the one successfully appealed to by the duke's come-on line: "LADIES AND CHILDREN NOT ADMITTED." But these amateurs are no match for the professional rogues, who anticipate their plans. The labels bestowed by the king and the duke—*greenhorns, flatheads*—prevail because they accurately describe the crowd.

The last line of the duke's Royal Nonesuch poster is literally truthful, but it is fraudulent on the level of usage where it is intended to function, as a code utterance to indicate obscene material in the show. Like other such calculated verbal deceptions, its success depends upon the creation of an interval of time during which the facts needed to expose the deception cannot be determined. Intentionally deceptive mislabeling is not necessarily harmful; it may instead be a convention of certain kinds of experience. Unlike the Royal Nonesuch fraud, the circus performer's impersonation of a drunk is legitimate entertainment which creates a welcome thrill of danger for the audience and then undeceives it by revealing the man to be an expert rider. In constructing a verbal universe of "empty names and facts," the king and the duke can gull an entire town into accepting them as the heirs of Peter Wilks because they use the same vocabulary that the real claimants would use. By langauge alone, as we see when the Wilks brothers arrive without their luggage, it is impossible for most people to distinguish the true brothers from the false. Almost everyone takes the king's outrageous etymology of *orgies*, like the duke's farrago of Shakespeare, to be authentic because it sounds right; a familiar rhetoric masks the absence of substance for the uneducated and unthoughtful majority.

The titles which the two confidence men assume for Huck and Jim's benefit are as deceptive as any of their schemes and utterances, but they work in a more complicated way than, for instance, LADIES AND CHILDREN NOT ADMITTED. In Jim's view the proper label for the king and the duke is *rapscallions* because they behave like rapscallions. Huck knows that the two are imposters, but with his smattering of information about historical figures, he concludes that they are just like real kings and dukes anyway. In spite of the technical mislabeling, the names point to a reality for Huck that Jim's ignorance rules out. What is literal for Huck—the fake king and duke are like real kings and dukes—is metaphorical for the reader, who can also perceive the larger linguistic irony that even when properly applied, a positive or neutral rubric can cover a number of negative examples. The nouns *king* and *rapscallion* are not mutually exclusive, although ideally they should be.

Huck's assimilation of the two confidence men to real kings and dukes, symbols of political and social authority, is another way of obliterating the distinction between the official, authorized practice, whose vehicle is public language, and other modes of power with varying degrees of legitimacy. Each of these unauthorized or semiauthorized

systems has an ersatz public language that attempts to clothe its enterprise in the social sanction that public language confers. As Henry
Nash Smith points out, "Different as the characters are in their natural
selves, when they fall into pretense they all sound alike because they
all begin to speak in a burlesque of the exalted rhetoric of the official
culture."[13] Planning to leave his crony Jim Turner tied up on a sink-
ing wreck, Jake Packard expresses satisfaction that this will obviate
the need to kill him: " 'He'll be drownded, and won't have nobody to
blame for it but his own self. I reckon that's a considerable sight better'n
killin' of him. I'm unfavorable to killin' a man as long as you can git
around it; it ain't good sense, it ain't good morals' " (59–84). Thus the
abandonment of Turner to an inevitable death is a way of "getting
around" the social and religious injunction against murder, a way that
public language facilitates. On the level of intention and result, Packard's plan and premeditated murder are identical; linguistically they
can be consigned to opposite camps, one for, the other against, sense
and morality. Tom's world of romantic illusion also replicates that of
respectable society: books of adventure constitute authority for Tom
just as society's authorized texts do for adults. In each of these cases
skepticism is distributed on both sides: the obviously untenable and
self-serving nature of Packard's private assertion of authority and the
intricate fantasy of Tom's romances pervert establishment authority to
antiestablishment ends.

In Stanley Fish's words, "Some stories . . . are more prestigious
than others; and one story is always the standard one, the one that
presents itself as uniquely true and is, in general, so accepted. Other,
non-standard stories will of course continue to be told, but they will
be regarded as non-factual when, in fact, they will only be non-autho-
rized."[14] To amend this extreme formulation somewhat, public language may convey truth, but truth is not constitutive of public language:
what confers authority is not factuality but some form of agreement.
Miss Watson calls Huck a fool for his failure to appreciate prayer with
just such reasoning—implicitly, an individual who questions one of
society's doctrines must be deficient. Both the widow and Pap categorize Huck according to what each wants to see, which is related to
their different dispositions, personal needs, and social contexts. For
the charitable widow, Huck is an object of compassion, "a poor lost
lamb." For his drunken reprobate father, he is an enemy, the "Angel
of Death." Subscribing to religious benevolence, society approves and

supports the widow's evaluative label; Pap's does not have the sanction of society but is enforced atavistically by physical power.

Although Jim is a naive observer, Twain often valorizes his perspective, much as he does Huck's, because it has an empirical basis. Jim confers labels on Huck, but unlike society, whose labels are prescriptive and inflexible (Pap must take custody of Huck because he is Huck's "father"), Jim can define experientially and change his mind when the facts warrant. When Huck fools Jim, Jim tells him that "trash is what people is dat puts dirt on de head er dey fren's en makes 'em ashamed" (105). But Huck apologizes, and Jim then redefines him as his best friend, "de ole true Huck; de on'y white gelman dat ever kep' his promise to ole Jim" (125). In associating himself with Jim's quest for freedom, Huck fears that society will apply the ultimate label of group enmity to him: *abolitionist*. Masking the suitability of this onerous name to his tacit support of Jim's escape, he composes fictive autobiographies designed to produce sympathy rather than antagonism on the part of the community, while under cover of these false but socially acceptable labels, he begins the process of defining a real self. Both Huck and Jim are seeking identities that are truer to themselves than the labels of identification society has applied to them. When Huck is true to himself, he is indeed Jim's friend, whose fidelity to their friendship makes him a truer gentleman than those distorted social versions of the species, Colonel Grangerford and Colonel Sherburn. Both Huck and Jim finally earn the right to be called men, the authoritative label that white males have preempted for themselves and denied to others. By selfless risk-taking to deliver another person from suffering, each proves his manhood and in the process transcends the derogatory labels society has applied to him.

To transcend is not to escape, as Twain reiterates most dramatically at novel's end by juxtaposing Jim's act of heroism with his society's response. Even when Jim's action is understood, it prompts no real mitigation of his severe treatment: he is returned to leg irons and a diet of bread and water. Only the legal document, the word of Miss Watson's will, changes his status.

■ As his relationship with Jim develops, Huck gradually frees himself from society's view of Jim; divesting himself of public language is more difficult. In the extended parody of Socratic dialogue on the subject of a Frenchman's speech, Jim grapples comically with the issues of language and humanity that Huck must seriously engage. Jim agrees that it is "natural and right" for cats, cows, and men to talk differently from one another, but he emphatically resists the idea that men should have different languages among themselves. To Jim it is self-evident that if a Frenchman is a man, he should "talk like a man." Another parodic examination of the issue of manhood takes place earlier in Pap's anecdote about the free mulatto who, to Pap's boundless indignation, is allowed to vote in Ohio. For Pap the label *nigger* outweighs the attributes of white success with which Twain pointedly endows his exemplum.

Huck's dilemma in his treatment of Jim is simply a more sophisticated version of the same problem of categorizing, that is, relating a particular kind of man, a *nigger*, to generic *man*. He must become aware of the essential attributes of humanity that demand recognition in spite of the differentiating labels society affixes. In the stages of Huck's growing awareness of Jim's full claim to humanity, we can almost see him ticking off aspects of a definition of man as he encounters them in Jim. Playing the trick on Jim in Chapter 15 prompts his discovery that Jim has the capacity to care and to be hurt, but this is not sufficient to undo social indoctrination. Huck is conscious of "humbling" himself to a *nigger* when he apologizes for the trick. Thinking of Jim abstractly as *nigger* rather than *man* or *Jim*, Huck has moments of stupefaction similar to Pap's over Jim's unproperty-like behavior, and the decision of Chapter 16 to help Jim escape from slavery is of necessity expressed in public language—that is, Huck labels it *wrongdoing*. Because it is based on Huck's experience and real feelings, the response to Jim as man and friend is ultimately stronger.

Huck's struggle against conscience in Chapter 31 follows the same pattern as that of Chapter 16, but the greater emotional intensity of the later episode, and the concluding resolution to steal Jim from slavery, mark a stage of greater commitment and deeper understanding, one that has been prepared for by repeated demonstrations of Jim's own capacity for feeling. Huck's immediate reaction to Jim's disappearance, the counterpart of Jim's bursts of feeling whenever the two have been reunited after a separation, reveals deep distress: "Jim was gone! I set up a shout—and then another—and then another one; and run this way and that in the woods, whooping and screeching; but it warn't no use—old Jim was gone. Then I set down and cried; I couldn't help it" (266–267). The purposeful shouting for Jim degenerates into whooping and screeching, then crying, a suggestion of loss of control and hysteria as well as genuine feeling.

After this spontaneous outburst, one expressed in sound alone, public language produces in Huck the predictable conflict between the authorized and the experiential. In Huck's meditation on the appeal of conscience, Jim is once again distanced by the label *nigger*, property that has no right to dispose of itself. (We may recall that from Pap's point of view, upheld by society, the label *son* means that Huck had no right to dispose of himself.) At this point the gulf between society's demands and Huck's own impulses results in his inability to "pray a lie." Public language, which recognizes the slaveholder as the victim in this situation, cannot express Huck's real feelings; consequently, when he tries to pray as social indoctrination prescribes, "the words wouldn't come." After resolving to inform "the nigger's owner" of his whereabouts, thus distancing Jim again, Huck remembers his experience of this *nigger* as a fellow human being and solicitous friend—in other words, as the individual Jim. It would be out of character for Huck to arrive at the conclusion that he is right and society is wrong. As James M. Cox observes, "Since Huck's entire identity is based on an inverted order of values . . . he cannot have any recognition of his own virtue." [15] He goes as far as he can go by embracing "wrongness," a rejection of society's values and its language. This does not mean, however, that Huck will no longer use public language at all; survival in society, as he well knows, depends upon it, and Huck is adept at divining what is required in a given situation. Immediately after his crucial decision to steal Jim out of slavery, he deflects the duke's suspicion skillfully by referring to Jim as "the only nigger I had in the world, and the only property" (181).

Although it jarringly violates the seriousness of the novel's core, the final episode of *Huckleberry Finn* does not give up the ground that Huck has won through his association with Jim; it reiterates the point that Twain has been obsessively making all along, "the mental and moral enslavement which is the lot of everyone in this society." [16] This society, even in its most benevolent form, the Phelpses, cannot tolerate the real Huck Finn, just as it cannot tolerate the extension of *man* to include *nigger*. Hearing Huck's tale about a steamboat accident, still another fiction to assure acceptability when Huck first arrives at the farm, Aunt Sally exclaims, " 'Good gracious! Anybody hurt?' " He replies: " 'No'm. Killed a nigger,' " and she rushes on: " 'Well it's lucky;

because sometimes people do get hurt'" (185). This casual bit of dialogue reminds us that even the most attractive members of a slaveholding society will implicitly deny humanity through their matter-of-fact
use of politicized labels like *nigger* and *slave*.[17] Twain's description of
his own mother seems relevant to his description of Aunt Sally here:
"Kind-hearted and compassionate as she was, I think that she was not
conscious that slavery was a bald, grotesque and unwarrantable usurpation. She had never heard it assailed in any pulpit but had heard it
defended and sanctified in a thousand."[18]

What may strike the reader as worse than Aunt Sally's unexam-
ined racism is the gratuitous embellishment of Huck's arrival fiction:
"Killed a nigger." It is tempting to conclude, as David Smith does, that
"Huck's off-hand remark is intended to exploit Aunt Sally's attitudes,
not to express Huck's own."[19] But this seems less convincing than Janet
Gabler-Hover's idea of Huck as a rhetorical artist and practitioner of
"evasive art."[20] In spite of his deference to Tom's derivative fictions,
Huck is himself an effective liar who knows that he must add some
believable detail to the bald assertion of an accident. Here, as elsewhere, the category represented by *nigger* is as devoid of emotional
engagement for him as the individual Jim is evocative of feeling. *Nigger*
as a category never attracts his speculation.[21] This is clearly a shocking limitation, but just as clearly it is appropriate to the character of
Huck Finn.

With his highly subversive motive of freeing a slave, Huck knows
that only through deceit, the assumption of still another proper identity
such as that of Tom Sawyer, can he remain a part of society. Because of
his overriding purpose, he accepts the role given to him and cooperates
with Tom's foolish schemes. The escape is aptly labeled *evasion*, for
it represents Tom's evasion of responsibility in not making Jim's freedom known and society's evasion of Jim's humanity. Does it similarly
establish Twain's evasion?[22]

The response of contemporary readers—outrage at the deflation of
seriousness and the insensitive treatment of Jim—refocuses the issues
usefully, reminding us that in slavery a man is indeed a thing, in this
case the plaything of "cute little white boys"[23] who fail to realize the
immorality of their behavior. I would accordingly modify Steven Mailloux's assertion—"if previously the text enacted its ideological critique
through the humor, now it does so *despite* the farce"[24]—to include the
farce as part of the text's comprehensive ideological critique, the final

statement of the individual's difficulty in escaping society's most insidious prescriptions.

In the novel's conclusion Jim has a chance to assert his humanity dramatically with an act of selfless heroism. He sacrifices his chance to escape because of Tom's injury, a pure emblem of the Golden Rule: "Ef it wuz *him* dat 'uz bein' sot free, en one er de boys wuz to git shot, would he say, 'Go on en save me, nemmine 'bout a doctor f'r to save dis one?' Is dat like Mars Tom Sawyer? Would he say dat? You *bet* he wouldn't! *Well,* den, is *Jim* gwyne to say it? No, sah" (340–41). Jim's imagining himself in the place of a white gentleman, "Mars Tom Sawyer," underscores their common manhood, which society has tried to obscure by its imposition of markedly different labels. Yet, Huck's confirmatory remark—"I knowd he was white inside" (341)—illustrates once again the impossibility not only of expressing Jim's humanity adequately in the language of a slaveholding society but of imagining it in other than racist terms.[25] As Alan Trachtenberg concludes, "The book is finally more persuasive as a document of enslavement, of the variety of imprisonments within verbal styles and fictions than as a testimony to freedom."[26] There is, of course, no value-free language, and consequently there is no total escape from verbal styles and fictions, or from ideology—save the radical choice of withdrawal from human community and communication.

Huck has freed his thought from the enslavement of society enough to participate actively in freeing Jim, but speaking is a social act, not undertaken in isolation. Where *Moby-Dick* offers a visual paradigm of life in the emblematic picture of Queequeg suspended between ship and sea, menaced by the denizens of both, *Huckleberry Finn* creates an equivalent vision of the dialectic between nature and society, a linguistic paradigm which suspends Huck between the silence of noncommunity and the corrupting language of the tribe.[27] After the multitude of diverse social contexts he has passed through, all of which have required false identities established only verbally, Huck knows that he "can't stand it." His recurrent spells of loneliness and silence throughout the novel portend that his marginal status in the community will plausibly be replaced by withdrawal and noncommunication.[28] Within society, even silence has a corrupt embodiment in the duke's counterfeiting of a deaf-mute. Only a total separation from the community offers the freedom from both restriction and deception that Huck requires. To "light out for the Territory ahead of the rest," where he will

be alone among Indians and thus have no one to talk to, is the choice
dictated by Huck's experience with society and with its instrument,
public language.[29]

As the long critical controversy attests, Twain undercuts the seriousness of Huck's flight with the comic mode of the final section of the
novel. Yet the greatness of *Huckleberry Finn* is "its power of telling
the truth,"[30] and although withdrawal from community is neither palatable nor pragmatic, it is a fitting response to a society of fools and
knaves and to that language which serves their purposes more than it
serves those of genuine community.

Part Two

The Devolution of Speech in the Twentieth-Century Novel

Prologue

■ The verbal skepticism of *Adventures of Huckleberry Finn* recurs paradigmatically in a number of significant twentieth-century American novels as a pattern of linguistic frustration whose origin is demonstrably more social than philosophical. During the early twentieth century it is conjoined with a preference for a vernacular style of simple words which also entered the mainstream of the American novel with *Huckleberry Finn*. Big words and vague abstractions are condemned as inappropriate to everyday speech and as characteristic of a debased form of language brought into being by those public figures who, according to John Dos Passos, "have taken the clean words our fathers spoke and made them slimy and foul."[1] The most famous expression of this idea is Frederic Henry's speech attacking abstract words in *A Farewell to Arms*:

> I was always embarrassed by the words sacred, glorious, and sacrifice and the expression in vain. We had heard them, sometimes standing in the rain almost out of earshot, so that only the shouted words came through, and had read them, on proclamations that were slapped up by billposters over other proclamations, now for a long time, and I had seen nothing sacred, and the things that were glorious had no glory and the sacrifices were like the stockyards at Chicago if nothing was done with the meat except to bury it. There were many words that you could not stand to hear and finally only the names of places had dignity. Certain numbers were the same way and certain dates and these with the names of places were all you could say and have them mean anything. Abstract words such as glory, honor, courage, or hallow were obscene besides the concrete names of villages, the numbers of roads, the names of rivers, the numbers of regiments and the dates. (184–85)[2]

In William Barrett's view, this passage became "the great statement of protest against the butchery of the First World War."[3] Neither Dos Passos nor Hemingway disallows the effort of language per se to describe a real world; their quarrel is with the distorted and politicized rhetoric of public language which falsifies such description. For Dos

Passos, the words "our fathers spoke" were "clean," i.e., serviceable for the traditional functions of communication, including art. Hemingway's many pronouncements on language, both in and out of his fiction, indicate a similar program to rehabilitate language, not to destroy its referentiality. Such rehabilitation does not include a position of "theological orthodoxy"[4] on signification because for twentieth-century writers language has a social, not a divine, imprimatur. Once Pierre had metaphorically violated the pyramid of the soul and confirmed the void that Ahab had feared, the mainstream of the American novel turned away from transcendent authority altogether.

Those novelists who came of age during the Great War follow Twain in attacking public language primarily through the speech of their characters. For numerous protagonists, linguistic alienation prefigures or accompanies physical or psychic withdrawal: since speaking is a social act, the discovery that the available language is inadequate or corrupt leads characters into some version of Huck's flight from society. Frederic Henry's minimalist vocabulary and his "separate peace" are both responses to social coercion just as Quentin Compson's insistence on a romantic language which does not correspond to the reality of his life demonstrates linguistically the personal dissociation exemplified by his suicide. These characters actively choose a stance vis-à-vis society, including linguistic behavior, while others like the grotesques of *Winesburg, Ohio* are simply inarticulate, defeated from the start by the impossibility of communicating with an instrument dedicated to institutional needs and often hostile to their efforts at self-expression. Linguistic breakdown is not restricted to the problematic and the alienated, the conventional protagonists of the American novel. Like Tom Sawyer's Aunt Sally, a benevolent woman who casually accepts a distinction between *nigger* and *person*, most characters participate unthinkingly in public language. Tom and Daisy Buchanan, the epitome of belongingness, nevertheless lack a meaningful language to order and clarify their confused ideas and feelings, while the copious speaking of the impressively verbal characters in Henry James's late novels serves to emphasize both the failure of language to express accurately and the tension between individual and collective values.

In the modern novel the loss of faith in public language assumes a number of diverse forms, but language is still used referentially about something ascertainable. The enemy can be identified and located, if not vanquished, and some individuals retain their integrity in the unequal combat. Frederic Henry is not misled by war rhetoric or reduced to silence; Nick Carraway has language enough to tell the story of the inarticulate people who surround him, one of whom—Gatsby— remains admirable in defeat: and the varied linguistic limitations of Faulkner's Compsons do not extend to Caddy, who speaks honestly about her self-destructive life, or for that matter, to Dilsey. In sum, characters more and more lack the power of speech as a consequence of alienation from society and from its language, but the text as a totality does not completely dissever language and society or social and individual speech. To use Herbert Marcuse's terms, the universe of discourse is closing but not yet closed.[5]

Chapter 4

Urbanity and Expatriation, Part 1: James and Wharton

That lying is a necessity of life is itself a part of the terrifying and problematic character of existence.

FRIEDRICH NIETZSCHE, *The Will to Power*

Speech in *The Ambassadors*: Woollett and Paris as Linguistic Communities

■ Lambert Strether, the protagonist of *The Ambassadors*, moves between two societies in dialectical opposition: Woollett, embodying an austere business ethic which subordinates personal and aesthetic experience to work and moneymaking; and Paris, promoting a civilization of art and life that allows greater individual autonomy. Although women are the dominant figures in both places, in terms of conventional stereotypes Woollett is a masculine or daylight world— presided over by the Queen Elizabeth-like Mrs. Newsome—and Paris is a feminine world, introduced to Strether by Maria Gostrey, who reminds him of that archromantic Mary Stuart, and later personified by the quintessential charming woman, Marie de Vionnet. As a fable of identity *The Ambassadors* is like a Shakespearean romantic comedy; it demonstrates that men must at least temporarily abandon the workaday world to acquire the feminine capacity for personal relations and aesthetic appreciation. Like a pastoral interlude, such an experience changes and completes the male sensibility, yet it cannot be an end in itself but must ultimately be assimilated into the necessarily corrupting and coarsening masculine world of endeavor and reward represented by the "rather provincial and somewhat contracted world" of Woollett.[1] James is not interested in this intolerant and unimaginative world, which Strether compares to a "reformatory for juvenile offenders"— i.e., those not fully mature or civilized—but he knows that most people must live in it, including, finally, Chad Newsome.

Paris as "some huge iridescent object," the locale and facilitator of individual development, is—we should keep in mind—an American tourist's or expatriate's Paris, self-indulgently imagined and incomplete. The Paris of French society, as Christopher Newman learned and Jeanne de Vionnet's arranged marriage illustrates, can be just as hard-headed and coercive as Woollett. In fact, by the standards of French society Woollett can be accused of sentimentality, for it does not regard affection and personal worth as irrelevant in proposing Mamie Pocock for Chad.[2] Physically the world of *The Ambassadors* is Paris, but socially it is a tertium quid in which a momentary suspension of the ordinary dynamic of the individual's relation to society has a liberating and enlarging effect.

Paris and Woollett speak languages that describe and interpret the world differently, not in terms of "the ontological and epistemological worlds of physical relationship . . . but the world of social relations . . . orientations towards persons, roles, statuses, rights and duties, deference and demeanor."[3] Rather than morality, these social distinctions are the heart of the divergence in their interpretations of reality. In Woollett social relations are rigidly prescribed, and its discourse consequently allows speakers little deviation from group norms. In Paris, Paris as tertium quid, a certain amount of social fluidity is reflected in a language of greater individual assertion and ambiguity. "Civilized Paris," as William Greenslade writes, "signals itself obliquely; interpretation necessitates a continued decoding of linguistic and visual ambiguity to penetrate further into the promised brilliance of its light."[4] Those who speak the language of Paris—Miss Barrace, Little Bilham, Madame de Vionnet, Chad, and Maria—all use their conversation with Strether to confound the preconceptions and certainties of Woollett and broach new interpretations: to enlarge not only the field of thought but also that of speech. Although Strether finally sees literally what the relationship of Chad and Madame de Vionnet is, the placing of this datum within a fully apprehended context is much more a matter of insight, arrived at through intellection and discourse, than visual apprehension. As such, it depends to a crucial extent upon his progress in learning to understand and speak a new language.

Given the long delay and careful buildup to Strether's enlightenment, it is easy to become preoccupied by the epistemological issue of Chad and Madame de Vionnet's relationship. But the reality of it, the crude and reductive stuff of Woollett's imaginings, constitutes the kind of commonplace donnée that life always made available to the transfor-

mative powers of James's art. What is important is not the brute fact of
the liaison but the institutional facts proceeding from it: the meaning
and value society confers on it and the effect that such social judgment
has.[5] These matters depend upon how it is described in language. As
Stanley Fish reminds us, "All facts are discourse specific (since no fact
is available apart from some dimension of assessment or other) and . . .
therefore no one can claim for any language a special relationship to
the facts as they 'simply are,' unmediated by social or conventional assumptions."[6] According to one's perspective the brute fact may be, in
Madame de Vionnet's words, "too ugly" or "too beautiful." The crucial
definition of a "virtuous attachment" is the point of juncture between
ethical and social requirements, the interface between the individual
and society that is James's typical fictive territory.

First assumed, then obscured, and finally revealed, the nature of the
liaison remains constant for the duration of the novel; what changes is
the shape that it assumes in words. In Woollett's single-minded determination to end Chad's life in Paris, actual evidence of an unsavoury
attachment is neither required nor wanted. Strether begins with the
Woollett assumption, which he merely expects to confirm in Paris, but
he moves through successive revelations that transform the relationship
in his vision and speech into a paramount value, transcending all other
claims and desiderata. When Strether discovers the pair to be lovers, he
is brought back to the starting point of the Woollett assumption without
repudiating what he has learned in the meantime.

■ That business is the chief value of Woollett is significantly apparent in the extent to which the language of commercial
transaction permeates its speech. Returning Chad to Woollett is presented as, first and foremost, a financially profitable venture: Chad will
take up "his definite material reward"; the family business will make
more money for the already rich Mrs. Newsome; and Strether, too, will
be paid for offering up the young man as a wedding present. Not the
least sign of Strether's change during the novel is his abandonment of
Mrs. Newsome's business in favor of his own, a business that will be
without the tangible profits of hers. Conversely, a presage of Chad's
return to Woollett is his application of a financial metaphor to his personal life.[7] When Strether tells him that his "value has quintupled,"
Chad responds, " 'If one *should* wish to live on one's accumulations?' "
(22: 312).

The language of Woollett, so quick to label Chad's life pejoratively, is noticeably reticent about its own concerns: the article whose manufacture sustains Mrs. Newsome's preeminence cannot be named because its vulgarity is incommensurate with that lady's dignity. Where Paris resorts to a deceptive verbal ambiguity, Woollett prefers silence. Strether's reiterated protestations of silence about Mrs. Newsome echo his earlier refusals to discuss her father and her husband. In all three instances the implication is that further speech would articulate more unworthy or unseemly particulars which would be, like the name of the vulgar object, incompatible with the dignity of wealth and position. More explicit language would establish that Mrs. Newsome's feminine gentility is directly related to and dependent upon a world of "practices" and vulgarity embodied in the masculine figures of business success: Chad's father and grandfather and the common but nevertheless highly valued Jim Pocock. When Strether commits himself to a statement about Mrs. Newsome's life, in response to Maria's urging, it again suggests the kind of association between money and charity that enables Maria to infer that "expiation" is involved.

Maria's direct and enthusiastic mode of speaking articulates what Strether prefers to leave vague or unsaid, habitually returning his financial idiom, as she does with *appreciate*, in a more extreme form or converting his own neutral utterance into commercial parlance. Like other Parisian speakers Maria employs the vocabulary of Woollett with tonal variations—light irony, exaggeration, affected disingenuousness—that are intended to confront Strether with the implications of Woollett's language. Strether's innocent description of his collaboration with Mrs. Newsome on the green Review thus becomes in Maria's retelling a business transaction in which Mrs. Newsome has bought Strether but would drop him if a more worthwhile investment became available. She concludes: "Therefore close with her—!" (21: 65), a directive redolent of the business deal.

Because of its devotion to a self-serving business ethos, Woollett is unable to assess correctly anything that cannot be translated into palpable profit and loss. This underlies Strether's indictment of the Woollett assumption in his speech to Sarah Pocock: "Our general state of mind had proceeded, on its side, from our queer ignorance, our queer misconceptions and confusions—from which, since then, an inexorable tide of light seems to have floated us into our perhaps still queerer knowledge" (22: 201).[8] Strether employs three nouns to indicate mis-

information, and he reiterates the qualifier *queer* to emphasize how
removed from reality Woollett's surmises have been. Yet the second half
of the sentences does not provide a completely positive counterpart: the
word *queerer* links the new truth to the previous error. The paradigms
Woollett applies to behavior are convenient but inadequate while the
truth, as conceptualized by Woollett, is "inexorable" but inconvenient.

■ Those speakers who speak the language of Paris—
Miss Barrace, Little Bilham, Chad, Madame de Vionnet, and Maria
Gostrey—are verbally adventurous, more playful and speculative.
Above all, they show themselves to be open to more possibilities than
are dreamed of in the language of Woollett: "Strether had never in his
life heard so many opinions on so many subjects. There were opinions
at Woollett, but only on three or four" (21: 173). In all the speakers who
tutor Strether in the ways of their world this openness takes the form of
an extravagant questioning and supposing markedly different from the
narrow certitudes of Woollett speakers. When Maria creates a verbal
fantasy about Strether's relationship with Mrs. Newsome, "she em-
broidered, she abounded" (21: 65). This is the style of all the Parisian
speakers.

   Strether begins his mission with total loyalty to the public language
of Woollett, but Maria's undermining of this position in the probing
language of Paris prepares the ground for his own reassessment. Before he has any firsthand information, Strether thinks of Chad's life
in the conventional stereotypes of a stage drama he witnesses: the
victim must naturally be weak as well as attractive, the woman bad,
the action "unspecified dreadful things"—all conveniently simplified
and absolute. The dialogue between Strether and Maria that follows—
their first on the subject—establishes the difference between the languages of Woollett and Paris not so much in vocabulary at this point
but in the manner of dealing with the world. Maria's method of questioning and insinuating, of suggesting other interpretations, undercuts
the starkly schematized and patently self-serving account of a wicked
woman preying upon innocent youth which gives the rescue mission
moral authority. While Strether dogmatically adheres to the official
view, answering Maria's first question with the collective *we*, Maria
challenges it by posing alternatives. Her approach is empirical: the
lack of information which has failed to inhibit Woollett from reaching
judgment causes Maria to reserve hers decisively; moreover, she rejects

the chiaroscuro of Woollett in favor of a more complex shading—the
woman may be "wicked" and good for Chad. Her bantering equation
of the woman to his life equally subverts Woollett values, which require
that Chad's life be his business career rather than a woman.[9] Strether
and Woollett might admit that a bad woman possessed a certain charm,
evil yet alluring, but in the context of Maria's refusal to subscribe to the
Woollett assumption, her remark implies that to be charming is reason
for a positive judgment on Chad's life. Although Chad reveals little,
his adversarial responses to Strether point up the myths and oversim-
plifications that Woollett affirms, according to which Chad can have
been deflected from the proper path only by a bad woman. If there is
no such woman, Strether assumes, there can be no obstacle to Chad's
departure.

The Woollett habit of mind in Strether often dictates a self-imposed
limitation—not to think a step further than he is obliged to. Although
he imagines himself to be proceeding "with scruples dismissed," in
reality he seeks to protect himself from an encounter with what is "too
ugly." Moving away from Woollett and towards Paris, Strether begins
to ask speculative questions, but with a note of hesitancy and timidity
in keeping with his reluctance to go beyond a certain point. Far from
diligently pursuing knowledge, Strether tries to escape it:

> But she [Maria] defended herself. "I don't pretend to know any-
> thing about it. Everything's possible. We must see."
> "See?" he echoed with a groan. "Haven't we seen enough?"
> (21: 188)

Maria is the aggressive speaker, eager to continue the investigation
until the truth, no matter what truth, is uncovered, willing to prod
and instruct Strether to do the same. He, in turn, is on the defensive,
fearful of what will be revealed in further pursuit. To her absolute—
everything—he responds with *enough*, for Woollett has no interest in
an exhaustive investigation. It has issued a command which Strether,
under Maria's tutelage, is transforming into an inquiry.[10]

■ Little Bilham's phrase "a virtuous attachment"
comes to encapsulate verbally the dispute between the languages of
Woollett and Paris over the meaning and value of Chad's life. In
Woollett's inflexible terms an illicit bond could never be designated as
"virtuous"; assuming that Little Bilham has spoken the language of

Woollett, Strether accepts the label for most of the novel as referring to a nonsexual relationship. This is a fruitful misunderstanding, for Strether's first attitude, that Chad must be in the clutches of a woman who is "base, venal—out of the streets," would have precluded his acceptance of Madame de Vionnet.[11] Armed with the reassuring label, Strether can approach her open-mindedly and succumb to a charm that he believes to be free from the overt eroticism condemned by Woollett.

Actually, there is little reason to misunderstand. Little Bilham himself soon qualifies the idea of the virtuous attachment unmistakably: " 'I can only tell you that it's what they pass for. But isn't that enough? What more than a vain appearance does the wisest of us know? I commend you,' the young man declared with a pleasant emphasis, 'the vain appearance' " (21: 202–203). And Strether himself has broached to Maria the possibility of Little Bilham's having lied. A speaker committed to the language of Woollett would have had no difficulty in penetrating Little Bilham's remark, but in both instances Strether's new desire to experience without judging leads to a willing suspension of disbelief. As Strether comes to understand, the term is a lie only in the language of Woollett: "It was but a technical lie—he [Little Bilham] classed the attachment as virtuous. That was a view for which there was much to be said—and the virtue came out for me hugely. There was of course a great deal of it. I got it full in the face, and I haven't . . . done with it yet" (22: 299). Strether can admit that by other standards than Woollett's, "virtuous attachment" is an accurate label, but he is nevertheless shocked by his encounter with virtue in such an unexpected guise. "I got it full in the face" suggests a physical thrusting of unwelcome revelation, the metaphoric blow that his sight of the lovers on an intimate outing administers. When Maria tells Strether that he "dressed up even the virtue," she confirms that he needed a certain amount of idealization to make this novel virtue palatable.

The difference the revelation makes to Strether is immediately apparent in his reaction to Madame de Vionnet's speaking in French: "The present result was odd, fairly veiling her identity, shifting her back into a mere voluble class or race to the intense audibility of which he was by this time inured" (22: 261). Stripped of her verbal uniqueness, Madame de Vionnet is also stripped of the power to create through language a picture of the situation that Strether can accept. Unable to understand her rapid French, he sees her as distanced, a representative figure categorized in the manner of Woollett as an excitable foreigner, devoid of any special significance for him. The dilemma of the awkward return journey that Strether and the lovers make together takes shape in Strether's mind as a choice between a socially proper lie and a truth that society prohibits the utterance of. The obviousness of the gap between the institutional fact created by social behavior and the underlying brute fact morally sickens Strether. What he feels retrospectively is the impossibility of escaping social dictates: "Their eminent 'lie,' Chad's and hers, was simply after all such an inevitable tribute to good taste as he couldn't have wished them not to render" (22: 277).[12] The tortured indirection of the final clause reflects a painful emotional confrontation: whether in Woollett, in Paris, or in the idyllic French countryside, the relationship of Chad and Madame de Vionnet cannot be openly acknowledged because it is socially proscribed. French society and the American expatriate community tacitly accept the resulting subterfuge and hypocrisy, but once Strether knows the full truth, he must leave to escape complicity in this "eminent 'lie.' "

Yet for Strether, the moral reason for repugnance and withdrawal is more compelling than the conventions of social decorum. Socially, the illicit sexual liaison is the paramount consideration; apart from this violation, the relationship of Madame de Vionnet and Chad represents the moral transgression of untrammeled egotism. As Madame de Vionnet herself recognizes, her selfish use of other people in order to keep Chad, the necessity of conniving and lying to satisfy the self, precludes genuine contentment: "What it comes to is that it's not, that it's never, a happiness, any happiness at all, to *take*. The only safe thing is to give. It's what plays you least false" (22: 282–83). Surely this principle—a secularized *caritas* that goes well beyond what society requires—is the abiding moral of James's diverse fictive worlds, as it is of Strether's conduct. He will not selfishly keep Paris, Madame de Vionnet, or Maria Gostrey: going makes him right, just as—he insists—staying makes Chad right, because, as the material rewards of Woollett beckon and he grows tired of Madame de Vionnet, staying becomes a matter of giving rather than taking.[13] Until Strether renounces advantage in order to be right, no one is disinterested or selfless or moral in either Woollett or Paris; his remarking to Little Bilham "I shan't live long" suggests the prescient understanding that he can no longer live in either place.

Strether comes to understand the language of Paris and to accept some of the revelations that its greater freedom makes available, but his reaction to the true state of affairs shows that he remains closer to the language of Woollett: "It had for me—it has still—such elements of strangeness. Her greater age than his, her different world, traditions, associations; her other opportunities, liabilities, standards" (22: 300–301). Although both societies unite in condemning an openly acknowledged liaison, Paris has more understanding, more flexibility, than Woollett.[14] In the language of Woollett, those differences in the world of social relations that Strether enumerates are the significant values; in the language of Paris that Maria speaks, passion is recognized as capable of overriding the social differences that put such a relationship almost beyond imagining for Strether. For Woollett what is strange cannot be entertained, much less spoken.

■ Analogous to *queer*, the word that most tellingly characterizes Strether's widening view is *strange*, a typical example of that late Jamesian language whose bland vagueness is, as David Lodge points out, "a treacherous medium of communication, concealing as much as it reveals."[15] For the purposes of social discourse this is its great virtue; a general connotation is established and nothing further because it is preferable to avoid confronting a set of embarrassing specifics. Such expressions can obviously be misunderstood: when Strether characterizes the Newsome women as "remarkably fine," Maria interprets this to mean "very handsome." Strether's reaction—his brief "drop" and subsequent rebound—makes it clear that this was not at all what he meant, nor do further questions pin down his meaning.

The stock epithets that all the characters employ—*strange, odd, queer, awful*, on the negative side; *wonderful, charming, admirable*, on the positive—are clichés that carry broad social meaning sufficient for polite discourse. "Remarkably fine" describes the social preeminence of Chad's mother and sister well enough, just as Jim Pocock's "awful" for Madame de Vionnet indicates her social unacceptability. *Abysses*, always used in the plural for intensification, invokes weighty and complex matters whose properties to some extent elude verbalization. When Strether refuses to discuss the business dealings of Chad's grandfather, Maria remarks, "Lord, what abysses!" Later, speaking about women, she says to Strether, "We're abysses." James also uses the term for Strether's thoughts on Chad's different duties to his mother and Madame de Vionnet: "It was rather much to deal with at once;

not only the question itself, but the sore abysses it revealed" (22: 200). *Abysses* are by definition *sore*, not only because they mark crucial hiatuses in knowledge but because they are irremediable. As Ruth Yeazell observes, "the full truth in James' late novels is never spoken,"[16] for words cannot eliminate the abysses of the Jamesian universe; they can only point to the void, the sore spot, and then fall silent.

Because there is much that cannot be spoken for reasons of decorum, social discourse in *The Ambassadors* exhibits numerous kinds of communication failure. In one instance James builds an entire conversation upon ambiguous antecedents, causing Strether to be continually uncertain whether pronouns refer to Chad, to Jeanne de Vionnet's prospective groom, or to her father. The verbal ambiguity reflects Strether's ignorance of Chad's true relationship to the household: is he attached to Jeanne and thus a possible son-in-law figure for Madame de Vionnet, or is he the mother's lover, i.e., a surrogate father to Jeanne? Chad's having made the arrangements for the forthcoming marriage confirms what the language of social discourse reveals only indirectly. When Madame de Vionnet remarks of the fiancé, "I quite adore him," Strether asks for clarification: "You mean your future son-in-law?" (22: 129) Behind the confusion is Chad's pervasive presence in the conversation, his filling unexpected roles in the Vionnet family's affairs, and in addition, Strether's unacknowledged sense that the words of perfunctory social approbation of the fiancé are literally true of Madame de Vionnet's feelings for Chad. Further confusion of the same sort occurs because Madame de Vionnet refers to Chad in language appropriate to the fiancé: "And do you suppose *he*—who loves her so—would do anything reckless or cruel? . . . He takes, thank God, the truest tenderest interest in her" (22: 130). Strether does not verbalize what he has learned; the authorial voice relates explicitly what presumably Strether does not tell himself, that he carries away "the refined disguised suppressed passion of her face"—the record of emotion which has been stifled and distorted by the requirements of social expression.

The imprecision of James's language, so necessary to the confined space of decorous speech, may explain why he tends to entrust climactic revelations to emblematic pictures instead of words. Isabel Archer's glimpse of her husband seated familiarly while Madame Merle stands impresses Isabel with the true nature of the relationship more than her sister-in-law's words of intended enlightenment. In *The Ambassadors*

Strether's endless verbal investigations of Chad and Madame de Vionnet do not prepare him for the truth that he learns, not through words, but through seeing the same kind of intimate tableau that undeceives Isabel.

Verbal reticence consciously chosen by the characters is paradoxically the distinctive quality of the copious speaking in *The Ambassadors*. It is not a philosophical position proceeding from a sense that language is unequal to experience; on the contrary, James's dicta that "art makes life" and "all life . . . comes back to the question of our speech" insist that language has supreme importance in creating the value of experience. Nevertheless, the mutual observance of silence to avoid breaking social taboos permits an intimacy that more explicit speech would make impossible: "These things, all the same, he wouldn't breathe to Madame de Vionnet—much as they might make him walk up and down. And what he didn't say—as well as what *she* didn't for she had also her high decencies—enhanced the effect of his being there with her at the end of ten minutes more intimately on the basis of saving her than he had yet had occasion to be. It ended in fact by being quite beautiful between them, the number of things they had a manifest consciousness of not saying" (22: 114). The very power of language to create reality, not its inadequacy, leads to verbal restraint in the Jamesian world. What James's characters renounce trying to express, in Leo Bersani's words, "is generally not an intuition that would expose the ambiguity of all efforts to understand, but rather a richness of understanding which would expand the dialogue to monstrous proportions."[17] Moreover, "high decencies" require that certain matters not be spoken of: "The maintenance of civility in speech," James writes, "costs what it must."[18] As Chad tells Strether at the end, "I spoke to you originally only as I *had* to speak. There's only one way—isn't there?—about such things" (22: 309). Although Paris may be more tolerant of personal deviation from group mores than Woollett is, neither society will allow these departures to be officially admitted into discourse. In the verbal universe of *The Ambassadors* silence and the lie are socially approved substitutes for an unspeakable truth.

In James's vision of life there is finally no alternative to the institutions, customs, and dictates of society—no matter how inimical they may be to individual self-realization. When Strether speaks to Little Bilham of Chad's being "saved," he explains that he is speaking of "his manners and morals, his character and life. I'm speaking of him as a person to deal with and talk with and live with—as a social animal" (21: 283). Society may curtail individual freedom and encourage deceptive behavior, but we are social beings whose lives, insofar as they are distinctively human, must be lived within its confines.[19] When Strether urges Chad to remain with Madame de Vionnet as a "sacred obligation," he asseverates his point by invoking both the nonsocial and the antisocial as terms of condemnation: "You'd not only be . . . a brute; you'd be . . . a criminal of the deepest dye" (22: 311). Through his encounter with the long-avoided truth Strether moves from the narrow collective vision of Woollett, the imagining of "horrors," to a personal liberation of mind and language, his supposing of "innumerable and wonderful things." But however positive the relationship of Chad and Madame de Vionnet may appear, its lawlessness is terrifying as well, and it must inevitably feel the pressures of social opprobrium that James brings to bear on all of his free spirits.

Language and Gender in
The House of Mirth

■ Edith Wharton's novels, like those of her friend and predecessor Henry James, are always speech-act dramas which turn upon what can and cannot be said according to the dictates of society: the code of verbal restraint that governs utterance is everywhere present. For both James and Wharton society is the coercive arbiter of individual behavior, but whereas in James's most characteristic fiction society is a generally diffused presence that never takes on the reality of a particular social milieu, in Wharton's it assumes the specific historical shape of turn-of-the-century upper-class New York. In *The House of Mirth* it is a fully realized character whose views at any given moment are as palpably presented as the furnishings of Mrs. Peniston's drawing room.

As her insistent light-and-dark imagery suggests, Wharton's treatment is compartmentalized.[20] She eschews the open-ended suggestiveness of James's evocation of the abyss in favor of a starkly elegant exploration of it, a difference reflected in their styles.[21] Hers is sharply focused and balanced, often to the point of epigram, an act of placement and clarification that decisively contains its materials in language. James's early style is similar, although never so epigrammatic as Wharton's; but the style of his late period, with its obscurings and complications, its vocabulary of vagueness and proliferation of syntactic elements—clauses, phrases, qualifiers—asserts the impossibility of such efforts of classification as Wharton habitually makes. While James constantly calls attention to the aporias of communication as unchartable regions where wraith-like abstractions rise out of concealing mists, Wharton gives such absences the weight and shape of precise definition. Predictably, her fictive speech is trenchant and climactic, a crystallization of narrative episode into a dramatic moment.[22]

The primary target of Wharton's pervasive irony is her society's ideological transvaluation of values. Reflecting a speech community that defines living well and dressing expensively as "inherited obligations," the language of this world elevates the superficial and the frivolous to the level of seriousness. Elderly dowagers like Mrs. Peniston talk about housekeeping; younger women discuss house parties; and travelers abroad inquire after the "best restaurant for peas" in Monte Carlo. Since there is no desire to engage genuinely serious matters such as Lily Bart's financial difficulties, there is no vocabulary for dealing with them. To her aunt, Lily's gambling debts are unimaginably shocking, while to Gus Trenor they are simply unimaginable, and thus the subject of a joking banter.

Measurements of value and status, which dominate the social discourse of this world, insist upon the assimilation of all other values to one standard, that of commodification.[23] Society is frankly and matter-of-factly permeated with an institutionalized commodification that requires no cloak of genteel expression to disguise its concerns.[24] Instead, the novel foregrounds the quid pro quos of social life, the principle of exchange that defines all relationships in some material way. In return for being best man at Jack Stepney's wedding, Rosedale will deliver a "thumping present"; Lily's mother expects her to get back the lost family fortune with her face; and newcomers are constantly buying their way into exclusive social circles. Commodification converts all personal relationships into quasi-commercial exchanges: where Mrs. Peniston rewards Lily's brilliant company with a clothing allowance, she compensates Grace Stepney's unexciting companionship with her cast-off clothing. Every encounter can be translated into material terms, however trivial. Giving her cousin the unwelcome news of Lily's debts, Grace has a "vision of forfeited dinners and a reduced wardrobe" (124–25).

The very name Lily Bart embodies the conflict between self and society, person and commodity, subject and object. Unlike the lilies of the field that neither toil nor spin, Lily cannot flourish effortlessly; she must barter her beauty for security. To do so, however, is to sacrifice that fineness of spirit that sets her apart from the habituées of her world as surely as her physical beauty does. Indeed, whenever Lily commits herself to the goals of her society she is inscribed in the text as an object. At the beginning of the novel when she is intent upon finding a rich husband, Selden constantly thinks of her in the language of things, precisely evaluated.[25] Lily is a more valuable object than other women because it seems, in her, "as though a fine glaze of beauty and fastidiousness had been applied to vulgar clay" (5). Later, succumbing once more to the lure of society, Lily undergoes a further stage in the process of reification: "Now its [her beauty's] impenetrable surface suggested a process of crystallization which had fused her whole being into one hard, brilliant substance" (191–92). As Robin Lakoff observes, in "language descriptive of women alone," a woman is treated "as an object—sexual or otherwise—but never [as] a serious person with individual views."[26] Objects, of course, do not speak, and Lily is never more successful as an ornament than when she is utterly silent in a *tableau vivant* of a Reynolds painting.[27] Her (changing) value is the subject of the novel and of everyone's appraisal. Selden tells her that she can "do better than Dilsworth," a former matrimonial prospect, and Rosedale calculates her worth in two ways, as a wife and as a painting.

Paradigmatically, Lily stakes an acceptable claim and then fails to pursue it to fruition: enticing Selden away from Bertha and consequently neglecting the serious business of acquiring a husband appears impulsive, but this violation of the code is more deeply motivated by Lily's developing desire to escape social definition and to express instead her own being. To a large extent this desire must be realized by freeing herself from public language, which discourages both individual self-expression and truthful communication, and by further freeing herself from a gendered discourse that denies her status as subject. "Indisputably," in Luce Irigaray's words, "this [denial] provides the financial backing for every irreducible constitution as an object: of representation, of discourse, of desire."[28]

■ Within the dominant materialistic discourse of society, gender-specific subcategories exist that reflect the role and status differences between men and women. Unlike sex, gender is a social construct, which emphasizes the authority of society in determining appropriate roles for men and women, including language behavior. In *The House of Mirth* the empirical power of men is expressed linguistically in their more forceful and direct speech as well as by a content of what Lakoff calls "real world information."[29] When women speak among themselves their subjects are the stereotypically feminine ones of adornment, domestic matters, and gossip.

In mixed conversation the subordinate position of women manifests itself, above all, in polite speech at the expense of other considerations. Generally, as Philip M. Smith writes, "masculinity tends to be expressed in terms of control-related skills and femininity in terms of affiliation."[30] Men speak openly of the matters that interest them, sacrificing conversational harmony to dominance, whereas women pursue their own agendas obliquely: the paradigm of overt subordination in the speech of women to men is often coupled with implicit manipulation.[31] With Percy Gryce, for example, Lily manages every aspect of the conversation according to her hidden agenda of impressing him as a suitable marriage prospect. Through the ritual of making tea, which allows her to be both domestic and graceful, Lily reassures and attracts the timid Gryce. She then offers him the opportunity to assume conversational dominance in his one area of expertise: "She questioned him intelligently, she heard him submissively. . . . He grew eloquent under her receptive gaze" (20). Wharton's description is infused with irony, but she leaves no doubt that this is a successful formula for conventional male-female conversation in which an enabling feminine discourse creates the space for the male to dominate the talk exchange and proffers the illusion that he has achieved this for himself.

Two critical conversations with Gus Trenor indicate that a more assertive and mature man requires more complicated versions of the same linguistic strategy. Picking Gus up at the station, Lily begins as she had with Gryce by giving him a chance to talk and be listened to attentively, an opportunity that men like Gryce and Trenor, economically powerful but boring and inarticulate, rarely encounter. Her suggestion of prolonging their drive initiates the second stage of this manipulative process. Having implicitly flattered Trenor by desiring to remain in his company, she explicitly does so by characterizing him as an intimate.[32] Her overture serves as an unobtrusive transition from Trenor's self-involved monologue to Lily's presentation of her case, a move made more effective by her introduction of a sham topic to disarm his suspicions of being made use of. Lily's decorous sexuality, combined with the reassurance that her appeal is not dangerous, works formulaically here as it did earlier with Gryce. Trenor dominates throughout this conversation in assertiveness and length of speeches, characteristics typical of masculine conversation with women; but behind an artful facade of subordination, Lily has orchestrated their talk exchange according to her own needs.

In the climactic dialogue on this subject, positions are partially reversed because Lily is taken unawares: Trenor has planned a scenario before the meeting and lured Lily to his town house with an invitation supposedly from his wife. When Lily first exposes this ruse, Trenor discards the decorum of polite speech and reproaches her in the terms of an unadulterated male discourse, blunt and demanding: "If Judy'd been here you'd have sat gossiping till all hours—and you can't even give me five minutes! . . . Very good, then; I'll take 'em. And as many more as I want" (146). Throughout Trenor's speeches to Lily the subject is ostensibly social rather than sexual intercourse—"you can't even give me five minutes!"—but, as the shift from assertives to declarations indicates, his language constantly veers away from the acceptable into a realm of forcible appropriation and satisfaction of desire. Nevertheless, even when he gives Lily an order, he adds an automatic "please": ultimately he cannot sustain an aggressive male speech at odds with long-established habits. When Lily invokes the decorum of polite discourse, a verbal prison that Trenor is seeking to escape, he admonishes her not to "talk stage-rot," yet in a sense Trenor himself is the victim of the "stage-rot" he dismisses, the polite treatment of women in his world that masks their economic dependence upon men. This acculturation as a man of honor customarily guided by social imperatives finally thwarts the realization of his intentions, for he cannot bring himself to speak plainly in the face of Lily's refusal to acknowledge his implicatures.[33] Since the only attention Trenor can legitimately claim from Lily is that of polite speech, he is reduced to reiterating this claim on her attention: "When I tried to come up and say a word, you never took any notice." Or: "I'm only asking for a word of thanks from you" (146). Although Lily's prompt "I *have* thanked you" shows the impossibility of speech's accomplishing Trenor's purpose, he cannot commit himself to plain speaking because the same conventions of social discourse that provide refuge for Lily constrain him. He is all too aware that he is "not talking the way a man is supposed to talk to a girl" (146).

The social climber Sim Rosedale is another male speaker whose lack of conversational polish causes him to speak more frankly than ordinary social discourse allows, and it is a measure of Lily's moral growth that she moves from a social view of his plain speaking as distasteful to an appreciation of its honesty that can overlook the violation of decorum. While Rosedale's expression of his real concerns comes to appeal to Lily as a contrast to social hypocrisy, the themes of his speech are the familiar ones of public language: the open embrace of acquisition, status, and wealth with a subtext of base manipulation that insidiously clothes itself in the language of business give-and-take.

To communicate her better self, the one stifled by the "tissue of social falsehoods" that she must speak in order to survive in society, Lily must find a language that reflects other values and a dialogue partner who shares it: "She felt the real difficulties of her situation to be incommunicable to any one whose theory of values was so different from her own" (263). Selden invokes a discourse whose values of personal autonomy and taste oppose those of public language and its social world; this language, he instructs Lily, serves a "Republic of the Spirit." As such, it is an ideal fleetingly glimpsed but unacknowledged by society and hence unspeakable—even, as it turns out, to Selden himself.

Selden, Lily's male counterpart, formed like her by "all the conditions of life" to be aloof and fastidious, is similarly unsuited to save Lily with a responsible love, one that moves beyond admiring spectatorship to the wholehearted commitment that Nettie Struther's husband makes to her. In their talk exchange at Bellomont each accuses the other of cowardice, and each is right: for different reasons neither Selden nor Lily can make a full commitment to the other although "an indwelling voice in each called to the other across unsounded depths of feeling." Articulating this voice always remains a teasing possibility in their discourse, but one that convention and misunderstanding keep from realization. In their last conversation Lily's "passionate desire to be understood," i.e., to be treated as a subject rather than as a commodity/object, cannot overcome Selden's passivity. She comes as close as she can to direct speech by referring in the third person to "the Lily Bart you knew" and asking Selden, "Will you let her stay with you?" (309). As well as an articulation of Lily's divided self, this is surely an unconscious proposal of marriage, and one with an awareness of Selden's impossible requirements: "She'll be no trouble, she'll take up no room" (309). Selden consistently responds to such overtures in the conventional terms of public language that preclude truthful discourse, much as Lily had responded to Trenor. He can imagine nothing more in this speech than an oblique reference to the customary salvation for distress such as Lily's—her approaching marriage.

Both find too late the word that will dissolve the distance between them: Lily's last coherent thought before death is that "there was something she must tell Selden, some word she had found that should make life clear between them" (323). He, in turn, hurries to her house the following morning with "the word he meant to say to her" (324). The novel ends with this word "which made all clear" passing in silence between Selden and the dead Lily, a pointed inscription of the discourse restraints that have governed their relationship.

Within the social world that the text has constructed there is in fact no solution to Lily's dilemma, no saving language. Lily cannot integrate her social and individual selves, nor can she, until the end of the novel, choose the individual over the social, the problematic status of subject over the prescribed role of object. As she realizes and accepts, Lily is irrevocably a social commodity, unfit in all respects to live other possible lives and equally unfit to live the life required by her world. She can emulate neither of the two women juxtaposed to her on her final evening, Bertha Dorset and Nettie Struthers, who represent negative and positive models, not only of survival but of language. Significantly, throughout the novel Bertha preserves herself and destroys others with socially acceptable lies while Nettie runs the risk of self-destruction by insisting upon the truth. Both women have husbands named George, one the recipient of a lying discourse that conceals infidelity and undermines relationship, the other of a truthful discourse which strengthens union. That the novel correlates these differing commitments to truthful speech with social class is an inescapable conclusion.

■ Where Wharton herself was able to create a "language of feminine growth and mastery," Elaine Showalter observes, "we are repeatedly reminded of the absence of this language in the world of *The House of Mirth* by Lily's ladylike self-silencing, her inability to rise above the 'word-play and evasion' that restrict her conversations with Selden and to tell her own story."[34] Lily *does* rise above this curtailing language by the end of the novel, and she does become capable of telling her own story honestly, both to herself and to others. But without a receptive dialogue partner she cannot effectively *communicate* her story, nor can she, in keeping with the recurring speech paradigms of the American novel, find another language, one that will free her from her story.

Although Lily's first reaction to misfortune is to preserve appearances, protecting the deceptive social self, she later admits candidly to Rosedale that she must work for a living, that she lives in a miserable boarding house, and that she owes all of the little money that she has inherited. Moreover, her confession is not part of the discourse of calculated feminine pathos that created an appealingly vulnerable image in order to manipulate Gus Trenor, for Lily wants no such favors from Rosedale. What she wants is to acknowledge her circumstances in truthful language to herself as much as to Rosedale, who is ultimately unsatisfactory as a dialogue partner.

Lily becomes unable to speak and live by the public language of her society and her sex, that feminine discourse that has the power to save her up to the very end. Its words are known to her—at the beginning of the novel they are automatically generated whenever she wants to manipulate a man, and at the end they are urged upon her by Rosedale and George Dorset. By speaking what she knows to Dorset she can openly save herself and ruin Bertha; by speaking to Bertha she can save herself clandestinely and marry Rosedale. Either alternative would preserve the social self/object in its traditional form, that of the married woman, at the expense of the individual self/subject that Lily has come to value so much that she cannot relinquish it in order to survive. Nor can she empower Selden to speak "the word which made all clear," to perform the speech act that would rescue this better self, Lily as subject. Her misfortune is to evoke only male discourse unworthy of her, like the "eloquence" she inspires in Percy Gryce; the crude admiration of Trenor, Rosedale, and other men; the uncommitted speech of Selden. Such discourse, Showalter writes, defines women:

> In one sense Lily's search for a suitable husband is an effort to be "spoken for," to be suitably articulated and defined in the social arena. Instead, she has the opposite fate: she is "spoken of" by men, and as Lily herself observes, "The truth about any girl is that once she's talked about, she's done for, and the more she explains her case the worse it looks." To become the object of male discourse is almost as bad as to become the victim of male lust.[35]

As a description of events in *The House of Mirth* this is persuasive but not entirely accurate, for although economic power is concentrated in the masculine kingdom of Wall Street, a feminine discourse controls the realm of social exclusivity represented by Fifth Avenue, albeit one that enunciates and upholds patriarchal values as a matter of self-interest.

The "talking about" that Showalter refers to is actually the province of women in the novel: Lily becomes the object of a censorious feminine discourse which adversely affects her at every critical moment.[36] Bertha Dorset begins the process by telling Percy Gryce "horrors" about Lily; later, her abrupt utterance that Lily will not return to the yacht severely undermines Lily's reputation; on subsequent occasions she continues to speak tellingly against Lily. In the major instance of the novel's inexorable process of marginalizing Lily, Mrs. Peniston revises her will to reduce her niece from chief beneficiary to mere legatee.

The female community of *The House of Mirth* makes the same demands that Susan Harding observed in the real verbal behavior of a Spanish village: "Girls must learn to decipher the degree of closeness offered by other girls, to recognize what is being withheld, and to recognize criticism. Girls who don't read these cues run the risk of public censure or ridicule."[37] For all of her success with men, Lily is not skillful in deciphering the cues offered by her own sex. In the crucial conversation with Bertha Dorset after the latter has stayed out all night with Ned Silverton and returned to the yacht the next morning, it is essential for Lily to decode Bertha's remarks correctly and to adapt herself to them, however fictional Bertha's account might be. Confident in the facts of the situation, Lily instead pursues her own reading and thus fails to understand Bertha. The language on both sides is often interrogatory, but Bertha's accusatory assertions and rhetorical questions constitute an aggression that Lily meets with genuine bafflement. Bertha's utterances have a theme and a strategy while Lily's are merely reactive, no more than a weak echo of Bertha's words:

B: Whenever anything upsetting happens. . . .
L: Anything upsetting? . .
B: I'm expected to take hints, not to give them: I've positively lived on them all these last months.
L: Hints—from me to you? (208)

Lily's questions betray her paralysis: as Geoffrey Leech and Michael Short point out, "typically people employ echo questions to indicate that they are not sure whether they have heard or understood the relevant part of the previous remark properly." [38] Lily moves from lame responses confined to the circle of Bertha's own words, and consequently of her controlling fiction, to the more passive role of silent witness, and then to a departure "without a word." Whereas Bertha has no need of verbal reinforcement, Lily literally cannot speak: "The words died under the impenetrable insolence of Bertha's smile" (208). This is not merely the silence of injured innocence: just as she was complicit in the relationship with Gus Trenor, here, too, Lily is culpable in having pursued the pleasures of society and forgotten her own vulnerability. The implicature indicated by her echo questions is that she can neither uphold her innocence in speech nor recognize her guilt.

This same inability to use the discourse of social power informs all of Lily's conversations with other women: those who have power—like Bertha, Mrs. Peniston, and even Grace Stepney—use it against Lily. Elizabeth Ammons comments that in *The House of Mirth* "women prey on each other—stealing reputations, opportunities, male admirers— all to parlay or retain status and financial security in a world arranged by men to keep women supplicant and therefore subordinate." [39] Since female power is indirect and fragile, based upon the manipulation of appearance and language rather than upon the manipulation of palpable goods that characterizes male power, the women of Wharton's Darwinian universe cannot risk generosity to a potential rival who may threaten their own survival.

A Woollett-like expediency predicated upon the power of status and wealth shapes the official version of events retailed by public language speakers of both sexes. When Lily suggests to Rosedale an alternative approach, namely, that the falsity of stories about her should "alter the situation," he responds: "I believe it does in novels, but I'm certain it don't in real life" (256). The false version of Lily's story becomes the authorized one because it is agreeable to powerful people and because it valorizes group mores by illustrating the essential wrongness of her pursuit of freedom, her seeming to claim "the privileges of marriage without assuming its obligations" (157).

For women, the prospect of marriage sanctions an unmarried "girl's" claim to a man, but Lily loses this legitimacy when she pursues Selden without such an aim and thereby places herself in conflict with a married woman. Because married women have more status, power, and freedom than unmarried "girls," Lily should have acquired the less vulnerable status before incurring an enmity she cannot afford. Lily is acutely aware that the designation "marriageable girl" is a temporary label which she has already worn far too long, one that she has assumed unwillingly because neither society nor her own imagination offers any other.[40] Her lack of enthusiasm for this role is an unconscious rejection of the responsibilities of feminine adulthood/wifehood that will reify her as an object once and for all.[41] This attitude also places her in the tradition of male social outsiders in the American novel—characters such as Natty Bumppo, Ishmael, and Huck Finn—who show a similar reluctance to be adults according to the terms of their respective societies and are thereby feminized in their refusal to assume masculine authority.

Wharton chooses a female protagonist and sympathetically focuses upon the special difficulties of women, yet her strategy to undermine patriarchal authority encompasses society as a system whose social determinants are just as insistent as those of sex. "So-called 'women's language,' is in large part a language of powerlessness," William O'Barr and Bowman Atkins write, "a condition that can apply to men as well as women."[42] It is always within Lily's power to make a rich marriage as her cousin Jack Stepney does, and the peripheral figure of Ned Silverton will probably end up on the same rubbish heap that Lily envisages for herself. Lily is not excluded from society because she is a woman but because she is a nonconformist who shrinks from her role as object and demands a latitude available only to women who *have* submitted themselves to men within the socially prescribed institution of marriage. Whereas society can make a place for the exceptional when it is conjoined with submission, Lily's experience demonstrates that even the highly valuable and valued cannot be accepted when conventions are flouted. Selden escapes Lily's fate not only because as a man he can support himself and refuse to marry but because he, unlike Lily, is content to live within the confines of society. He, too, is wasted, if not destroyed as dramatically as Lily. As a reminder that "growth and mastery" in the sense that Showalter applies to Wharton's own language are not tolerated in either sex in the society of *The House of Mirth*, the novel ends with the absence of the word that would save Lily and Selden equally. Representing a bond that would contravene the social requirement of wealth, it remains unuttered and unutterable.

Chapter 5 ═══

Urbanity and Expatriation,
Part 2: Fitzgerald and Hemingway

"Major, there's no way to express thirty million dead.
No words. So certain men are recruited to reinvent the
language."

DON DELILLO, *End Zone*

The Great Gatsby and the Speech of Self

■ *The Great Gatsby* contains a spectrum of inarticulate characters whose inability to use language in traditional ways indicates gross social malfunction "under the red, white and blue."[1] Gatsby's monstrous dream, the chief example of the novel's pervasive Eckleburgian vision, is a banal reduction of American idealism: its goal is not to create a vital future but to repeat a mythicized past; not to explore the potential richness of experience that the "fresh green breast" of the new world once promised but to acquire a conventional security, no matter how corrupt; not to establish a new social order but to enter one that is so empty and trivial that the behavior of even the most exclusive people seems to be parodic, and it is replicated on lower levels of society in increasingly grotesque forms.

Although the novel ends in violent death, it is a speech act that destroys Gatsby's dream by stripping him of his self-created identity and redefining him as a criminal. Tom Buchanan first associates Gatsby with that other interloper who said he knew Daisy, "Blocks" Biloxi; then he exposes the tenuousness of Gatsby's identity as an Oxford man, suggesting finally that a more appropriate description would be the boy who delivered groceries to Daisy's back door. Having deprived Gatsby of any foothold in proper society, Tom next labels him a bootlegger and a common swindler, with the implication of more dangerous unspoken activities. When Tom challenges Gatsby with "Who are you, anyhow?" Gatsby fails to produce any credentials. As Richard Godden has observed, his name, in fact, suggests nothingness: "Gat, the root shared by Gatz and Gatsby, in German means 'hole' and in Dutch 'hole, gap, break.' "[2] Through his greater capital of authority, Tom can thus enforce his own definition of Gatsby, "Mr. Nobody from Nowhere," and pull Daisy back into the conspiratorial union of the rich and careless. His assertion has the perloctionary effect of a declaration: it transforms Gatsby's self-created identity into a nonself. Dying, Gatsby is less than ever himself, a victim of Wilson's twofold delusion that he has been Myrtle's lover and was responsible for her death. Only by artistic fiat through the narrator's intuitive apprehension of his unexpressed self does he become "the great Gatsby," measured by a standard he is incapable of imagining.

■ As testimony to the difficulty of sustaining the socially acceptable identity Gatsby has tried to invent, it is appropriate that he first speaks in the novel as an unidentified man, taken by Nick Carraway to be a fellow guest at a Gatsby party. The hackneyed quality of Gatsby's language reflects the staleness of the American dream at this historical moment and reveals Gatsby's status as a social interloper. As Nick reports, Gatsby chooses his words "with care," fearful of giving away his outsider status by conspicuous speech. Typically, he assembles his utterances from a ragbag of clichés and polite formulas whose lack of real meaning makes them seem safe and acceptable. He uses "old sport" indiscriminately because it is a conveniently familiar, pleasing British term, but also because *sport* is the province of the elite, hence his immediate reference to his hydroplane when he first meets Nick.[3] Gatsby describes Jordan Baker the golfer as "a great sportswoman," the very thing she isn't but an image that conforms to Gatsby's fiction of the upper class. Flaunting Tom as a social acquisition to other guests at one of his parties, Gatsby persists in introducing him as "the polo player" in spite of Tom's annoyance at the label.[4]

Gatsby is an outsider in any group, alone with his vision even in the midst of his parties. Employed to make him always correct, his colorless, self-effacing speech cannot go beyond a limited protective function. When more is needed, Gatsby fails miserably.[5] Brian Way's description of Gatsby as "overwhelmingly comic"[6] unfairly reduces him to his worst verbal mannerisms. It is Nick's contention, which I believe the text valorizes, that Gatsby has no language for genuine self-expression. Because his "romantic readiness" can find no adequate speech, the verbal fantasy he creates in his first attempt to establish his

identity in Nick's eyes is unconvincing, not only ludicrous in its formulaic language and extravagant events but suspicious in its manner
of delivery: "He hurried the phrase 'educated at Oxford' or swallowed
it, or choked on it, as though it had bothered him before" (65). Nick
believes, finally, only because Gatsby produces tangible supporting evidence—the Montenegrin medal inscribed to himself, the photograph
placing him at Oxford. Rather than speaking unconvincingly at the re-
union with Daisy, Gatsby simply lapses into a tense silence, then takes
Nick aside to repeat ineffectually, "This is a terrible mistake . . . a
terrible, terrible mistake" (88). When Tom puts Gatsby on the defensive by defining him as a bootlegger, Gatsby is seemingly unaware that
his habitual "polite" mode of response, this safe and correct defense
mechanism, is unsuited to the occasion; he corroborates Tom's verbal
pictures by looking, even in Nick's friendly eyes, like someone who has
"killed a man." Once Tom has triumphed, Gatsby "began to talk excit-
edly to Daisy, denying everything" (135); but unlike a confidence man,
who can make a verbal fiction credible, he cannot overcome through
words his real vulnerability. The weakness of Gatsby's speech reflects
the actual weakness of his capital of authority, a weakness his apparent
substance would seem to contest.

Gatsby's real character eludes verbal expression. His extraordinary
smile, his emblematic postures of yearning for Daisy, the misdirected
magnificence of his life all speak more eloquently about him than his
speech. Society's verdict, rendered in its refusal to participate in the
rituals of burial and mourning for Gatsby, is essentially Tom's limited
view of him as a common crook. Elevating the partial into a total self,
it is unaware of the "incorruptible dream" that redeems him in Nick's
eyes. Gatsby never speaks of the dream directly; instead, Nick translates it into his own elegant idiom, surely far removed from any speech
Gatsby could conceivably use. When Gatsby does attempt to express
his feelings, he can only stammer inconsequentially: " 'It's the funniest
thing, old sport,' he said hilariously. 'I can't—when I try to—' " (93).[7]
Mired in his inarticulateness, he breaks off, and Nick helpfully takes
over to explain Gatsby's feelings: "He had been full of the idea so long,
dreamed it right through to the end, waited with his teeth set, so to
speak, at an inconceivable pitch of intensity. Now in the reaction, he
was running down like an overwound clock" (93). When Gatsby later
tells Nick the history of his involvement with Daisy, it is undoubtedly in
a style akin to that of his "young rajah" narrative. According to Kenneth

Eble, in a surviving draft of the novel "much of Gatsby's story is told in dialogue as he talks to Nick," and most of this material was later eliminated.[8] At one point in this earlier version Gatsby abruptly invokes his own name: " 'Jay Gatsby!' he cried suddenly in a ringing voice. 'There goes the great Jay Gatsby! That's what people are going to say—wait and see.' "[9] Such a fantasy is plausible to account for Gatsby's career, but as an utterance it reduces him to an obnoxious parvenu, the way that Tom and his class want to see him. Gatsby's styling himself great in speech is unthinkable; he must not tell his own story because he has no language to transcend the banal ambition of that story qua story.

Nick's shaping imagination translates Gatsby's "unutterable visions" into a language bearing little resemblance to Gatsby's own.[10] What, we might wonder, might be Gatsby's version of the following accomplished description: "Out of the corner of his eye Gatsby saw that the blocks of the sidewalks really formed a ladder and mounted to a secret place above the trees—he could climb to it, if he climbed alone, and once there he could suck on the pap of life, gulp down the incomparable milk of wonder" (112). The dream-like quality and sustained metaphoric mode make clear that the essence of Gatsby's experience as reimagined by Nick is a fiction remote from the actuality of his encounter with Daisy. According to Nick, Gatsby has the vision of art without its power of expression; his only medium is the meretricious display of things that fails to establish either individual or social identity.

When he tells his own story, Gatsby's language is uninspired, yet his far more fluent narrator also finds its core inexpressible: "Through all he said, even through his appalling sentimentality, I was reminded of something—an elusive rhythm, a fragment of lost words, that I had heard somewhere a long time ago. For a moment a phrase tried to take shape in my mouth and my lips parted like a dumb man's, as though there was more struggling upon them than a wisp of startled air. But they made no sound, and what I had almost remembered was uncommunicable forever" (102). What Nick may be reaching for is a worthy objective correlative of the incorruptible dream, an unknown entity in the same relation to Gatsby's involvement with Daisy as the fresh green breast of the new world is to the debased pastoral landscape of East Egg and West Egg. The vision remains unutterable because any positive formulation of it has been closed off: only the stream of energy, the impetus toward self-creation and fulfillment, is actually pure; any container it finds, any tangible expression, must be part of the sterility

and decadence of the time. That Gatsby's genuinely valuable character is squandered and destroyed in the service of the unattainable is
ironic, but the greater irony lies in the nature of his image of the self:
reaching for a vision he comes up with this diminished thing—to be the
gold-hatted, high-bouncing lover who wins the golden girl. " 'They're
a rotten crowd,' Nick tells Gatsby, and " 'you're worth the whole damn
bunch put together' " (154), yet "they" must of necessity represent what
Gatsby aspires to. In post-World War I America it is no longer possible
to be a discoverer like the Dutch sailors, or even a *pioneer debauchee*
like Dan Cody, that oxymoronic figure who retains some of the grandeur of the American dream compounded with its degeneration. What
is left is a chain of corruption in which the pivotal figure of Wolfsheim
reaches downward into the underworld and upward through Walter
Chase into the circle of Tom Buchanan.

■ Tom Buchanan is inarticulate in a different way
than Gatsby is because his speech accurately expresses the void within,
but unlike Gatsby, he has no need to protect himself through language.
With the confidence of old money and established position, his speech,
like his whole demeanor, is assertive, bullying, tinged with "paternal
contempt." [11] Whatever the words, the implicit message is dominance
and coercion: " 'Now don't think my opinion on these matters is final,'
he seemed to say, 'just because I'm stronger and more of a man than
you are' " (7). Tom's habitual verbal assertiveness often shades into
aggression: in addition to frequently *demanding*, on various occasions
he speaks *harshly, savagely, insultingly*. He *insists impatiently, mutters
fiercely, objects crossly, interrupts, breaks in, interposes, cries roughly,
snorts contemptuously,* and *snaps*.

In fact Tom has no verbal resources other than the ability to enunci-
ate simple statements and questions; sustained reasoning and wordplay
are equally beyond him. His sarcastic reference to Gatsby's business—
"you can buy anything at a drug store nowadays"—is flat-footed; his
few attempts at joking are similarly obvious and feeble. When Daisy
twits him with *hulking* or makes fun of his deep reading, he can only
respond directly—"I hate that word hulking"—or plod on with his
argument, countering any objections with his talismanic word *scientific*. Attracted to apocalyptic theories which he assimilates imperfectly,
Tom asserts that the sun is getting hotter, then reverses himself in
the next sentence; his mind leaps from the discovery that Gatsby and

Daisy have been seeing each other to a spectacle of interracial marriage. In both cases the actual specifics are unconsciously transformed into a vision of general doom while for his own conduct such specifics are arbitrarily subsumed under positive generalizations. Tom's flagrant unfaithfulness is merely "going off on a spree" once in a while, and he styles himself the defender of "family life and family institutions." Like Gatsby's sentimental narrative about Daisy, Tom's description of his and Daisy's marital relationship is a fiction, but whereas Gatsby's fiction is the fruit of a romantic impulse which can find no worthy expression, Tom's is the result of a self-serving hypocrisy and insensitivity. Gatsby's fiction overvalues Daisy; Tom's is the operative fiction, the story society valorizes, and his words correspondingly carry the authority of his secure social rank and the collective desire of his group to remain closed to outsiders When Tom directs Wilson to Gatsby, he is acting against a class enemy, the interloper, and against an enemy of society, the would-be homewrecker. He can feel "entirely justified," as he tells Nick, because, as in the case of Pap's claiming Huck by right of paternity, society and public language support his patriarchal view.

Poised between lover and husband, Daisy Buchanan shares a romantic sensibility with Gatsby and a position of social invulnerability with Tom. Whereas for Gatsby the romantic vision must encompass all of the accoutrements of social approval, for Daisy it has the opposite meaning of personal fulfillment divorced from the advantages of belongingness. Where Gatsby moves toward a public confirmation of his fantasy which will legitimize it and himself, Daisy is apparently content to dally with Gatsby privately, as Tom does with Myrtle, while enjoying the life of social respectability which she already has. Class loyalty in Daisy is ultimately stronger than the individualistic, antisocial impulse Gatsby represents, but her language reflects both of these forces.

Daisy's romanticism finds release in a verbal style that cultivates hyperbole and fancy. Whatever she says tends to be less important (if important at all) than her manner of saying it, buttressed by the context that she creates to enhance her words. When Nick arrives for dinner, she greets him with a playful exaggeration, prefaced by a charming laugh and followed up with seductive behavior that carries more meaning than the banal expressive:

"I'm p-paralyzed with happiness."
She laughed again, as if she said something very witty, and held

my hand for a moment, looking up into my face, promising that there was no one in the world she so much wanted to see. That was a way she had. (9)

Daisy's manner is as exaggerated as her words, but this is irrelevant. Gatsby fails to compel belief in the story of his life that he first tells Nick because his specifics are implausible, his language a tissue of romantic storybook clichés. Daisy compels belief because she communicates feeling rather than fact, and the feeling is nebulous, a promise of excitement. She appears to have the same "heightened sensitivity to the promise of life" that Nick finds attractive in Gatsby, but the charismatic quality of Daisy's utterance is actually an end in itself—the thrilling voice summons to no thrill beyond its own music. Or, like the other promises/dreams/potentials of the once new world, Daisy's voice is only "full of money." Unlike Gatsby's, her voice is assured because the money has always been there; possessing her would be like converting new money into old, guaranteeing belongingness.[12] Stripped of this charisma, Daisy's speech is random and foolish, typically marked by a vapidity of language without real meaning:

> She looked at us all radiantly. "Do you always watch for the longest day of the year and then miss it? I always watch for the longest day in the year and then miss it."
> "We ought to plan something," yawned Miss Baker. . . .
> "All right," said Daisy. "What'll we plan?" She turned to me helplessly: "What do people plan?"
> Before I could answer her eyes fastened with an awed expression on her little finger.
> "Look!" she complained; "I hurt it." (12)

Daisy's disjointed speech is one form of an inability to sustain or follow through on anything. Before Nick can reply to her question, she has lost interest and become self-absorbed. Later, when she speaks to Nick alone about her cynical outlook, he senses a "basic insincerity." For Daisy, performance and gesture are all: the capacity for romantic readiness that produces Gatsby's unutterable vision is only skin deep in Daisy, a series of impulsive whims that call for no narrative shape. Raised as the golden girl in the king's palace, Daisy has no need to obliterate her reality with a made-up story.

The other side of Daisy's speech, equally irresponsible in terms of the actual referents of her words, expresses the more enduring social identity to which her romantic individualism gives way. Gatsby's means of wooing Daisy by displaying his material possessions, the accessories of a social acceptability he lacks, shows his awareness of her values and his own desire to conform to them. The desperately overdone quality of the performance, which stamps Gatsby as a parvenu, culminates in the profusion of extravagantly colored shirts that causes Daisy to sob, " 'They're such beautiful shirts. . . . It makes me sad because I've never seen such—such beautiful shirts before' " (93–94). Daisy's attempt to express her pleasure in finding Gatsby again is deformed into praise of his shirts. To praise his possessions is to praise him, a metonymic assumption that the man who has all of this has the other credentials of belongingness as well. At the same time as Daisy's exclamation illustrates the social deflection of feeling into an appreciation of material worth, it also suggests an aesthetic richness that the world of the Buchanans excludes, a world where pink suits and the shirts that go with them are a violation of decorum.[13] Daisy is fleetingly sad for the lost opportunity of this fuller but less respectable life, but she—like her world—sees no way of having both.

Daisy's concentration on Jay Gatsby the individual is constantly processed into such materialistic expression. Seeing his picture, she exclaims, "I adore it. . . . The pompadour! You never told me you had a pompadour—or a yacht" (95). Gatsby's hairstyle makes the first impression, but this is quickly followed by attention to the implied status symbol. Her later compliment on Gatsby's personal appearance—"You always look so cool"—is quickly transformed into an image with social and economic implications: "You resemble the advertisement of the man" (119). Tom dismisses Gatsby in the same manner by categorizing him socially as a man who wears a pink suit.

■ The speech of Gatsby and both the Buchanans illustrates Bakhtin's dictum that "individualistic confidence in oneself, one's sense of personal value, is drawn not from within, not from the depths of one's personality, but from the outside world."[14] In society's terms there are no words that can make Gatsby acceptable. His facade of polite language, his unsuccessful fictions, his final inability to defend himself to Tom are the verbal manifestations of his lack of the credentials that have meaning in the Buchanans' world. Nothing he could say would establish his right to belong there, and knowing this, he tries to say little and thereby avoid self-incrimination. Tom can speak fool-ishly and behave brutally without threatening his social position, and Daisy's childish and irresponsible speech is a function of class and sex which both relieve her of the adult obligations to make decisions and keep commitments. For all three characters, the word means little to social identity.

If speech in *Gatsby* cannot materially affect social position, it does reveal the pressures of social values which distort utterances. Although Gatsby typically assesses people inaccurately, he is perceptive about the compelling quality of Daisy's voice: it is "full of money." Nick ex-pands this to include the mythic: "That was the inexhaustible charm that rose and fell in it, the tingle of it, the cymbals' song of it. . . . (120). The American dream, the other-than-old-world vision, is now simply a copy of it, replete with aristocratic exclusiveness.

The materiality of this world insistently permeates speech: houses, cars, jewels, horses, clothes, boats—all are invoked as icons of social position, but they are, after all, only accessories, not the thing itself. Gatsby and Myrtle, two outsiders who covet belongingness, exagger-ate the Buchanans' sumptuous standard of living. Myrtle responds to a compliment about her dress as she imagines her social better would: "It's just a crazy old thing. I just slip it on sometimes when I don't care what I look like" (31). A misguided sense of social decorum deforms Myrtle's speech from a sincere expression of her pleasure in wearing the showy garment to a comment exhibiting her grasp of the principle that rightful possession is matter of fact; she errs on the side of over-deprecation. The right tone is acquired not by intellect or will but by upbringing, the early external shaping of the self.[15] Tom and Gatsby both refer to their possessions, but Gatsby's speech has a hint of naive pride that is absent from Tom's, as well as an appeal for agreement:

> "My house looks well, doesn't it?" he demanded. "See how the whole front of it catches the light."
> I agreed that it was splendid.
> "Yes." His eyes went over it, every arched door and square tower. "It took me just three years to earn the money that bought it." (91)

Demand is a verb usually associated with Tom's verbal bullying, but Gatsby needs to have Nick confirm his worth, a portent of and prelude to its confirmation by Daisy. Gatsby uses his house, which he visu-ally fondles, part by part, as a proof that he is entitled to the capital of authority it seems to demonstrate. He has acquired his possessions to make himself right, and he remains aware of their cost. Tom asserts value without the need for approval: " 'I've got a nice place here,' he said, his eyes flashing about restlessly. Turning me around by one arm, he moved a broad flat hand along the front vista, including in its sweep a sunken Italian garden, a half acre of deep, pungent roses, and a snub-nosed motor-boat that bumped the tide offshore" (7–8). Tom's possessions are illustrations rather than proofs; because he is right to begin with, he naturally has such things and can make casual reference to them with a gesture—there is no need for specific enumeration.

■ *The Great Gatsby* ultimately images the powerlessness of language to create the self or to affect reality in the way that Gatsby desires. As Nick realizes, Gatsby's proper sphere is fiction; in the autonomous world of art, words have the power to create the complete and totally controlled dream that in his own life Gatsby can bring into being only as a series of material possessions and inadequate gestures. Value for Nick lies in a return to the American heartland, a return that is, at least in part another variation on Gatsby's desire to repeat the past. The novel's celebrated closing image—"so we beat on, boats against the current, borne back ceaselessly into the past" (182)— reaches out to implicate the reader, too, in this exercise in futility, just as American society finally embraces the legal and the illegal alike under a common rubric of chicanery and gain.

The Dialectic of Discourse in
The Sun Also Rises

■ As my readings of their novels indicate, I believe that James, Wharton, and Fitzgerald—along with other modern writers like Dreiser and Dos Passos—consider society to be the inescapable place where the individual must live his life; and as such, it is a presence and a force in their fictive worlds. The constraints that James's Woollett and Wharton's and Fitzgerald's New York impose upon individual behavior are painfully clear. Just as clear is the impossibility of living apart from these constraints.[16] Strether observes that he will not live long; Lily and Gatsby die; Nick retreats to the smaller, safer, and more comfortable society he came from. Hemingway, in so many respects more exemplary of the modern spirit than any of his literary

contemporaries and hence the most widely imitated writer of the first
half of the twentieth century, rejects this traditional perspective to follow the most radical implications of *Adventures of Huckleberry Finn*:
namely, that society cannot provide, either physically or metaphorically, the context for individual self-realization. Moreover, society is no
longer any place that matters. While it remains an external antagonist
capable of destroying the individual and a physical backdrop for his or
her activities, it does not provoke the kind of internal conflict between
collective and personal imperatives that Huck experienced.

In keeping with the characters' alienation from society, both responsibilities of ordinary speech—that language mean something and
that this meaning be communicated—are atrophied in *The Sun Also
Rises*. An avoidance of institutional meaning linguistically exemplifies
distance from society, a response to the paradox that language either
means too much by involving the speaker in social commitments or
means too little in failing to express the truly significant. The assumption that language is inimical to the discussion of those few matters
which are important, i.e., feelings and personal experiences, leads to
numerous injunctions not to speak and to verbal behavior which consciously attempts to exclude much of the common conversational fare.
In part this attitude springs from a philosophical position that the level
of empirical reality, as Alfred Korzybski states, "is not words and cannot be reached by words alone. We must point our finger and be silent
or we shall never reach this level." [17] The inability of language to reach
what Korzybski calls the "objective level" motivates much of the verbal
restraint in Hemingway's fiction, but more threatening than this impotence and irrelevance of language is its active power to destroy the
most valuable experiences. Roland Barthes's distinction between pleasure and bliss is germane to Hemingway's practice: "Pleasure can be
expressed in words, bliss cannot. Bliss is unspeakable, interdicted." [18]
Brett's reiterated plea to Jake after she has sent Pedro Romero away is
that they never talk about it, but she constantly returns to the subject
until Jake finally reminds her:

> "I thought you weren't going to ever talk about it."
> "How can I help it?"
> "You'll lose it if you talk about it." (245)

This is the dialectic of discourse in *The Sun Also Rises*: the felt necessity of imposing discipline on speech wars with the desire to ex-

press and communicate. Bliss, that which is most worth having and remembering, is asocial and inexpressible, but the characters' (human) need to speak produces a felt tension in the dialogue. Focusing upon the experience of others, Jake's narrative voice embodies the writer's struggle to articulate within the limits imposed by the nature of language. Avoiding large areas of experience and emotionally flattening out others, it creates a smaller, safer, controllable world out of the chaotic and dangerous universe, yet one that points beyond itself to the larger, unexpressed territory.[19] As narrator, Jake knows what Hemingway knows, the difference between what can and cannot be said; but as character, when he is emotionally involved in events, he intermittently forgets.[20]

The other aspect of language as the enemy is its role as "a space already occupied by the public."[21] Hemingway characters may disregard social imperatives to pray, work, or marry, but they cannot completely escape what Locke calls "the great Instrument and common Tye of Society."[22] Speaking entails participating in the "reciprocal web of obligations that is the content of the system of conventional speech acts";[23] hence the content of discourse in *The Sun Also Rises* must be purged of all but certain categories of immediate experience in order to escape the burden of social responsibility that language usually carries. Language is thus drained of social coloration or hollowed out so that a denotative meaning remains while ordinary connotations are lost. For example, Brett and Mike are *engaged*, a word implicated in the basic structure of society, yet they observe none of the protocols expected of an affianced couple. The meaning of *engaged* in their case is restricted to the expressed intention to marry, unsupported by the usual confirmatory behavior. Brett as Mike's fiancée going off with one man after another becomes analogous to Georgette, the prostitute Jake casually picks up and introduces as his fiancée. Both cases mock the institutional meaning of the word.

The same attitude of distrust is implicit in the nature of speech throughout the novel, as exemplified in a brief exchange between Jake and Georgette:

> "I got hurt in the war," I said.
> "Oh, that dirty war."
> We would probably have gone on and discussed the war and agreed that it was in reality a calamity for civilization, and perhaps would have been better avoided. I was bored enough. (17)[24]

The war as Jake's personal calamity, a specific physical injury that changes his life, recedes before an all-embracing, remote abstraction, the war as "calamity for civilization." As the ironic understatement of "perhaps would have been better avoided" emphasizes, the war cannot be talked about without falling into conventional formulas that close off the possibilities of individual expression. Such a discussion suits boredom because it requires no personal investment of thought or feeling. "For this generation," Mark Spilka observes, "boredom has become more plausible than love." [25]

This distrust of institutional meaning is the thesis of Larzer Ziff in "The Social Basis of Hemingway's Style." [26] However, I disagree with Ziff's conclusion that this style "works effectively only in conjunction with material that supports the view that public ideals are false and truth resides solely in unverbalized private experience." [27] Once again, Barthes's distinctions seem more accurate and, I believe, more applicable to Hemingway. Unlike the isms and abstractions Hemingway eschews, simple specifics—like the place names and numbers of Frederic Henry's linguistic credo—enforce "the final state of matter, what cannot be transcended, withdrawn." [28]

Jake makes light of "large statements" and "fine philosophies" whose extrapolation from living experience engulfs the meaningful particular. He gets bogged down in just such a process when he moves from the specific sensations of pleasure and disgust at Mike's baiting of Cohn to a general formulation of value: "That was morality; things that made you disgusted afterward. No, that must be immorality. That was a large statement. What a lot of bilge I could think up at night. What rot, I could hear Brett say it" (149). Jake appropriately thinks of Brett because her refrain—"Let's not talk. Talking's all bilge"—expresses the inability of speech to describe meaningful experience and the anarchic sense of its powerlessness to order this experience. This particular denial of language comes at a pivotal point in a discussion whose full extent reveals both the dynamic of their relationship and their attitudes toward language:

> "Couldn't we live together, Brett? Couldn't we just live together?"
> "I don't think so. I'd just *tromper* you with everybody. You couldn't stand it."
> "I stand it now."
> "That would be different. It's my fault, Jake. It's the way I'm made."

"Couldn't we go off in the country for a while?"

"It wouldn't be any good. I'll go if you like. But I couldn't live quietly in the country. Not with my own true love."

"I know."

"Isn't it rotten? There isn't any use my telling you I love you."

"You know I love you."

"Let's not talk. Talking's all bilge. I'm going away from you, and then Michael's coming back."

"Why are you going away?"

"Better for you. Better for me."

"When are you going?"

"Soon as I can."

"Where?"

"San Sebastian."

"Can't we go together?"

"No. That would be a hell of an idea after we'd just talked it out."

"We never agreed."

"Oh, you know as well as I do. Don't be obstinate, darling."

"Oh, sure," I said. "I know you're right. I'm just low, and when I'm low I talk like a fool." (55–56) [29]

The requirements of speech-act theory and sociolinguistics come together in the extralinguistic considerations that govern the dialogue. Jake's capital of authority for Brett is diminished by his impotence. Because he can have no authority for her as a lover, his speech acts are accordingly flawed. He becomes the speaker who fulfills the sincerity and essential conditions but not those of preparation. For the proposals he makes to Brett to be felicitous speech acts, Jake would have to be sexually able.

Brett controls the dialogue totally: she first responds to Jake's urgings negatively, then, after the assertion that "talking's all bilge," announces her own plan of action, which does not include him. By "talking," Brett means informing; she is willing to use speech to communicate her plans or desires, not to discuss them. For Brett, discussing or arguing is futile because her determination to do what she wants to do, regardless of what might be said about it, repudiates the social bonds embodied in language, the recognition of responsibility to subordinate individual impulse to a larger, social concern and to rules of meaning inherent in language. As John R. Searle writes, "The retreat from the committed use of words ultimately must involve a retreat from language itself, for speaking a language . . . consists of performing speech acts according to rules, and there is no separating those speech acts from the commitments which form essential parts of them."[30] Brett's statement "There isn't any use my telling you I love you" means that this conventionally powerful assertion actually has no power to affect her behavior or their situation and thus might as well remain unsaid. When Jake tries once more to impose on Brett his fantasy of their going away together, she responds more sharply, without the palliations of the first part of the conversation. His maintaining that no agreement has been reached prompts her to say, "Oh, you know as well as I do," i.e., know through an acquaintance with brute facts, the givens of his impotence and her need for a sexual relationship, rather than through their speech together.

Brett's language conforms to the world while Jake's unsuccessfully attempts to get the world (in this case Brett) to conform to his words. Given the gulf between desire and reality in Jake's life, he has trouble achieving a disciplined language, and he does so only through the kind of conscious effort seen in his self-mocking rejection of "fine philosophies." Initially, his overtures to Brett represent attenuated forms of social commitment, first in the idea of their living together, then in the absolute assertion of his love for her, while Brett's mode of declaring love effectively cancels it. When Brett takes the initiative by announcing her decision to leave, Jake is reduced to asking for details of her plan rather than proposing a plan of his own. Significantly, he fails to ask or learn the critical fact that Brett is going away with Robert Cohn. Although Jake's part of the dialogue reveals his yearning for some version of commitment, the conversation ends with his acknowledgment that he has been "talking like a fool," verbalizing fantasies of conventional behavior, the linguistic relics of a society that no longer represents value or authority for the war survivors.

Linguistic authority, as the famous *Farewell to Arms* passage asserts, resides only in the simple factuality of numbers and names. Thus Jake returns to his apartment after a frustrating encounter with Brett to find two letters, both common institutional forms of communication, one a bank statement, the other a wedding announcement. The first is relevant to balancing Jake's checkbook; the other is irrelevant because he does not know the subjects of the announced marriage. The form of the second message communicates in spite of the inappropriateness of the content to this particular receiver just as, if the bank's figures were in error, the form of communication known as a bank statement would still be valid. But when Jake thinks about Brett, he can find no satisfactory linguistic form and therefore abandons the effort to order his thoughts about her in language: "Lady Ashley. To hell with Brett. To hell with you. Lady Ashley. . . . I suppose she only wanted what she couldn't have. Well, people were that way. To hell with people" (30–31). Jake's speculations are always broken off with an expression of dismissal or passive resignation in the face of the human dilemma that "nobody ever knows anything" (27).

Like Captain Ahab, the Hemingway protagonist confronts the inscrutability and seeming malice of the universe, but he sees no way of conquering or making sense of it, even through the ordering process of language. As Jake says about his wound, "I was pretty well through with the subject. At one time or another I had probably considered it from most of its various angles" (27). Because he also sees no way of influencing the behavior of others, Jake tends to accept their assertions of will passively: "I try and play it along and just not make trouble for people" (31).[31] All of these positions diminish the efficacy of speech and consequently circumscribe its territory, but it is necessary to distinguish the experience itself from the report. When Jake sums up his relationship with Brett, his words impose only a minimal degree of linguistic order because, as the emphatic closure reminds, to go beyond an austerely defined factuality is to risk the betrayal of experience through falsification: "That was it. Send a girl off with one man. Introduce her to another to go off with him Now go and bring her back. And sign the wire with love. That was it all right" (239). The framing comment places sharply defined boundaries around actions which are depersonalized and schematically presented, evidence of conscious discipline; yet as a sequence the actions bear an emotional charge that the frame rigidly holds in check.

Nevertheless, Hemingway's severe economy and control do not diminish the experience in the interest of avoiding self-justification and subjective distortion. William Barrett, among others, implies that the price Hemingway pays for such avoidance is inconsequentiality; he characterizes the "real feelings" presented as "humble and impoverished," although he goes on to laud Hemingway's style for "its ability . . . to see what it is one really senses and feels."[32] To reverse the sequence of Barrett's remarks, what one really senses and feels is humble and impoverished, but since it is the truth, Hemingway deserves credit

for representing it. Such a reading seems to be based entirely upon vocabulary and to ignore the creative space between narrator and text,
and correspondingly between text and reader. This darkness visible is
a dynamic silence, a consciously contrived artifact of restraint. The *expression* may be considered "humble and impoverished" insofar as it
is strongly monosyllabic and unembellished, but the *feelings* evoked
by passages of this sort are neither—nor are they "exposed," to use
Barrett's word, so much as palpable.

       ■ Simply not speaking about what matters, as Jake
and Brett try to do, is one form of linguistic alienation; another extends
the abstract rhetoric of social discourse beyond its customary sphere
because it is too vague and clichéd to have retained more than the
crudest kind of signification. Having no color of its own, this vapid,
timeworn language is made to yield a number of different effects, "one
phrase to mean everything," as Jake says about English speech.[33] On
being introduced to Brett, Count Mippipopolous uses the conventional
language of such an occasion straightforwardly while she passively responds in kind:

> "Well, does your Ladyship have a good time here in Paris?" . . .
> "Rather," said Brett.
> "Paris is a fine town all right," said the count. "But I guess you
> have pretty big doings yourself over in London."
> "Oh, yes," said Brett. "Enormous." (28)

This kind of perfunctory response which requires no effort, meaning,
or commitment simply fills up what would otherwise be a socially awkward linguistic vacuum when two people are introduced, although the
extreme lack of effort Brett exhibits could be construed as mockery. Between intimates like Jake and Brett the same sort of dialogue acquires
meaning through an irony perfectly understood because the speakers
share such values as the deprecation of people outside their own circle:

> "It's a fine crowd you're with, Brett," I said.
> "Aren't they lovely? And you, my dear. Where did you get it?"
> "At the Napolitain."
> "And have you had a lovely evening?"
> "Oh, priceless," I said. (22)

Peter Messent observes that "Jake and his crowd communicate via a
type of language which—in its use of shared conventions, coded ter-

minology . . . catch phrases, and stylistic nuance—asserts their membership of a particular closed community."[34] This vocabulary is also used to convey genuine feeling. When Jake and Bill prepare to leave Burguete, Harris reiterates that it is "rotten luck." They've had such a "jolly time." Elsewhere Jake tells us that Harris was "very pleasant" and "nice," and Harris himself says several times that Jake can't know how much their fishing together has meant to him: "Barnes. Really, Barnes, you can't know. That's all" (129). After this emphatic closure, Harris expresses his feelings by giving each man an envelope containing trout flies he has tied himself. The familiar basic vocabulary Hemingway has appropriated—*fine, nice, lovely, rotten*—can refer to and categorize affective experience, but it cannot describe or assess it beyond the elementary distinction between positive and negative.

Language can relate what happens, as opposed to what is felt, but it is rarely worth the trouble. given the narrowing of value to certain immediate personal experiences. Jake's work is referred to only in passing; Paris exists as a topos of streets and cafés; and the novel's typical discourse is about movement and liquor—what has been, is, or will be drunk, and where. In other areas conversational inertia obtains either because the subject isn't worth pursuing or because it falls beyond the pale of what can be spoken about at all:

> Cohn looked at the bottles in bins around the wall. "This is a good place," he said.
> "There's a lot of liquor," I agreed. . . .
> "Do you know that in about thirty-five years more we'll be dead?"
> "What the hell, Robert," I said. "What the hell." (11)

Jake's first reply is reductive, his second characteristically dismissive. In neither case does he want to contribute or respond to Cohn's thought; he speaks for the usual social reason of acknowledging being spoken to. Such conventions of social discourse still govern speech in *The Sun Also Rises* although the province of speech has been radically curtailed to eliminate what cannot be profitably expressed; like the vocabulary of social discourse, the form of communication persists without the message of social commitment it usually carries.[35] In speech-act terms the regulative rules are observed, but not necessarily the constitutive.

Given their lack of interest in living through words, each of the members of Jake's group except Bill has only a single verbal style; Bill has a repertory of voices and a sense of linguistic fun that the others lack.[36] (Jake sometimes feeds Bill lines, but he tends to model them after Bill's

and to participate only to the extent of stimulating Bill's inventiveness.)
Rather than genuinely witty, Bill is facile and playful; when Jake describes him to Brett as a taxidermist, he replies, "That was in another
country . . . and besides all the animals were dead" (75). The allusion
is not functional; it is simply a clever rejoinder in the spirit of Jake's
sportive identification. Bill mocks collective values relentlessly from his
initial appearance recounting the story of the "big sporting evening"
in which a Viennese audience throws chairs at a black boxer who dares
to knock out the local boy: "Injustice everywhere. Promoter claimed
nigger promised let local boy stay. Claimed nigger violated contract.
Can't knock out Vienna boy in Vienna. . . . All we could get was nigger's
clothes. Somebody took his watch, too. Splendid nigger. Big mistake to
have come to Vienna" (71). The unsportsmanlike behavior at the fight,
with its suggestion of racial as well as national chauvinism, the promoter's attempt to fix the fight and then to avoid his obligation to pay,
the theft of the watch—all characterize society as unjust, while Bill's
extravagant praise of the boxer—*wonderful, awful noble-looking, splendid*—establishes him as heroic. The simplified vocabulary and syntax
which are hallmarks of the group's verbal style suit the starkly polarized
terms of conflict which, in Bill's telling, are transvalued. In contrast
to the official values of public language, black becomes superior both
physically and morally; white is weak, conniving, and treacherous. "Big
mistake to have come to Vienna" represents any social involvement.

In a joking banter that looks forward to Nathanael West's character
Shrike, Bill also parodies religious commonplaces and the ritualistic
form such utterances take: "Let us not doubt, brother. Let us not pry
into the holy mysteries of the hencoop with simian figures. Let us accept on faith and simply say—I want you to join with me in saying—
What shall we say, brother?" (122). Bill hesitates momentarily because
there is no prescribed dogma to insert in his parodic ritual. He similarly mocks consumerism with a sales pitch to buy a "nice stuffed dog"
and the New York literary establishment with his litany of the latest
catchwords, "irony and pity." Historical figures and contemporary public men receive fancifully irreverent treatment: "Abraham Lincoln was
a faggot. He was in love with General Grant" (116). In this respect
too, uttering nonsense meant to beguile and entertain through its out-
rageousness, Bill is a singular character in the novel. Uninvolved with
his material, as Jake cannot be, he allows his imagination verbal expression without inhibition. His ability to use language satirically pro-

vides Bill with an organizing approach to experience that shields him from the destructiveness of Brett but also keeps him from the deeper enjoyment of *afición* that Jake feels.

Mike is the least conscious member of Jake's group, his disvaluing of society more a blend of the casual contempt and lack of personal discipline of someone who has inherited wealth. Whereas Bill's criticism of society is the basis for consciously contrived and polished verbal performances, in Mike's one extended speech, a long anecdote about some medals he borrowed and gave away, disdain for such prestigious symbols as badges of valor and formal dinners attended by royalty is part of the narrative texture, not the point of the story. In contrast to Bill, Mike is an uncertain narrator who continually explains or seeks reassurance that his audience understands his story and who has no real sense of its shape or point. Yet both their long anecdotes, like the narrative that contains them, belong to the same paradigm in which the narrator is distanced from his own participation in the events recounted by his detachment from the social code that structures them. There is a drama within each story concerning people who operate within the code, but no meaningful involvement for Bill or Mike.

Mike's opening assertion, logically and grammatically one sentence but conveying more emphatic rejection as two, sets the tone of offhand dismissal of collective values: "I suppose I've the usual medals. But I never sent in for them." (135). When Mike's tailor wants to provide him with the medals he has rightfully earned, Mike protests that any medals will do. Justifying his ignorance about his own medals, Mike interrupts his story at this point to solicit agreement from his like-minded audience: "Did he think I spent all my time reading the bloody gazette?" (135). Once the tailor has given him some medals, he puts them in his pocket and promptly forgets them:

> "Well, I went to the dinner, and it was the night they'd shot
> Henry Wilson, so the Prince didn't come and the King didn't come,
> and no one wore any medals, and all these coves were busy taking
> off their medals, and I had mine in my pocket."
> He stopped for us to laugh.
> "Is that all?"
> "That's all. Perhaps I didn't tell it right."
> "You didn't," said Brett. "But no matter."
> We were all laughing.

"Ah yes," said Mike. "I know now. It was a damn dull dinner, and I couldn't stick it, so I left. Later on in the evening I found the box in my pocket. What's this? I said. Medals? Bloody military medals? So I cut them all off their backing—you know, they put them on a strip—and gave them all around. Gave one to each girl. Form of souvenir. They thought I was hell's own shakes of a soldier. Give away medals in a night club. Dashing fellow."

"Tell the rest," Brett said.

"Don't you think that was funny?" Mike asked. We were all laughing. "It was. I swear it was. Any rate, my tailor wrote me and wanted the medals back. Sent a man around. Kept on writing for months. Seems some chap had left them to be cleaned. Frightfully military cove. Set hell's own store by them." (135–36)

Mike's audience laughs first at his naiveté as a fabulist; what he perceives to be the climax of his story is the least dramatic of three illustrations of opposition to the social valuing of medals. Actually, since the ironic intersection of Mike's bungled attempt to follow protocol with the unforeseeable circumstance that medals are not worn after all occurs in a context of high seriousness and formality, whose magnitude intensifies the divergence of values, Mike's intuition of its thematic weight is valid.[37] The true climax is the scene in the nightclub, a sudden drop from the official world of pomp and ceremony into a milieu of hedonistic gratification and social fluidity where Mike can be himself, impulsively desecrating the medals and dispersing them among girls casually encountered, yet still passing for a socially respectable figure: the dashing soldier who generously gives away the tokens of his bravery and patriotism.

The epilogue to the story, which Brett must also elicit, reveals Mike without the misleading public personae of the earlier events. In the privacy of his relation to a tradesman, he is seen to be a man whom society can neither approve nor trust, but since speaker and audience do not share the social values symbolized by the medals, the "serious discrediting" of Mike is inverted to become a tripartite demonstration of Mike's superiority to those who accept the official valuation. At the dinner he is spared the awkwardness of the others, who must publicly remove the medals he has forgotten to put on, and in the nightclub he is taken for a "dashing fellow" when he gives them away. Finally, in the aftermath of the evening Mike's aplomb compares favorably to the importunings of the tailor and the consternation of the medals' owner, caricatured as a "frightfully military cove."

Like Mike, Robert Cohn behaves badly, but according to another standard of conduct altogether, one predicated upon the assumption that the ordinary, socially approved ways of conferring value are meaningful.[38] Because he has not had the defining experience of the war, which all of Jake's circle have in common, his is the only personal history Hemingway presents in detail; for the others the war has deprived the past of relevance. His protected and in a way make-believe experience—his wealth, the elitist world of Princeton, amateur boxing, literary magazines—leads him to want the conventional existence of professional success, love, and going home that the others have abandoned. In Pamplona he is briefly able to live the romantic fantasy that eluded him in Paris, "ready to do battle for his lady love," but he is ultimately defeated by the realization that his affair with Brett had no meaning for her and has no future. This denial of the world of commitments and significances that Cohn perhaps unwillingly represents is his true initiation into the expatriate circle, one that sends him back to a more conventional existence.

In keeping with his embodiment of traditional social values beneath a bohemian exterior, Cohn uses language with its social freight of responsibility. Although he now finds Frances a burden, to Jake's suggestion that he break with her, he replies, "I can't. I've got certain obligations to her" (38). When Cohn takes umbrage at Jake's description of Brett and Jake tells him to go to hell, Cohn rises from the table in anger:

> "Sit down," I said. "Don't be a fool."
> "You've got to take that back."
> "Oh, cut out the prep-school stuff."
> "Take it back."
> "Sure. Anything. I never heard of Brett Ashley. How's that?"
> "No. Not that. About me going to hell."
> "Oh, don't go to hell," I said. "Stick around. We're just starting lunch." (39)

For Cohn, Jake's "go to hell" is a personal insult, seriously meant and provocative; its constitutive rules require that he take offense.[39] For Jake, this interpretation is immature romanticism, but when Cohn persists, Jake becomes so extravagantly accommodating that his retraction is clearly as casual as the original provocation had been. Through mockery the act of capitulation is rendered harmless, more meaningless language. Cohn is placated, however, because he is operating according to the conventional rules of language use whereby Jake's "taking it back" nullifies the imagined offense. He wants no trouble with Jake, his "best friend," but his espousal of the standard linguistic code demands that the form of retraction and apology be carried out before the conversation can be resumed.

The scene is reversed in Pamplona when Cohn truly insults Jake by calling him a pimp and Jake responds by swinging at him. For the moment Jake's personal code and that of society converge, although later Jake reverts to his customary passivity by distancing the insult and foregrounding an incident in his past. The two episodes are equally submerged in his desire for the physical gratification of a hot bath. In this instance it is Cohn who apologizes and Jake who accepts the apology, but linguistically and emotionally the outcome replicates the earlier scene. In both cases Cohn is the one to insist upon conventional social rituals, the verbal apology and shaking hands, and to obtain relief and a sense of closure through their performance, no matter how devoid of real substance. Jake appears indifferent throughout in contrast to Cohn's obvious emotion; neither a verbal formula nor a social gesture has meaning for him. What matters, Brett's affair with Pedro Romero and his own part in it, is like other things that matter—outside the domain of words.[40]

If Robert Cohn represents conventional values neurotically displaced to the expatriate circle, Pedro Romero is the ideal man of a simpler world, one whose successful functioning within society does not preclude living his life "all the way up." This firm social grounding, which buttresses rather than counters his individuality, allows him to be a serious person; even when making a joke he speaks soberly, and even at a table full of drunks he politely shakes hands and takes their toast "very seriously," surely without any idea that they could make such a ritualistic gesture frivolously. Among Spaniards Romero conceals his knowledge of English because it would not be proper for a bullfighter, a figure of the national mythos, to know a foreign language so well. Where Jake must retreat from speech about himself because it brings him too close to the pain of his condition, and Cohn boasts about his prowess as a writer and a bridge player out of insecurity, Romero can discuss his work dispassionately and unself-consciously because he does not rely on speech to establish his identity. Although he meticulously observes the proprieties of language, employing words as meaningful signifiers, he does not confuse sign and substance. He communicates personal authority silently: "He seated himself, asking Brett's permission without saying anything" (185). His mastery of the bulls, which also becomes a communication to Brett, is equally wordless.

Only Romero has dignity in the confrontation over Brett. Both Jake and Cohn assign it to meaninglessness, Cohn by imposing the social ritual of closure, a perfunctory handshake, Jake by simply shrugging it off. Romero refuses to shake hands in order to invest the fight and the social gesture with significance: to acquiesce would be to forgive or dismiss Cohn's attack as unimportant. Because he experiences no conflict between communal and individual values and can thus draw certitude from traditional sources as well as from his own power, Romero alone is capable of loving Brett without diminishing himself.[41] Adhering to the prescribed masculine and feminine roles that have become blurred in the postwar expatriate circle, he wants to place her within the conventional context of womanliness and marriage.

■ For the free-floating expatriate existence Paris and Burguete are topographies of self-gratification abstracted from social context.[42] Pamplona, on the other hand, is a harmonious whole whose pleasures are generated by the communal fiesta rather than egocentrically pursued. This setting presents society in its traditional forms: rituals of celebration and mourning, institutional edifices like the cathedral and the bullring, collective purpose. In Pamplona the veneer of decorum which vestigially cloaks the expatriates' irresponsibility wears thin, and they are all diminished by juxtaposition with the explicit standards of an enduring, established world, one that offers an ideal in Romero, a judge in Montoya. Romero is the catalyst who causes Brett to be most flagrantly a bitch, Mike and Cohn to behave badly, and even Jake— who is at first "forgiven his friends" by Montoya—to forfeit Montoya's approval. Early in the stay Jake had advised Montoya not to give the bullfighter a message to mingle with potentially corrupting foreigners at the Grand Hotel, essentially the same message Jake himself later delivers for Brett. Like her other admirers Jake, too, is transformed into a swine, albeit one who refuses to distort or sentimentalize his condition.

In Madrid Jake's comment to Brett reinvokes the sense of society as a world apart: "Some people have God. . . . Quite a lot" (245). As Brett and Jake's unsuccessful efforts to pray have demonstrated, even with the disposition to do so they cannot respond to institutional systems of valorization. Social rituals fail to work for them; their own rituals are personal and nonverbal. Jake confirms this when he chooses Brett's self-indulgence over the institutional obligation concerning the bull-fighter that he had earlier subscribed to. Although in leaving Romero Brett atypically renounces something she wants, she, too, rejects social commitment in the traditional forms of womanliness and marriage that Romero seeks to impose upon her. In closing the Romero episode Brett and Jake reestablish their familiar world: the rituals of eating and drinking well; the reassuringly empty social discourse interspersed with the painful talking around what is significant; and finally, the taxi ride which emblematically restores them to their habitual ambience, a moving vehicle passing through society, subject to its language and laws (the policeman raising his baton) but removed from involvement with it.

As the novel's last exchange between Brett and Jake confirms, the narrow private space of the taxi is further emblematic of their linguistic confinement:

> "Oh, Jake," Brett said, "we could have had such a damned good time together." . . .
> "Yes," I said. "Isn't it pretty to think so?" (247)

The suppressed protasis of Brett's assertion recapitulates the dynamic of silence in Hemingway discourse, while the past-tense expression of potential incapable of fulfillment typifies the situation of the Hemingway protagonist, whose theoretically manageable hedonism is brought down by whatever real-life condition the language avoids. In *The Sun Also Rises* Barthes's idea that a narrative is a long sentence applies equally to life.[43]

The last bit of dialogue thus encapsulates the dialectic of discourse that structures the entire novel. Like all of the characters at various times, including Jake, Brett cannot stop herself from "talking rot." Jake, whom elsewhere Brett admonishes to silence, is here able to resist the temptations of verbal fantasy, yet his rhetorical question also reminds us once more of the interface between what can and what cannot be said, the need for restraint versus the desire to embody thought and feeling in words. While Jake's response ironically emphasizes the inherent foolishness of any contrary-to-fact speech, it affirms unironically the autotelic nature of language and the seductiveness of its power to create sustaining and consoling fictions.

Chapter 6

Rural Speech Communities:
Faulkner and Hurston

I used to think there was a direct link between
Language and Reality.

> LUDWIG WITTGENSTEIN,
> *Conversations with Friedrich Waismann*

■ Both *The Hamlet* and *Their Eyes Were Watching God* take place in poor rural Southern communities: Frenchman's Bend is an entirely white village whose inhabitants characteristically express themselves through action, often of a violent and desperate kind. Eatonville, the entirely black town of Hurston's novel, is almost as isolated and self-contained as Frenchman's Bend, but its speech is not similarly restricted. On the contrary, its exuberant metaphorical language infuses and vivifies even the most mundane utterances. In both communities linguistic capital is part of a larger capital of authority. Class, gender, and race are all conditions that allow speech or impose silence, but these two texts reflect that social capital is based upon gender more than class; that is, those in positions of authority, like Will Varner and Jody Starks in their respective communities, have the tacit right to monopolize speech if they see fit. Women acquire no such right along with their status as the wives or daughters of their community's preeminent men. Moreover, when Janie Crawford marries a man of a lower class, the relationship begins democratically but eventually incorporates his admittedly token physical abuse of her "to show he was boss."

Where Faulkner's powerful authorial discourse sharply distinguishes itself from and points up his characters' lack of language, enforcing a gulf between its voice and theirs, Hurston's authorial voice merges with the voices of the text, democratically erasing the distance between itself and them and thereby valorizing the characters' speech. Faulkner's practice reminds us of his characters' limitations and frustrations:

while they have an intense need to escape the terms of their existence, with the exception of Ratliff they lack not only the linguistic resources to voice their discontent but the resources of imagination to shape an alternative vision. The pervasive poverty of the hamlet also encompasses this resource. Silence underscores the irrelevance of speech to the inhabitants' lives, that is, its inability to change their condition. The blacks of Eatonville are equally—or arguably more—vulnerable than the whites of Frenchman's Bend, but they seem less frustrated because they have linguistic resources unavailable to Faulkner's characters.

■ *The Hamlet* presents the most isolated of Faulkner's speech communities, a narrow rural world that speaks most eloquently as a spectrum of the inarticulate and unexpressed.[1] The only romantic language in the novel is the author's; the characters speak a literary equivalent of the slowly unwinding, repetitive vernacular that gets country people through their ordinary activities. This is a fictive speech that Faulkner, like Mark Twain, perfectly commands—earthy, utilitarian, prosaic, and limited, for, as Coleridge observed, "the distinct knowledge of an uneducated rustic would furnish a very scanty vocabulary."[2]

In fact, in pointed contrast to Faulkner's verbal expansiveness the people of Frenchman's Bend are parsimonious with language. Locked into the quotidian, they seldom waste words or even speak their desires. Their speech is suited to their lives: plain, terse, circumscribed, occasionally violent, and preponderantly transactional. Unlike Balzac's peasants of the Vendée, who Faulkner said had much in common with Southerners,[3] these villagers have no political consciousness or institutional targets; the dominant feeling of rage that life engenders in Frenchman's Bend is more apt to manifest itself in the criminal violence of a personal vendetta, such as Ab's barn burning or Mink's killing Houston, or be given socially acceptable expression in the pervasive matching of wits—encounters which depend on things more than on words.[4] The horse that Pat Stamper's "nigger magician" transforms, the wild horses of Texas, the gold coins buried by Flem—all are objects that exert a compelling influence over various inhabitants of the Bend in spite of their association with known tricksters whose words in their favor would be regarded with suspicion. What is significant in this world is *seen*, not spoken; phenomena of nature, whether Eula Varner or the spotted horses, impact upon the community directly, through a physical presence that requires no expression or validation in language. Supremely inactive and almost mute, Eula drives to desperation the schoolteacher Labove, the one man in her environs who has an "invincible conviction in the power of words as a principle worth dying for if necessary" (105). The humbling of articulate intellect by mute nature is the pattern of more than one of *The Hamlet*'s tales.

More than speakers, the community is a collection of onlookers whose passivity toward the events they observe from the gallery of Will Varner's store precludes all but minimal comment. As if speaking entails complicity, a primitive sense of taboo operates to prevent the utterance of what is threatening or shameful; hence no one but Ratliff will draw conclusions about Flem Snopes out loud, and Ratliff must see for himself what is going on in Mrs. Littlejohn's barn because no one will tell him. When Henry Armstid coerces his wife into the pen with the dangerous horses, and when Flem refuses to return her money, community mores are flagrantly violated, yet the response is merely looking away and keeping silent. Sharecroppers, tenant farmers, small landowners—these are powerless people, essentially inarticulate beyond the minimal demands of a life of hard labor for small gains.

The celebrated episode of the spotted horses, Flem's victimization of the village residents as a group, demonstrates most forcibly the small part that language plays in a major community event. The men clearly believe the evidence of their senses that the horses are wild and dangerous rather than the Texan's claims, which are always disputed verbally or through silence rather than agreed with.[5] Faulkner successfully develops the episode to an outrageous extreme through his power of complete visualization. He gives us, as James wrote of Balzac, "a reproduction of the real on the scale of the real."[6] Dense, weighty, alive, the world of the horse auction leaves no gaps for the reader's conjecture and thus compels belief in spite of the blatantly comic gulf between reality and language. After every violent encounter with the ponies, the Texan emerges from the dust of the corral to say: "Them's good, gentle ponies" (273). His words only provoke mockery and have no more effect than Eck's reiterated command to his little boy to stay out of the corral. Nor do the men talk themselves into buying the horses. When they discuss the man who once brought back a pair from Texas and worked them for ten years, they are justifying for the benefit of the skeptic Ratliff a decision already made. The seemingly plausible words are remote from the real attraction of the horses, the fearsome energy and anarchic aggressiveness that the passive men covet. The men never *say* they will buy the horses, but they do buy them, and Eck, who strongly denies three times that he will, also becomes a purchaser.

The attraction of the spotted horses to the community reveals the interrelationship of economic status, language, and psychic life, for the only person immune other than the affluent Varners is Ratliff, whose margin of security as an independent small businessman and his command of linguistic resources no one else has mediate the frustration and rage that erupt destructively in the other men. Ratliff can get away physically, routinely escaping the geographic confines of the village as no one else does, and he can also escape through language: he is the only character able to use language nontransactionally to a positive end. Conveying the news and gossip from one place to another he is a welcome speaker, who also serves as the voice of the community in saying what others feel but cannot or will not express. This power to formulate and articulate is linked to a more active stance toward life; verbalization clarifies Ratliff's perception and makes possible confrontations that the other men avoid.

Ratliff is more likely than others to initiate and direct discourse because in addition to giving and receiving information he likes the play of speech itself, a correlative to his "pleasure of the shrewd dealing which far transcended mere gross profit" (68). His speech is not the common brief parlance but a more leisurely and expansive personal style, embellished with humor and detail:

> "Well, well," Ratliff said. "Well well well. So Will couldn't do nothing to the next succeeding Snopes but stop him from talking. Not that any more would have done any good, Snopes can come and Snopes can go, but Will Varner looks like he is fixing to snopes forever. Or Varner will Snopes forever—take your pick. What is it the fellow says? off with the old and on with the new; the old job at the old stand, maybe a new fellow doing the jobbing but it's the same old stern getting reamed out?" Bookwright was looking at him.
>
> "If you would stand closer to the door, he could hear you a heap better," he said.
>
> "Sholy," Ratliff said. "Big ears have little pitchers, the world beats a track to the rich man's hog-pen but it aint every family has a new lawyer, not to mention a prophet. Waste not want not, except that a full waist dont need no prophet to prophesy a profit and just

whose." Now they were all watching him—the smooth, impenetrable face with something about the eyes and the lines beside the
mouth which they could not read.

"Look here," Bookwright said. "What's the matter with you?"
(161–62)

Although nominally in conversation with Bookwright, Ratliff is not
speaking for any listener so much as for himself, transforming his outrage at the marriage of Eula to Flem into satiric fantasy. The sheer
extravagance of the puns, word play, alliteration, repetition, parody,
double entendre—Elizabethan rhetoric transmogrified into rural Mis-
sissippian—obscures the message of Flem's profiting from Eula's preg-
nancy and strikes the close-mouthed denizens of the Bend only as a
sign that something is wrong with the speaker. Ineffective as communication (the fable of Flem in hell isn't even spoken aloud), Ratliff's
verbal fantasies are an aesthetic equivalent of the violent or irrational
actions that relieve desperation in other villagers, and as such they link
Ratliff to the authorial voice which is similarly powerless to save the
world it turns into tall tale and myth.

Because he is the sole member of the community to use and value
language beyond the most basic practical level, it is fitting that Ratliff's
buying the Old Frenchman's place from Flem comes about through a
linguistic error, the mistaken assumption that Will Varner lied about
the property's lack of value. Ratliff's refusal to take Will's utterance at
face value assimilates him to other gulls in the novel, defeated as much
by a fiction of his own making as by the machinations of a trickster.
Committed to his interpretation of Will's words, he fails to be equally
suspicious of what he sees. Thus, in still another Faulknerian image of
the modern world, the most concerned and articulate member of the
community is bested by a man who has no commitment to it or to its
language.

Flem Snopes, the Faulkner character who is completely identified
with the modern business world, is the most prominent member of
a family of outsiders as linguistically extreme as they are socially removed from the other folk of the Bend. In a community of few words
Flem is a man of fewer: unlike those confidence men who depend upon
deceptive speech or a persuasive verbal charisma to gull the public, the
physically unimpressive and verbally reticent Flem manipulates and
accumulates money according to the impersonal rules of modern capi-

talism. In Floyd Watkins's words, "His silence is the inarticulateness of pure materialism and negation,"[7] yet "inarticulateness" suggests inability to speak or unexpressed content—neither of which accurately applies to Flem's lack of speech. Other communication than figures or the brief speech necessary to convey figures is simply beside the point to Flem: he "answered Yes and No to direct questions and . . . apparently never looked directly or long enough at any face to remember the name that went with it, yet [he] . . . never made mistakes in any matter pertaining to money" (56). Flem never looks at people directly because they exist for him only as configurations of profit and loss, not as flesh and blood. What communication he has with others is consequently stripped of social amenities, not in order to be hostile or aggressive like his relatives Ab and Mink but to be efficient. Flem's lack of speech is not a protest or a sign of frustration, nor is it totally attributable to his evident desire to conceal his financial affairs. He literally has nothing to discuss with others except the terms of business transactions. He is never surprised, never hurries, never seems to exert himself as he rises to economic preeminence in Frenchman's Bend, nor does he display any of the gamut of passions which agitate the other characters.[8] Removed from the living texture of the novel Flem would be an allegorical monster, a personified abstraction of Acquisition who lacks all other interests or human qualities.[9] Yet, by describing his appearance in detail, having other characters speak of him constantly, and maintaining the reader's distance, Faulkner establishes Flem as a real presence, an omnipresent factor in the affairs of Frenchman's Bend.

The embodiment of the new economic order replacing the old paternalistic system of Will Varner, Flem encapsulates the irrelevance of language to a system devoid of humanistic values and devoted solely to amoral aggrandizement. The joke of the village gossip that "Flem Snopes dont even tell himself what he is up to" (280) is a laughable exaggeration of close-mouthed prudence, but the truth is that "telling" for Flem is always superfluous, acquisition everything. When Varner tenants challenge his figures, he takes pencil and paper and proves them wrong without speaking. In any group Flem remains physically apart in "his small yet definite isolation," within the community yet never accepted by it. The little speaking he does in a social context is still about money and property although it consistently fails to answer conversational expectations. When he is accused of owning some cattle, he merely replies that they are in Varner's lot; when his cousin tells him that Ratliff wonders who owns the Texas horses, he remarks that Ratliff "was there too. . . . He knows as much as anybody else" (312). Although speakers employ an information-eliciting form of discourse, the dialogue is clearly a kind of play designed to entertain rather than provide information. Everyone knows that Flem will reveal nothing: Ratliff accordingly makes his accusation to Lump rather than to Flem, and the cousin gleefully acts as intermediary, voicing the speculation that Ratliff will not make directly to Flem. Such exchanges simply confirm the attitude of evasion; Flem will withhold what his audience wants to know but knows that it will not get, and the real expectations—rather than those of the form of discourse—are fulfilled by hearing him do so. Flem's one moment of public self-revelation is his interjection into the horse auction when the Texan returns Mrs. Armstid's five dollars. Even the alarming sight of money flowing the wrong way provokes only the guarded question "What's that for?"

Flem's behavior is outrageous because its perfect mechanicality is inserted into a human and social context in which it is jarringly inappropriate.[10] "The steady motion of his jaws" is like the hum of a computer, the sign that the machinery is running smoothly; the spitting which punctuates the chewing is Flem's routine gesture toward the world, all that he ever gives it of himself and an expression more probably of indifference than contempt. He spits past the pathetic Mrs. Armstid and, as he leaves Frenchman's Bend for the city, pauses to observe his final victim, Henry Armstid, and spit—his farewell to the now fully exploited community.

Lack of speech also marks Flem's membership in the Snopes family, whose head he becomes by virtue of economic power. In Faulkner's mythology Snopesism as an abstraction stands for the "incorrigible and unflagging conviction of the inherent constant active dishonesty of all men including [themselves]" (160).[11] Such a profoundly antisocial view entails a rejection of speech. As J. L. Austin writes, "It is fundamental in talking (as in other matters) that we are entitled to trust others, except in so far as there is some concrete reason to distrust them. Believing persons, accepting testimony, is the, or one main, point of talking."[12] Whatever their different verbal styles, Snopeses cannot be trusted, and in one way or another all are deeply estranged from society and diminished in terms of human possibility. As a group they represent a new predatory breed that usurps the position and power of the traditional order—of humanity, we might almost say, since Faulkner constantly associates Snopeses with rodent-like animals and the behavior suited to such species.[13]

Given their guiding principle of distrust, the Snopeses differ from the indigenous inhabitants of Frenchman's Bend most markedly in their lack of community, and because "linguistic cooperation . . . is one kind of social cooperation,"[14] their lack of speech reflects this condition. Although natives of the community are severely limited in their use of speech, they do use language according to the conventional expectations of conversational exchange. Representatives of a new order or antiorder based on ruthless self-assertion at the expense of traditional communal values, the Snopeses habitually violate such conventional expectations. When Ratliff renews his old acquaintance with the newly settled Ab Snopes, he goes through an entire ritual of welcoming which Ab rebuffs at every point. When he proffers a bottle of moonshine as a gift, Ab not only fails to accept it graciously, he implicitly demands that the ritual justify itself:

> "You brought it to me?"
> "Sholy," Ratliff said. "Take it."
> The other did not move. "What for?" (49)

When Ratliff tries again, politely voicing the formulaic hope that Ab will prosper in his new location, Ab retorts: "What's it to you if I do or dont?" (49) Before turning back to the plowing as an abrupt closure to the conversation, Ab does thank Ratliff for the bottle and peremptorily suggest that he get his dinner at the house, but what impresses Ratliff most forcibly is that Ab has conspicuously neglected to invite him to visit again. The thread of social contact offered by Ratliff will not be woven into the fabric of community relationships, for in meeting Ratliff's overtures with suspicious questions Ab challenges the underlying assumption of the ritual that there is a bond of community between Ratliff and himself or, by extension, between himself and any other men.

Similarly, Jody Varner's attempt to find out about Ab's past is a study in the law of diminishing returns, each question producing less of a response than the one before:

> "Where you been farming?" Varner asked.
> "West." He did not speak shortly. He merely pronounced the one word with a complete inflectionless finality, as if he had closed a door behind himself.

"You mean Texas?"

"No." . . .

"Little anxious to get settled, ain't you?" The other said nothing. (8) [15]

Ab's voice is *inflectionless* (uncolored by feeling or emphasis), *dead, lifeless, rusty from infrequent use*—all indications of his withdrawal from the community of speech. He always says as little as possible, in this case only the bare minimum necessary to become Jody's tenant; but unlike the taciturnity of the natives of Frenchman's Bend, a shared and comfortable verbal reticence, Ab's uncommunicativeness is hostile. He defines and asserts himself through antisocial behavior, not language; his resistance to social discourse is the passive form of an impulse which is aggressively expressed in his gross violation of social decorum at Major DeSpain's—tracking manure into the house and wiping it off on the rug—and in the criminal activity of barn burning.

Mink Snopes also reveals his status as an outsider through language that denies community, even the primal community of kin. In contrast to Ab, Mink does make attempts to speak, but he seeks an absolute assertion of self (as his conspicuous painting of MINKSNOPES on the old mailbox reveals), not the give-and-take of talk exchange. His utterances tend to be isolated assertives or directives rather than parts of an ongoing conversation, and they accordingly reveal Mink's desire to make the world conform to his will, a desire that is constantly thwarted. His first message to Flem, implicitly threatening his cousin's property, is one of a series of abortive communications that sum up Mink's linguistic commerce with the world, the embodiment of perlocutionary failure. Flem refuses even to listen to the communication Ratliff seeks to deliver; the later message Mink has for Flem—"Tell that son of a bitch"—is appropriately unfinished. On several occasions Mink answers a passionate torrent of words from his wife with blows or simple commands such as "Get back in the house." When she threatens to leave him, he replies, "Go." A barrage of words from his greedy cousin is at first ignored, then answered in a "flat, absolutely toneless" voice like Ab's: "I ask you to let me alone" (242). His most important assertion, one that would express his sense of retributive justice and claim responsibility for his most significant act, is never uttered: "What he would have liked to do would be to leave a printed placard on the breast itself: *This is what happens to the men who impound Mink Snopes's cattle*, with his name signed to it. But he could not and here again . . .

was that conspiracy to frustrate and outrage his rights as a man and his feelings as a sentient creature" (218). Self-expression in language as well as in deed, voicing the words that existentially claim the act and thereby create identity, seems to Mink to be a necessary completion and an inalienable right denied to him by society.

Such words as Mink has only confirm the gulf between his expansive vision of self and that of a society which has constantly coerced and diminished him, forcing him to flee his own community, decreeing that he must pay Houston for feeding his bull, and finally sending him to prison for an act that he regards as "the vindication of his rights and the liquidation of his injuries" (218). The man he kills, his wife, and his cousin all curse him, not for committing murder but for failing to do so in a reasonable fashion: to have enough ammunition for more than one shot, enough money to make a getaway, enough sense of self-interest to take the dead man's wallet. Such reasonableness would presuppose an expectation of benefit that Mink's face—"wasted, seemingly without life" (247)—denies.

Mink's self-interest is focused upon communicating an image of self, not in reaping those material benefits which preoccupy others. When he makes one last effort to tell his story, to utter a hero's boast, his audience of black prisoners has no desire to hear or, of course, the context to make his broken utterance meaningful. " 'I was all right,' " he says twice, following each statement with an incipient narrative which is broken off after a few words. Then, a shift from the indicative to the subjunctive acknowledges that the posture of capability he has tried to create in words is contrary to fact:

> "I would have been all right," he said, harsh, whispering. Then his voice failed altogether again and he held to the bars with one hand, holding his throat with the other, while the Negroes watched him, huddled, their eyeballs white and still in the failing light. Then with one accord they turned and rushed toward the stairs and he heard the slow steps too and then he smelled the food. (258)

Mink's physical inability to speak reflects his inherent inability to express himself, just as his total posture is emblematic of his existential condition of mute imprisonment. Momentarily an object of curiosity to his uncomprehending audience, he is displaced first in their attention and then in his own by the arrival of dinner. Like the rushing Negroes, the narrative perspective recedes from Mink and turns its attention elsewhere. At the trial, his last chance to speak, he is an inert exhibit, distanced by his own withdrawal from the space of his life as well as by the narrative distance which disallows a glimpse of the thought process that might complete his final outcry.

The speechlessness of Mink and Ab reflects their commitment to an antisocial individualism whose object is a leveling or equalizing of advantage. Having lost out in the initial conquest of the country, they seek to perpetuate an atavistic lawlessness and denial of community, to achieve through force what is unobtainable by the more civilized means of law or speech. They are Melvillian *isolatos,* whose unused voices and lifeless faces emphasize that society must deny their aspirations. To quote Stanley Fish, "There is no world . . . where it is possible to stand freely, unencumbered by obligations and dependencies. There are only other speech act communities, and every one of them exacts as the price of membership acceptance of its values and meanings."[16]

Ike, another member of the tribe, is a Snopes in name only, released from the ordinary parameters of humanity and kinship by his idiocy. With difficulty he can say his name and nothing else; he has been given "the wordless passions but not the specious words" (196), or, Faulkner's comment suggests, the truth of feeling as opposed to the deception or inadequacy of language. Like Mink he goes on a quest, but where Mink is frustrated in his intention to create his act in words as a heroic deed, Ike has a primal purity, the direct experience of passion without the impulse or the ability to falsify that experience by speaking it.[17] Language is inherently inadequate in its failure to render perfectly act or feeling, inner or outer reality, but Faulkner's *specious* conveys something more—the appearance of logic and plausibility, the misplaced authority that language arrogates, even when it is used without the intention to deceive.

The Snopeses who use language speciously by intention are the loquacious cousins I. O. and Lump, linguistic opposites of their taciturn kinsmen Ab, Mink, and Flem, but excluded from the belongingness of communal parlance just as surely. I. O. masks a void of signification with popular clichés intended to ally suspicion and enforce agreement. Through this caricaturing of ordinary forms of discourse his speech makes no more contact with the community than the few words of other Snopeses: "His voice [was] voluble and rapid and meaningless like something talking to itself about nothing in a deserted cavern" (65). Unlike I. O., Lump uses the forms of discourse correctly; it is the defective "sincerity condition" of his speech that sets him apart from the community and from his cousin Mink as well.[18] He abuses language opportunistically, lying for Flem at the trial in support of the same five-dollar theft and alternately threatening and cajoling Mink in order to get Houston's money. Moreover, when other inhabitants of Frenchman's Bend look away from the spectacle of Flem substituting five cents' worth of candy for the five dollars belonging to Mrs. Armstid, Lump verbally applauds the action, an explicit admission of the predatory rapacity that informs the Snopes worldview.

Although Frenchman's Bend never accepts them, the Snopeses are unstoppable because their lack of belongingness is immaterial to the conditions of the modern world, where society no longer entails community. Trampling upon all the values of the quasi-feudal agrarian society that the new commercial order is replacing, Snopeses unhesitatingly do whatever a non-Snopes, however imperfect, would shrink from doing: cheating the pathetic Armstids; marrying a woman made pregnant by another man; and, climactically, failing to come to the aid of a kinsman in trouble. As their deliberate withdrawal from the community of language reveals, there is no solidarity in the modern world, only the interaction necessary for exploiting others and advancing the isolated self.

■ In its celebration of speech, *Their Eyes Were Watching God* does not at first appear to belong to the paradigm that I have applied to the twentieth-century American novel, whose primary characteristic is the devolution of speech. The deviance of Hurston from what is typical in authors of traditionally canonical twentieth-century American novels correlates with this divergence of the text without necessarily accounting for it in any complete fashion; that is, her experience as a minority woman writer cum anthropologist and her sense of relationship to a literary tradition were significantly different from those of male, predominantly white, novelists.[19] Nevertheless, the treatment of public language, the voice of the community, links *Their Eyes* with the mainstream tradition.[20] By the end of the novel Janie asserts that the public speech of Eatonville, so expansively imaginative in comparison with the public speech of Frenchman's Bend, is a substitute for reality—not the appealing, playful fantasies that the mule stories represent, but a negative phenomenon that conceals the lack of genuine experience and empowerment. Those who speak it, the occupants of the porch, are "sitters-and-talkers," who *"got* tuh rattle tuh make out they's alive" (183). This speech, however appealing in its vivacity of metaphor, is the bankrupt mask of an experiential void, the same void that the inhabitants of Frenchman's Bend cover over with silence.

Where *The Hamlet* preserves a sharp distinction between the authorial voice and the speech of characters, *Their Eyes Were Watching God* relies heavily on free indirect discourse, "a third or mediating term between narrative commentary and direct discourse."[21] And where speech is curtailed, suspect, and generally inefficacious in *The Hamlet*, unable to create a fructifying vision or express the self, in *Their Eyes Were Watching God* it is eloquent, repeatedly appropriated to assert identity. The voice that Mink fails to gain, that in Ratliff is no match for the silent chicanery of Flem Snopes, develops in Janie to become the instrument of self-realization. By speaking her own narrative, an oral text that preserves Tea Cake and consoles her for his loss, she confirms this act of creation and possession of the self although, as some commentators have argued, this victory is qualified by Janie's failure to speak publicly in the hostile forums of the white courtroom and the black community she returns to after Tea Cake's death.[22]

Janie's construction of an authoritative voice, one that will challenge male speakers successfully, is recounted within the frame narrative as an extended speech made to Janie's friend Pheoby. Although presumably this good friend would already know something of Janie's life before her disappearance from Eatonville, Janie begins at the beginning because what is significant in her story requires more than the record of the period when she was away: who she is now depends upon who she was originally, a person deprived of the ordinary bases of identity— parents, a name, a racial group. She is referred to as "Alphabet" because everyone gives her a different name. This suggests her unformed state, her lack of definition, but the nickname "Alphabet" also contains the potential of verbal communication. Significantly, Janie is unable to recognize herself in a photograph and must rely on Miss Nellie's identification: "Dat's you, Alphabet, don't you know yo' ownself?" (9) Janie will not know her "ownself," nor will she own this self, until she finds the voice that can create and uphold this self in opposition to the dominant male discourse of her community.

Although every opponent—Nanny, Logan Killicks, Jody Starks—accuses Janie of a perverse independence, she is unable to verbalize her feelings because they are still incoherent. Others who can articulate their positions succeed in imposing their will upon her, beginning with Nanny, who insists that she marry an old man and expects that she should be content with the identity of a married woman. Janie's two husbands successively expect the same thing: that she will be content to subordinate her voice to theirs, to live upon their capital of authority. Her first husband, Logan Killicks, cannot admit to any weakness by responding honestly to her truthful supposition—"S'posin' Ah wuz to run off and leave yuh sometime" (29)—but instead retreats into his patriarchal role, accusing her of not knowing her place and thus losing the chance for genuine communication. Rather than face their differences, Killicks constructs a fiction of personal power according to which he is "too honest and hard-workin' for anybody in yo' family" (30). Class buttresses his gender-based authority over Janie.

This insistence on a male superiority that denies identity and voice also erodes the initially more desirable marriage with Jody Starks. Jody has always known that he wants to be a "big voice,"[23] a single-minded ambition that gives him the advantage over the still unformed Janie and over other men as well.[24] As much as an acquisition of property and prestige, Jody's rise to power is an extension of his voice over others and a concomitant denial of voice to Janie. He preempts occasions for speechmaking; her role is to do what he tells her, the silent activities of the store. "Mrs. Mayor" has more status than "Mrs. Killicks" did, but as Jody defines this role, it submerges Janie's own identity while he is free to exact "obedience out of everybody under de sound of his voice" (46). Worse, some of the initiatives that bring Jody the most communal admiration—such as his buying Matt's abused mule in order to free it from labor—are actually Janie's ideas.

Although on one occasion when he is displeased Jody "slapped Janie until she had a ringing sound in her ears" (67), his verbal abuse—according to which Janie and all women are lumped with chickens and cows in their inability to think—is far more damaging.[25] The discourse of the male porch sitters is more directly and violently misogynistic. Speaking of a woman who has come to the store to beg food, one of the men remarks, "If dat wuz *mah* wife . . . Ah'd kill her cemetery dead." Another continues, "Ah'd break her if she wuz mine. Ah'd break her or kill her" (70). When Janie intervenes with a mild defensive remark, Jody does not respond to its implicit accusation but instead dismisses her as "too moufy."

There can be no speech of substance between husband and wife: all their speaking is an issue of authority which Janie, whose only capital is borrowed from Jody, is bound to lose. For years under this provocation she reconciles herself to silence and detachment, watching "the shadow of herself . . . prostrating itself before Jody" (73) while her real self, now discovered but not articulated, withdraws to sit "under a shady tree" (73). This split between public and private selves is healed when Jody sacrifices her in words to hide his own physical decline: Janie finally challenges him, although not without giving him three warnings beforehand. Jody's repeated failure to end the contest as Janie offers leads to her final, terrible accusation of sexual lack. In the public arena where he has held sway, Janie verbally emasculates her husband, redefining him from an envied and wealthy leader to a figure of ridicule. Because Janie introduces the private space of sexual intimacy in which she will be accepted as an authoritative speaker, her words have the power to negate Jody's "big voice." Ironically, Jody's substantial capital of authority works against him by making the community savor the gulf between his social position and his humiliation.

By finally challenging Jody in public, Janie establishes her own authentic speech, but she cannot similarly acquire authority in a male-dominated society. The more primitive social organization of "the muck" and the more egalitarian relationship with Tea Cake allow her to progress further: "She got so she could tell big stories herself" (128). Yet when she returns to Eatonville, she tells her story privately. The community is still a problematic arena for a woman "speaking herself free"[26] because authorized speech is usually individual male speech or a collective voice that expresses patriarchal values. Indicative of their suppression, female voices are rarely heard in the text. Other than Janie's voice, there is Pheoby's within the framing narrative and Nanny's, both heard only briefly. Otherwise, Janie's verbal interactions are with men.

At the beginning of the novel the authorial voice characterizes the community's initial response to Janie's reappearance in Eatonville as "mass cruelty," words used as "killing tools" and "burning statements" in the form of questions:

"What she doin' coming back here in dem overhalls? Can't she find no dress to put on?—Where's dat blue satin dress she left here in?—Where all dat money her husband took and died and left her?—What dat ole forty year ole 'oman doin' wid her hair swingin'

down her back lak some young gal?—Where she left dat young
lad of a boy she went off here wid?—Thought she was going to
marry? (2)[27]

These are "words walking without masters" because whatever individual speakers utter them, they reflect a communal view, "altogether
like harmony in a song" (2), and they further reflect a conservative,
patriarchal value system. In the form of questions the community cri-
tiques Janie's behavior as unfeminine: she should wear a dress, not
overalls; she should not have run off with the money her late husband
earned; she should not wear her hair in a style suitable to younger
women; and she should not have made a liaison with a younger man.
This is all speech *about* Janie. What they say *to* her is merely the neutral greeting "Good evenin." When Janie fails to provide any answers
to their questions, "the porch"—a synecdoche for the community but
always identified as a space of masculine performance—simply assesses her body as a collection of sexually relevant parts: buttocks, hair,
breasts. This reduction controls Janie's image in the voyeuristic gaze of
the men; the women present criticize her unwillingness to subsume her
identity in the female group by stopping and talking. Janie's independence, established here by her inappropriate attire—suitable neither
to her sex nor to her position as the late mayor's wife—the allusions
to unconventional behavior, and her refusal to participate in a social
ritual uniting her with other women, cause the community to hope that
the answers to their unasked questions are "cruel and strange."

As she prepares to tell her story to Pheoby, her closest friend, Janie
speaks contemptuously of this communal chorus, which she labels
"Mouth-Almighty." When she has concluded her narrative, she is
equally contemptuous of the kind of speech they represent: " 'Let 'em
consolate theyselves wid talk. 'Course, talkin' don't amount tuh uh
hill uh beans when yuh can't do nothin' else. And listenin' tuh dat
kind uh talk is jus' lak openin' yo' mouth and lettin' de moon shine
down yo' throat. It's uh known fact, Pheoby, you got tuh *go* there tuh
know there' " (183).[28] The loquacity of Eatonsville and the silence of
Frenchman's Bend are two versions of the same male impotence. Public
speech, both the playful dialoguing that Janie once longed to join and
the censorious judgments, have a common origin in these two communities in a lack of meaningful life experience: "dey's parched up from

not knowin' things" (183). This also characterizes the black community of the muck that condemns Janie's shooting of Tea Cake without "having been there": "They were there with their tongues cocked and loaded, the only real weapon left to weak folks" (176).

In the final movement of the text, killing the man she loves becomes the painful necessity that allows Janie to live and requires her to complete the process of self-realization in language in order to do justice to what she has experienced. Through her authoritative narrative, in opposition to the malicious and distorted version of the black community, literal justice is done: she moves the white audience with her story and is acquitted of Tea Cake's murder. Nevertheless, it is unclear why Janie is exonerated. Rather than her eloquence, it may be the corroborative testimony of the white doctor, or, as the black community cynically believes, it may be true that a black woman's killing a black man is of no concern to whites.[29]

The text avoids a climactic moment by failing to present Janie's speech to the court. Like Dimmesdale's Election Day sermon and numerous withheld utterances in Melville's fiction, this utterance may be more important to the narrative as a reported effect.[30] The court is a white institution where blacks are threatened and demeaned, not a venue of choice for Janie to tell her story but one where she is constrained to appear and argue for her life. Her speaking here must of necessity be distorted to conform to institutional requirements.

Such instances and others have caused some disagreement on the extent of Janie's self-realization in speech. In summing up her own history as a reader of the text, Mary Helen Washington writes, "In 1989, I find myself asking new questions about *Their Eyes*—questions about Hurston's ambivalence toward her female protagonist, about its uncritical depiction of violence toward women, about the ways in which Janie's voice is dominated by men even in passages that are about her own inner growth."[31] These are valid concerns, but I believe that the text subordinates them to Janie's success. Realistically, her story can be told only in private, to the sympathetic ear of her friend Pheoby, because the community, authorizing a speech that conceals its weakness or deflects it into banter, cannot accommodate an empowered Janie or an assertive female discourse. It *wants* Janie's story to affirm its own values. From the vantage point of having gone there, Janie can now speak from knowing: when she begins to speak, she tells Pheoby,

"Ah know exactly what Ah got to tell yuh" (8). Her concluding speech
asserts her present discourse as superior and repudiates her earlier behavior of passive listening and acceptance of male dominance.

■ When Hurston describes in *Dust Tracks on a Road*
the personal experience that contributed to *Their Eyes*, she refers to it
retrospectively: "I have the satisfaction of knowing that I have loved
and been loved by the perfect man. If I never hear of love again, I have
known the real thing."[32] Once again the emphasis is on the genuine
experience of the self, but here Hurston asserts an additional element
of preservation more forthrightly than in the novel, which she speaks
of as her effort to "*embalm* all the tenderness of my passion for him"
(my emphasis).[33] Joking about her lover's modest weight gain in her
absence, she observes, "If he had been crippled in both legs, it would
have suited me even better."[34] It might have suited Hurston better because such a condition of complete dependence and immobility would
have subdued the male desire for dominance that had often disrupted
her relationships with men.

What is presented as a comic fantasy in Hurston's autobiography
becomes the tragedy that leads to the last stage of self-realization for
Janie. In the final movement of the text, killing the man she loves
becomes the painful necessity that allows Janie to save her own life
and requires her to realize herself completely in language in order to
communicate what she has experienced.

Pheoby is not simply Janie's confidante but a mediator between her
and the community. She returns to her husband, to communal life,
while Janie experiences the lyrical renewal of Tea Cake's memory. She
is now the agent of this experience, pulling in her horizon "like a great
fish-net. . . . So much of life in its meshes!" (184). Tea Cake has been
reconstituted as an entirely valuable image, "embalmed" in Janie's
controlling idiom like the "perfect man" preserved in Hurston's mem-
oir.[35] This verbal artifact represents the satisfaction of self-expression
without the compromises required by the community or by even the
best lover.[36]

Chapter 7

Nathanael West and the Urban Apocalypse of the Word

Most lives are guided by clichés. They have a soothing
effect on the mind and they express the kind of widely
accepted sentiment that, when peeled back, is seen to be
a denial of silence.

DON DELILLO, *End Zone*

■ Because the authorial language of the modern
American novel supports rather than undermines characters, valuing
them as a preeminent part of the fiction, their identity is established
in spite of their inability to use language effectively in speech. Their
withdrawal from or defeat by language has a certain stoical dignity,
nowhere more impressive than in James, whose characters discover
the parameters of their social and lingistic prisons, a bleak knowledge
that nevertheless compensates for losing the world of signifieds that
language ambiguously refers to. Paradoxically, as John Carlos Rowe
asserts, "James's novels demonstrate that individuals are free only to
the extent that they recognize their bondage to a language that is never
their own." [1] More radically, Hemingway's protagonists rigorously deny
themselves the sham consolations of public language and consciously
choose more limited vocabularies in the interest of truth and self-
discipline. Other characters go down with vigorous self-assertion, like
the hopelessly thwarted Mink Snopes, whose final, uncompleted utterance—"Flem Snopes! . . . Tell that son of a bitch"—is nevertheless
a message, and one that expresses his life. Even Jay Gatsby, with his
phony social persona and artficial idiom, is valorized by a nobility that
can be separated not only from the role he plays but from his misguided
and unworthy goal.

Characters in the modern American novel have their authors' attention and sympathy in that their viability as characters, their sense of
reality, is central to the fictions they are a part of. Their speech may
be increasingly futile, but it is memorable as idiosyncractic expression,

testimony to a continuing belief in the individual. For the inhabitants of postmodern fiction, linguistic failure is unrelieved by other forms of authorial attention. Undercutting and overshadowing characters, an authorial voice intent upon its own performance transforms traditional omniscience into postmodernist verbal omnipotence.

That characters are diminished by the world that they inhabit and not by their authors as well marks a crucial separation between modernism and postmodernism and between the modernists of the first three decades of the twentieth century and Nathanael West. West, whose brief career was over by 1940, is a genuinely transitional figure, typically but not entirely postmodern in his distanced handling of character and mechanical treatment of other novelistic elements.

In their mixture of postmodernist assumptions about the world and modernist sensibility, the novels of Nathanael West challenge Roland Barthes's assertion that "the Book is a High Mass, and it matters little whether or not it is said with piety, provided every element proceeds in order."[2] In spite of the reassurance of orderly procedure, the absence of piety may be disturbing, for West dramatizes the bankruptcy of society, public language, and traditional protagonists while organizing the text as if society, language, and characters were credible entities. Practicing "a kind of verbal terrorism which murders sense without even disrupting legitimate verbal orders and sequences,"[3] West reveals the difficulty of carrying the abjuration of public language to its logical conclusion without simultaneously changing other aspects of the novel. It remained for the postmodern novel to take the final step: to assimilate the break with society implicit in modernism by refusing to impose formal order on a fragmentary vision, and by mediating public language with the literary devices of indirect presentation.

All four of West's prose fictions are efforts to encapsulate social criticism in a special vocabulary. *The Dream Life of Balso Snell*, a postmodernist fabulation, is confined within a discourse of literary parody and pastiche, fittingly symbolized by the interior of that consummate imaginative structure, the Trojan horse. The incoherence and brevity of the text indicate how limiting West found this restricted perspective, whose double mediation keeps society at a remote distance. *A Cool Million*, on the other hand, foregrounds social failure too insistently and simplistically. What could have been a dynamic tension between the novel's optimistic language of Horatio Alger clichés and its sequence of disastrous events is instead monotonously static. Both language and event are too stereotypical to transcend the level of surface cleverness, except when West briefly substitutes for the dominant voice of the text the individual flavor of a peripheral ethnic idiom—Chief Satinpenny, a sinister Chinaman, a foreign "red." *Balso Snell* and *A Cool Million* are equally trapped within verbal styles too narrowly conceived to sustain novelistic development. Turning from literature to the mass media in *Miss Lonelyhearts* and *The Day of the Locust*, West found the controlling public language that he needed without restricting the novel to this media voice.

The two novels compose a dyptich, complementary views of contemporary urban society rendered in terms of two different kinds of linguistic failure, deceptive language and silence. An American dream rhetoric disseminated by the media victimizes the pathetic characters, yet in the recurring dilemma of Huck Finn, as long as society establishes the context of human existence there is no way to avoid its language(s). As Bakhtin reminds us, "Directly intentional, reservationless, unrefracted speech appears to be a barbaric, coarse, bizarre kind of speech. Cultured speech is speech refracted through the authoritative canonical medium."[4] Frustration in West's fiction has two modes, linguistic and physical, and no character escapes injury from an abuse of language that is commensurate with the high level of physical violence.

Miss Lonelyhearts juxtaposes the desperate appeals for meaning and solace in the letters written to a newspaper advice columnist with diverse public rhetorics, none of which has the power to respond truthfully or effectively. For West's protagonist, consciousness of this failure of words impels to desperate action: Miss Lonelyhearts's intervention into the affairs of the Doyle family leads to madness and, presumably, death; but before the climactic confrontation, he has renounced language and retreated into a condition of wordlessness. Appropriately, the novel ends violently in miscommunication. In *The Day of the Locust* language as a means of communication among characters almost ceases to exist: the inarticulate characters are cinematic images who express themselves in contrived appearances modeled on movie stereotypes. Everyone has a mask, an act, a costume whose misleading surface temporarily conceals an unvoiced substance of unrealistic hopes and rage. Where the false visions of media language in *Miss Lonelyhearts* reveal their insubstantiality in the face of powerfully drawn pictures of suffering, the images of *The Day of the Locust* are themselves deceptive facades that can be dissolved only by violence.

The passive sufferers of *Miss Lonelyhearts* become the destructive mob of *The Day of the Locust.*

■ The submerged antiphonal structure of questions and responses in *Miss Lonelyhearts* embodies a dialectic of entropy and order, or more accurately, entropy and false forms of order. The questions shape in language all of the miseries of life whose common denominator is that they are undeserved: men sexually abuse women; women tease and belittle men; the sadistic prey upon the vulnerable; and the cosmos, in its random and inscrutable operation, inflicts illness and deformity. Social responsibility for these misfortunes is at best indirect. Although acculturation fosters the sexually exploitative attitudes repeatedly depicted, the text does not focus on cause so much as consequence. What can anyone do for a girl without a nose, who is an object of horror even to herself? What is the answer to her question, "What did I do to deserve such a terrible bad fate?" (67). Clearly, West intends that the assorted ills of the letters Miss Lonelyhearts receives, like the dilemma of Miss Lonelyhearts himself, resist ordinary solutions. The exploitation in the novel is both immediately personal and cosmic rather than social, but society is culpable in its inability to assuage individual anguish and in its substitution of the meretricious and the delusory for an order-creating myth. As Shrike advises Miss Lonelyhearts, "Give your readers stones. When they ask for bread don't give them crackers as does the Church, and don't, like the State, tell them to eat cake. Explain that man cannot live by bread alone and give them stones. Teach them to pray each morning: 'Give us this day our daily stone'" (70–71).[5] When the myths of Church and State as order and meaning-producing institutions are rejected, Shrike implies, nothing remains but meaningless repetition and reification.

The simple language of incontestable data that Frederic Henry extols in *A Farewell to Arms* is the authentic idiom in which the letter writers powerfully express their impossible woes.[6] "I have 7 children in 12 yrs and ever since the last 2 I have been so sick" (66); "She plays on the roof of our house and don't go to school except to deaf and dumb school twice a week on tuesdays and thursdays" (68); "The doctor told me I ought to rest it for six months but who will pay me when I am resting it" (125). The letter writers illustrate John Searle's category of "the simplest cases of meaning . . . those in which the speaker . . . means exactly and literally what he says."[7] They alone in the novel observe the ideal conditions of successful linguistic communication: they express themselves sincerely, and they are understood.[8] At the same time, the writers make pathetic attempts to express themselves within the conventional genre of a letter to a newspaper columnist, a genre that is grotesquely inadequate to their narratives and to the writers' needs.[9]

Only the letter writers speak the truth, and the truth is unbearable; their barren world is the reality of suffering and victimization that society tries to obscure with the paraphernalia of romantic illusion—"guitars, bright shawls, exotic foods, outlandish costumes"—material fakery that corresponds to the evasive language of the other voices in the text. In terms of the deceptive world that media language creates and society accepts as a desirable version of the world, the letter writers are ironically the novel's least successful speakers, truthful by default because they have no linguistic resources for avoiding the truth. They, too, seek an escape route, a reassuring and sustaining word that will palliate their desperation, but this naive faith that such a word exists is simply another aspect of their victimization. It is the dilemma of Miss Lonelyhearts and of the text that public language does not wish to confer recognition upon the reality of their suffering.

Even the mode of discourse appropriate to their situation has been deformed from speaking to writing, from the personal context of a face-to-face conversation to an impersonal dialogue in print between parties stripped of identification.[10] Since there is no message in the commercialized modern world of *Miss Lonelyhearts* that is not a merchandized commodity, the basis of this exchange is economic rather than altruistic: in return for buying the paper, readers can write for advice. What they get from Miss Lonelyhearts is neither genuine comfort, an impossibility, nor the illusion that everywhere substitutes for it. Instead, they are given a facile invocation of religious experience couched in the comfortably distanced abstractions of official piety, a bankrupt version of public language analogous to the rhetoric that Frederic Henry condemns.

In the direct brutality of its signification, the language of the letters is a naturalistic floor upon which the verbal codes of indirection dance. The other fictive voices transform and eclipse experiential reality elsewhere in the text, promulgating their own self-confirming stories, but they can neither answer nor alter the world created by the letters. The readers of Miss Lonelyhearts's column have already been given the stone of reality, heavy and immutable, and Shrike's advice is to make a virtue of necessity by accepting it.

Instead of the hoped-for sustenance, society adds its own stone to their misery, the false world projected by the media. Culture, as Yuri Lotman writes, "creates a social sphere around man which, like the biosphere, makes life possible; that is, not organic life but social life." [11] When the social sphere fails to nourish, social life becomes increasingly difficult—*life* becomes increasingly difficult. Such social failure is the donnée of *Miss Lonelyhearts*, as West deftly dramatizes and then heavy-handedly explicates in a memorable passage:

> He saw a man who appeared to be on the verge of death stagger into a movie theater that was showing a picture called *Blonde Beauty*. He saw a ragged woman with an enormous goiter pick a love story magazine out of a garbage can and seem very excited by her find.
>
> Prodded by his conscience, he began to generalize. Men have always fought their misery with dreams. Although dreams were once powerful, they have been made puerile by the movies, radio and newspapers. Among many betrayals, this one is the worst. (115)

West's emblematic glimpses of the city streets reveal an unconscionable manipulation of the vulnerable: love and beauty are desperately sought by the poor and the ill, staggered after and rummaged for in refuse, but the visual images and words that are mass produced to exploit these desires for profit are sterile fantasies.[12] "Dreams" have been turned into the "business of dreams" while the "Christ dream" has similarly become the "Christ business," retailed by a Lonelyhearts columnist in the daily paper.

The phenomenon *Miss Lonelyhearts* indicts is essentially the same betrayal that *A Farewell to Arms* describes, transposed from the war world to the civilian cityscape. Where Frederic Henry pronounces the rhetoric of patriotism "obscene," the authorial voice of *Miss Lonelyhearts* calls media rhetoric "puerile": both discourses fail the test of accountability. The common denominator of all the novel's voices other than those of the letter writers is this lack of linguistic accountability; each speaker has his or her own verbal code that reflects the mode of escape chosen. For Betty, the Virgin/Mother figure, speech asserts a sincerely felt vision of superficial order: "Whenever he mentioned the letters or Christ, she changed the subject to tell long stories about life on a farm" (111). Her remedy for Miss Lonelyhearts' angst is William James's "healthymindedness"—chicken soup, a visit to the zoo, a weekend in Connecticut, and a conventional middle-class marriage met-

onymically dichotomized into "his job and her gingham apron," the
sanitized world of a Dick and Jane primer. Whereas Betty pursues
a stereotyped normality in keeping with her image of well-scrubbed
innocence, Mary Shrike, a sexual tease, prefers the ersatz exoticism of
the El Gaucho Club. In each case the presentation of self is designed
to elicit the desired response from men: for Betty a marriage proposal,
for Mary the masculine attention that will give her an opportunity to
tell her own lonelyhearts story.

■ Shrike is the novel's most successful speaker in
maintaining a consistent attitude that deflects the serious into word-
play. His description of a letter from an old woman whose son has
just died first caricatures her condition and then renders it comical
with a pun: "She has no stockings and wears heavy boots on her torn
and bleeding feet. She has rheum in her eyes. Have you room in your
heart for her?" (134).[13] Always a self-conscious performer and maker
of fictions, Shrike is distanced from his speech by the imposition of
these inappropriate roles on talk exchange: "No matter how fantas-
tic or excited his speech, he never changed his expression" (72). In
Shrike the withdrawal from language that modern novelists approach
has reached one kind of completion, not silence but a total repudiation
of the linguistic social contract conjoined with a continued commitment to speech. Shrike's word is never his bond (the assumption of
ordinary talk exchange), nor does he observe those conversational principles that enable speakers to interact harmoniously. Instead, like the
bird he is named after, which impales its prey on thorns, Shrike impales his conversational victims on needling words. His conversation
with Miss Lonelyhearts and Miss Farkis in Delehanty's bristles with
such verbal aggression:

"Ah, my young friend!" he shouted. "How do I find you? Brooding again, I take it."
"For Christ's sake, shut up."
Shrike ignored the interruption. "You're morbid, my friend, morbid. Forget the crucifixion, remember the Renaissance. There were
no brooders then." . . .
"To the Renaissance!" he kept shouting. "To the Renaissance! To
the brown Greek manuscripts and mistresses with the great smooth
marbly limbs. . . . But that reminds me, I'm expecting one of my
admirers—a cow-eyed girl of great intelligence." He illustrated the

word *intelligence* by carving two enormous breasts in the air with his hands. "She works in a book store, but wait until you see her behind." (71–72)

Shrike's shouting is a form of bullying that violates the decorum of social discourse. Similarly, the question "How do I find you?" would ordinarily be a variant on the formulaic "How are you," demanding a response—however perfunctory—from the person addressed. But since Shrike has egocentrically shifted the subject to himself and posed the question for rhetorical emphasis, he thwarts the conventions of talk exchange by answering his own question. Miss Lonelyhearts expresses his distaste for the topic forthrightly, but Shrike pays no attention to this unmistakable signal and continues with his performance. His repeated assertion, "You're morbid," contravenes one of Austin's criteria of felicity, namely that the speaker be the proper person to make a particular statement.[14]

In fact Shrike's discourse flouts any number of conditions that speech-act theorists posit. Grice's maxims of quantity, quality, relation, and manner, for example, require that a conversational contribution be of the proper length, be truthful, be suited in terms of content to the talk exchange in progress, and be appropriate in terms of form (how rather than what).[15] None of these typically applies to Shrike's speech because, while it ostensibly occurs as part of a conversation, it is not actually conversational. Disregarding the basic character of talk exchange as a mutually cooperative social interaction in which all parties have the same overall goal, Shrike either ignores the attempt of another speaker to introduce a topic or uses the other speaker's contribution for his own monologic purpose.[16] Denying other speakers their conversational rights, he superimposes the frame of performance upon talk exchange.

Shrike is the novel's author-surrogate, the voice of postmodernism who creates his own world in language, one of arbitrary definition and surrealistic juxtaposition that wittily challenges the claims of reality and ordinary discourse. In Shrike's language, both of word and of gesture, the intellectual and the intangible are reductively transformed into the physical; in this case *intelligence/breasts* and *bookstore/behind* demonstrate the split between the socially acceptable and the real attractions of Miss Farkis. The soul similarly becomes a jungle bird in Shrike's mock sermon, the positioning of which between the newspaper account of a bizarre religious ritual and Miss Lonelyhearts's grisly dream about sacrificing a lamb valorizes the need for violent fantasies. The language of the flanking episodes is the unadorned vehicle of extreme actions, aberrations symptomatic of the modern impossibility of religious normality, whereas Shrike's verbal extravagance foregrounds expression to create an aesthetic construct that exists for its own sake.[17] Like the "calmly decorative" Christ hanging on Miss Lonelyhearts's wall, its religious content is not functional.

■ The common denominator of the novel's verbal codes is dissociation, epitomized by the conversation between Miss Lonelyhearts and Mary Shrike. Mary's clothing and gestures are seductive, but like the romantic atmosphere of the El Gaucho Club they are fake; she speaks, instead, of her mother's death from cancer. Miss Lonelyhearts alternates between passively offering conventional responses to her words—"Tell me about your mother," "You poor kid"—and aggressively challenging her with his own desire—"Sleep with me." The icon presiding over their uncommunicating dialogue is a medal "awarded by the Boston Latin School for first place in the 100 yd. dash" but used by Mary to call attention to her breasts. The medal thus symbolizes conflictive identification with her father's achievement and her mother's sexuality. When Miss Lonelyhearts accompanies her home, she insists on talking, not in order to have a conversation with Miss Lonelyhearts, who is oblivious to her words, but to create the illusion of speech in case her husband is listening behind the door: " 'She died leaning over a table. My father was a portrait painter. He led a very gay life. He mistreated my mother. She had cancer of the breast. She . . .' He tore at her clothes and she began to mumble and repeat herself" (96). Mary's unconnected and obsessive sentences reveal that her fear of the emotional abuse and physical pain that her mother suffered overwhelms her desire to be gay like her father.[18]

There is no normal conversation anywhere in *Miss Lonelyhearts*, no successful linguistic communication beyond the Word that is central to the novel, the plaint of the letter writers to Miss Lonelyhearts, whose problems stem from his receiving so clearly the message that everyone else is able to ignore. Each character has a story in which he is either sufferer or fantasied revenger or both; what is everywhere lacking is a receptive ear for such stories.[19] When characters speak, they tend to be monologists aggressively imposing their own needs without respect for the context or the rights of other listener/speakers. People in this speech are reduced to objects verbally used and abused, as women are in the misogynistic fantasies of the writers in the speakeasy who were "aware of their childishness but did not know how else to avenge themselves" (83). Peter Doyle also uses language to express a hostility now divorced from its occasion, "a jumble of the retorts he had meant to make when insulted and the private curses against fate that experience had taught him to swallow" (124). His gestures are equally dissociated from his speech, either anticipating or lagging behind his words.

In the authorial voice, a language of arresting unpleasantness and lack of feeling whose metaphors transform the living into the inanimate, the natural into the man-made, consciously and consistently enforces distance from the world of the text. Goldsmith's cheeks are like "twin rolls of smooth pink toilet paper"; Shrike's features are "huddled together in a dead, gray triangle"; a singing thrush—potentially a positive image—sounds like "a flute choked with saliva." Miss Lonelyhearts thinks of Mrs. Doyle "as a tent, hair-covered and veined, and of himself as the skeleton in a water closet, the skull and cross-bones on a scholar's bookplate" (26). In the dignified simplicity of their stories the letter writers merit sympathy, but they are shadowy actors in vivid dramas who remain abstractions behind such general designations as *Sick-of-it-All* and *Desperate*. Like the authorial voice Shrike constructs fictions he is detached from, extravagant verbal constructs that he delivers with much energy but no expression. While the language of fiction protects its speakers from the harshness of brute reality *and* from the equally inimical palliations of public language, the price of this linguistic mastery in *Miss Lonelyhearts*, as in much postmodern fiction, appears to be experiential deadness.

Because he can find no words in which to answer his readers and thus justify his own existence, the language of Miss Lonelyhearts is always dissociated from his experience and his aspirations. His visions of the yearned-for order are always arrangements of objects or abstract patterns, "square replacing oblong and being replaced by circle," or his vision of the wasteland, a fenced-in desert of "rust and body dirt" in which his readers "were gravely forming the letters MISS LONELY-HEARTS out of white-washed clam shells, as if decorating the lawn of a rural depot" (97).[20] "Beloved junk" replaces the clam shells and itself gives way, in a later daydream, to the contents of a pawnshop window and then to detritus washed up on shore. The materials become more remote from human possession and at the same time more intractable to human purpose.

Like other protagonists of the modern American novel, Miss Lonelyhearts discovers that some form of public language prevents genuine self-expression; his own efforts to create a religious idiom always fail to penetrate the "thick glove of words" which Shrike has slipped over the image of Christ. Pursuing him from office to speakeasy to sickroom, Shrike's inescapable voice undermines and infiltrates his own speech. Shrike's written words, a parodic prayer to Miss Lonelyhearts as secular deity, preside over the desk where Miss Lonelyhearts struggles to write his column about Christ, who has already been preempted by Shrike as his "particular joke." When Miss Lonelyhearts has the opportunity to deliver his message in person to two letter writers, he finds to his horror that he has "substituted the rhetoric of Shrike" for his own. This happens more often than he acknowledges, for most of Miss Lonelyhearts's verbal encounters create fictive identities from which he is, like Shrike, self-consciously distanced. With Peter Doyle he plays the role of saintly confidant. at Shrike's party he is a rock, and afterwards with Betty he acts the part of a model would-be husband. He bullies an old man in the guise of a "scientist" and imagines himself to be a detective while waiting to meet Fay Doyle in the park. Both of these roles stress an objective examination of data which would purge the encounter with reality of emotional pain. Unlike Shrike's performances, all of Miss Lonelyhearts's roles are versions of an absolute, modes of perfection he yearns for but cannot sustain. He oscillates between these evasive postures of the moment and painful confrontations with reality for which he finds no adequate language.

The resolution is madness. which leads inevitably to a death brought on by his failure to understand a message from the world he wishes to succor: "[Doyle] shouted some kind of warning, but Miss Lonelyhearts continued his charge. He did not understand the cripple's shout and heard it as a cry for help from Desperate, Harold S., Catholic-mother, Broken-hearted, Broad-shoulders, Sick-of-it-all, Disillusioned-with-tubercular-husband" (140). The reprise of Miss Lonelyhearts's petitioners in the novel's final scene reminds us that Doyle's misguided revenge is only an accidental instrument of Miss Lonelyhearts's death. By ignoring Doyle's literal message and responding to his condition as victim, Miss Lonelyhearts reaches out to the world's suffering and is engulfed by it. Betty, who has narrowed her vision to exclude this reality, becomes the unwitting catalyst of Miss Lonelyhearts's destruction, her advance on Doyle blocking his escape and forcing him to enact the fantasy of revenge he has expressed in his letter. In spite of himself, Doyle's words become truth.

Chapter 8

Postmodernist Speech: The Universe of Discourse as a Closed System

What it means to be a man. In a city. In a century. In
transition. In a mass. Transformed by science. Under
organized power. Subject to tremendous controls. In a
condition caused by mechanization. After the late failure
of radical hopes. In a society that was no community and
devalued the person.

SAUL BELLOW, *Herzog*

It comes to pass then that the denizen of a scientific-
technological society finds himself in the strangest of
predicaments: he lives in a cocoon of dead silence, in
which no one can speak to him nor can he reply.

WALKER PERCY, *The Message in the Bottle*

■ Style, or more comprehensively, technique, becomes
the ideology of postmodernist fiction not only as the perfection of art
for art's sake, the fulfillment of the romantic ego of the writer, who
now preempts all attention in propria persona, but as a further, more
radical response to the ongoing thrust of modern technology towards
dehumanization and to the continuing crisis of institutional authority.[1]
Because, as John Barth has written, one of its major premises is the
"used-upness of certain forms or exhaustion of certain possibilities,"[2] a
number of postmodernist texts refuse to impose conventional forms of
literary order upon their fragmentary visions of reality, a step implicit
in modernism. Embracing the disruptions that modernism contained
within a controlling structure, postmodernism employs such staples
of fictive praxis as plot, character, theme, and referential language
playfully or sporadically rather than straightforwardly or "believably."
Mimesis, for example, is not so much abandoned as stylized or paro-
died. It becomes simply one of many techniques serving at authorial
pleasure rather than a sustained position organizing an entire text. Or,

more radically, it becomes a concept irrelevant to a world view "which has effaced the distinction between the real and the imaginary."[3]

Language in the postmodernist text is an end in itself, a purely aesthetic rather than a social instrument, the stuff of a world whose relation to reality is arbitrary. In this respect, too, the postmodern novel carries further the tenets of modernism: it accepts a more complete break with society by mediating public language with literary devices of indirect presentation. Fictive speech in particular becomes the vehicle for the writer's alienation from public language, words that function for him "as something completely reified."[4] Treated ironically, parodically, or sportively, public language is no longer used seriously; its speakers, along with their customary areas of concern, are correspondingly diminished by the textual politics that grants them less space or devalued by their own self-mockery. The devolution of social discourse evident within the still character-oriented modern novel becomes part of a new set of novelistic conventions reflecting this change in the power structure of the text, one that empowers the author's voice and attenuates the voices of characters.[5] To compensate for the diminishing space and significance of characters and their utterances, the authorial voice has enlarged its own province and resources by bringing an array of special discourses and techniques for manipulating them to the construction of the fictive world.

In the modern novel the mode of reaction to society on the part of characters is some form of withdrawal from the arena of public performance into a nonheroic, usually private sphere. In the postmodern novel, such avenues of escape have been closed off or deprived of meaning as alternatives. Where Nick Carraway can leave the East for the simpler life of the Midwest, characters in the postmodern novel find that what Fitzgerald meant by "the East" in *The Great Gatsby* is now everywhere and inescapable—or nowhere, dethematized completely.

As the novelistic enterprise marginalizes characters, their speech ceases to be a means of significant communication, a deemphasizing of propositional content that reveals more starkly than in previous literary periods the nature of conversation as, in Roger Fowler's words, "a negotiation for power."[6] The postmodernist texts that I consider—Kurt Vonnegut's *Breakfast of Champions*, Thomas Pynchon's *The Crying of Lot 49*, and Donald Barthelme's *Snow White*—share the premise that speech is part of this exitless universe, a closed system. Each images a condition of verbal exhaustion in society in which automatic responses, endlessly recycled, have supplanted individual expression to the extent that almost all utterances are predictable and clichéd.[7] "The more probable the message, the less information it gives";[8] consequently, no discourse has the power to bring about action or understanding.

Hunger for the word nevertheless persists. Each novel also records some attempt on the part of a character to escape into communication, or, in terms of the text, to recover referentiality: Dwayne Hoover's desire to be given "the message," Oedipa Maas's quest to solve the mystery of the secret mail delivery system, Snow White's desire to hear new words. These linguistic initiatives to achieve connection and to explain the world, however futile or misguided, are efforts to overcome entropy and to restore the social institution of language to its traditional functions. But in the "chaos of competing voices," to cite Allon White's felicitous phrase, these efforts come to nothing.[9] Their failure suggests that, quite aside from the question of its desirability, postmodernist writers regard such a restoration as impossible. Communication, these texts imply, is a fiction of both literary and real world discourse, one that has long been conventional but is now outmoded.

Fictive characters have always been vulnerable to the afflictions of real life visited upon them by mimetically-inclined authors, but in the postmodern novel they are more vulnerable to authors themselves, who create characters as foolish automatons, parodic stereotypes, inarticulate speakers, or at best, baffled and unheroic searchers for signification/significance: pathetic creatures in texts that allow them neither serious speech nor individualized voices. Instead, the speech of "things" is privileged, the specialized vocabularies of—in White's list— "technology, psychoanalysis, business, administration and military jargon."[10] As Bakhtin notes, only purely mechanistic relationships are not dialogic,[11] and while the postmodern novel preserves a heteroglot surface, it actually dissipates dialogism by reducing the utterances of characters to a dead level of insignificance or meaninglessness— what Fredric Jameson has called "degraded practical speech"[12]—and by contaminating their voices with an all-encompassing authorial discourse. In this way it continues to be identifiable as belonging to the genre of the novel while also suggesting a generic endpoint.

Breakfast of Champions

■ Among contemporary novels *Breakfast of Champions* is the most reminiscent of the Twain who moves from legitimate targets of satire to indict "the damned human race." Although the constant breaking of the fiction defines *Breakfast of Champions* as a postmodernist text, the pervasive satire, overt didacticism, and emphasis on linguistic abuse place it in the tradition of *Adventures of Huckleberry Finn*—less removed from a real society than either *The Crying of Lot 49* or *Snow White*. Vonnegut updates and expands the evils that preoccupied Twain—the oppression of racism, the materialism of the Gilded Age, American imperialism, and the susceptibility to bad ideas disseminated primarily through language—in order to reflect the conditions of American society in the early 1970s: the mass media, consumerism, and—a new area of concern—destruction of the environment. Like Twain, Vonnegut also satirizes unrealistic literary conventions that seem to him to be pernicious influences on actual behavior.

The crucial distinction between *Adventures of Huckleberry Finn* and *Breakfast of Champions* is that the language of Twain's novelistic world, however politicized and inescapable, has meanings that could be rejected or changed: *nigger*, meaning property, could be redefined to mean human being, and had been so redefined officially in American society by the time Twain composed his narrative of a boy's successful struggle to free his intuitive judgments from the bad ideas and language of his culture. A comparable situation is unimaginable in the world that Vonnegut constructs, in which *nigger* refers to a free human being, but active prejudice against black people is widespread, language is too indeterminate to be held accountable to meaning, and all human behavior is determined by forces beyond individual consciousness or control.

A logical evolution from *Miss Lonelyhearts*, *Breakfast of Champions* presents a society whose public language, shaped and disseminated by the media, is either meaningless or misleading. The contact between two speakers is so fleeting and superficial that the minimal obligation of utterance is observed, an exchange of words that merely acknowledges a face-to-face encounter:

> "How's it going, fella?" Governor Rockefeller asked him.
> "About the same," said Kilgore Trout. (106)

There is no meaningful talk exchange because there is no necessity beyond the unfleshed paradigm of greeting and response imposed by the social frame: as a politician the Governor speaks to whoever crosses his path, and as a person spoken to, Trout automatically responds. Even such brief, mechanical exchanges are open to misunderstanding, but given their restricted function, it does not matter.[13]

The text presents speech as a closed system primarily through such utterances without substance. Speech is not vacuous in *Breakfast of Champions* in spite of the efforts of speakers to convey substance; it is vacuous because most of the time there is nothing to convey, and if speakers have expectations beyond the social compulsion to avoid silence, they are expectations that can be satisfied within a closed system, the verbal assertion of self that requires no response or the expression of agreement. (Dwayne Hoover and his employee Vernon Garr would rather talk to their dogs than to other people; Kilgore Trout talks to his parakeet.) The closed system can even absorb a certain amount of eccentricity because the line of least resistance is to absorb it: "It didn't matter much what most people in Midland City said out loud, except when they were talking about money or structures or travel or machinery—or other measurable things. . . . If a person stopped living up to expectations, because of bad chemicals or one thing or another, everybody went on imagining that the person was living up to expectations anyway" (142).[14] The narrator's "measurable things" corresponds to Frederic Henry's "place names and some numbers" in a division of language between precise and imprecise signification, one realm of direct equivalence between word and verifiable thing and another of vague and unreliable referentiality.[15]

But modern and postmodern diverge from this common basis. In the Hemingway text, abstract words are obscene because they are easily misused in ways that have real-life consequences; in the affluent consumer society that *Breakfast of Champions* shares with *The Crying of Lot 49* and *Snow White* they are without consequence, ignorable.[16] Thus, when Dwayne Hoover begins to speak and act inappropriately, no one assumes that he is insane because this would be a troublesome assumption. Dwayne's "capital of authority," which includes linguistic capital,[17] legitimates his behavior up to the point of violent breakdown. Since the people who remark his strangeness are his employees, they view his aberrations in the light of his status and the privileges it confers: the bellhops regard his loud singing in the Holiday Inn as a right of his proprietorship; his secretary interprets his criticism of the sales manager's wardrobe as the boss's right to inflict his bad humor on a subordinate. Dwayne's ecolalia, a symbol of the condition of contemporary utterance, is simply absorbed into the familiar linguistic sludge that characterizes all speech: the waitress who hears it is so conscious of her own powerlessness vis-à-vis Dwayne's capital of authority and so insecure about her own ability to speak "correctly" that she apologizes for her language rather than questioning his. Throughout the novel people are concerned with grammatical correctness rather than propositional content.[18]

Because of such insecurity about language, most white adults in Midland City "kept their sentences short and their words simple" (138), but this verbal parsimony does not eliminate miscommunication. When Francine Pefko responds to Dwayne's accusations with the simple assertion "You're my man," the authorial voice explains that it "meant that she was willing to agree about anything with Dwayne, to do anything for him, no matter how difficult or disgusting, to think up nice things to do for him that he didn't even notice, to die for him if necessary, and so on" (160)—a wealth of meaning in marked contrast to the poverty of her words. What it suggests to Dwayne is a sharply different set of connotations: the responsibilities of caring for her materially in an expensive fashion.

An underlying lack of imagination clothes itself in the convenient language of advertising, now the common currency of public language.[19] The title slogan, "breakfast of champions," creates a signification intended to sell a cereal product by identifying it with excellence in sports, an arbitrary and misleading association that masquerades as a word-to-world fit but is actually world-to-word.[20] The cocktail waitress's saying "breakfast of champions" whenever she serves a martini changes the signified to a product presumably more appealing to adults, a tongue-in-cheek defamiliarization that does not alter the arbitrary and untruthful claims of the commercial signification although it perhaps makes its real nature more apparent. Whether the signified is a cereal or alcohol, the communication is inaccurate; but at the same time, neither assertion matters *as* communication. Most labels (including book titles), the text implies, are equally arbitrary, yet this disjunction is unimportant because by now no one expects a logical relationship between language and reality.

All of the conversation in *Breakfast of Champions* is doomed to be pseudo-conversation because the characters, unlike Huck Finn, lack the linguistic innocence or conviction or imagination to eschew public language. Moreover, the universal media discourse—fuzzy, glamorous, and convenient—is more subtle than the polarizing vocabularies of racism or political ideology. Milo Maritimo seems delighted to meet Kilgore Trout, but he can express himself only in television clichés: "Oh, Mr. Trout . . . . teach us to sing and dance and laugh and cry. We've tried to survive so long on money and sex and envy and real estate and football and basketball and automobiles and television and alcohol—on sawdust and broken glass!" (233). Milo's hackneyed romantic metaphors transform Trout's odd appearance and disclaiming words into a fulfillment of the expected, a process similar to the verbal justification of Dwayne's behavior. In the texts of modernism, words themselves will point to the inexpressible and to the characters' awareness of it, but Milo speaks on and on without any realization that his facile clichés have no referents and convey nothing beyond the inchoate desire to find a saviour.

Since most talk exchange is empty, most propositional content trivial or false, the characters in the novel (including Vonnegut himself)[21] harbor a desire to encounter real authority and substance, to receive the Word. Often what passes for this truth are merely advertising claims—"You can always trust Dwayne"—or statistics that establish norms in all areas; hence the penile measurements that are comically gratuitous to the narrative and suggest not only the pervasive anxiety about masculinity in our society but the extent to which norms of quantification govern all judgments.[22]

The message that Dwayne Hoover mistakes for truth, like the omnipresent commercial messages that dominate communication, is false and unregenerative. In Trout's book *Now It Can Be Told*, the one creature in the universe with free will, "The Man," has nothing to express. It hardly matters that the Creator never knows in advance what The Man will say when what he does say is "Wouldn't you really rather drive a Buick" or "cheese." Dwayne has nothing to say either: his sense of isolation and anomie prompts him to a rampage of violence, a one-way communicative street that connects with others only physically.

Not surprisingly, the one genuine message of the text, Kilgore Trout's answer to the question scrawled on the lavatory wall of a pornographic movie theater, is communicated to the reader alone. Since Trout has nothing to write with, he can respond only mentally to the question "What is the purpose of life?" with the answer "To be the eyes and ears and conscience of the Creator of the Universe, you fool" (67). The epithet of address reflects Trout's feeling that even if such a message could be articulated, people would be unreceptive to it—although they welcome a simplistic version delivered by the painter Rabo Karabekian. In defending his minimalist creation with an elaborate intellectual rationale, Karabekian employs a strategy that has much in common with those of Twain's king and duke, whose empty eloquence in the service of their own profit overwhelms their uneducated targets much as Karabekian's glib rhetoric overcomes the objections of his unsophisticated critics.

In remarking that a five-year-old could have painted a better picture, the waitress utters the equivalent of "The Emperor has no clothes." But where the speaking of truth shatters the illusion in the fairy tale, and ultimately the king and the duke are brought to account in *Adventures of Huckleberry Finn*, in the unverifiable realm of aesthetic value a confidence man need never fear exposure. The enthusiasm that Karabekian inspires springs more from his rhetorical skill and his audience's need for authority than from his explanation.

When Karabekian addresses the hostile group, he has already revealed himself to be a cynical manipulator who defines truth as "some crazy thing my neighbor believes" (209) and mocks the waitress with a pretense of interest in her anecdotes. His defense of his painting contains two slighting references to her, in one of which a waitress is interchangeable with a cockroach. That the essential point about any creature is its "immaterial core," its "I am," its "awareness," is hardly an original idea of Rabo Karabekian's, and his assertion that its perfect embodiment in paint will always be an unwavering band of light belongs with the uncreative uniformity and numbing banality of the novel's world. Art, too, is subject to entropy, and Karabekian's speech, the longest in *Breakfast of Champions*, perfectly encapsulates the deterioration of both language and creative conceptualization as well as the pervasive anxiety about value in a world of commodity fetishism.

No one responds more enthusiastically to Karabekian's explanation than the character Vonnegut, a measure of the gullibility that Trout's science fiction exempla illustrate repeatedly and which a number of commentators on the text have shared.[23] The credulousness of Vonnegut as character contaminates the reliability of Vonnegut as author, but the "unified creative will" directing the text has clearly contrived this episode as an ersatz spiritual climax, the only kind possible in the world constructed by the text.[24] The obvious parallel with the insane Dwayne Hoover, yearning for just such a revelation of meaning, hardly inspires a belief in its authenticity.

By maintaining authorial privilege over one of the characters in the novel's final conversation, Vonnegut does not seriously question the distinction between actuality and fiction so much as sport with the literary conventions that interdict such flagrant illusion-breaking. Enjoying obvious advantages over Kilgore Trout, "Vonnegut" monopolizes speech while Trout responds noncommittally until a display of authorial omnipotence convinces him that he is speaking to his creator. Then, when he has an opportunity for the momentous discourse that other characters have repeatedly desired, that Ahab sought monomaniacally to the point of destruction, Trout can only cry out, "Make me young!" (295). A comically infelicitous directive, these last spoken words of the novel assimilate Trout to other futile speakers of the twentieth-century American novel whose unrealistic desires are governed by and expressed in media language.

The Crying of Lot 49

■ Oedipus answered the riddle in a brilliant verbal performance that caused the sphinx to kill herself and the city of Thebes to welcome him as a hero. Oedipa Maas, the protagonist of Thomas Pynchon's *The Crying of Lot 49*, cannot answer her riddle; she can only recontextualize it.[25] The brilliant performance here is Pynchon's alone, but unlike Oedipus's, it is one of open-ended signification. The sphinx's riddle, although couched in a trope to make it appear obscure, ultimately yields a precise meaning to the hearer who recognizes its nonliteral code. In *The Crying of Lot 49* the existence of a secret network of true communication, like the existence of Vheissu, the fabled land of Pynchon's earlier novel *V.*, is neither verified nor disproved. Crouching over the text like the sphinx on the rock outside of Thebes, the Trystero is an image of meaningfulness that never reveals its meaning.[26]

■ Like most postmodernist novels, *The Crying of Lot 49* partially abrogates the conventional contract between reader and text by defamiliarizing the familiar elements of traditional fiction.[27] The title, for example, will be intelligible only at the novel's end, and then its intelligibility is too limited to be genuinely informative: rather than identifying a major character or theme, "the crying of lot 49" refers to an event that takes place after the book ends. This potentially clarifying event is thus proffered as a traditional climax, but the novel then ends preclimactically without dispelling its mysteries. *The Crying of Lot 49* also subverts the bildungsroman process of acquiring knowledge. What is learned in the space of Oedipa's quest is simply the nature of the problem; the familiar world is defamiliarized to reveal its strangeness, but it is not reconstituted into new orders of coherence and meaning. What Jameson has called "random pluralism" perfectly describes the novel, which images "a coexistence not even of multiple and alternate worlds so much as of unrelated fuzzy sets and semiautonomous sub-systems whose overlap is perceptually maintained like hallucinogenic depth planes in a space of many dimensions." [28]

In a curious way *The Crying of Lot 49* is a postmodernist rewriting of *Moby-Dick*, an exploration into the nature and meaning of its universe—in this case that of twentieth-century technology, whose matrix, inevitably, is California. The elusive Trystero, like the whale, is seemingly omnipresent and omnipotent, a symbol that once understood will unlock the secret workings of the world. But there is no climactic confrontation with this adversary, who is even more hidden and inscrutable than the powers Ahab addresses. Nor is there a true Ahabean hero. Oedipa Maas is neither aggressive nor vengeful, but her idea of a vast conspiracy organized for her benefit is as egocentric, or paranoid, as Ahab's personalistic universe, and her quest becomes as much a single-minded preoccupation as his. Like Ahab she sees the potential for concealed meaning everywhere and dreads the conclusion of meaninglessness: "Behind the hieroglyphic streets there would either be a transcendent meaning, or only the earth" (181).[29] Still, Oedipa is more akin to Ishmael, a wanderer through the mysterious world observing and ultimately accepting it, although the fragmented nature of modern existence precludes the salvation of community that Ishmael embraces.

The Crying of Lot 49 is a structure whose parts replicate its whole, itself a tantalizing Nefastis Machine that promises but does not deliver "information" to the reader/sensitive. Communication may be the key, as Nefastis proclaims, but the text is a model of communication failure. Its series of thwarted messages, disjunctions, and incompletions that range from the inevitable distortions of technology to the intentional secrecy of conspiracy could serve as the perfect exemplum of Norbert Wiener's assertion that "as efficient as communications' mechanisms become, they are still . . . subject to the overwhelming tendency for entropy to increase, for information to leak in transit."[30]

Behavior in the novel is subsumed under the twin poles of entropy and paranoia, which according to the text's idiosyncratic definition represent uniformity as death and fantasy or deviance as life. The official world that communicates through public language is entropic in its valorizing of uniformity and dehumanized technology. Whether or not a sinister design governs this world, certainly a number of characters believe that they have reasons for secrecy in their affairs. As Oedipa comes to agree, paranoia represents creativity, possibly the only escape from an arid, humdrum normality equated with the death of individuality.

The relationship of consciousness to word, and secondarily of word to signified, is one aspect of the text's own inquiry into communication. At one end of the linguistic spectrum are the Puritans, "utterly devoted, like literary critics, to the Word" (156), while at the other end is the director Randolph Driblette, who "felt hardly any responsibility toward the word" (152). The distinction is between denotation and connotation, or between a restricted, dogmatic, textual reading and a contextual approach that sees the word as only a point of departure. The Puritans invest authority in the "direct, epileptic Word," a practice that assumes the existence of an uncorrupted text. Driblette elevates above a demythologized word "the invisible field surrounding the play, its spirit" (152). When he asks Oedipa why everyone is "so interested in texts," his assumption is that all texts are corrupt. The "direct, epileptic Word" has been lost, its original energy broken up into fragments of discourse that cannot unite society into a harmonious whole: the Puritan vision of the city on a hill obeying the Word of God.

Words either organize and explain the world, or they are merely the pasteboard masks of *Moby-Dick* that teasingly hint at but finally conceal reality. Like the universe of *Moby-Dick*, that of *The Crying of Lot 49* constantly suggests but never confirms the existence of transcendent meaning. The "gem-like 'clues'" that Oedipa painstakingly accumulates are not enough, do not compensate for the loss of the Word, do not cohere into signification.

The primal unity of discourse has been irrevocably shattered, at least in part by the failure of society to accommodate diversity, a failure that drives underground into an alternate system of communication any sort of deviation: the disgruntled inventors who perceive themselves to be exploited by industry, the Inamorati Anonymous, the Mexican "CIA" anarchists, the Peter Pinguid Society, and countless isolates who fit nowhere in the ranks of society. All may be leading radically split lives, communicating their real concerns through W.A.S.T.E., an acronym appropriate to their peripheral status, "whilst reserving their lies, recitations of routine, arid betrayals of spiritual poverty, for the official government delivery system" (170).[31] Public life may thus be an elaborate sham, a false rhetoric masking private lives of counter-cultural nonconformity and concealing its own insufficiency. Yet this remains only a hypothesis. The inconclusive communication that does take place simply dramatizes the need for an unverifiable universe of true discourse.

■ The mundane reality of Kinneret, where Oedipa Maas is a typical middle-class housewife, appears to be a solid and knowable world of familiar objects and activities: lasagna, television news commentators, the latest *Scientific American*, Tupperware parties, shopping, making dinner: "a fat deckful of days which seemed . . . more or less identical" (11). Pynchon's style is always heavily specific yet not reassuring for all of its detail; the more physical texture his fictive universe acquires, the more problematic and frightening it becomes. The objects that thickly populate this world can come to violent and menacing life, like the caroming aerosol can in a motel bathroom, but even an ordinary environment such as the Yoyodyne factory is passively ominous: "The air-conditioning hummed on, IBM typewriters chiggered away, swivel chairs squeaked, fat reference manuals were slammed shut, rattling blueprints folded and refolded, while high overhead the long silent fluorescent bulbs glared merrily; all with Yoyodyne was normal" (87).

Into this seeming normality the announcement that Oedipa has been named executor of a former boyfriend's will introduces the quest or question of the novel. Attempting to solve the mystery of the will, Oedipa will reevaluate her world, see her identical suburban days as an unsatisfying partial existence, and drift into isolation. Like Oedipus, she will acquire a terrible knowledge, but not, as in his case, a knowledge that explains the signification of enigmatic signs and stabilizes the text of the world. Oedipus belatedly discovers that his role in a system of family relationships is not single, as he had assumed, but double; he is husband and son to the same woman, son and murderer of the same man, father and brother to the same children. One role has been superimposed over the other, but both are real; one, however unfortunate and proscribed, does not cancel out the other. Oedipus becomes truly, if horrifyingly, enlightened. In *The Crying of Lot 49* there is no such definite revelation or firm knowledge because the penetration of one level of ambiguous signification simply betokens another indeterminate field: uncertainty of voice exemplifies uncertainty of identity, which in turn reflects the fundamental ambiguity of the world. There is no striking through the pasteboard mask to uncover reality.

Uncertainty of voice extends to most of the novel's characters, who are usually disembodied voices, fleetingly heard. When Oedipa's psychiatrist, Dr. Hilarius, calls her, "he sounded like Pierce doing a Gestapo officer" (16). (Later he is revealed to be a former Gestapo officer.) Pierce did any number of voices, none of which was the authentic Pierce Invararity, whose name suggests a process of arriving at the truth.[32] It is never clear who Pierce actually was: he exists in the text only as a series of assumed voices remembered by Oedipa and as a tangle of mysterious business enterprises left behind at his death.

The existence of other characters is equally unstable—or fictitious. The California rock musicians Oedipa meets, the Paranoids, are recreating themselves as an English group. Dr. Hilarius, too, has reinvented himself to escape his past as a Nazi doctor. And Metzger, Oedipa's co-executor, describes a condition of role change that resembles an infinite regress:

> "A lawyer in a courtroom, in front of any jury, becomes an actor, right? . . . Me, I'm a former actor who became a lawyer. They've done the pilot film of a TV series, in fact, based loosely on my career, starring my friend Manny Di Presso, a one-time lawyer who quit his firm to become an actor. Who in this pilot plays me, an actor become a lawyer reverting periodically to being an actor." (33)

Oedipa can never be certain whether she is talking to the lawyer acting or the actor playing the role of lawyer, and while Metzger himself confesses to uncertainty about his identity, this may simply be part of his approach to her: "all words."

The instability and unknowability of identity is one of the difficulties in evaluating communications, from the initial problem of Pierce's will—is it a straightforward or deceptive document—to the final non-encounter: would the mysterious bidder be an agent of the Trystero or not? When Oedipa infelicitously asks Dr. Hilarius, "Do I trust you?" and concludes that she does not (17), the issue is once more whether or not another speaker's intentions are benevolent or exploitative. Oedipa's "trusted family lawyer," whose preoccupation with the fictive lawyer Perry Mason is a typical Pynchonesque eccentricity, hastily conceals some notes when she enters his office:

> "You might have been one of Perry Mason's spies," said Roseman. After thinking a moment he added, "Ha, ha."
> "Ha, ha," said Oedipa. They looked at each other. (19)

Whether Roseman distrusts Oedipa, is somewhat suspicious, or is merely joking cannot be determined from this unadorned dialogue, but throughout the novel suspicion is the dominant response to conversational gambits.[33]

"In conversation," Roger Fowler writes, "any appearance of intimacy, solidarity and co-operation is generally illusory,"[34] an extreme formulation that accurately describes the talk exchanges of *The Crying of Lot 49*. Fictive speech has traditionally maintained the conventions of polite discourse, but Oedipa's encounters are invariably with speakers who, for whatever reason—sensible caution or paranoid delusion—will not cooperate in talk exchange. Since she is both a stranger and an outsider, the reluctance of some of her putative informants concerns the issue of trust and identification, while for others a lack of real knowledge is probable. Oedipa's own inability to articulate what she is looking for contributes to the ineffective communication of most of her conversations:

> "What then?" Metzger challenged. . . .
> "I don't know," she said, a little desperate. "Metzger, don't harass me. Be on my side."
> "Against whom?" inquired Metzger. . . .
> "I want to see if there's a connection. I'm curious."
> "Yes, you're curious," Metzger said. (76)

Neither question of the conversation is answered; the exchange probes Oedipa's confusion and establishes her failure to fulfill the necessary conditions of her speech acts: the illocutionary intent of her utterance—"Be on my side"—is too vaguely expressed to gain the compliance of her less than fully committed associate. Since only we ourselves can speak with authority about our own feelings, Metzger's reiteration of Oedipa's remark is merely an echo, a version of empty closure.[35]

Oedipa's ambivalence about the goal of her quest also contributes to conversational hiatuses. Seeking an uncorrupted text of the Wharfinger play, she inquires for the book at Zapf's Bookstore:

> "It's been very much in demand," Zapf told her. The skull on the cover watched them, through the dim light.
> Did he only mean Driblette? She opened her mouth to ask, but didn't. It was to be the first of many demurs. (65)

Oedipa is equally fearful of an overdetermined world in which everything harbors a secret and perhaps sinister meaning, essentially the world of Ahab, and a void of signification in which there are no messages or meanings. Thus whatever answer Zapf might give to her unspoken question would be menacing, although only in the same unfocused way that the casually intruded description of the skull on the book's cover is portentously charged.

The prevailing inanity of the novel's speech carries a greater comic weight than the same vacuous language in James or Hemingway. Instructing Oedipa to "just be herself" in the radio interview following Dr. Hilarius's breakdown, Mucho then addresses her as "Mrs. Edna Mosh." He begins routinely:

> "How do you feel about this terrible thing?"
> "Terrible," said Oedipa.
> "Wonderful," said Mucho. (139)

Mucho's response is absurd as an unexpected positive in a speech situation calling for a negative, i.e., a doctor gone mad and become dangerous, but its meaning is nevertheless clear as a comment on the metalinguistic priority of ritualized format over propositional content and of media image over real event. What is "wonderful" is that Oedipa is reacting appropriately to the situation and to the expectations of the listening audience about such events.

Ironically, the Maas' conversation as husband and wife is no more satisfactory as communication than their formalized exchange as interviewer and subject. The reiterative and aimless speech in *The Crying of Lot 49* is another manifestation of entropy, a closed system in which the endless recycling of predictable words in their expected conversational slots substantiates a loss of verbal and mental energy.

All of the novel's conversations are futile, either playfully gratuitous, circular, or incomplete, usually sliding quietly into anticlimax:

> "No husband, no shrink?"
> "Both," Oedipa said, "but they don't know."
> "You can't tell them?"
> She met his eyes' void for a second after all, and shrugged. (112)

Oedipa no longer has a common language with those institutional pillars—husband, psychiatrist, lawyer—but she is equally unable to communicate with the alienated of W.A.S.T.E. Stanley Koteks disregards her attempt at a password, "Kirby sent me," and the old sailor for whom she feels a nurturing affection ends by roughly dismissing her.

The authorial voice usually overwhelms the brief and incomplete utterances of the characters, creating a Jamesian aura of the unspoken and interdicted. When a story is told, it is typically begun by a character and continued in indirect discourse:

> She knew the pattern because it had happened a few times already, though Oedipa had been most scrupulously fair about it, mentioning the practice only once, in fact, another three in the morning and out of a dark dawn sky, asking if he wasn't worried about the penal code. "Of course," said Mucho after awhile, that was all; but in his tone of voice she thought she heard more, something between annoyance and agony. (46)

The burden of the episode is carried by the narrative, which surrounds and envelopes an utterance that would be meaningless without the description of how it was uttered. The example is parodic James, and also paradigmatic: the novel's banal speech relies heavily on the authorial voice to give it what limited meaning it has. In this case signification moves uncertainly over the expanse of possibility between annoyance and agony.

In *The Sun Also Rises* the narrator patiently allows Mike to tell his story about the medals in his own voice and in the awkward style suited to his character. Where Pynchon's characters speak at length, they do so in voices indistinguishable from that of the narrative. Barricaded in his office, Dr. Hilarius conducts a question-and-answer dialogue with Oedipa in the simple phrases of ordinary talk, but his long monologue about his past becomes increasingly Pynchonesque and remote from speech: "Buchenwald, according to Freud, once the light was let in, would become a soccer field, fat children would learn flower-arranging and solfeggio in the strangling rooms. At Auschwitz the ovens would be converted over to petit fours and wedding cakes, and the V-2 missiles to public housing for the elves" (137–38). Eclipsing the character Hilarius, the authentic voice of the narrative creates arresting combinations of history and fantasy that exhibit what Shoshana Felman calls "the pleasure of linguistic *doing*."[36] *The Crying of Lot 49* is finally revealed to us as an example of another world that collides with the agreed-upon reality of society, an exit of the imagination which, like the W.A.S.T.E. letters, is made of words.

Oedipa's final effort to understand through speech, a naked plea for help addressed to the Inamorato Anonymous in the San Francisco bar, is repulsed with still another cryptic reiteration:

"It's too late," he said.
"For me?"
"For me." Before she could ask what he meant, he'd hung up. (177)

This pattern of frustration—enlightenment offered, then denied—informs all of Oedipa's conversations and the text's verbal strategies as well.

Oedipa is thrown back upon her own resources for making meaning, aware that there is no way to verify her hypotheses but certain that if the Trystero conspiracy does not exist, it is necessary to invent it through some private paranoia, some means of expanding life beyond its social boundaries, its mundanity. For everyone in the technological wasteland of America desperately wants to make contact with "that magical Other who would reveal herself out of the roar of relays, monotone litanies of insult, filth, fantasy, love whose brute repetition must someday call into being the trigger for the unnameable act, the recognition, the Word" (180). *Act, recognition, Word:* these free-floating signs toward which the sentence moves climactically through a typical Pynchonesque catalogue of contemporary detritus both promise and thwart signification, a reminder of the closed system of the self-referential text and the pleasure of the writer writing.

Snow White

■ Pynchon's postmodernist subversion of the familiar form that structures *The Crying of Lot 49*, the quest cum bildungsroman narrative, is not fully experienced until the novel's end denies the expectation of resolution that the narrative structure has teasingly proffered. In Donald Barthelme's *Snow White*, a quintessential post-modernist text, the intention of the fiction is never unclear: from the beginning the text subjects actuality and literary conventions to kaleido-scopic distortions. Like Pynchon's style, Barthelme's contains a heavy weight of contemporary phenomena, but where things have an aura of menace in Pynchon, asserting vague claims over human space and preempting attention, in Barthelme, as Richard Gilman writes, they are "abstracted into comic helplessness, deprived, by being turned into *mere* language, of their tyranny as fashionable facts.[37] "Abstracted," these bits of cultural detritus are recycled and oddly juxtaposed in ways that suggest collage, a technique in which, Barthelme states, "unlike things are stuck together to make, in the best case, a new reality."[38] In its insistence on the material, *Snow White* could have been written to illustrate Jameson's proposition that "culture itself is one of those things whose fundamental materiality is now for us not merely evident but quite inescapable."[39] Language and other aspects of contemporary life have become so lacking in individual value and imaginative energy that only the extreme defamiliarization of Barthelme's technique can reanimate them.

Pynchon's novel predictably reduces the role of speech, but although the narrative voice is more audible, the territories of the two forms of discourse are conventionally demarcated.[40] Barthelme's practice is more radical and more overt: he enlarges the province of speech while effectively blurring its distinctiveness from narration. Most of what is presented as speech in *Snow White* is actually interior monologue with the characteristics of indirect rather than direct discourse; there is little talk exchange. Moreover, speech is not set apart in the custom-ary manner but is instead buried in paragraphs of narrative while the unstabilized authorial voice moves erratically between first and third person.

The effect of these departures from traditional praxis is to minimize both the special condition and the special contribution of any particular aspect: the elements of fiction become to some degree interchangeable, like the dwarfs themselves and like so many of the words.[41] The sub-stitution of *horsewife* for *housewife* prompts Jerome Klinkowitz to ob-serve that deadened terms can be brought back to life by little twists of defamiliarization."[42] On the contrary, the defamiliarization fails to reenergize *housewife;* it emphasizes that it does not matter whether Snow White calls herself a housewife or a horsewife: there is always "some other word that would do as well . . . or maybe a number of them" (96). Since the language of ordinary speech is so uniform, most speakers can use it unthinkingly on most occasions: " 'That's true Roger,' Kevin said a hundred times. Then he was covered with embarrassment. 'No I mean that's true Clem. Excuse me. Roger is somebody else. You're not Roger. You're Clem. That's true Clem' " (67). The confusion of address, comically prolonged by its repetition "a hundred times," is socially embarrassing but functionally meaningless since the same bland remark can be made as fittingly to Clem as to Roger.[43]

In *The Crying of Lot 49*, as I have already observed, the voices of the characters sometimes merge with the authorial voice, as if the author has become impatient with his characters' limitations and preempts their discourse with bursts of eloquence beyond their capabilities. Barthelme's more extreme practice continually mixes these voices. When Bill says, "I had in mind launching a three-pronged assault, but the prongs wandered away seduced by fires and clowns" (53), the author's own wit infuses and transforms his character's clichés to remind us that the only voice to heed in the text is his.

Snow White's version of entropy is the "trash phenomenon," a situation in the near future when everything has become trash: "Now at such a point, you will agree, the question turns from a question of disposing of this 'trash' to a question of appreciating its qualities, because, after all, it's 100 per-cent, right? And there can no longer be any question of 'disposing' of it, because it's all there is, and we will simply have to learn how to 'dig' it" (97). Language, too, participates in this condition, being increasingly overtaken by such forms of linguistic trash as "stuffing" and "sludge," filler words and the drag that they impose upon the intention to communicate.

By its own logic then, *Snow White* is itself trash since there is no other possibility in the closed world that the text posits. Traditional forms of literature—a great fairy tale like the original "Snow White," an epic poem, a national novel—are no longer viable, although they can still be made use of, incorporated into what Brian McHale calls a "*heterotopia,* the disorder that is made up of fragments of a number of incommensurable orders."[44] The issue now, *Snow White* implies, is between different kinds of trash: postmodernist metafictions like *Snow White* on one hand, perhaps harlequin romances and other genres of mass appeal on the other. In Gerald Graff's words, "Barthelme's irony toward official institutional, professional, and artistic jargon does not stop at these targets but spreads and envelops all language, including Barthelme's own authorial prose."[45] Graff concludes that literature now finds itself "virtually deprived of uncontaminated language,"[46] yet this is misleading in its failure to recognize the imaginative use to which this language can be put. The status of *Snow White* as aesthetic artifact, its self-reflexiveness and sense of performance, forestalls an equation of the text with the banal materials from which it is made. The collage is more than the sum of its parts: "It's an *itself*," Barthelme says, "if it's successful: Harold Rosenberg's 'anxious object,' which doesn't know whether it's a work of art or a pile of junk."[47]

Graff's observations restate those of the *Snow White* narrator on trash: it is a given of the situation that there is no "uncontaminated language," and therefore the authorial voice is necessarily implicated in the debasement of language insofar as it employs language *straightforwardly and unself-consciously*. It is no longer possible to make a separate peace, proscribing a certain limited vocabulary: Hemingway's abstract words or West's media rhetoric. Jane's letter to Mr. Quistgaard, in which she threatens to "inject discourse" from her universe of discourse into his, diluting and ultimately replacing his own language, illustrates the potential of language as an infiltrating and corrupting agent. Her conclusion—"You are, essentially, in my power" (46)—is a reminder of the individual speaker's helplessness to purify and police language or to escape it.

The text of *Snow White* performs an analogous contamination. By its self-conscious absorption of critical discourse it collapses the distinction between criticism and fiction, depriving criticism of discovery and reducing it to repetition. Rather than transforming the fiction into the stuff of criticism, the critic can only repeat the text's remarks, remarks made banal by their prior usage, in the same mode of critical discourse that the text itself employs.

More than any other text, *Snow White* is an encyclopedia of postmodernist fictive speech and a reflection of real spoken language—the redundancy, repetition, formula, and lack of fluency that novelists formerly excluded in the interest of telling a story or revealing character. In keeping with the pervasive trash phenomenon, these aspects of speech are now foregrounded and parodically intensified so that little else remains. Talk exchange in the world of *Snow White* is the giving and receiving of clichés: " 'He is certainly a well-integrated personality, Paul,' she said. 'Yes,' we said. 'He makes contact, you must grant him that.' 'Yes,' we said" (49). The uttering of and acquiescing to clichés is the only paradigm of successful communication in *Snow White* because the same lack of substance that precludes meaning insures agreement.

As long as the dwarfs can think of their new shower curtain as "adequate" or "nice" or even "splendid," they are content, because these vague positives demand nothing beyond perfunctory agreement —neither action nor controversy. Once a "professor of esthetics," i.e., an expert, describes their property as "the best-looking shower curtain in town" (123), the truth of the statement becomes important, but they find that its verification presents "a thousand problems." Ridding themselves of the difficulty by expunging the statement is equally impossible because words, once uttered, quickly move beyond the control of any single consciousness. The comfortable, unverifiable cliché of public language is thus preferable to the individualized utterance that entails the dilemma and responsibility of evaluation. The shower curtain that is "nice" is satisfactory without being singular, a locus of easy agreement among speakers, but if it is officially proclaimed the best-looking shower curtain in the entire city, then the issue of its status cries out for resolution, and opportunities for divisiveness multiply.

Even the most banal exchanges lead to misunderstanding. Dan mishears *bed* when Henry says *bend*, and a direct question elicits an unexpected answer in keeping with Ogden and Richards's pessimistic contention that speakers seldom use words in the same way:[48]

> "What sort of actors?"
> "Do you mean good or bad?"
> "I didn't mean that but what is the answer?"
> "Bad, I'm afraid," the chief actor said, and we turned away. That wasn't what we'd wanted to hear. Everything was complex and netlike. (154)[49]

Each speaker pursues an individual rather than a common agenda, not because of the endemic distrust and desire to conceal that are present in *The Crying of Lot 49* but simply because common ground of any sort seems inconceivable. As it did in *The Crying of Lot 49*, reiteration in *Snow White* often indicates a solipsistic failure of language to bridge the gap between speakers:

"All right Jane get into the car." "Hogo you are making stains on
my new white-duck love seat with pillows of white-on-white Indian
crewel!" . . . "That's all you know Hogo isn't it. How to take a thing
that was white, and stain it until it is black. That's a pretty strong
metaphor of what you would like to do with me, too. I understand.
If you think for one moment that your capability of staining the
thing you love has escaped me, from the very beginning, you have
grossly misperceived our situation. Get out of here Hogo forever!"
"All right Jane get into the car." (113)

Hogo's banal directive exemplifies what Herbert Marcuse calls "the
closed language," which "does not demonstrate and explain—it communicates decision, dictum, command,"[50] enacting the power differ-
ential between Hogo and Jane by literally enclosing and disregarding
her lengthy speech. Hogo's directive can be translated into action because it expresses his capital of authority: he satisfies the preparatory
conditions necessary for the performance of this speech act while Jane's
verbally stronger directive remains on the level of words alone, an infelicitous speech act.

Discourse in *Snow White* is closed, however, in more than Marcuse's
sense. It is a closed system because it demonstrates a linguistic exhaustion or complacency that is one facet of a pervasive mental numbness:

"Snow White," we said, "why do you remain with us? here? in
this house?" There was a silence. Then she said: "It must be laid,
I suppose, to a failure of the imagination. I have not been able to
imagine anything better." *I have not been able to imagine anything
better.* We were pleased by this powerful statement of our essential
mutuality. (59)

There are no truly powerful statements in the direct discourse of the
novel, but the power of the underlying myth informs *Snow White*'s
parodic fragments and can occasionally be directly glimpsed:

WHAT SNOW WHITE REMEMBERS:

THE HUNTSMAN

THE FOREST

THE STEAMING KNIFE

The vivid particularity of these significant images momentarily reproaches the enervation and role-playing of the world of *Snow White*

and the nonreferentiality of its language; at the same time these are allusions to pop culture, drawn from Walt Disney's feature cartoon film *Snow White and the Seven Dwarfs*, rather than unmediated natural images.

With their contemporary penchant for self-analysis, all of the characters find their lives lacking, and all express the hackneyed yearnings of their society for "more," for "something better." Yet none has a tenable vision, and their dreams are static, bogged down in the usual banal formulae that everyone can agree to: " 'Most life is unextraordinary,' Clem said to Snow White, in the kitchen. 'Yes,' Snow White said, 'I know. Most life is unextraordinary looked at with a woman's desperate eye too it might interest you to know' " (21). The possibility of overcoming the unextraordinary is a major reason for speaking, yet the speech it yields is always banal.

One of the manifestations of Snow White's dissatisfaction is a desire to escape from this closed discourse of predictability and exhaustion: "Oh I wish there were some words in the world that were not the words I always hear!" (6). The dwarfs respond with "things that were more or less satisfactory, or at least adequate, to serve the purpose, for the time being" (6), a metastatement of conversational sludge that emphasizes the impossibility of realizing Snow White's wish. The random words they speak, while answering her requirement of not belonging to their usual discourse, are useless by virtue of their very lack of integration into meaningful dialogue.

The designs of the speakers come to nothing because they inhabit a circumscribed verbal universe in which they are servants rather than masters of their clichés. The authorial voice transcends this linguistic trash by reframing it within a revitalizing comic context.

Conclusion

> The Apostle tells us that in the beginning was the Word.
> He gives no assurance as to the end.
>
> GEORGE STEINER, *Language and Silence*

■ In the endless arguing over chaws of tobacco in the Brickville episode of *Adventures of Huckleberry Finn*, one sorry loafer says to another: "*You* give him a chaw, did you? so did your sister's cat's grandmother" (188). The subject is trivial, but the speech is both convincingly realistic and pungently energetic, the utterance of a voice that Twain respects at the same time as he mocks the speaker's tobacco-centered worldview. As banal as this character's reality is, he can articulate it without banality. Verbal vitality at least partially redeems even those characters in *Huck Finn* who employ some form of deceptive speech: the duke declaiming his outrageous pastiche of Shakespeare, the king heatedly defending his use of "funeral orgies," and Pap becoming so engrossed in his speechifying about "a govment that calls itself a govment, and lets on to be a govment and thinks it is a govment" (25) that he goes head over heels over the tub of salt pork. These are memorable voices which Twain valorizes as individual expression while at the same time condemning the public language that shapes their deceptions and prejudices. (Deceptive speakers always find public language suited to their illegitimate perlocutionary intentions because they can use it to appeal to common values: their word is not their bond, but they rely on this principles holding for their victims.)

From Twain on, realistic speech is the norm in American prose fiction, but as characters become devalued, their utterances lose both individual expressiveness and meaningfulness until only the form of realistic speech remains. Good-faith speakers increasingly embody a dialogic tension between some unacceptable kind of public language and self-expression. What disappears is the fusion of passionate speaking with successful communication. The diverse verbal styles of Deerslayer, Hester Prynne, Uncle Tom, and Captain Ahab succeed in both these respects, although each achievement is associated, tellingly, with social alienation. All are characters divorced from community in some respect, and all are forceful enough personalities to impose their own definitions upon language in crucial instances. Hester's use of *consecration* in a private sense runs completely counter to its ritualistic public nature, while Natty Bumppo, Uncle Tom, and Captain Ahab preempt social authority, Natty and Tom as versions of God's spokesman, Ahab as society's (and God's) subverter. The rhetorical formality of these characters gives way to colloquial speech, vivacious at first with the expansiveness of oral humor and regional expression in *Adventures of Huckleberry Finn*, but increasingly guarded and uncertain in twentieth-century texts.

The fusion of passion with successful expression disappears first: in the social constraints weighing upon the speech of characters in James and Wharton, the inability to find the right idiom in *Gatsby*, the austere requirements of the code in Hemingway. Insofar as characters have something to say in the modern novel, language is a source of frustration and difficulty rather than a resource, an instrument shaped by social intentionalities that coerce and distort individual expression. Faulkner brings back the passion, but in a character like Ratliff, in but not of his speech community, utterance is severed from effective communication, a manifestation of self-indulgence and solipsism.[1] Moreover, this futile verbal extravagance is swallowed up by a powerful authorial discourse that monopolizes attention and authority far more than the typical omniscient voice of earlier, traditional authors.

As fictive speech moves from the modern to the postmodern novel, it continues to devolve as an adequate vehicle of meaning or feeling. Where characters in the modern novel struggle for self-expression, albeit in increasingly circumscribed terms, postmodernist characters either have nothing to say or are resigned to the impossibility of saying it. From being the straightforward testimony of a failure to communicate, which at the same time attempts to express individuality, the text embraces and institutionalizes this failure in speech that makes little or no claim to signification/significance or feeling. Denied the contextualization that suggests unexpressed meaning in James and Hemingway, the clichés that make up the linguistic currency of postmodern fictive speech become opaque and perfunctory indicators of the void.

One key to this process is the shift from language as representation to a self-reflexive discourse. All fictive characters are verbal constructs, obviously, but in the modern novel, as in earlier texts, they are representations of reality whose authors accord them ordinary human rights, among them the importance of humanity and the dignity of individuality. In the postmodern novel characters have no such entitlements. Their vitality is that of the word alone, not that of the human representation that we distinguish in the memorable characters of traditional literature. They tend to be stereotypes speaking clichés, who enact human behavior only in abstract paradigms.

The attenuation of speech in the twentieth-century American novel continues beyond the period I have discussed in the "minimalist" fiction of the eighties, a spare and unsettling blend of postmodernist attitudes and traditional formal elements. But it also leads to another kind of fiction, texts that are about writing, like *The Death of Che Guevara*, or about *not* writing, like *The Anatomy Lesson*.[2] People can lose faith in the possibility of reforming their institutions, as John Lukacs contends,[3] yet they may continue to believe in the idea or myth of such institutions and to act upon this belief. The crisis of contemporary society is one of legitimation more than belief: the will to believe endures although no compelling loci of authority have appeared to replace those institutions which have become unworkable and untenable. The response of the novel, itself an institution, to the disillusionment with public language that is its own version of this condition has been to leave the ground occupied by society and its authoritative discourse and seek its own space with its own authority, a parallel universe in which fictive speech has become increasingly marginalized. Nevertheless, change in art does not have an absolute and inescapable quality; just as representational painters did not disappear with the invention of photography or with the development of non-representational movements in painting, so some serious novelists continue to construct traditional narratives in our own post-Joycean and now postmodern or postpostmodern time. I find it unlikely, though, that an age in which increasingly sophisticated technology and electronic media proliferate will find any incentive or means of returning to a confident eloquence in fictive speech or to an untroubled relationship with the social authority embodied in public language.

Notes

■ Introduction

1. Pierre Bourdieu, *Ce que parler veut dire: l'économie des échanges linguistiques* (Paris: Fayard, 1982), p. 46, refers to "the unequal distribution of linguistic capital" as a significant factor in discourse. He continues, "It is necessary to distinguish between the capital necessary to the simple production of a more or less legitimate *ordinary speech* and the capital of instruments of expression . . . necessary to the production of a written discourse worthy of being *published*, that is to say, officialized" (my translation).

2. Monosyllabic responses and unadorned imperatives fall into this category. As John R. Searle observes, "Ordinary conversational requirements of politeness normally make it awkward to issue flat imperative sentences . . . or explicit performatives." "Induced Speech Acts," *Speech Acts*, vol. 3 of *Syntax and Semantics*, ed. Peter Cole and Jerry L. Morgan (New York: Academic Press, 1975), p. 64. See also M. M. Bakhtin, "Discourse Typology in Prose," *Readings in Russian Poetics: Formalist and Structuralist Views*, ed. Ladislav Matejka and Krystyna Pomorska (Cambridge: M.I.T. Press, 1971), pp. 176–96; and Susan Ervin-Tripp, "Is Sybil There? The Structure of Some American English Directives," *Language and Society*, 5 (1976), 26. Ervin-Tripp notes that "conversational transcripts reveal that people do not often literally say what they mean. We can accomplish the same ends by various means, many of them indirect."

3. Stanley E. Fish, *Is There a Text in This Class? The Authority of Interpretive Communities* (Cambridge, Mass.: Harvard University Press, 1980), p. 245. Fish's essay, the best discussion of speech-act theory in literary criticism, is on pp. 197–245.

4. *Expression and Meaning: Studies in the Theory of Speech Acts* (Cambridge: Cambridge University Press, 1979), p. viii.

5. *Speech Acts: An Essay in the Philosophy of Language* (Cambridge: Cambridge University Press, 1969), p. 64.

6. "A Classification of Illocutionary Acts," *Language in Society*, 5 (1976), 2.

7. *Speech Acts*, pp. 42–49.

8. Ibid., p. 46.

9. My position may simply represent the desire of the nonphilosopher to be less rigorous. Geoffrey N. Leech and Michael H. Short, *Style in Fiction: A Linguistic Introduction to English Fictional Prose* (London: Longman, 1981), exhibit the same tendency when they write that "a command or a question is

successful if it elicits an appropriate response" (293). Austin and Searle would say that these speech acts are successful if they are performed felicitously. The response is irrelevant to the assessment of the speech act qua speech act.

10. *Philosophical Papers* (Oxford: Clarendon Press, 1961), p. 143.

11. Mary Louise Pratt, "Ideology and Speech-Act Theory," *Poetics Today*, 7 (1986), 63. See also Michelle Z. Rosaldo, "The Things we do with Words: Ilongot Speech Acts and Speech Act Theory in Philosophy," *Language in Society*, 11 (1982), 204: "They [speech-act theorists] think of 'doing things with words' as the achievement of autonomous selves, whose deeds are not significantly constrained by the relationships and expectations that define their local world"; and Pierre Bourdieu, "The Economics of Linguistic Exchange," trans. Richard Nice, *Social Science Information*, 16 (1977), 657: "It can be seen that what determines discourse is not the spuriously concrete relationship between an ideal competence and an all-purpose situation, but the objective relationship, different each time, between a competence and a market, actualized practically through the mediation of the spontaneous semiology that gives practical mastery of the social level of the interaction." Fish, pp. 220–31, provides a lucid discussion of the limitations of speech-act theory.

12. Pratt, p. 67.

13. "The Economics of Linguistic Exchange," p. 646.

14. Ibid., p. 648.

15. Austin's "doctrine of the *Infelicities*" concerns the successful completion of a speech act; for example, "the procedure must be executed by all participants both correctly and completely." *How to Do Things with Words* (Cambridge, Mass.: Harvard University Press, 1962), pp. 14, 15.

16. "Bakhtin, Sociolinguistics and Deconstruction," *The Theory of Reading*, ed. Frank Gloversmith (Sussex: Harvester Press, 1984), p. 123.

17. Ibid., p. 140.

18. *The Dialogic Imagination*, ed. Michael Holquist, trans. Caryl Emerson and Michael Holquist (Austin: University of Texas Press, 1981), p. 294.

19. Fred G. See, *Desire and the Sign: Nineteenth-Century American Fiction* (Baton Rouge: Louisiana State University Press, 1987), formulates this struggle in terms of the sign. He describes "a central and structural dilemma, that of reshaping literary signs, which always consist not only of the energy of an imagination but also of the immense pressure of inherited forms, of ideas become sedimented, knowledge become inert. These two imperatives work against one another to engender a field of possibilities" (26).

20. *Class, Codes and Control: Theoretical Studies Towards a Sociology of Language* (New York: Schocken Books, 1971), pp. 47–48. M. M. Bakhtin's undialogized language, "privileged language that approaches us from without" (*The Dialogic Imagination*, p. 424), Bourdieu's "authorized language" ("The Economics of Linguistic Exchange," p. 648), and Michel Foucault's "le dis-

cours vrai" are similar concepts that emphasize the social production of an authorized discourse (*L'ordre du discours* [Paris: Gallimard, 1971], p. 22).

21. *Society in the Novel* (Chapel Hill: University of North Carolina Press, 1984), p. 210.

22. *The Rise of the Novel: Studies in Defoe, Richardson and Fielding* (Berkeley: University of California Press, 1967), p. 32.

23. "From Realism to Expressionism: Toward a History of the Novel," *NLH*, 6 (1975), 425.

24. *A Future for Astynax: Character and Desire in Literature* (Boston: Little, Brown, 1976), p. 7; see also Roland Barthes, "Literal Literature," *Critical Essays*, trans. Richard Howard (Evanston: Northwestern University Press, 1972), p. 58: "Literature always ends by succumbing under the weight of a traditional form which compromises it insofar as it serves as an alibi for the alienated society which produces, consumes, and justifies it."

25. Peter Messent, *New Readings of the American Novel: Narrative Theory and Its Application* (New York: St. Martin's, 1990), pp. 208, 209, observes that Bakhtin makes a fundamental distinction between centripetal and centrifugal forces. The centripetal is a "movement towards monoglossia" while the centrifugal embodies "the forces of disunification and decentralization."

26. Shlomith Rimmon-Kenan, *Narrative Fiction: Contemporary Poetics* (London: Methuen, 1983), pp. 29–31, has a useful reprise of commentary on the idea of the death of character in the modern novel.

27. Joel Weinsheimer, "Theory of Character: Emma," *Poetics Today*, 1 (1979), 195.

28. Rimmon-Kenan, p. 33: "In the text characters are nodes in the verbal design; in the story they are—by definition—non (or pre-) verbal abstractions, constructs. . . . In the text, characters are inextricable from the rest of the design, whereas in the story they are extricated from their textuality." Rimmon-Kenan's approach is applied to *The Sun Also Rises* by Messent, pp. 86–129.

29. *Writing Degree Zero/Elements of Semiology*, trans. Annette Lavers and Colin Smith (Boston: Beacon Press, 1970), p. 40.

30. It should be noted, however, that silence has always been an important part of discourse, from the pregnant pause to the finality of closure.

31. Modern linguistics takes the specialized meaning of *langue* and *parole*, language and speech, from Ferdinand de Saussure, *Course in General Linguistics*, ed. Charles Bally and Albert Sechehaye, trans. Wade Baskin. (New York: McGraw-Hill, 1966), pp. 7–15.

32. *Ce que parler veut dire*, p. 18; "Discourse Typology in Prose," p. 195.

33. Pratt, *Toward a Speech Act Theory of Literary Discourse* (Bloomington: Indiana University Press, 1977), p. 211.

34. As Pratt writes in *Toward*, p. 121: "The plain fact that the literary speech situation conventionally presupposes preparation and pre-selection explains a

great deal about how readers respond to and cooperate with works of literature."

35. "An Introduction to the Structural Analysis of Narrative," *NLH*, 6
(1975), 245.

36. *Speech in the English Novel* (London: Longman, 1973), p. 18. I am using
the idea of communicability in its broadest sense. Some of the verbal behavior Page discusses would interfere in the clear communication of an intended
message but would convey much about the speaker's feelings, personality, and
effectiveness as a speaker.

37. Quoted by John C. Gerber, "The Relation between Point of View and
Style in the Works of Mark Twain," *Style in Prose Fiction*, ed. Harold C. Martin
(New York: Columbia University Press, 1959), p. 163.

38. "The Logical Status of Fictional Discourse," *New Literary History*, 6
(1975), p. 326.

39. Bakhtin, *The Dialogic Imagination*, p. 323, refers to fictive speech as
"a special type of *double-voiced discourse* . . . [which] serves two speakers at
the same time and expresses simultaneously two different intentions: the direct
intention of the character who is speaking, and the refracted intention of the
author." Boris Uspensky, *A Poetics of Composition: The Structure of the Artistic Text and Typology of a Compositional Form*, trans. Valentina Zavarin and
Susan Wittig (Berkeley: University of California Press, 1973), p. 42, discusses
an interim voice between author and character: "The reworking of direct discourse by the author." He calls this "narrated monologue." Most narratologists
prefer the term "free indirect discourse." See Rimmon-Kenan, p. 110.

40. I am speaking only in terms of authors versus characters here. See
Wayne C. Booth's discussion of unreliable narration in *The Rhetoric of Fic-
tion* (Chicago: University of Chicago Press, 1961), pp. 221–40, 339–74; and
Rimmon-Kenan, pp. 100–103.

41. Ernest Hemingway, *A Farewell to Arms* (New York: Charles Scribner's
Sons, 1929), p. 31. Subsequent references are to this edition and will follow
citations in the text.

42. Plausibility is itself a convention, differing from one genre to another: it
will not be the same for an adventure romance and a realistic novel of everyday
life except for a common acceptance of what philosophers call "brute existence"—facts of the natural universe which prescribe, for example, that human
beings will be subject to gravity and incapable of walking on water.

43. Catherine's speeches in sequence contain the following number of
words: 5-8-5-9-8-12-11; while Frederic's responses, also in sequence, contain
1-4-1-8-1-5-4, a total of 47 and 24 respectively.

44. The certainty I refer to is of a much more limited formal sort than that
discussed by Booth. In his treatment of modern fiction he writes that *The Am-*

bassadors "presages many works which, by removing the traditional certainties that might be provided in a play, heighten the reader's sense of the character's isolation as he faces his moral problems and thus heighten the reader's own dilemma as he reads" (p. 293). Booth is concerned primarily with moral evaluation, the reader's ability to know the author's attitude toward the materials he presents.

Modern fiction often abolishes moral certainty while retaining an empirical certainty that the text will distinguish between what actually happens in the fiction and what is only thought, hallucinated, or imagined. In other words, the reader accepts the dialogue between Frederic Henry and Catherine Barkley as the product of Ernest Hemingway's imagination, not Frederic Henry's, and accepts further that the authorial voice reports Frederic's thoughts accurately in the passage which follows the conversation. Where the authorial voice is unreliable, it will usually be in matters of interpretation; empirical certainty still exists in modern fiction although it, too, is radically circumscribed in postmodern writing.

45. *Marxism and the Philosophy of Language*, trans. Ladislav Matejka and I. R. Titunik (New York: Seminar Press, 1973), p. 87.

46. I exempt the post–World War II novels from this assessment since they are too close to the present to have withstood "the test of time."

47. *The Body in Pain: The Making and Unmaking of the World* (New York: Oxford University Press, 1985), p. 43.

Part One

■ Prologue

1. *The Quest for Nationality* (Syracuse: Syracuse University Press, 1957), p. 25.

2. Alan Swingewood, *The Sociology of Literature* (New York: Schochen, 1972), p. 212.

3. *Democracy in America*, ed. J. P. Mayer and Max Lerner, trans. George Lawrence (New York: Harper & Row, 1966), pp. 440–41.

4. William Charvat, *The Profession of Authorship in America, 1800–1870: The Papers of William Charvat*, ed. Matthew J. Bruccoli (Columbus: Ohio State University Press, 1968), p. 211.

5. Cooper, who was the first commercially successful novelist, voiced one of the most vehement complaints in *Notions of the Americans*, 2 vols. (Philadelphia, 1841), II, 108: "There is scarcely an ore which contributes to the wealth of the author, that is found, here, in veins as rich as in Europe. There are no annals for the historian; no follies (beyond the most vulgar and commonplace)

for the satirist; no manners for the dramatist; no obscure fictions for the writer
of romance; no gross and hardy offenses against decorum for the moralist; nor
any of the rich artificial auxiliaries of poetry."

6. *The Puritan Origins of the American Self* (New Haven: Yale University
Press, 1975), p. 185.

7. The poets wished to remove their art from the prosaic world of utilitarian
communication, whose language they thought good enough for its mundane
purposes but unsuitable for poetry. In Stephane Mallarmé's words, "language,
in the hands of the mob, leads to the same facility and directness as does
money, but in the Poet's hands, it is turned, above all, to dream and song."
Selected Prose Poems, Essays, and Letters, trans. Bradford Cook (Baltimore:
Johns Hopkins University Press, 1956), p. 43. Cf. Julia Kristeva, *Desire in Language: A Semiotic Approach to Literature and Art*, ed. Leon S. Roudiez, trans.
Thomas Gora, Alice Jardine, and Leon S. Roudiez (New York: Columbia University Press, 1980), p. 31: "The poet is put to death because . . . he wants to
make language perceive what it doesn't want to say, provide it with its matter
independently of the sign, and free it from denotation."

8. *The Philosophy of Symbolic Forms*, vol. 1: *Language* (New Haven: Yale
University Press, 1953), p. 81.

9. J. D. Salinger, *The Catcher in the Rye* (New York: Bantam Books, 1964),
p. 198.

10. *A Farewell to Arms*, p. 185; *As I Lay Dying* (New York: Random House,
1946), pp. 463, 464.

■ Chapter One. Verbal Confidence

1. *An Essay Concerning Human Understanding*, ed. Peter H. Nidditch (Oxford: Clarendon Press, 1975), III.i.133.

2. D. H. Lawrence, *Studies in Classic American Literature* (New York: Viking
Press, 1964), p. 60.

3. In his preface to *The Deerslayer* Cooper describes Deerslayer as follows:
"Removed from nearly all the temptations of civilized life, placed in the best
associations of that which is deemed savage and favorably disposed by nature
to improve such advantages, it appeared to the writer that his hero was a fit subject to represent the better qualities of both conditions without pushing either
to extremes" (p. v.).

4. Donald Darnell, "Cooper's Tragedy of Manners," *Studies in the Novel*,
11 (1979), 406. Most criticism of the novel has defined itself around the issue
of Cooper's attitude toward the dichotomy between nature and civilization
embodied in the novel, beginning with D. H. Lawrence's influential essay extolling the Leatherstocking Tales as a "wish-fulfillment vision" (51). For an
opposing point of view, see Henry Nash Smith, *Virgin Land: The American*

West as Symbol and Myth (Cambridge, Mass.: Harvard University Press, 1951) and Allan M. Axelrad, "Wish Fulfillment in the Wilderness: D. H. Lawrence and the Leatherstocking Tales," *American Quarterly*, 39 (Winter 1987), 563–85. For Smith, Cooper's "strongest commitment is to the forces of order" (68). Axelrad writes, "No matter how disquieted he [Cooper] might have been about the world in which he lived, unlike Lawrence he placed his limited hope and faith in civilized society, and civilized men and women, not in wishful thinking about the wilderness" (581). Recent critics tend to see Cooper as ultimately unable to resolve the conflict between wilderness and society. For David Simpson, " 'Natty's career' is founded on a lifelong attempt to bring together appearances and reality, and his failure to do so is an index of Cooper's despair at the sophisticated deceptions of the society Cooper saw coming into being around him." *The Politics of American English 1776–1850* (New York: Oxford University Press, 1986), p. 183. Similarly, Wayne Franklin, *The New World of James Fenimore Cooper* (Chicago: University of Chicago Press, 1982), p. 202, finds a "pattern of erasure" which led Cooper to "leave out of *The Deerslayer* the social landscape he had sought to repossess in *The Pioneers*. Geoffrey Rans, *Cooper's Leather-Stocking Novels: A Secular Reading* (Chapel Hill: University of North Carolina Press, 1991), p. 205, concludes that "Cooper's refusal to resolve fictionally what history has not resolved and to reconcile intellectually or emotionally the mutually exclusive claims of Natty and the civilization that destroys him enables the reader to grasp the unendurable conflict."

5. As Nina Baym comments, "Chiefly, Cooper divides women into those who can be married and those who cannot." "The Women of Cooper's Leatherstocking Tales," *American Quarterly*, 23 (December 1971), 698.

6. Baym, p. 706, describes Judith as "restless, intelligent, experienced, impatient, moody, and yet with keen sensibilities and a sharp appreciation of high moral qualities . . . she combines enough qualities to take on the semblance of a rich life."

7. Roland Barthes, *A Lover's Discourse: Fragments*, trans. Richard Howard (New York: Hill and Wang, 1978), p. 6.

8. The central passage distinguishing gifts from nature is the following: "A natur' is the creatur' itself; its wishes, wants, idees, and feelin's, as all are born in him. This natur' never can be changed in the main, though it may undergo some increase or lessening. Now, gifts come of sarcumstances. Thus, if you put a man in a town, he gets town gifts; in a settlement, settlement gifts. . . . All these increase and strengthen until they get to fortify natur'. . . . Still the creatur' is the same at the bottom; just as a man who is clad in regimentals is the same as the man that is clad in skins" (455).

9. Notoriously in the Cooper/Deerslayer worldview, Indians lack the natural ability to master the white technology of the gun. In a shooting competition with Chingachgook, Deerslayer repeatedly triumphs. As he tells Judith,

" 'Chingachgook, now, though far from being parfect sartainty with a rifle—
for few redskins ever get to be *that*—though far from being parfect sartainty,
he is respectable, and is coming on' " (457).

10. Cf. Cooper in *The American Democrat* [1838], ed. George Dekker and
Larry Johnston (Baltimore: Penguin, 1969), p. 112: "It is seldom any good arises
from a misapprehension of the real circumstances under which we exist."

11. Deerslayer's various Indian names, one of which is Straight Tongue,
overtly suggest personified abstractions, and his own description of himself
and Hurry all but denominates them as Good Deeds and Good Looks. Other
characters may also be labeled: Hutter as Rapacity, Rivenoak as Guile, Chingachgook as Fidelity, Hetty as Simplicity. The only character to develop is
Judith, who moves from Vanity to Humility.

12. In *The American Democrat*, p. 110, Cooper advances the more hierarchical view that the ideal of linguistic excellence is reserved for polite society:
"A just, clear and simple expression of our ideas is a necessary accomplishment for all who aspire to be classed with gentlemen and ladies. It renders all
more respectable, beside making intercourse more intelligible, safer and more
agreeable."

13. Cooper's Littlepage trilogy—*Satanstoe, The Chainbearer*, and *The Redskins*—single-mindedly illustrates the corruption of language as one consequence of the antirent movement. Interests of various sorts deflect words
from their common meanings; for example, "shaving" means extortion except
among certain Wall Street money dealers, who use the term to refer to the
legal transaction of buying a note at less than its face value. In a recent case,
Cooper writes autobiographically, the New York Court of Appeals ruled that
to call a man a "shaver" was not pejorative, hence not libelous, "thus making
a conventional dignification of the brokers of Wall Street higher authority for
the use of the English language than the standard lexicographers, and all the
rest of those who use the language!" *The Redskins, or Indian and Injin* (Boston:
Houghton, Mifflin, 1898), p. 195.

The Littlepage trilogy both chronicles and condemns the antirenters' manipulation of language in this fashion, but even Cooper's pessimistic assessment of the current state of affairs does not cause him to retreat from verbal
confidence. The fact that some characters can recognize the linguistic abuse
for what it is and communicate it clearly differentiates Cooper's perspective
from that of Twain and later writers.

14. William P. Kelly writes of this passage, "There is, Cooper implies, a
bond between naming and destruction which transcends the inevitable process of wilderness clearing." *Plotting America's Past: Fenimore Cooper and the
Leatherstocking Tales* (Carbondale: Southern Illinois University Press, 1983),
p. 185.

15. David Brion Davis, "The Deerslayer, A Democratic Knight of the Wilderness: Cooper, 1841," *Twelve Original Essays on Great American Novels*, ed. Charles Shapiro (Detroit: Wayne State University Press, 1958), p. 7, describes Hetty as "impotent and inarticulate," suggesting "the nobility of mute nature itself." Actually, Hetty is surprisingly articulate. Rather than "mute nature," she embodies unswerving devotion to an institutional value—religion—and although she is incapable of understanding that it cannot be applied everywhere, her discourse is far from impotent.

16. The quoted description is from R. W. B. Lewis, *The American Adam: Innocence, Tragedy and Tradition in the Nineteenth Century* (Chicago: University of Chicago Press, 1955), p. 104. Natty is not master of all of the names of civilization, however. He imagines the chess pieces to be idols and has never heard of a buccaneer.

17. John Searle, "A Classification of Illocutionary Acts," *Language in Society*, 5 (1976), 10.

18. "Fenimore Cooper's Literary Offenses," *The Portable Mark Twain*, ed. Bernard DeVoto (New York: Viking Press, 1946), p. 553. Harold C. Martin correlates the leisureliness and prolixity of Cooper's style with a separation from direct observation, "energy distributed rather than focused." "The Development of Style in Nineteenth-Century American Fiction," *Style in Prose Fiction*, ed. Harold C. Martin (New York: Columbia University Press, 1959), p. 122.

19. Judith, who has been unduly influenced by settlement life, observes the conventions of social discourse until her proposal of marriage to Deerslayer.

20. Unlike Hurry's remarks, Hutter's message is not objectionable, only its form, which implies distrust. As Deerslayer agrees, the father of two daughters has a right to know why a stranger comes into his territory during a time of crisis.

21. Alan F. Sandy, Jr., "The Voices of Cooper's *The Deerslayer*," *ESQ*, 60 (1970), 5–9, distinguishes three levels of diction in dialogue: "the frontier-dialect of Natty and Hurry Harry, the Indian dialect, and the more or less standard English of the Hutters" (6).

22. *Biographia Literaria, Complete Works of Samuel Taylor Coleridge*, ed. Professor Shedd, 7 vols. (New York: Harper and Brothers, 1864), III: 405.

23. " 'Voice' in Narrative Texts: The Example of *As I Lay Dying*," *PMLA*, 94 (1979), 302–3.

24. *Political Justice in a Republic: James Fenimore Cooper's America* (Berkeley: University of California Press 1972), p. 280.

25. *Harriet Beecher Stowe and American Literature* (Hartford: Stowe-Day Foundation, 1978), p. 4. Moers enumerates a number of ways in which Stowe's life differed from the lives of her male counterparts. Not all are persuasive; for example, Stowe's "obsession with money and work" because of having to pro-

vide for her family is a condition shared with Hawthorne and Melville. Moers does accurately point out that Stowe was "the only writer of the American Renaissance really to experience life in the West" (4).

I have chosen to violate chronology by considering *Uncle Tom's Cabin* before, rather than after, *The Scarlet Letter* and *Moby-Dick* because Hawthorne and Melville so much more consciously write within an ongoing tradition, the romance, and are interconnected in so many other ways. Although as a male writer who also saw himself as part of a literary tradition, Cooper has more in common with Hawthorne and Melville than he does with Stowe, he is closer to her in his conception of the authority of language and the stability of the sign.

26. Thomas F. Gossett, *Uncle Tom's Cabin and American Culture* (Dallas: Southern Methodist University Press, 1985), pp. 89–90, recapitulates the story of Stowe's decision to write: "Toward the end of 1850, Mrs. Edward Beecher, Harriet's sister-in-law, wrote a letter to her. 'If I could use a pen as you can,' she is quoted as saying, 'I would write something that would make this whole nation feel what an accursed thing slavery is'. . . . [Stowe responded,] 'I will write something. I will if I live.' " During the writing of *Uncle Tom's Cabin* she wrote to Dr. Gamaliel Bailey, who was publishing it in installments in the *National Era*, that "the time is come when even a woman or a child who can speak a word for freedom and humanity is bound to speak." Letter of March 9, 1851, quoted by Robert Forrest Wilson, *Crusader in Crinoline: The Life of Harriet Beecher Stowe* (Philadelphia: Lippincott, 1941), pp. 259–60.

27. Letter to Dr. Wardlow, 4 December 1852, rpt. as "Letter from Mrs. Stowe," *New-York Times*, 17 February 1853, p. 3, cited from Gossett, p. 420, n. 3.

28. *Oldtown Folks*, ed. Henry F. May (Cambridge, Mass.: Harvard University Press, 1966), p. 133.

29. Fred G. See, *Desire and the Sign: Nineteenth-Century American Fiction* (Baton Rouge: Louisiana State University Press, 1987), p. 43.

30. The romantic thesis illustrated by Huck Finn, that society destroys natural goodness, informs *Uncle Tom's Cabin* as well. After Shelby's neighbor helps the runaway slave Eliza, the authorial voice ironically comments on "this poor, heathenish Kentuckian, who has not been instructed in his constitutional relations, and consequently was betrayed into acting in a sort of Christianized manner, which, if he had been better situated and more enlightened, he would not have been left to do" (63).

31. As Peter L. Berger and Thomas Luckmann write in *The Social Construction of Reality: A Treatise in the Sociology of Knowledge* (New York: Doubleday, 1966), p. 44, "As a businessman I know that it pays to be inconsiderate of others. I may laugh at a joke in which this maxim leads to failure, I may be moved by an actor or a preacher extolling the virtues of consideration, and I may concede in a philosophical mood that all social relations should be gov-

erned by the Golden Rule. Having laughed, having been moved and having philosophized, I return to the 'serious' world of business, once more recognize the logic of its maxims, and act accordingly." This passage could serve as a description of the lawyer's behavior in Melville's "Bartleby the Scrivener." See pp. 77–87.

32. *Benito Cereno*, published in 1855, makes a similar point: "Captain Delano took to negroes, not philanthropically, but generally, just as other men to Newfoundland dogs" (*PT*, 100). He compares the slave Babo to "a shepherd's dog" (60).

33. Stowe's intentional irony is always more pointed. A male slave is described as "the article enumerated as 'John, aged thirty'" (199) and later referred to as "that unfortunate piece of merchandise before enumerated" (202). Anticipating Huck's reaction to Jim's love of his family, the authorial voice also remarks that his tears "came as naturally as if he had been a white man" (199).

34. Philip Fisher, *Hard Facts: Setting and Form in the American Novel* (New York: Oxford University Press, 1985), p. 101. Fisher's reading of *Uncle Tom's Cabin* as sentimental representation that "installed the slave system in the public realm" (6) is particularly rich and illuminating.

35. The majority of critics writing about *Uncle Tom's Cabin* during the past decade have remarked this quality. See, among others, Myra Jehlen, "The Family Militant: Domesticity Versus Slavery in *Uncle Tom's Cabin*," *Criticism*, 31 (Fall 1989), 383–400; Gillian Brown, "Getting in the Kitchen with Dinah: Domestic Politics in *Uncle Tom's Cabin*," *American Quarterly*, 36 (Fall 1984), 503–23; Amy Schrager Lang, "Slavery and Sentimentalism: The Strange Career of Augustine St. Clare," *Women's Studies*, 12 (1986), 31–54; Jane Tompkins, *Sensational Designs: The Cultural Work of American Fiction 1790–1860* (New York: Oxford, 1985), pp. 122–46; and Elizabeth Ammons, "Heroines in *Uncle Tom's Cabin*," *New Essays on Harriet Beecher Stowe*, ed. Elizabeth Ammons (Boston: Hall, 1981), pp. 152–65, and her "'Stowe's Dream of the Mother-Savior': *Uncle Tom's Cabin* and American Women Writers Before the 1920s," *New Essays on Uncle Tom's Cabin*, ed. Eric J. Sundquist (Cambridge: Cambridge University Press, 1986), pp. 155–95.

The gender distinction is not crudely schematized, however: the discourse of Marie St. Clare adopts the values of the marketplace, but only because they serve her narcissism, not as ends in themselves or abstractly correct principles.

36. Brook Thomas, *Cross-examination of Law and Literature: Cooper, Hawthorne, Stowe, and Melville* (Cambridge: Cambridge University Press, 1987), pp. 113–37, provides a thoughtful analysis of Stowe's relation to capitalism. As he observes, "Not trained in the logic of business or the law, women felt especially helpless when confronted by the power of the market" (124).

37. Lang, p. 38.

38. However distasteful contemporary readers may find the passivity of

Tom's religious behavior (see especially James Baldwin's "Everybody's Protest Novel," *Critical Essays on Harriet Beecher Stowe*, ed. Elizabeth Ammons [Boston: G. K. Hall, 1980] pp. 92–97), his death as a Christian martyr is no less meritorious because of the constraints of slavery. Examples of the degradations of slavery unilluminated by Christian morality occur repeatedly in the text from the despair of old Pru and the slave mother who drowns herself to the sadism of Legree's black henchmen.

39. So much so that James Baldwin complains that George and Eliza "may be dismissed immediately, since we have only the author's word that they are Negro and they are, in all other respects, as white as she can make them" Ibid., p. 94. The exasperation of a twentieth-century black reader like Baldwin is understandable; nevertheless, through George Harris, Stowe employs another strategy for reducing the distance between owners and slaves. Although she sends him to Liberia, it is clear that George and his family are well equipped to flourish in American society. Cf. *Adventures of Huckleberry Finn* (24), where Pap tells Huck about a light-skinned black who in every respect but his categorization is a superior exemplar of whiteness. In describing this impeccably dressed, well educated "mulatter," Pap becomes so absorbed in his indignation that the man can't be immediately sold as a slave that he falls over the tub of salt pork. Without Twain's humorous treatment, Stowe presents George as in every way superior to his master.

40. Referring to the St. Clare household, Fisher, p. 124, makes a similar point: "Shiftlessness and leisure are the same events framed in the language of regional perceptions and moral geography."

41. Christina Zwark, "Fathering and Blackface in *Uncle Tom's Cabin*, NOVEL, 22 (Spring 1989), p. 280, notes George's use of this rhetoric in the speech that he makes to his pursuers (298).

42. *The Life and Letters of Harriet Beecher Stowe*, ed. Annie Fields (Boston: Houghton-Mifflin, 1897), p. 377.

43. "Toward a Theory of the Engaging Narrator: Earnest Interventions in Gaskell, Stowe, and Eliot," *PMLA*, 101 (1986), 813.

44. Ibid., p. 816.

45. Preface to *Twice-Told Tales, The Centenary Edition of the Works of Nathaniel Hawthorne*, ed. William Charvat et al., vol. 9 (Columbus: Ohio State University Press, 1974), 6.

46. Indeterminacy is advocated by Millicent Bell, "The Obliquity of Signs: *The Scarlet Letter*," *Massachusetts Review*, 23 (1982), 9–26; Evan Carton, *The Rhetoric of American Romance: Dialectic and Identity in Emerson, Dickinson, Poe, and Hawthorne* (Baltimore: Johns Hopkins Press, 1985), pp. 191–216; and Jonathan Arac, "The Politics of *The Scarlet Letter*," *Ideology and Classic American Literature*, ed. Sacvan Bercovitch and Myra Jehlen (Cambridge: Cambridge University Press, 1986), pp. 247–66. I will discuss Bell and Carton in

the body of my text; Arac, exploring connections between the novel and Hawthorne's *Life of Pierce*, propounds indeterminacy from the original perspective of "the political impasse of the 1850s" (259).

47. Bell, p. 3.

48. Carton, pp. 209, 202.

49. Bell, p. 12.

50. Cf. M. M. Bakhtin, *Problems of Dostoevsky's Poetics*, ed. and trans. Caryl Emerson (Minneapolis: University of Minnesota Press, 1984), p. 184: "Dialogic relationship can permeate inside the utterance, even inside the individual word, as long as two voices collide within it dialogically."

51. See, p. 15; cf. Bell, who concedes that in his treatment of signs Hawthorne "was still formally committed to older views" (12).

52. *The Shape of Hawthorne's Career* (Ithaca: Cornell University Press, 1976), p. 124. I agree with many aspects of Baym's reading although I disagree that Pearl and Chillingworth are imaginative projections of Hester's sin and Dimmesdale's guilt respectively. This seems to me to be needlessly reductive.

53. Gabler-Hover, *Truth in American Fiction: The Legacy of Rhetorical Idealism* (Athens, Ga.: University of Georgia Press, 1990), pp. 85–120; citations, pp. 86, 120.

54. Michael Ragussis, "Family Discourse and Fiction in *The Scarlet Letter*," *ELH*, 49 (Winter 1982), 863–888, sees the crime of silence concerning family relationships as central to the novel. Dimmesdale is guilty of "the refusal to name oneself, to recognize one's family, to confess" (883). Our readings of the dynamic of speech and silence differ in his greater emphasis on individual responsibility, a position he shares with Gabler-Hover, and mine on societal responsibility.

55. John G. Bayer, "Narrative Techniques and the Oral Tradition in *The Scarlet Letter*," *American Literature*, 52 (1980), 252, points out that Hawthorne refers to speech early on in "The Custom House." He quotes the authorial comment that "thoughts are frozen and utterance benumbed, unless the speaker stand in some true relation with his audience" (*SL*, 4). But it should be further noted that this oratorical ideal does not obtain in the romance proper. Dimmesdale, for example, achieves new heights of eloquence in his sinful and hypocritical state.

56. "The Scarlet Letter," *Hawthorne Centenary Essays*, ed. Roy Harvey Pearce (Columbus: Ohio State University Press, 1964), p. 455.

57. Dimmesdale characterizes his death with the oxymoron "triumphant ignominy." Hester has had unmediated ignominy inflicted on her without the free choice that he exercises.

58. *Truth in American Fiction*, p. 100.

59. It is Hawthorne's failure to follow through on the implications of this position that keeps him in the traditional camp.

60. Robin Lakoff, *Language and Woman's Place* (New York: Harper, 1975), p. 25, remarks that "women's speech is devised to prevent the expression of strong statements."

61. *The Imperial Self: An Essay in American Literary and Cultural History* (New York: Knopf, 1971), pp. 81–82.

62. For a dissenting view of speech in Hawthorne see Richard Bridgman, *The Colloquial Style in America* (New York: Oxford University Press, 1966), pp. 63–66. Bridgman writes of *The Scarlet Letter*, pp. 65–66: "Hawthorne's is drayhorse dialogue laboring faithfully for the narrative. It says what needs to be said to advance the plot, and very little more."

63. This process is characteristic of Hester, as Richard H. Brodhead points out in *Hawthorne, Melville, and the Novel* (Chicago: University of Chicago Press, 1976), p. 62. Describing Hester's rationalizing to maintain her love for Dimmesdale, he writes, "She employs Puritan terminology in a most un-Puritan strategy of consciousness, using it to perpetuate an inner need which she is unable to act out and unwilling to relinquish."

64. In the climactic encounter of Dimmesdale's homeward journey, Mistress Hibbins both assumes that the minister understands her own allusive speech and refers to the necessity of public and private languages: "Well, well, we must needs talk thus in the daytime! You carry it off like an old hand! But at midnight, and in the forest, we shall have other talk together!' " (221–22).

65. David Leverenz, *The Language of Puritan Feeling: An Exploration in Literature, Psychology, and Social History* (New Brunswick: Rutgers University Press, 1980), p. 164.

66. Pearl's fantasy that she "had been plucked by her mother off the bush of wild roses, that grew by the prison-door" (111) links Pearl to another social rebel, "the sainted Ann Hutchinson," from whose footstep it had supposedly sprung, and links both to the world of nature. In keeping with her lack of socialization Pearl's language consistently fails as social communication: "Perversity . . . closed her lips or impelled her to speak words amiss" (111).

67. Ragussis, p. 880, equates Hawthorne's denial of authorship with Dimmesdale's "criminal concealment, a casting off of the child, a withholding of the father's name." I would argue that unlike Dimmesdale's, Hawthorne's evasion is meant to be exposed.

68. Michael J. Colacurcio, "Footsteps of Ann Hutchinson: The Context of *The Scarlet Letter*," *ELH*, 39 (1972), 459–94, examines a number of parallels between Hester and Hutchinson.

69. See Sacvan Bercovitch, p. 120: "Self-examination leads to the assertion of a social-divine selfhood which certifies their calling as introspection alone could never do."

70. Basil Bernstein, "Aspects of Language and Learning in the Genesis of the Social Process," *Language in Culture and Society*, ed. Dell Hymes (New York: Harper & Row, 1964), p. 255.

71. Dimmesdale's spurious sanctity may be contrasted with the genuine sanctity of Ann Hutchinson, whose outspoken opposition to Puritan dogma earned her banishment from the Massachusetts Bay colony in 1638. Where "some hideous secret" taken to the grave produces ugly weeds in Roger Chillingworth's fantasy, the footsteps of Ann Hutchinson are reputed to have produced the rose bush by the prison door.

72. Michael Small, "Hawthorne's *The Scarlet Letter*: Arthur Dimmesdale's Manipulation of Language," *American Imago*, 37 (1980), 121, sees Dimmesdale's confession as "simply another manipulation"; however, "manipulation" suggests too much calculation.

73. Leverenz, p. 110.

74. *A Future for Astynax: Character and Desire in Literature* (Boston: Little, Brown, 1976), p. 80.

75. *Truth in American Fiction*, p. 117.

76. Dimmesdale's influence is undoubtedly mixed, since—as Gabler-Hover points out (117)—the virgins who gather around him are misguided victims of passion, but the novel alludes to other examples too vaguely to justify an absolute conclusion. It would seem likely that the numbers who regard Dimmesdale as a saint are inspired by his eloquence in some positive fashion.

77. This is also true in an earlier description of Dimmesdale's power as a public speaker: "But this very burden it was, that gave him sympathies so intimate with the sinful brotherhood of mankind; so that his heart vibrated in unison with theirs, and received their pain into itself, and sent its own throb of pain through a thousand other hearts, in gushes of sad, persuasive eloquence" (141).

78. *Sins of the Fathers: Hawthorne's Psychological Themes* (New York: Oxford University Press, 1966), p. 147.

79. Baym, pp. 136–37, Carton, p. 216, and Small, p. 113, are other critics who reject the either/or reading of Dimmesdale's character.

80. "Our Hawthorne," *Hawthorne Centenary Essays*, p. 455.

81. A number of commentators have discussed the different kinds of language in *Moby-Dick*. Among the most insightful are Walter E. Bezanson, "*Moby-Dick*: Work of Art," in *Moby-Dick: Centennial Essays*, ed. Tyrus Hillway and Luther S. Mansfield (Dallas: Southern Methodist University Press, 1953), pp. 31–58, and James Guetti, *The Limits of Metaphor: A Study of Melville, Conrad, and Faulkner* (Ithaca: Cornell University Press, 1967), pp. 12–45.

82. Philip F. Gura, *The Wisdom of Words: Language, Theology, and Literature in the New England Renaissance* (Middletown: Wesleyan University Press, 1981) examines the nineteenth-century shift in the concept of language from one of divine origin and empirical verification to a relativity and ambiguity that deny ultimate linguistic authority. Of the writers of this period, Melville, he writes, "best understood the effects of the revolution in language and meaning that occurred when the centrifugal forces of romanticism were unleashed in theology and philosophy both" (p. 158).

83. *Philosophical Papers* (Oxford: Clarendon Press, 1961), p. 65.

84. Letter of April 16, 1851, *The Letters of Herman Melville*, ed. Merrell R. Davis and William H. Gilman (New Haven: Yale University Press, 1960), p. 125.

85. Ibid.

86. Although Cooper is not part of his scheme, See, pp. 15ff. finds a similar progression from Stowe to Melville in terms of radicalizing the sign. His instructive argument is as follows: "Sensibility and scandal are the opposite capacities of language, and of desire: they cause the annealment and the fragmentation of significance. And sensibility, up until the middle of the nineteenth century . . . was always manifest as law—a law so homogeneous and sedimented that scandal is required to make it reflect upon its own order. So Melville and Hawthorne realized, though Melville stood more openly for scandal, and more resolutely against the sentimental canon epitomized by Mrs. Stowe. He and she constitute the brackets of literary signifying, one could scarcely go farther toward either extreme . . . and Hawthorne . . . falls somewhere between . . . in terms of his failure either to release language from the rule of signified spirituality or, on the other hand, convincingly to validate his own faith in a universe of metaphoric ideals."

87. Melville wrote of his discovery to Evert A. Duyckinck in his letter of February 24, 1849, *Letters*, p. 77: "Dolt and ass that I am I have lived more than 29 years, & until a few days ago, never made close acquaintance with the divine William. . . . I take such men to be inspired. I fancy that this moment Shakespeare in heaven ranks with Gabriel Raphael and Michael. And if another Messiah ever comes twill be in Shakespeare's person." See F. O. Matthiessen's valuable discussion of Shakespeare's influence on the language of *Moby-Dick* in *American Renaissance* (New York: Oxford University Press, 1941), pp. 421–31, 432–33.

88. As Warner Berthoff writes in *The Example of Melville* (Princeton: Princeton University Press, 1962), p. 170: "The qualities that sustain *Moby-Dick*, the sensuous charm, the verbal music, the kinetic tension and urgency, seem relatively muted, even withheld in the later stories."

89. Bridgman, p. 69, gives a good sense of the variety of verbal styles: "Father Mapple is equipped with a racy but eloquent discourse; the commands and shouts of the mates as they pursue the whales are colorful and animated; Ishmael on several occasions indulges in verbal slapstick; Queequeg speaks a pidgin English; Old Fleece mumbles in the grossest of Negro dialects; and Tashtego rumbles out sounds virtually indistinguishable from the thunder overhead."

90. In its presentation of soliloquies *Moby-Dick* has an authorial speaker masquerading as a narrator, although Melville undoubtedly is less concerned to escape a blatant violation of narrative convention than to give his ideas the drama of utterance.

91. See, for instance, Ahab's speech on the general injustice of the universe in "The Sphynx" (311–12), and on the "creative libertines" responsible for Pip's loss of sanity (522).

92. "Nervous" in the nineteenth century sense of "vigorous, powerful, forcible; free from weakness and diffuseness" admirably describes Ahab's speech. See *The Oxford English Dictionary*, 7 (Oxford: Clarendon Press, 1933), 96.

93. *Is There a Text in This Class? The Authority of Interpretive Communities* (Cambridge, Mass.: Harvard University Press, 1980), p. 206.

94. See, for example, Ahab's instructions to the carpenter on constructing an ideal man: " 'Shall I order eyes to see outwards? No, but put a sky-light on top of his head to illuminate inwards' " (470).

95. John Searle, *Speech Acts: An Essay in the Philosophy of Language* (Cambridge: Cambridge University Press, 1969), p. 124n.

96. In contrast to my reading. Herbert Rothschild, Jr., "The Language of Mesmerism in 'The Quarter-Deck' Scene in *Moby-Dick*," *English Studies*, 53 (1972), 235–38, discusses this scene as an example of the magnetizer-somnambulist relationship.

97. *Philosophical Papers*, p. 256. A preparatory condition of all speech acts, Austin also says, is that "the particular persons and circumstances in a given case must be appropriate for the invocation of the particular procedure invoked." *How to Do Things with Words* (Cambridge, Mass.: Harvard University Press, 1962), p. 15.

98. The one exception is Ahab's further effort to convince Starbuck to support his deflection of the whaling voyage from commerce to the pursuit of Moby Dick, and it proceeds from Ahab's calculation that the first mate is the one man who has the capital of authority and the motivation to challenge his plan successfully.

99. Boomer is the most significant counterpart of Ahab, a captain his own age who has also lost a limb to Moby Dick and whose injury with his own whaling weapon prefigures Ahab's death. Like Ahab, Boomer interrupts and directs the narrative of Dr. Bunger, but as affectionate byplay rather than egocentric intrusion.

100. *Philosophical Papers*, p. 256.

101. *The Interpreted Design as a Structural Principle in American Prose* (New Haven: Yale University Press, 1969), pp. 3–4.

102. *Melville's Thematics of Form: The Great Art of Telling the Truth* (Baltimore: Johns Hopkins University Press, 1968), p. 101. There are good discussions of the difference between Ishmael and Ahab in perception and language in Guetti, pp. 12–45 and passim. and in Brodhead, pp. 134–62. For Guetti, Ishmael's approximate use of language is "simile" whereas Ahab's imposition of his imagination upon reality is "metaphor" (102–3). For Brodhead, Ahab's

"determinate version of reality" is "one fiction among many" in Ishmael's story (162).

103. Cf. Stubb's remark about the doubloon: "Here's another reading now; but still one text" (434).

104. There are numerous instances where Ishmael's narrative adopts Ahab's point of view as its own. Although Ishmael often prefaces these passages with "it seemed," he does not do so here or do so consistently.

■ Chapter Two. "Truth Is Voiceless": Speech and Silence in Melville's Later Fiction

1. See Nina Baym, "Melville's Quarrel with Fiction," *PMLA*, 94 (1979), 915: "The doubting of language itself is what makes the skepticism of *Pierre* so much more thoroughgoing and corrosive than the naysaying of Ismael." I am indebted to Baym's seminal essay throughout this chapter. Fred G. See, *Desire and the Sign: Nineteenth-Century American Fiction* (Baton Rouge: Louisiana State University Press, 1987), pp. 64–94, analyzes *Pierre* in terms of Melville's discovery that the sign is indeterminate: "Melville moves to replace these two versions of an optimistic universe [sentimentalism and Emersonianism] with a new epistemology based not on reciprocal exchange but on dispersion" (84). See finds a central metaphor for the destabilization of the sign in the soul's interpretation of itself: "By vast pains we mine into the pyramid; by horrible gropings we come to the central room; with joy we espy the sarcophagus; but we lift the lid—and no body is there!—appallingly vast as vacant is the soul of a man!" (285)

2. *Symbolism and American Literature* (Chicago: University of Chicago Press, 1966), pp. 199, 206.

3. Ibid., p. 108.

4. Feidelson examines the difference between logical and symbolic uses of language in *Symbolism and American Literature*, p. 68ff. Barbara Foley points out that Feidelson's approach absorbs the historical world into a "boundless textuality." "From New Criticism to Deconstruction: The Example of Charles Feidelson's *Symbolism and American Literature*," *American Quarterly*, 36 (1984), 62.

5. *Progress into Silence: A Study of Melville's Heroes* (Bloomington: Indiana University Press, 1970), p. 152. Lebowitz's study reasonably concludes that Melville came to realize that the hero is useless in "an increasingly non-heroic world" (148).

6. *Hawthorne, Melville and the Novel* (Chicago: University of Chicago Press, 1976), p. 123.

7. In a study of the novel it may seem perverse to ignore Melville's novel of this period, *Israel Potter*, in favor of his short fiction. Nevertheless, it seems to

me that the successful tales illuminate Melville's development more than the unsuccessful novel, especially in the area of direct discourse.

8. *The Profession of Authorship in America, 1800–1870: The Papers of William Charvat*, ed. Matthew J. Bruccoli (Columbus: Ohio State University Press, 1968), p. 257.

9. See Chapter 1, note 81.

10. *The Poetics of Prose*, trans. Richard Howard (Ithaca: Cornell University Press, 1977), p. 195.

11. Carolyn L. Karcher writes in *Shadow over the Promised Land: Slavery, Race, and Violence in Melville's America* (Baton Rouge: Louisiana State University Press, 1980), p. 138, "The chief lesson Benito Cereno should have learned from his initiation into the feelings of a man who finds himself totally at the mercy of another man's will—that slavery is an intolerable condition— has completely eluded him." Karcher links *Benito Cereno* to attitudes held by Southern slaveholders (127). See also Eric J. Sundquist, "*Benito Cereno* and New World Slavery," in *Reconstructing American Literary History*, ed. Sacvan Bercovitch (Cambridge, Mass.: Harvard University Press, 1986), pp. 93–122, for a detailed discussion of *Benito Cereno* in relation to New World slavery, and to Caribbean history in particular, during the first half of the nineteenth century. Sundquist believes that this background plays a "critical role" in the story (122).

12. *How to Do Things with Words* (Cambridge, Mass.: Harvard University Press, 1962), p. 15.

13. Sundquist, "Suspense and Tautology in *Benito Cereno*," *Glyph*, 8 (1981), 103–26, is illuminating throughout on the narrative voice. He writes, p. 111, "The cunning narrative voice lures the reader in only to discount suddenly the perception it has projected."

14. James H. Kavanaugh, "That Hive of Subtlety: 'Benito Cereno' and the Liberal Hero," *Ideology and Classic American Literature*, ed. Sacvan Bercovitch and Myra Jehlen (Cambridge: Harvard University Press, 1986), p. 276, writes, "Cereno, like Babo, stands mute, knowing the futility of speech in the face of an infinite, closed ideological discourse."

15. The tale follows hard upon the novels. "Bartleby the Scrivener" appeared in *Putnam's Monthly Magazine* in November and December, 1853; *Pierre* was published on August 6, 1852; *Moby-Dick* on or about November 14, 1851 (*The Whale* was published in London on October 18, 1851). Martin Pops, *The Melville Archetype* (Kent: Kent State University Press, 1970), p. 127, describes Bartleby as "Pierre made passive."

16. "Melville's Quarrel with Fiction," p. 915.

17. A recent reprise of a number of such readings is given in Dan McCall, *The Silence of Bartleby* (Ithaca: Cornell University Press, 1989). He discusses Bartleby as possibly schizophrenic, autistic, a portrait of Thoreau, of Haw-

thorne, or of Melville himself. His own preference is for Bartleby as a son figure.

18. For treatments of the business world in "Bartleby" see my essay "Bartleby as Alienated Worker," *Studies in Short Fiction*, 11 (1974), 379–85; H. Bruce Franklin, *The Victim as Criminal and Artist: Literature from the American Prison* (New York: Oxford University Press, 1978), pp. 56–60; Stephen Zelnick, "Melville's 'Bartleby, the Scrivener': A Study in History, Ideology, and Literature," *Marxist Perspectives*, 8 (1979/80), 74–92; James C. Wilson, " 'Bartleby': The Walls of Wall Street," *Arizona Quarterly*, 37 (Winter, 1981), 335–46; and Michael T. Gilmore, *American Romanticism and the Marketplace* (Chicago: University of Chicago Press, 1985), pp. 130–45. Wilson characterizes the story as "one of the bitterest indictments of American capitalism ever published" (346).

19. *The Language of Puritan Feeling: An Exploration in Literature, Psychology, and Social History* (New Brunswick: Rutgers University Press, 1980), p. 226.

20. Zelnick, p. 82. See also Leedice Kissane, "Dangling Constructions in Herman Melville's 'Bartleby,' " *American Speech*, 36 (1961), 195–200. Kissane finds that the lawyer "is at intervals shaken into incoherency, his faulty sentences registering progressive changes in his attitude" (p. 196). I see the "faulty sentences" as demonstrating the lawyer's troubled state of mind in a repetitive fashion without change or illumination.

21. Two other notable examples of the lawyer's indirect style have other occasions. The talismanic name of Astor is invoked in this manner: "I was not unemployed in my profession by the late John Jacob Astor. . . . I was not insensible to the late John Jacob Astor's good opinion" (14). Here the motive seems to be the ordinary social injunction to refrain from blatant self-praise. Later, when the lawyer discovers that Bartleby lives in his office, he is overwhelmed by the unfamiliar sensation of melancholy: "Before, I had never experienced aught but a not unpleasing sadness" (28). In this case the indirection seems attributable to a desire to avoid the idea that he has ever had an explicitly negative feeling.

22. The paragraph's second sentence is its longest, forty-six words; the next highest number is thirty-three, but six of the ten sentences are a dozen words or less.

23. Susan Ervin-Tripp, "Is Sybil There? The Structure of Some American English Directives," *Language in Society*, 5 (1976), 59–64, discusses ranking of directives according to politeness. The narrator's directives to Bartleby would rank as among the least polite.

24. Herbert F. Smith, "Melville's Master in Chancery and His Recalcitrant Clerk," *American Quarterly*, 17 (1966), 734–41, finds legal rhetoric markedly present in the lawyer's narrative. See also McCall, pp. 119–20, for a list of legal expressions the lawyer uses.

25. *The Oxford English Dictionary*, 12 vols. (Oxford: Clarendon Press, 1961), 8: 1268.

26. *Through the Custom-House: Nineteenth-Century American Fiction and Modern Theory* (Baltimore: Johns Hopkins Press, 1982), p. 126.

27. John R. Searle, "Indirect Speech Acts," in *Speech Acts*, vol. 3 of *Syntax and Semantics*, ed. Peter Cole and Jerry L. Morgan (New York: Academic Press, 1975), p. 60, defines indirect speech acts as "cases in which one illocutionary act is performed indirectly by way of performing another."

28. Edwards does not distinguish between volition and preference. See Jonathan Edwards, *A Careful and Strict Inquiry into the Prevailing Notions of the Freedom of the Will* (1754), rpt. in *Works*, 4 vols. (New York: Leavitt and Allen, 1843), 2: 1–3.

29. A similar moment of paralysis occurs when Bartleby announces his continued presence in the lawyer's office, again denying the power of the lawyer's order: "I was thunderstruck. For an instant I stood like the man who, pipe in mouth, was killed one cloudless afternoon long ago in Virginia by summer lightning; at his own warm open window he was killed" (34–35). The image of domestic comfort and security conveyed by pipe, window, and cloudless sky shows how deep a sense of violation the lawyer experiences.

30. This occurs most tellingly when the criticism of professional acquaintances comes to the lawyer's attention ("This worried me very much," p. 38). Later, he is forced to return to deal with Bartleby because of group pressure, which confirms that Bartleby is indeed a problem for society.

31. Sanford Pinsker, " 'Bartleby the Scrivener': Language as Wall," *College Literature*, 2 (1975), 18. In Pinsker's illuminating reading, "walls are the central motif . . . extending from the Wall Street locale suggested by the sub-title, through a maze of physical walls which separate one man from another and, finally, to those walls of language which make human understanding impossible" (17). As the above comment indicates, Pinsker's concern with language is more philosophical than social.

32. *Is There a Text in This Class: The Authority of Interpretive Communities* (Cambridge, Mass.: Harvard University Press, 1980), p. 202.

33. Pinsker, p. 24, maintains that Bartleby's *prefer* "gets picked up as a grim office joke," but the narrator makes clear that his own use is unconscious. Turkey, in a speech full of "prefers," seems to straightforwardly deny that he ever uses the word.

34. Searle, *Speech Acts: An Essay in the Philosophy of Language* (Cambridge: Cambridge University Press, 1969), pp. 50–52.

35. Gilmore, p. 137, remarks that what the narrator "does *not* propose is as significant as what he does: a job in a factory, the kind of work which in the American economy of 1853 was more and more frequently the lot of men . . . like Bartleby."

36. This is H. Paul Grice's term for a basic convention of talk exchange:

"Make your contribution such as is required, at the stage at which it occurs, by the accepted purpose or direction of the talk exchange in which you are engaged." "Logic and Conversation," in *Speech Acts*, p. 45.

37. Erving Goffman, *Frame Analysis: An Essay on the Organization of Experience* (Cambridge, Mass.: Harvard University Press, 1974), p. 124, notes that an "obligation to show visual respect . . . characterizes the frame of ordinary face-to-face interaction."

38. The lawyer's remarks take the form of assertions but are actually disguised directives. See Searle, *Speech Acts*, p. 124n., who writes that the aim of directives "is to get the world to conform to words."

39. Ann Douglas, *The Feminization of American Culture* (New York: Knopf, 1977), p. 298, states that Melville in his fictions without women characters "is interested primarily in questions of class: the clash between employer and employed, master and slave." Cf. Gilmore, p. 132: " 'Bartleby' is a story about class relations and their consequences."

40. I agree with Hershel Parker, "The 'Sequel' in 'Bartleby,' " in *Bartleby the Inscrutable*, ed. M. Thomas Inge (Hamden: Archon, 1979), p. 164, that this final exclamation is sentimental rather than profoundly insightful. Parker writes, "The concluding words reduce his experience with the strange scrivener to manageable, not-unpleasing terms; they show that he is at last in control."

41. The majority of contemporary reviews complained that the author of *Typee* and *Omoo*, as he was still known, had disappointed audience expectations. See the *Albany Evening Journal*, April 2, 1857; *New York Dispatch*, April 5, 1857; *Literary Gazette*, and *Journal of Archaeology, Science, and Art* (London), April 11, 1857; *Burlington Free Press*, April 25, 1857; *New York Day Book*, April 17, 1857; *London Illustrated Times*, April 25, 1857; *Cincinnati Enquirer*, February 3, 1858.

Among many interpretations advanced by modern critics, there have been numerous treatments of the novel as allegory and satire: foremost among these is Elizabeth S. Foster's introduction to *The Confidence-Man* (New York: Hendricks House, 1954), pp. xiii–xcv. Other notable readings are the following: H. Bruce Franklin, *The Wake of the Gods: Melville's Mythology* (Stanford: Stanford University Press, 1963), pp. 153–87, explains the novel in terms of Hindu myth; John D. Seelye, *Melville: The Ironic Diagram* (Evanston: Northwestern University Press, 1970), pp. 117–30, sees it as a picaresque novel; Helen P. Trimpi, "Harlequin-Confidence-Man: The Satirical Tradition of Commedia Dell'Arte and Pantomime in Melville's *The Confidence-Man*," *Texas Studies in Literature and Language*, 16 (1974–75), 147–93, is an original and provocative reading, as is Henry Sussman, "The Deconstructor as Politician: Melville's *Confidence-Man*," *Glyph*, 4 (1978), 32–56. More recently, Tom Quirk, *Melville's Confidence Man: From Knave to Knight* (Columbia: University of Missouri Press, 1982), is particularly comprehensive on possible sources for the novel; William B. Dillingham, *Melville's Later Novels* (Athens, Ga.: University of Georgia Press, 1986), pp. 297–364, iconoclastically regards the confidence man as a truthteller and those who resist him as lost; Jean-Christophe Agnew, *Worlds Apart: The Market and the Theater in Anglo-American Thought, 1550–1750* (Cambridge: Cambridge University Press, 1986), pp. 195–203, discusses the interweaving of theatricality and commerciality in the novel; Brook Thomas, *Cross-examinations of Law and Literature: Cooper, Hawthorne, Stowe, and Melville* (Cambridge: Cambridge University Press, 1987), pp. 182–98, reads the novel as "Melville's most realistic response to the conditions of a market economy" (183); Wai-chee Dimock, *Empire of Liberty: Melville and the Poetics of Individualism* (Princeton: Princeton University Press, 1989), pp. 176–214, also sees a kinship between the novel and the market economy. In her reading the victims of the confidence man freely enter into contracts: their "folly of contract can only be an expression of their own foolish wants" (188); Janet Gabler-Hover, *Truth in American Fiction: The Legacy of Rhetorical Idealism* (Athens, Ga.: University of Georgia Press, 1990), pp. 9–34, persuasively establishes the central role of rhetoric in the novel. Gabler-Hover's reading also contains an extensive application of Jacques Derrida's version of Plato's *Phaedrus* in *Dissemination*, trans. Barbara Johnson (Chicago: University of Chicago Press, 1981).

42. *The Poetics of Prose*, p. 118.

43. "The Last Word on 'The Confidence-Man'?" *Illinois Quarterly*, 35 (1972), 15.

44. Ibid., p. 20.

45. As Quentin Anderson writes, "Melville's magnificent power to negate, as in *Bartleby*, is witness to his power to affirm." *The Imperial Self: An Essay in American Literary and Cultural History* (New York: Knopf, 1971), p. 241.

46. Quirk, p. 32.

47. "Melville's Quarrel with Fiction," p. 920.

48. Melville has dropped a number of clues to suggest that the novel follows the masquerade of one confidence man; however, on several occasions this central figure is joined by other (lesser) swindlers.

49. Sussman, p. 37, points out that "the operators collectively contribute to a mutually-confirming fictive utopia."

50. Warner Berthoff's comment about the postmodern novel *Gravity's Rainbow* applies equally well to *The Confidence-Man. A Literature Without Qualities: American Writing Since 1945* (Berkeley: University of California Press, 1979), p. 71.

51. *Subversive Genealogy: The Politics and Art of Herman Melville* (Berkeley: University of California Press, 1979), p. 239.

52. Agnew's assertion that the *Fidèle* is "beyond the pale of respectable society" (196) strikes me as overstatement. The conventions of respectable society, including polite speech, are in full force.

53. This description is pointedly directed toward the Cosmopolitan, the final

and longest-sustained guise of the confidence man. Denounced as a masquer-ader by the Missouri bachelor and described as "quite an original" by the barber, he is addressed as a confrere by the boy peddler: " 'Don't care about a Counterfeit Detector, do ye? or is the wind East, d'ye think?' " (247).

54. Ernst Cassirer, *Language*, vol. 1 of *The Philosophy of Symbolic Forms* (New Haven: Yale University Press, 1953), p. 188, writes, "The road to language seems to lead us, not upward into spiritual universality, but downward to the commonplace: for only this, only what is not peculiar to an individual intuition or sensation, but is common to it and others, is accessible to language."

55. C. K. Ogden and I. A. Richards, *The Meaning of Meaning*, 4th ed. rev. (London: Routledge & Kegan Paul, 1936), p. 125.

56. *Philosophical Papers* (Oxford: Clarendon Press, 1961), p. 50.

57. *How to Do Things with Words* (Cambridge, Mass.: Harvard University Press, 1962), p. 10. As Barbara Herrnstein Smith elaborates, "Lying is a social transgression of the first order precisely because it undermines the commu-nity's confidence in that verbal medium of exchange so basic to social trans-actions." *On the Margins of Discourse: The Relation of Literature to Language* (Chicago and London: University of Chicago Press, 1978), p. 100.

58. As Cecelia Tichi writes, "Mark Winsome's language, a private code that circumvents the sociality of a verbal interchange, is his means of retreat into a wholly private world." "Melville's Craft and Theme of Language Debased in *The Confidence-Man*," *ELH*, 39 (1972), 657.

59. *Melville's Thematics of Form: The Great Art of Telling the Truth* (Balti-more: Johns Hopkins University Press, 1968), p. 195.

60. *Truth in American Fiction*, p. 34.

61. Rogin, p. 302, also sees a resemblance between *Billy Budd* and Melville's fiction of the 1850s: "*Billy Budd* confines us in a denuded, mundane world, from which all possibility of transformation has fled. But unlike the earlier stories, *Billy Budd* gives that world its blessing." This does not seem to me to accurately describe the text's attitude towards its world, which I would char-acterize as acceptance rather than "blessing." The world of *Billy Budd* should not be confused with the totality of the text, which accomplishes an aesthetic transformation of the denuded and the mundane.

62. Barbara Johnson, *The Critical Difference: Essays in the Contemporary Rhetoric of Reading* (Baltimore: Johns Hopkins University Press, 1980), p. 102: "While Billy kills through verbal impotence, Vere kills through the very potency and sophistication of rhetoric."

63. *Philosophical Papers*, p. 36.

■ Chapter Three. Verbal Skepticism in
Adventures of Huckleberry Finn

1. Richard Bridgman's *The Colloquial Style in America* (New York: Oxford University Press, 1966) remains the standard account of the development of the vernacular in American prose fiction in general and in Twain in particular. More recently, Janet Holmgren McKay, "'An Art So High': Style in *Adventures of Huckleberry Finn*," *New Essays on Adventures of Huckleberry Finn*, ed. Louis J. Budd (Cambridge: Cambridge University Press, 1985), pp. 61–81, analyzes the speech of characters in terms of vernacular and standard features. The most systematic treatment of language as speech in the novel is David R. Sewell's *Mark Twain's Languages: Discourse, Dialogue, and Linguistic Variety* (Berkeley: University of California Press, 1987). Primarily concerned with levels of English and what they reflect, Sewell divides the vernacular into three categories: folk speech (Huck's), the speech of pretentious ignorance (Tom's), and ornery speech (that of depraved characters such as Pap), "marked by its tedious repetition" (93). I agree that these three categories can be distinguished in the text, but I find that "ornery speech" has far more vitality than Sewell allows, particularly when spoken by Pap or the king. Writers who devote significant attention to speech for other than reasons of dialectal differentiation include the following: Janet Gabler-Hover, *Truth in American Fiction: The Legacy of Rhetorical Idealism* (Athens: University of Georgia Press, 1990), pp. 121–54, who discusses the novel in relation to nineteenth-century rhetoric; John Bird, "'These Leather-Face People': Huck and the Moral Act of Lying," *Studies in American Fiction*, 15 (Spring 1987), 71–80, who analyzes lying as "central to [Huck's] character" (76); and Peter Messent, *New Readings of the American Novel: Narrative Theory and its Application* (New York: St. Martin's, 1990), pp. 204–42.

2. To cite only a few salient examples, Hemingway and Faulkner both identify Twain as the father of the American novel. Hemingway asserts that "all modern American literature comes from one book by Mark Twain called *Huckleberry Finn*" (*Green Hills of Africa* [New York: Scribner, 1935], p. 22). According to Faulkner, Twain was the father of both Dresier and Anderson and hence the beginning point of the "tradition of writing which our successors will carry on" (Jean Stein, "The Art of Fiction XII: William Faulkner," *Paris Review*, 12 [1956], 46). Malcolm Cowley also identifies Twain as the source of the vernacular style popularized by Hemingway ("The Middle American Style: D. Crockett to E. Hemingway," *New York Times Book Review*, July 15, 1945, p. 3). And Lionel Trilling writes "Out of his knowledge of the actual speech of America Mark Twain forged a classic prose. . . . It may be said that almost every contemporary American writer who deals conscientiously with the problems and possibility of prose must feel, directly or indirectly, the influence of

Mark Twain" (*The Liberal Imagination: Essays on Literature and Society* [New York: Scribner's, 1976], p. 117).

3. "American Literature and the American Language," *To Criticize the Critic and Other Writings* (New York: Farrar, Straus & Giroux, 1965), p. 54.

4. In a Bakhtinian reading similar to my own, Peter Messent uses the term "double voicedness" to describe the conflict in Huck between the voice of society and the community constituted by himself and Jim on the raft (231). As he states, these communities (and, by implication, their languages) are "irreconcilable" (232). *New Readings of the American Novel* (New York: St. Martin's, 1990).

5. *Phenomenology of Language* (Pittsburgh: Duquesne University Press, 1965), p. 123.

6. According to Kenneth Burke, *Permanence and Change* (New York: New Republic, 1935), p. 224, "To call a man a friend or an enemy is *per se* to suggest a program of action with regard to him. An important ingredient in the meaning of such words is precisely the attitudes and acts which go with them."

7. Lotman with B. A. Uspensky, "On the Semiotic Mechanism of Culture," trans. George Mehaychuk, *New Literary History*, 9 (1978), 217.

8. Stuart Chase writes in *The Tyranny of Words* (New York: Harcourt, Brace, 1938), p. 115, "In dealing with the physical world the test of fact is generally accepted as supreme. In dealing with the world of social control it is widely believed that there are other tests more to be respected—authority, internal consistency, rationalistic thinking, historic principles."

9. *Language and Control* (London: Routledge and Kegan Paul, 1979), p. 195.

10. Lee Clark Mitchell, " 'Nobody but Our Gang Warn't Around': The Authority of Language in *Huckleberry Finn*," *New Essays on Adventures of Huckleberry Finn*, ed. Louis J. Budd (Cambridge: Cambridge University Press, 1985), p. 92. Gabler-Hover, p. 136, finds that "Tom's artistry does not really involve belief so much as a haughty indifference to reality."

11. John Searle, *Expression and Meaning: Studies in the Theory of Speech* (Cambridge: Cambridge University Press, 1979), p. 3: "Some illocutions have as part of their illocutionary point to get the words . . . to match the world, others to get the world to match the words."

12. Colonel Sherburn also has a critical perspective on society, but unlike Huck, he is within its ranks, socially secure because of his status as a gentleman and his personal courage.

13. Introduction, *Adventures of Huckleberry Finn* (Cambridge, Mass.: Houghton, Mifflin, 1958), p. xxiv. They all sound pretentious, but their speech reproduces different authorized rhetorics depending upon the context (religion, theater, politics, etc.). Sewell, p. 94, uses the term "speech of pretentious ignorance."

14. *Is There a Text in This Class: The Authority of Interpretive Communities* (Cambridge, Mass.: Harvard University Press, 1980), p. 239.

15. *Mark Twain: The Fate of Humor* (Princeton: Princeton University Press, 1966), p. 172. Cox further remarks that "if Huck ever begins to think he is doing a good thing by helping Jim, he will become a good boy like Sid—one knowingly engaged in virtuous action; or a bad boy like Tom—one who can seem to go against society because he really knows that he is doing right" (170–71).

16. Joyce A. Rowe, *Equivocal Endings in Classic American Novels* (Cambridge: Cambridge University Press, 1988), p. 54. See also, Mitchell, p. 103: "Not slavery alone, but all codes and structures, are exposed as arbitrary human conventions, denying therefore the inherent validity of any institution."

17. The pointed and explicit denial of humanity to blacks in Aunt Sally's response seems implausible although the assumptions that whites are of greater value and have more human potential are everywhere implicit in the novel's public language.

18. *The Autobiography of Mark Twain*, ed. Charles Neider (New York: Harper & Row, 1959), p. 30.

19. "Huck, Jim, and American Racial Discourse," *Mark Twain Journal*, 22 (Fall 1984), 4.

20. Gabler-Hover, p. 135.

21. Richard Bridgman, *The Colloquial Style in America* (New York: Oxford University Press, 1966), p. 111, describes Huck's "powers of generalization" as "almost nil."

22. Among recent critics who think so are Wayne C. Booth, *The Company We Keep: An Ethics of Fiction* (Berkeley: University of California Press, 1988) and Forrest G. Robinson, *In Bad Faith: The Dynamics of Deception in Mark Twain's America* (Cambridge, Mass.: Harvard University Press, 1986). Robinson includes the reader in this evasion: "In dismissing Tom as childish we join him in the 'evasion' of the grave moral significance of his behavior" (177). Booth's thoughtful engagement with the text has been responded to by Gabler-Hover, pp. 140–45, who believes—as I do—that "Twain's moral orderings *are* clear" (144). For me, the aesthetic argument for the ending made by Cox, pp. 170ff., is more persuasive than Robinson's single-minded focus on an amalgam he calls "race-slavery." That "the bottomless craving for entertainment" is caused by slavery (163), for example, is too sweeping. "Race-slavery" should be acknowledged as the greatest social issue of the novel, but it does not explain loafers tormenting dogs or townspeople flocking to the Royal Nonesuch.

23. Booth, p. 466.

24. "Reading *Huckleberry Finn*: The Rhetoric of Performed Ideology," *New Essays on Adventures of Huckleberry Finn*, p. 129.

25. Cf. Huck's comment on Jim as a father: "I do believe he cared just as

much for his people as white folks does for theirn. It don't seem natural, but I reckon it's so" (201).

26. "The Form of Freedom in *Adventures of Huckleberry Finn*," *Southern Review*, N. S. 6 (1970), 971. Trachtenberg examines the language of the novel in terms of the technical conflict between Huck as narrative voice and Huck as character.

27. Messent, p. 232, notes that Huck "cannot avoid this prior discourse."

28. Robinson, p. 181, criticizes Huck because he "makes no place for Jim in his plans for 'The Territory.'" But, as Laurence B. Holland points out, Jim wants the opposite of what Huck wants, i.e., "to escape from slavery and enter *into* the civilization that chafes Huck." "A 'Raft of Trouble': Word and Deed in *Huckleberry Finn*," *American Realism: New Essays*, ed. Eric J. Sundquist (Baltimore: Johns Hopkins University Press, 1982), p. 70.

29. Cf. the novel's opening: "The Widow Douglas, she took me for her son, and allowed she would sivilize me; but it was rough living in the house all the time, considering how dismal regular and decent the widow was in all her ways; and so when I couldn't stand it no longer, I lit out" (1). Later, when Pap takes him away, Huck is content to be in the woods: "I didn't want to go back to the widow's any more and be so cramped up and sivilized, as they called it" (31).

Among others, Alan Ostrom, "Huck Finn and the Modern Ethos," *Centennial Review*, 16 (1972), 178, assumes that "the territory will be a temporary respite." A Twain projection of Huck's return, however, suggests a life of insanity-producing isolation: "Huck comes back sixty years old, from nobody knows where—and crazy." *Mark Twain's Notebook*, ed. Albert Bigelow Paine (New York and London: Harper and Brothers, 1935), p. 212.

30. Trilling, p. 105.

Part Two

■ Prologue

1. Quoted by Malcolm Cowley, *A Second Flowering* (New York: Viking Press, 1973), p. 18.

2. Cf. Don DeLillo, *End Zone* (Boston: Houghton Mifflin, 1972), p. 54: "The words were old and true, full of reassurance, comfort, consolation. Men followed such words to their death because other men before them had done the same, and perhaps it was easier to die than admit that words could lose their meaning." See also Hugh Kenner, *A Homemade World: The American Modernist Writers* (New York: Knopf, 1975), p. 156: "To write off the big empty words is to return to the small full words, small because Saxon and rooted, full because

intimate with physical sensation, the ground, the knowable. But the small full words have dangers of their own; they tend to contract and grow fewer, and approximate to the grunt."

3. *Irrational Man: A Study in Existential Philosophy* (Garden City: Doubleday, 1962), p. 45.

4. This is Fred See's term for transcendent referentiality. *Desire and the Sign: Nineteenth-Century American Fiction* (Baton Rouge: Louisiana State University Press, 1987), p. 26.

5. *One-Dimensional Man: Studies in the Ideology of Advanced Industrial Society* (Boston: Beacon Press, 1964). In a chapter entitled "The Closing of the Universe of Discourse," Marcuse writes, "The unification of opposites which characterizes the commercial and political style is one of the many ways in which discourse and communication make themselves immune against the expression of protest and refusal. . . . In exhibiting its contradictions as the token of its truth, this universe of discourse closes itself against any other discourse which is not on its own terms" (90).

■ Chapter Four. Urbanity and Expatriation,
Part 1: James and Wharton

1. Henry James, *The Notebooks of Henry James*, ed. F. O. Matthiessen and Kenneth B. Murdoch (New York: Oxford University Press, 1947), p. 375.

2. Strether tells Maria Gostrey that Mamie is "our prettiest brightest girl. He adds: "'We don't miss money much . . . in general, in America, in pretty girls" (21:72).

3. Dell Hymes, "Speech and Language: On the Origins and Foundations of Inequality among Speakers," *Daedalus*, 102 (1973), 75.

4. "The Power of Advertising: Chad Newsome and the Meaning of Paris in *The Ambassadors*," *ELH*, 49 (1982), 103.

5. I use these terms according to *The distinction between brute and institutional facts* in John R. Searle, *Speech Acts: An Essay in the Philosophy of Language* (Cambridge: Cambridge University Press, 1969), pp. 50–53. As Searle explains, brute facts are "essentially physical," and the model for identifying them comes from the empirical method of the natural sciences. Institutional facts presuppose "the existence of certain human institutions." For example, Searle writes, "It is only given the institution of money that I now have a five dollar bill in my hand. Take away the institution and all I have is a piece of paper with various gray and green markings" (p. 51).

6. *Is There a Text in This Class? The Authority of Interpretive Communities* (Cambridge, Mass.: Harvard University Press, 1981), p. 199.

7. Another is Chad's lack of imagination. Strether, on the other hand, has too much imagination for the life of Woollett. In her persuasive reading of

The Ambassadors, Millicent Bell remarks on the chiasmus of Strether's urging Chad to stay in Paris. As she comments, "the real crossover of plots is that it is Strether who is ready to offer Madame de Vionnet . . . devotion and sacrifice. Chad, on the other hand, wants to take up the plot of Woollett." *Meaning in Henry James* (Cambridge, Mass.: Harvard University Press, 1991), p. 340.

8. As Seymour Chatman observes in *The Later Style of Henry James* (New York: Barnes and Noble, 1972), p. 24, "Characters leave—and abstractions enter—the grammatical limelight." The shift diminishes personal agency so that in this passage *truth* becomes the active principle that bears a passive Strether and his Woollett compatriots into unknown territory.

9. Mamie Pocock is clearly put forward as the girl who will bring Chad back to the business, subordinating personal claims. As Strether explains to Maria, "His marriage is what his mother most desires—that is if it will help. And oughtn't *any* marriage to help? . . . Almost any girl he may marry will have a direct interest in his taking up his chances. It won't suit *her* at least that he shall miss them" (21: 184).

10. According to Basil Bernstein, *Class, Codes and Control: Theoretical Studies Towards a Sociology of Language* (New York: Schocken Books, 1971), p. 45, in a public language, authority, rather than reason or empirical observation, legitimates categoric statements.

11. This is the novel's principal example of James's "general novelistic method," described by Ian Watt as "progressive and yet artfully delayed clarification." "The First Paragraph of *The Ambassadors*: An Explication," *Essays in Criticism*, 10 (1960), 266. See also Ruth Bernard Yeazell, *Language and Knowledge in the Late Novels of Henry James* (Chicago: University of Chicago Press, 1976), p. 75: "A sufficiently ambiguous language ensures that no hasty judgment will be made."

12. The quoting of *lie* in this passage, like the enclosure of key words throughout the novel, enables James to refer to both languages simultaneously. As George Knox notes in "James's Rhetoric of 'Quotes,'" *College English*, 17 (1956), 294, "Strether's meditations are peppered with quotes," a mark of the speculative Parisian speaker.

13. It is possible to see the situation as more ambiguous than Strether's sharp dichotomy. In *Meaning in Henry James*, p. 352, Bell notes that in leaving, Strether "has duplicated Chad's own casting off of the woman who has done so much for the man she has loved, educated, and refined—and he is no less a 'brute.'"

14. See Sarah Pocock's description of Madame de Vionnet as "not even an apology for a decent woman" (22: 202).

15. *The Language of Fiction: Essays in Criticism and Verbal Analysis of the English Novel* (London: Routledge & Kegan Paul, 1966), p. 197.

16. Yeazell, p. 86. In Strether's last meeting with Madame de Vionnet, "he

felt what he had felt before with her, that there was always more behind what she showed, and more and more again behind that" (22: 283).

17. *A Future for Astynax: Character and Desire in Literature* (Boston: Little, Brown, 1976), p. 131.

18. *The Question of our Speech and The Lesson of Balzac: Two Lectures* (New York: Haskell House, 1972), p. 32.

19. Without social forms to structure behavior and the eternal vigilance to maintain them, James indicates in *The Question of our Speech*, we would be little better than animals: "Abate a jot of the quantity, and, much more of the quality, of the consecration required, and we practically find ourselves emulating the beasts, who prosper as well without a vocabulary as without a marriage-service" (p. 47).

20. See Diana Trilling, "*The House of Mirth* Revisited," *Edith Wharton: A Collection of Essays*, ed. Irving Howe (Englewood Cliffs: Prentice-Hall, 1962), p. 115: "Except for *Othello*, or perhaps *Romeo and Juliet*, one can think of no other work of the literary imagination which makes this much verbal play between the images of night and day."

21. Millicent Bell, *Edith Wharton and Henry James: The Story of Their Friendship* (New York: George Braziller, 1965), pp. 227–28, describes the style of *The House of Mirth* as "as far as could be conceived from the late or even the early Henry James . . . a defiantly different style."

22. Wharton's comments about fictive speech in *The Writing of Fiction* [1925] (New York: Octagon, 1966) emphasize its adjunct nature: "The use of dialogue in fiction seems to be one of the few things about which a fairly definite rule may be laid down. It should be reserved for the culminating moments. . . . The sparing use of dialogue not only serves to emphasize the crises of the tale but to give it as a whole a greater effect of continuous development" (73). She complains of a dialogue forced to bear the burden of narrative development and consequently "so diluted with irrelevant touches of realistic commonplace [that] . . . it rambles on for page after page" (74).

23. Georg Lukács writes that commodification "stamps its imprint upon the whole consciousness of man; his qualities and abilities are no longer an organic part of his personality, they are things which he can 'own' or 'dispose of' like the various objects of the external world. And there is no way in which man can bring his physical and psychic 'qualities' into play without their being subjected increasingly to this reifying process." *History and Class Consciousness: Studies in Marxist Dialectics*, trans. Rodney Livingstone (Cambridge, Mass.: M.I.T. Press, 1971), p. 100.

24. For an excellent treatment of this theme see Wai-Chee Dimock, "Debasing Exchange: Edith Wharton's *The House of Mirth*," *PMLA*, 100 (1985), 783–92. Dimock writes, "The realm of human relations is fully contained within an all-encompassing business ethic" (783). Gus Trenor's comment on

Rosedale's entrance into society confirms the pervasiveness and inevitability of this ethic: "A few years from now he'll be in whether we want him or not" (82).

25. See Cynthia Griffin Wolff, *A Feast of Words: The Triumph of Edith Wharton* (New York: Oxford University Press, 1977), pp. 109–33, for a detailed discussion of "the woman as self-creating artistic object" in *The House of Mirth* (111). Cf. Luce Irigaray, *Speculum of the Other Woman*, trans. Gillian C. Gill (Ithaca: Cornell University Press, 1985), p. 125: "Woman's special form of neurosis would be to 'mimic' a work of art" (125).

26. Robin Lakoff, *Language and Woman's Place* (New York: Harper & Row, 1975), p. 7.

27. In his important discussion of *The House of Mirth* Walter Benn Michaels defines the moment of the *tableau vivant* as "a moment of speculation," a "moment of risk when intentions and actions may come apart." He sees the novel as a series of such moments, and writing as "a paradigm for an exciting loss of self-control." *The Gold Standard and the Logic of Naturalism: American Literature at the Turn of the Century* (Berkeley: University of California Press, 1987), pp. 240, 241.

28. Irigaray, p. 133.

29. Lakoff, p. 70.

30. *Language, the Sexes and Society* (Oxford: Basil Blackwell, 1985), p. 160.

31. Sociolinguistic studies indicate that real male speakers conversing with women take longer speech turns, interrupt more frequently, and are generally more assertive speakers. See Don H. Zimmerman and Candace West, "Sex Roles, Interruptions and Silences in Conversation," *Language and Sex: Difference and Dominance*, ed. Barrie Thorne and Nancy Henley (Rowley, Mass.: Newbury House, 1975), pp. 105–25; see also John J. Gumperz, *Discourse Strategies* (Cambridge: Cambridge University Press, 1982), pp. 154–55. Such empirical studies ignore the kind of speech situations seen here in which a subtle form of dominance undermines superficial control.

32. Amy Kaplan, "Edith Wharton's Profession of Authorship," *ELH*, 53 (1986), 449, observes that in *The House of Mirth* "social intercourse depends on the use of intimacy as a medium of exchange." She sees Lily's withdrawal from this economy as leading to her death.

33. *Implicature* is H. P. Grice's term for implied as opposed to overtly stated meanings. Geoffrey N. Leech and Michael H. Short see Gricean implicature as at odds with the Cooperative Principle, which posits in talk exchange a condition of cooperation to achieve mutual goals. See Chapter 2, n. 36. *Style in Fiction: A Linguistic Introduction to English Fictional Prose* (London: Longman, 1981), p. 299.

34. Elaine Showalter, "The Death of the Lady (Novelist): Wharton's *House of Mirth*," *representations*, 9 (1985), 136.

35. Ibid.

36. At the same time, each stage of Lily's movement down the social lad-

der produces a potential male rescuer, and while none is disinterested, none is villainous, either. Where her former good women friends abandon her, these men reveal themselves reluctant to believe the worst and willing to help her.

37. "Women and Words in a Spanish Village," *Towards an Anthropology of Women*, ed. R. Reiter (New York: Monthly Review Press, 1975), p. 207.

38. Leech and Short, p. 297.

39. *Edith Wharton's Argument with America* (Athens, Georgia: University of Georgia Press, 1980), p. 39.

40. Lakoff, p. 25, remarks of the label *girl* that "in stressing the idea of immaturity, it removes the sexual connotations lurking in *woman*." It also removes the adult connotations of autonomy, responsibility, and maturity associated with masculinity.

41. See Jacques Lacan, *Ecrits* (Paris: Seuil, 1966), p. 222: "Both for every woman and for reasons which are at the very foundation of the most basic social exchanges . . . the problem of her condition is at bottom that of accepting herself as the object of man's desire" (my translation).

42. " 'Women's Language' or 'Powerless Language' "? *Women and Language in Literature and Society*, ed. Sally McConnell-Ginet, Ruth Borker, Nelly Furman (New York: Praeger, 1980), p. 94.

■ Chapter Five. Urbanity and Expatriation, Part 2: Fitzgerald and Hemingway

1. According to Milton R. Stern, *The Golden Moment: The Novels of F. Scott Fitzgerald* (Urbana: University of Illinois Press, 1970), p. 287, Fitzgerald wanted to change the novel's title to "Under the Red White and Blue" at a time when it was too late to do so.

2. Richard Godden, "*The Great Gatsby*: Glamor on the Turn," *Journal of American Studies*, 16 (December 1982), 354.

3. Sport as a mark of rank is a recurring motif. Tom's stables, which he invariably calls to people's attention, testify to his power to go, in Fitzgerald's memorable phrase, "wherever people played polo and were rich together." Wolfsheim, who takes Gatsby for the real thing, excuses himself after lunch by saying, "You sit here and discuss your sports" (73).

4. Tom also bridles at the familiarity of being addressed by Gatsby as "old sport," but the expression characterizes him accurately. He is an old jock who can excel at nothing else.

5. Brian Way, *F. Scott Fitzgerald and the Art of Social Fiction* (New York: St. Martin's, 1980), p. 105, observes that when Gatsby "talks about his feelings to Nick Carraway, the words he uses retain echoes from many cheap and vulgar styles."

6. Ibid., p. 110.

7. Cf. Prufrock's analogous speech: "It is impossible to say just what I mean." T. S. Eliot, "The Love Song of J. Alfred Prufrock," *Collected Poems 1909–1962* (New York: Harcourt, Brace, 1968), p. 6.

8. "The Craft of Revision: *The Great Gatsby,*" *Fitzgerald's The Great Gatsby: The Novel, The Critics, The Background,* ed. Henry Dan Piper (New York: Charles Scribner's Sons, 1970), p. 116.

9. Ibid.

10. Peter Messent, *New Readings of the American Novel: Narrative Theory and its Application* (New York: St. Martin's, 1990), pp. 14–18, discusses the relationship of Nick's voice to Gatsby's at some length. I agree with his conclusion that "it is finally impossible to say to what extent the narrating instance (Carraway's voice) obliterates character (Gatsby); exactly how far Nick integrates the latter's words into his own speech, and thus *expresses* them in his own style" (18). Messent is primarily concerned with aspects of narrative in *Gatsby,* applying Gérard Genette's terminology to the text. Godden, p. 346, asserts that "Carraway writes 'a life' that Gatsby does not deserve." His essay is an original and insightful discussion of Nick as author, who needs to write Gatsby's story to escape his own failures.

11. Tom momentarily loses this quality on the threshold of his confrontation with Gatsby: " 'Sit down Daisy,' Tom's voice groped unsuccessfully for the paternal note. 'What's been going on? I want to hear all about it' " (131).

12. In *Il testo e la voce: oralità, scrittura e democrazia nella letteratura americana* (Rome: Manifestolibri, 1992), p. 242, Alessandro Portelli uses the image of "a voice full of money" to develop the relationship between money and language in the novel. He writes, "Like money, language is inflated, falsified, voided" (my translation). Roger Lewis notes that "even when the sentiments are genuine, they are formulated in monetary terms." "Money, Love, and Aspiration in *The Great Gatsby,*" *New Essays on The Great Gatsby,* ed. Matthew J. Bruccoli (Cambridge: Cambridge Univ. Press, 1985), p. 46.

13. Godden, p. 348, writes, "The shirts are a Trimalchian and necessary overplaying of [Gatsby's] wealth."

14. V. N. Volosinov [M. M. Bakhtin], *Marxism and the Philosophy of Language,* trans. Ladislav Matejka and I. R. Titunik (New York: Seminar Press, 1973), p. 89; cf. Pierre Bourdieu, "The Economics of Linguistic Exchange," *Social Science Information,* 16 (1977), 659: "The dominant class learns the dominant language at home."

15. Cf. Natty Bumppo's constant reflection of his author's strong sense of a rigid social hierarchy: inborn "gifts" dictate one's place in life, and it is folly to aspire above this. Ironically, Natty's general maxim could apply to both Gatsby and Myrtle: "Onequal matches . . . can't often tarminate kindly" (*Deerslayer,* 425).

16. Writing about *What Maisie Knew,* Donna Przybylowicz asserts that "man

is a creature of society and must learn to live within its confines or perish," a statement that I would apply to all three of these texts. Przybylowicz divides late Jamesian texts into impressionistic works such as *The Ambassadors*, in which society still has meaning, and expressionistic works in which "the objective world is now contained by the subjectivity of the consciousness and becomes a projection of individual desire " *Desire and Repression: The Dialectic of Self and Other in the Late Works of Henry James* (University, Ala.: University of Alabama Press, 1986), p. 293.

17. *Science and Sanity*, 4th ed. (Lakeville, Conn.: The International Non-Aristotelian Library, 1958), p. 399.

18. Roland Barthes, *The Pleasure of the Text*, trans. Richard Miller (New York: Hill and Wang, 1975), p. 21.

19. As Hemingway wrote in *Death in the Afternoon* (New York: Scribner's, 1932), p. 192, "If a writer of prose knows enough about what he is writing about he may omit things that he knows and the reader, if the writing is written truly enough, will have a feeling of those things as strongly as though the writer had stated them."

20. Not as much as other, less disciplined characters, however. For John W. Aldridge, "Jake's strength as a character largely derives from his capacity for withholding information." "Revaluation: *The Sun Also Rises*—Sixty Years Later," *Sewanee Review*, 94 (1986), 343. Jake's speech is notably terse, but he withholds evaluation more than "information."

21. Stanley E. Fish, *Is There a Text in This Class? The Authority of Interpretive Communities* (Cambridge, Mass.: Harvard University Press, 1980), p. 207.

22. John Locke, *An Essay Concerning Human Understanding*, ed. Peter H. Nidditch (Oxford: Clarendon Press, 1975), p. 402.

23. Fish, p. 213.

24. Nina Schwartz comments on this same passage in her psychoanalytic reading of *The Sun Also Rises*: "The narration's refusal to speak directly of the war and the wound, its evocation of those topics only as 'the unspeakable,' invests them with a potent and compelling fascination." "Lovers' Discourse in *The Sun Also Rises*: A Cock and Bull Story," *Criticism*, 26 (Winter, 1984), 53.

25. Mark Spilka, "The Death of Love in *The Sun Also Rises*," *Hemingway and His Critics: An International Anthology*, ed. Carlos Baker (New York: Hill and Wang, 1961), p. 82. I acknowledge a debt throughout my reading to Spilka's seminal essay.

26. Larzer Ziff, *Poetics*, 7 (1978), 417–23.

27. Ziff, p. 422.

28. Barthes, p. 45.

29. Examining part of this same passage, Messent, p. 103, finds that "these patterns of physical and emotional advance and retreat suggest the highly unstable nature of both Jake and Brett's emotional state in the first part of the

novel." Messent's compelling reading focuses on character, especially on Brett and Jake as self-divided characters whose portrayal reveals a modern conception of the nonunitary nature of all character.

30. *Speech Acts: An Essay in the Philosophy of Language* (Cambridge: Cambridge University Press, 1969), p. 198.

31. Cf. Huck Finn: "I never said nothing, never let on; kept it to myself; it's the best way; then you don't have no quarrels and don't get into no trouble." *Adventures of Huckleberry Finn*, p. 165.

32. *Irrational Man: A Study in Existential Philosophy* (Garden City: Doubleday, 1962), p. 45.

33. Cf. David Lodge's discussion of *wonderful* as just such an all-purpose word in *The Ambassadors. The Language of Fiction* (London: Routledge & Kegan Paul, 1966), pp. 210–213. Hemingway, too, finds it a useful word for a range of situations. When an American tourist asks Bill if he's having a good trip, Bill replies, "Wonderful." Jake's comment "He's wonderful" when Brett tells him that Cohn is looking forward to joining the group in Pamplona is typically Jamesian.

34. Messent, p. 125.

35. Even at the minimal level of obligation the characters recognize, their arrangements to meet each other, commitments are frequently broken (notably by Brett and Mike).

36. Scott Donaldson, "Humor in *The Sun Also Rises*," *New Essays on The Sun Also Rises*, ed. Linda Wagner-Martin (Cambridge: Cambridge University Press, 1987), pp. 19–41, discusses Bill's role as "the most consistently funny character" in the novel (34). According to Donaldson, a salient characteristic of Bill's humor is that it "directs jokes at ideas and institutions, not human beings" (37).

37. Mike may subconsciously wish to end his story here in order to hold back what is truly discrediting—the mutilation and disposal of property belonging to and highly valued by someone else.

38. In a world which has left such values behind, Cohn's embodiment of socially acceptable behavior and goals is represented pejoratively as infantile, in Harvey Stone's words, "a case of arrested development." Jake says that Cohn had a "funny sort of undergraduate quality about him," and he wears polo shirts, "the kind he'd worn at Princeton" (194).

39. Distinguishing between personal and ritualistic insults, William Labov writes: "The appropriate responses are quite different. Ritual insults are answered by other ritual insults while a personal insult is answered by denial, excuse or mitigation." *Language in the Inner City* (University Park: University of Pennsylvania Press, 1972), p. 335.

40. Jake's only immediate thought when he confirms that Brett and Romero have gone off together is that "it was not pleasant."

41. While both Jake and Montoya invoke the stereotype of the young man corrupted by the older woman, Hemingway makes clear in an embarrassingly overwritten passage (the only one of its kind in the novel) that this does not happen to Pedro Romero: "Everything of which he could control the locality [in the bullring] he did in front of her that afternoon. Never once did he look up. He made it stronger that way, and did it for himself, too, as well as for her. Because he did not look up to ask if it pleased he did it all for himself inside, and it strengthened him, and yet he did it for her, too. But he did not do it for her at any loss to himself. He gained by it all through the afternoon" (216).

42. As such they are completely different, however. Burguete is a pastoral environment free of the excesses of Brett, Mike, and Cohn. Paris is an urban world where the expatriates are most at home.

43. "An Introduction to the Structural Analysis of Narrative," *New Literary History*, 6 (1975), 241.

■ Chapter Six. Rural Speech Communities: Faulkner and Hurston

1. *As I Lay Dying*, with which it might be compared in this respect, releases its characters from physical confinement by taking them on a journey. And although the novel's actual speech is similar to that of *The Hamlet*, in *As I Lay Dying* Faulkner's own voice has infiltrated the characters' monologues and enlarged their powers of expression considerably.

2. *The Complete Works of Samuel Taylor Coleridge*, ed. Professor Shedd, 7 vols. (New York: Harper and Bros., 1864), III: 405.

3. Maurice Coindreau, "The Faulkner I Knew," *Shenandoah*, 16 (1965), 29.

4. Forrest G. Robinson's description of the inhabitants of Bricksville in *Adventures of Huckleberry Finn* also applies to the community of Frenchman's Bend: "Spectacles of violence draw their attention away from the grinding torpor of their lives, and at the same time express the rage that those pointless lives must breed" (p. 141). *In Bad Faith: The Dynamics of Deception in Mark Twain's America* (Cambridge. Mass.: Harvard University Press, 1986).

5. Some of the reason for *The Hamlet*'s verbal parsimony may be a distrust, especially of outsiders, that militates against speech.

6. *The Question of Our Speech, The Lesson of Balzac: Two Lectures* (New York: Haskell House, 1972), p. 78

7. *The Flesh and the Word: Eliot, Hemingway, Faulkner* (Nashville: Vanderbilt University Press, 1971), p. 262.

8. Flem is both phlegmatic and phlegm-producing, constantly chewing and spitting. As John T. Matthews aptly characterizes him in *The Play of Faulkner's Language* (Ithaca: Cornell University Press, 1982), p. 174, Flem "has no inter-

est in games, art, magic, talk, passion, or romance—all of the forms of play that enliven the mind."

9. Faulkner humanizes Flem in *The Town* (1957) by having his narrators recreate Flem's state of mind and changing his quest from simple and ruthless gain to respectability. Although Flem remains an antipathetic loner and outsider, Faulkner's portrayal of him thinking and speaking diminishes the distance between him and the reader. Moreover, Flem is now actively dishonest rather than simply exploiting the humanly destructive potential of the business ethos. From the terrifying phenomenon of *The Hamlet* Flem dwindles into merely a particularly objectionable human being.

10. See Henri Bergson, *Laughter*, in *Comedy* (Garden City: Doubleday Anchor, 1956), pp. 78–79: "[Matter] would fain immobilize the intelligently varied movements of the body in stupidly contracted grooves . . . imprint on the whole person such an attitude as to make it appear immersed and absorbed in the materiality of some mechanical occupation instead of ceaselessly renewing its vitality by keeping in touch with a living ideal."

11. Cf. Jason Compson's view that he at least is exempt from an otherwise universal human untrustworthiness: "All the rest of the town and the world and the human race too except himself were Compsons, inexplicable yet quite predictable in that they were in no sense whatever to be trusted." Appendix to *The Sound and the Fury* (New York: Random House, 1956), p. 421.

12. *Philosophical Papers* (Oxford: Clarendon Press, 1961), p. 50.

13. The actual Snopes characters cannot be entirely subsumed under Snopesism, a paradigm that only Flem illustrates completely. His cousins I. O. and Lump are lesser versions of Flem who model themselves on his success within the village; other kinsmen notably deviate from the pattern. Both Ab and Mink are subsistence farmers, neither successful nor rapacious, and Eck, who Faulkner later insisted is not a true Snopes at all, is kind and decent. Accordingly, Matthews's descriptive tag, "the imaginative sterility of Snopesism" (p. 177), applies to Flem and his emulators within the clan, but it does not accurately characterize Ab, Mink, or Ike—all of whom have imaginative visions and aspirations, albeit antisocial in nature.

14. Mary Louise Pratt, *Toward a Speech Act Theory of Literary Discourse* (Bloomington: Indiana University Press, 1977), p. 214.

15. Within the context of social discourse a monosyllabic reply is invariably awkward. As Leech and Short comment, "It is generally true that to be polite, one has to be prolix and indirect." Geoffrey N. Leech and Michael H. Short, *Style in Fiction: A Linguistic Introduction to English Fictional Prose* (London: Longman, 1981), p. 312.

16. Stanley E. Fish, *Is There a Text in This Class? The Authority of Interpretive Communities* (Cambridge, Mass.: Harvard University Press, 1980), p. 218.

17. If Ratliff's verbal playfulness and fiction-making suggest that he is one

kind of author surrogate, Ike is surely another—the pure artist who creates in life itself rather than in the medium of language.

18. Searle, *Speech Acts*, p. 65: "In the performance of any illocutionary act, the speaker implies that the preparatory conditions of the act are satisfied. Thus, for example, when I make a statement I imply that I can back it up."

19. It differed from black male writers as well, who criticized Hurston, as Richard Wright did in a review for *New Masses*, for her embrace of "the Negro folk-mind" and lack of bitterness. Cited by Robert E. Hemenway, *Zora Neale Hurston: A Literary Biography* (Urbana: University of Illinois Press, 1977), p. 241. Such critics failed to appreciate that Hurston's attitude was that of the field anthropologist, not the urban intellectual.

20. Peter Messent reads the novel as "a Bakhtinian decentering of official values and official language," a reading I agree with. However, he explicitly excludes "issues of narration, speech representation, and focalization" from his discussion. *New Readings of the American Novel* (New York: St. Martin's Press, 1990), p. 244.

21. Henry Louis Gates, Jr., *The Signifying Monkey: A Theory of Afro-American Literary Criticism* (New York: Oxford University Press, 1988), pp. 191–92. Gates has the fullest discussion of this phenomenon, which he sees as functioning in a number of ways: as "a dramatic way of expressing a divided self" (p. 207) and as a strategy to resolve "implicit tension between standard English and black dialect" (p. 192), and the opposition between diegesis and mimesis (p. 207). Karla F. C. Holloway, *The Character of the Word: The Texts of Zora Neale Hurston* (Westport, Conn.: Greenwood Press, 1987), p. 56, refers to passages that are "more like dialogue than narration," as examples of "the blending narrative voice."

22. See in particular Mary Helen Washington, "'I Love the Way Janie Crawford Left Her Husbands': Zora Neale Hurston's Emergent Female Hero," *Invented Lives: Narratives of Black Women, 1860–1960* (Garden City: Doubleday, 1987), pp. 237–54, and her foreword to *Their Eyes Were Watching God* (New York: Harper and Row, 1990), pp. vii–xiv; see also Robert B. Stepto, *From Behind the Veil: A Study of Afro-American Narrative* (Urbana: University of Illinois Press, 1979), p. 166. Stepto write, "Hurston's curious insistence on having Janie's tale . . . told by an omniscient third person, rather than by a first person narrator, implies that Janie has not really won her voice and self after all—that her author cannot see her way clear to giving Janie her voice outright."

23. The text punctures Jody's pomposity, treating him like a mock god who creates a world (the land that he acquires and then sells in lots), brings light to it (the single street lamp that he purchases at Sears, Roebuck), and applies retribution to the unfortunate thief Henry Pitts, running him out of town. With a little prompting, he also dispenses mercy to a broken down mule. His favorite interjection is "I god."

24. When Janie repulses Hicks's seductive overture shortly after she and Jody arrive in Eatonville, one of Hicks's friends ignores the volitional element in Janie's behavior and stresses the power of her husband: "You oughta know you can't take no 'oman lak dat from no man lak him. A man dat ups and buys two hundred acres uh land at one whack and pays cash for it" (36). In his ambition and class consciousness Jody is clearly meant to identify with white values.

25. Similarly, the novel links women and mules as beasts of burden in the service of men.

26. Gates, p. 207.

27. When Janie is tried for the killing of Tea Cake, the black community is similarly hostile: "They were there with their tongues cocked and loaded, the only real weapons left to weak folks. The only killing tool they are allowed to use in the presence of white folks" (176).

28. Cf. Hurston's similar statement about Alain Locke, the Harvard and Oxford educated scholar who criticized *Their Eyes* as "folklore fiction" in his survey of "literature by and about the Negro" for the year 1937. Hurston responded by characterizing him as "one who lives by quotations trying to criticize people who live by life." In Hemenway, pp. 241–42.

29. Hurston says as much when she writes that "Negro women are punished . . . for killing men, but only if they exceed the quota. . . . One woman had killed five when I left that turpentine still where she lived. The sheriff was thinking of calling on her and scolding her severely." *Mules and Men* (New York: Negro Universities Press, 1935), p. 86.

30. The narrator of "The Encantadas" reports the effect of Hunilla's speech while deliberately withholding its contents. Cf. Captain Vere's parting words to Billy Budd, an important communication that remains mysterious.

31. Foreward, *Their Eyes Were Watching God*, pp. xiii–xiv.

32. *Dust Tracks on a Road* (Philadelphia: Lippincott, 1942), p. 270.

33. Ibid., p. 268.

34. Ibid., p. 269.

35. This artistic objectification is what must compensate Janie for Tea Cake's death and should not be confused with the exploitative male objectification of living women.

36. Although I place more emphasis on gender, I agree with Klaus Benesch that the final emphasis of the text is on the achievement of Janie telling her story. "Oral Narrative and Literary Text: Afro-American Folklore in *Their Eyes Were Watching God*," *Callaloo*, 11: 3 (Winter 1988), 634. Another positive view of the ending is Holloway's, p. 73: "Janie is surrounded with imagery that is bright. Natural symbols like the pine tree point toward the universe. She is enclosed in the protective warmth of her home, and we understand that within

its walls is a place that shines with her own awakening and is brightened by the poetry of her spirit."

■ Chapter Seven. Nathanael West and the Urban Apocalypse of the Word

1. *Through the Custom-House: Nineteenth-Century American Fiction and Modern Theory* (Baltimore: Johns Hopkins University Press, 1982), p. 178.

2. "Literature and Discontinuity," *Critical Essays*, trans. Richard Howard (Evanston: Northwestern University Press, 1972), p. 173.

3. Leo Bersani, *A Future for Astyanax: Character and Desire in Literature* (Boston: Little, Brown, 1976), p. 195.

4. "Discourse Typology in Prose," *Readings in Russian Poetics: Formalist and Structuralist Views*, ed. Ladislav Matejka and Krystyna Pomorska (Cambridge, Mass.: M.I.T. Press, 1971), p. 195.

5. Miss Lonelyhearts himself becomes the stone Shrike speaks of when he transforms himself into a rock in order to escape suffering.

6. Ernest Hemingway, *A Farewell to Arms* (New York: Charles Scribner's Sons, 1969), p. 185: "Finally only the names of places had dignity. Certain numbers were the same way and certain dates and these with the names of places were all you could say and have them mean anything."

7. "Indirect Speech Acts," *Speech Acts*, vol. 3 of *Syntax and Semantics*, ed. Peter Cole and Jerry L. Morgan (New York: Academic Press, 1975), p. 60.

8. For a dissenting view of the letters as humorous and not necessarily sincere or truthful, see Jeffrey L. Duncan, "The Problem of Language in *Miss Lonelyhearts*," *Iowa Review*, 8 (1977), 116–28. Commenting on the "letters in the flesh" spoken by Mary Shrike and Fay Doyle, he writes, "They reveal a reality, unarguably, but it is hardly one of genuine suffering, much less of profound humility. Instead they betray mere attitudes struck, postures assumed, poses wantonly displayed, a comic pornography of suffering and trouble" (117–18). I draw a different conclusion. Duncan's description does not fit the other "letter in the flesh," Peter Doyle, any more than it does the letters whose writers remain unseen. But it does suggest the novel's central issue: how to express (and deal with) the reality of suffering in public language.

9. West constantly mixes these discourses with the effect that William Gass has described in characterizing postmodernist fiction: "If you take really bowel-turning material, from the point of view of its pragmatic importance in the world, and surround it like kitty litter with stuff that is there purely for play, then you get an electric line between the two poles clothes would turn white simply hanging on." "An Interview with William Gass," *Anything Can Hap-*

pen: Interviews with American Novelists, ed. Tom LeClair and Larry McCaffery (Urbana: University of Illinois Press, 1983), p. 160.

10. Those letter writers Miss Lonelyhearts encounters personally are unable to improve upon their letters with speech. Fay Doyle delivers a self-justifying narrative which reveals her insensitivity and brutality. When Peter Doyle "labored into speech, Miss Lonelyhearts was unable to understand him" (45).

11. Lotman with B. A. Uspensky, "On the Semiotic Mechanism of Culture," *New Literary History*, 9 (1978), 213.

12. *Blonde Beauty* encapsulates the Wasp fantasy of sexual perfection in the American cultural tradition.

13. Shrike's banter has a nasty edge, but it is otherwise reminiscent of Bill's in *The Sun Also Rises*.

14. J. L. Austin, *How to Do Things with Words* (Cambridge, Mass.: Harvard University Press, 1962), p. 15; see also Searle, "Indirect Speech Acts," p. 77: "Since normally you are never in as good a position as I am to assert what I want, believe, intend, and so on, and since I am normally not in as good a position as you to assert what you want, believe, intend, and so on, it is, in general, odd for me to ask you about my states or tell you about yours."

15. H. Paul Grice, "Logic and Conversation," *Speech Acts*, vol. 3 of *Syntax and Semantics*, ed. Peter Cole and Jerry L. Morgan (New York: Academic Press, 1975), p. 47.

16. Parties to a conversation commonly have the same goal while the conversation lasts. This can also apply to quarrels because the disputants share the goal of expressing individual positions on a particular matter (with varying motives: self-justification, proselytization, hostility toward the dialogue partner). Should the quarrel reach a point of open conflict, the norms of social discourse will no longer apply since they depend upon a threshold of politeness. As Erving Goffman writes in *Frame Analysis: An Essay on the Organization of Experience* (Cambridge, Mass.: Harvard University Press, 1974), p. 124, "It is . . . the obligation to show visual respect which characterizes the frame of ordinary face-to-face interaction."

17. As West described his method in "Some Notes on *Miss Lonelyhearts*," *Contempo*, 3 (1933), 1, "Violent images are used to illustrate commonplace events. Violent acts are left almost bald."

18. Syntactically the medial positioning of Mary's statements about her father conveys the impossibility of emulating masculine achievement and freedom. Her destiny is the feminine one of abuse and suffering which occupies both positions of primacy in the speech. Mary's verbal dissociation from her own life is rendered most dramatically here: while she voices her fears of this role she is playing it.

19. In contrast, Shrike never speaks about himself. He escapes this other-

wise endemic verbal self-preoccupation by directing his language away from himself, making others his theme.

20. The word *gravely*, which occurs in both visions of order, suggests a seriousness that Miss Lonelyhearts cannot achieve. Whereas he often dismisses his serious thoughts with a laugh when they become uncomfortable, the children dancing and the readers forming his name are engaged in constructive enterprises, imposing a pattern on the flux of experience: "All order is doomed, yet the battle is worth while" (209).

■ Chapter Eight. Postmodernist Speech:
The Universe of Discourse as a Closed System

1. This is not the place for an extended discussion of what postmodernism is. I have found some definitions more useful than others, but more importantly, I agree with Brian McHale that postmodernism follows "*from* modernism more than *after*." *Postmodernist Fiction* (New York: Methuen, 1987), p. 5. For diverse perspectives, see Richard Gilman, *The Confusion of Realms* (New York: Oxford University Press, 1969); Ihab Hassan, *The Dismemberment of Orpheus: Toward a Postmodern Literature* (New York: Oxford University Press, 1971); Tony Tanner, *City of Words: American Fiction, 1950–1970* (New York: Harper & Row, 1971); Albert J. Guerard, "Notes on the Rhetoric of Anti-realist Fiction," *Tri-Quarterly*, 30 (1974), 3–50; Gerald Graff, *Literature Against Itself: Literary Ideas in Modern Society* (Chicago: University of Chicago Press, 1979); Fredric Jameson, "Postmodernism and Consumer Society," *The Anti-Aesthetic: Essays on Postmodernist Culture*, ed. Hal Foster (Port Townsend, Wash.: Bay Press, 1983), pp. 111–25, and *Postmodernism, or, the Cultural Logic of Late Capitalism* (Durham: Duke University Press, 1991); Jean François Lyotard, *The Postmodern Condition: A Report on Knowledge* trans. Geoff Bennington and Brian Massumi (Minneapolis: University of Minnesota Press, 1984), and Douwe W. Fokkema, *Literary History, Modernism, and Postmodernism* (Amsterdam: John Benjamins, 1984). Alain Robbe-Grillet, *For a New Novel: Essays on Fiction*, trans. Richard Howard (New York: Grove Press, 1965) remains the classic statement of the postmodernist position by a practicing novelist, while Richard A. Lanham's definition of "rhetorical man" in *The Motives of Eloquence: Literary Rhetoric in the Renaissance* (New Haven: Yale University Press, 1976) seems remarkably apt as a description of the postmodernist writer: "He can play freely with language. For him it owes no transcendent loyalties" (4).

2. "The Literature of Exhaustion," *The American Novel Since World War I*, ed. Marcus Klein (New York: Fawcett, 1969), p. 267.

3. Mike Featherstone, "Postmodernism, Cultural Change, and Social Practice," *Postmodernism/Jameson/Critique*, ed. Douglas Kellner (Washington,

D.C.: Maisonneuve Press, 1989), p. 122; cf. Fokkema, p. 42: "[Postmodernism] is based on a preference for nonselection or quasi-nonselection, on a rejection of discriminating hierarchies, and a refusal to distinguish between truth and fiction."

4. M. M. Bakhtin, *The Dialogic Imagination*, ed. Michael Holquist, trans. Caryl Emerson and Michael Holquist (Austin: University of Texas Press, 1981), p. 299.

5. As McHale writes, p. 39, "The dimension of speakers, voices, and positions is especially foregrounded in modernist poetics, but while of course still present and functional in postmodernist poetics, relatively backgrounded there."

6. *Language and Control* (London: Routledge and Kegan Paul, 1979), p. 63.

7. Emile Benveniste, *Problems in General Linguistics*, trans. M. E. Meek (Coral Gables: University of Miami Press, 1971), p. 234, regards clichés as so meaningless that he excludes them from the category of performatives.

8. Norbert Wiener, *The Human Use of Human Beings: Cybernetics and Society* (New York: Discus Books, 1954), p. 21.

9. "Bakhtin, Sociolinguistics and Deconstruction," *The Theory of Reading*, ed. Frank Gloversmith (Sussex and New York: Harvester Press and Barnes and Noble, 1984), p. 133. White's description of Pynchon's novels could serve for the majority of postmodernist texts: "The 'high' languages of modern America— technology, psychoanalysis, business, administration and military jargon—are 'carnivalized' by a set of rampant, irreverent, inebriate discourses from low life" (135).

10. Ibid., p. 135.

11. *Problems of Dostoevsky's Poetics*, ed. and trans. Caryl Emerson (Minneapolis: University of Minnesota Press, 1984), p. 40.

12. *Fables of Aggression: Wyndham Lewis, The Modernist as Fascist* (Berkeley: University of California Press, 1979), p. 14.

13. Stanley Schatt, *Kurt Vonnegut, Jr.* (Boston: Twayne, 1976), p. 100, remarks that "Vonnegut's conversations illustrate the hopelessness of communication."

14. Peter L. Berger and Thomas Luckmann observe in *The Social Construction of Reality: A Treatise in the Sociology of Knowledge* (New York: Doubleday, 1966), that we assume that others are sharing "the common world of everyday life" (25).

15. Clinton S. Burhans, Jr., "Hemingway and Vonnegut: Diminishing Vision in a Dying Age," *Modern Fiction Studies*, 21 (1975), 181, observes that Hemingway, unlike Vonnegut, espouses the nineteenth-century belief that "man can find or create patterns of meaning and order and value."

16. Dwayne Hoover's capricious and eventually violent treatment of others

has its counterpart in the writer/character's treatment of the characters he manipulates and interacts with in the text.

17. Pierre Bourdieu, "The Economics of Linguistic Exchange," trans. Richard Nice, *Social Science Information*, 16 (1977), 648.

18. As Bourdieu notes, *ibid.*, p. 667n., "this is one aspect of the anxious vigilance which the dominated invest in their relations with the dominant."

19. See also Vonnegut, in *Wampeters, Foma and Granfalloons* (New York: Delacorte, 1974), p. 281: "What I say didactically in the introduction to *Breakfast of Champions* is that I can't live without a culture anymore, that I realize I don't have one. What passes for a culture in my head is really a bunch of commercials, and this is intolerable."

20. See Chapter 5, p. 248 (n. 11).

21. Wayne Booth's categories of intruding, dramatized, and unreliable narrators are not designed to encompass such postmodernist subversions as Vonnegut's creation of the character Vonnegut who retains authorial omnipotence within the text at the same time as he becomes the victim of another character. (See *The Rhetoric of Fiction* [Chicago: University of Chicago Press, 1961], pp. 169–240.) It is typical of postmodernist fiction to take the traditional aspects of fiction to extremes, as if to determine how much it is possible to distort a particular convention without destroying its usefulness altogether. See McHale, p. 204: "The author as a character in his own fiction signals the paradoxical interpenetration of two realms that are mutually inaccessible, or ought to be."

22. In the area of literary satire, the measurements of the penis may be a comic reduction of Melville's statistics about whales in *Moby-Dick*. As Charles Berryman has pointed out, a tourist attraction named Moby Dick is being destroyed by industrial pollution elsewhere in the novel. "Vonnegut's Comic Persona in *Breakfast of Champions*," *Critical Essays on Kurt Vonnegut*, ed. Robert Merrill (Boston: G. K. Hall, 1990), p. 164.

23. The difficulty of distinguishing between the writer and the character is borne out by the number of commentators who take the character Vonnegut's assertion that he was "born again" as a serious utterance of the author about himself. See Peter B. Messent, "*Breakfast of Champions*: The Direction of Kurt Vonnegut's Fiction," *Journal of American Studies*, 8 (1974), 109; Lynn Buck, "Vonnegut's World of Comic Futility," *Studies in American Fiction*, 3 (1975), 183; Stanley Schatt, p. 109; Robert Merrill, "Vonnegut's *Breakfast of Champions*: The Conversion of Heliogabalus," *Critique*, 18 (1977), 107; Kathryn Hume, "Kurt Vonnegut and the Myths and Symbols of Meaning," *Texas Studies in Literature and Language*, 24 (1982), 436; and David Cowart, "Culture and Anarchy: Vonnegut's Later Career," *Critical Essays*, p. 174. Berryman, p. 166, believes that Vonnegut creates a persona in the novel who is "an obtuse, comic self-parody of the novelist." I believe, instead, that the relationship between

Vonnegut as author and Vonnegut as character is not so clear-cut, a characteristic that destabilizes the authorial voice in a typically postmodern way.

24. The term is Bakhtin's in *Problems of Doestoevsky's Poetics*, p. 184.

25. Jane Gallop's description of Oedipus and the riddle in *The Daughter's Seduction: Feminism and Psychoanalysis* (Ithaca: Cornell University Press, 1982), p. 61, works equally well for *The Crying of Lot 49*: "A 'solved' riddle is the reduction of heterogeneous material to logic, to the homogeneity of logical thought, which produces a blind spot, the inability to see the otherness that gets lost in the reduction. Only the unsolved riddle, the process of riddle-work before its final completion, is a confrontation with otherness." The text of the novel is a sustained piece of riddle-work in which Oedipa confronts various forms of otherness without, however, arriving at a way of mastering their heterogeneity.

26. The text contains two spellings, both suggestive: tristero (*triste*, sadness) and trystero (tryst). The first reflects the common denominator of dissatisfaction with society on the part of the alienated; the second, the possibility of meaningful encounter that Oedipa seeks.

27. Molly Hite, *Ideas of Order in the Novels of Thomas Pynchon* (Athens, Ohio: Ohio State University Press, 1983), p. 78, describes the novel's structure as parodic but finds that Pynchon "allows the initial level of parody to be muted into pathos." Frank Palmieri, "Neither Literally nor as Metaphor: Pynchon's *Crying* and the Structure of Scientific Revolutions," *ELH*, 54 (Winter, 1987), 984, believes that the novel "expresses a modern anxiety about the efficacy of metaphor."

28. *Postmodernism, or the Cultural Logic of Late Capitalism*, p. 372.

29. Cf. Alain Robbe-Grillet, p. 19: "The world is neither significant or absurd. It *is*. . . ."

30. *The Human Use of Human Beings*, p. 92.

31. Hite, p. 83, points out that the only W.A.S.T.E. letter Oedipa sees is banal (*Crying*, p. 53). Given the novel's atmosphere, this is hardly definitive since the letter could easily be part of the plot to deceive Oedipa. The letters received by the founder of Inamorati Anonymous from failed suicides are described as genuine messages as opposed to the "sucker-list stuff" that comes through regular deliveries (*Crying*, p. 114).

32. Stefano Tani, *The Doomed Detective* (Carbondale: Southern Illinois University Press, 1984), p. 95, notes that the Italian verb *inverare* means "to make true."

33. See Erving Goffman, p. 488: "Suspicion . . . would seem to be a universal and basic structural possibility in social life, and its analysis a best way of beginning to appreciate the framed character of our realms of meaning, including our realities."

34. *Language and Control*, p. 63.

35. Both Austin and Searle take this position. See J. L. Austin, *Philosophical Papers* (Oxford: Clarendon Press, 1961), p. 236, and John Searle, "Indirect Speech Acts," *Speech Acts*, vol. 3 of *Syntax and Semantics*, ed. Peter Cole and Jerry L. Morgan (New York: Academic Press, 1975), p. 77.

36. *The Literary Speech Act: Don Juan with J. L. Austin, or Seduction in Two Languages*, trans. Catherine Porter (Ithaca: Cornell University Press, 1983), p. 112.

37. *The Confusion of Realms*, p. 51. Any later critic must acknowledge an indebtedness to Gilman's brief consideration of *Snow White*, an early treatment (1969) that contains a number of valuable insights into the novel's structure and technique.

38. "Interview with Donald Barthelme," in Joe David Bellamy, *The New Fiction: Interviews with Innovative American Writers* (Urbana: University of Illinois Press, 1974), pp. 51–52. Charles Molesworth, *Donald Barthelme's Fiction: The Ironist Saved From Drowning* (Columbia, Mo.: University of Missouri Press, 1982), pp. 46–47, describes collage as Barthelme's chief stylistic device." This holds true for the early short stories and *Snow White*, but not for Barthelme's later work.

39. *Postmodernism, or the Logic of Late Capitalism*, p. 67.

40. With rare exceptions for short utterances, in *The Crying of Lot 49* speech is separated from narrative by the use of quotation marks and indentation.

41. Feelings are also the same. Clem thinks of Snow White: "I cannot help feeling that, when everything is said and done, she is essentially mine. Even though I am aware that each of the others feels the same way" (22).

42. *Donald Barthelme: An Exhibition* (Durham: Duke University Press, 1991), p. 86.

43. As Fokkema writes, "Much of the meaning of the story consists of learning to understand its code—a code that opens our eyes to our habit of repeating semantic waste without being aware of it" (47).

44. McHale, p. 163.

45. *Literature Against Itself*, p. 236.

46. Ibid., p. 239.

47. Bellamy, *The New Fiction*, p. 52.

48. C. K. Ogden and I. A. Richards, *The Meaning of Meaning*, 4th ed. rev. (London: Routledge and Kegan Paul, 1936), p. 15: "Normally, whenever we hear anything said we spring spontaneously to an immediate conclusion, namely, that the speaker is referring to what we should be referring to were we speaking the words ourselves. . . . in most discussions which attempt greater subtleties than could be handled in a gesture language this will not be so."

49. Like all speech in the novel this passage is part of a paragraph. I have

presented it in the conventional form of fictive direct discourse in order to focus on it as speech.

50. *One-Dimensional Man: Studies in the Ideology of Advanced Industrial Society* (Boston: Beacon Press, 1964), p. 101.

■ Conclusion

1. Ratliff, it is true, can communicate effectively, but most of the time he prefers a fanciful self-pleasuring idiom that puzzles the plain folk of the Bend.

2. Jay Cantor, *The Death of Che Guevara* (New York: Knopf, 1983); Philip Roth, *The Anatomy Lesson* (New York: Farrar, Straus & Giroux, 1983). Cantor's novel may well be the most undervalued significant work of the eighties.

3. *The Passing of the Modern Age* (New York: Harper & Row, 1970), p. 31.

Bibliography

Agnew, Jean-Christophe. *World's Apart: The Market and the Theater in Anglo-American Thought, 1550–1750*. Cambridge: Cambridge University Press, 1986.

Aldridge, John W. "Revaluation: *The Sun Also Rises*—Sixty Years Later," *Sewanee Review*, 94 (1986), 337–45.

Ammons, Elizabeth. *Edith Wharton's Argument with America*. Athens: University of Georgia Press, 1980.

———. "Heroines in *Uncle Tom's Cabin*," *Critical Essays on Harriet Beecher Stowe*. Ed. Elizabeth Ammons. Boston: G. K. Hall, 1981, pp. 152–65.

———. "'Stowe's Dream of the Mother-Savior': *Uncle Tom's Cabin* and American Women Writers Before the 1920s," *New Essays on Uncle Tom's Cabin*. Ed. Eric J. Sundquist. Cambridge: Cambridge University Press, 1986, pp. 155–95.

Anderson, Quentin. *The Imperial Self: An Essay in American Literary and Cultural History*. New York: Knopf, 1971.

Arac, Jonathan. "The Politics of *The Scarlet Letter*," *Ideology and Classic American Literature*. Ed. Sacvan Bercovitch and Myra Jehlen. Cambridge: Cambridge University Press, 1986, pp. 247–66.

Austin, J. L. *How to Do Things with Words*. Cambridge, Mass.: Harvard University Press, 1962.

———. *Philosophical Papers*. Oxford: Clarendon Press, 1961.

Axelrad, Allan M. "Wish Fulfillment in the Wilderness: D. H. Lawrence and the Leatherstocking Tales," *American Quarterly*, 39 (Winter 1987), 563–85.

Bakhtin, M. M. *The Dialogic Imagination*. Ed. Michael Holquist. Trans. Caryl Emerson and Michael Holquist. Austin: University of Texas Press, 1981.

———. "Discourse Typology in Prose," *Readings in Russian Poetics: Formalist and Structuralist Views*. Ed. Ladislav Matejka and Krystyna Pomorska. Cambridge, Mass.: M.I.T. Press, 1971, pp. 176–96.

———. *Problems of Dostoevsky's Poetics*. Ed. and trans. Caryl Emerson. Minneapolis: University of Minnesota Press, 1984.

Baldwin, James. "Everybody's Protest Novel," *Critical Essays on Harriet Beecher Stowe*. Ed. Elizabeth Ammons. Boston: G. K. Hall, 1980, pp. 92–97.

Barnett, Louise K. "Bartleby as Alienated Worker," *Studies in Short Fiction*, 11 (1974), 379–85.

Barrett, William. *Irrational Man: A Study in Existential Philosophy*. Garden City: Doubleday, 1962.

Barth, John. "The Literature of Exhaustion," *The American Novel Since World War I*. Ed. Marcus Klein. New York: Fawcett, 1969, pp. 267–79.

Barthelme, Donald. *Snow White*. New York: Atheneum, 1967.

Barthes, Roland. *Critical Essays*. Trans. Richard Howard. Evanston: Northwestern University Press, 1972.

———. "An Introduction to the Structural Analysis of Narrative," trans. Lionel Duisit, *NLH*, 6 (1975), 237–72.

———. *A Lover's Discourse: Fragments*. Trans. Richard Howard. New York: Hill and Wang, 1978.

———. *The Pleasure of the Text*. Trans. Richard Miller. New York: Hill and Wang, 1975.

———. *Writing Degree Zero/Elements of Semiology*. Trans. Annette Lavers and Colin Smith. Boston: Beacon Press, 1970.

Baumgarten, Murray. "From Realism to Expressionism: Toward a History of the Novel," *ELH*, 6 (1975), 415–27.

Bayer, John G. "Narrative Techniques and the Oral Tradition in *The Scarlet Letter*," *American Literature*, 52 (1980), 250–63.

Baym, Nina. "Melville's Quarrel with Fiction," *PMLA*, 94 (1979), 909–23.

———. *The Shape of Hawthorne's Career*. Ithaca: Cornell University Press, 1976.

———. "The Women of Cooper's Leatherstocking Tales," *American Quarterly*, 23 (December 1971), 696–709.

Bell, Millicent. *Edith Wharton and Henry James: The Story of Their Friendship*. New York: George Braziller, 1965.

———. *Meaning in Henry James*. Cambridge, Mass.: Harvard University Press, 1991.

———. "The Obliquity of Signs: *The Scarlet Letter*," *Massachusetts Review*, 23 (1982), 9–26.

Bellamy, Joe David. *The New Fiction: Interviews with Innovative American Writers*. Urbana: University of Illinois Press, 1974, pp. 51–52.

Benesch, Klaus. "Oral Narrative and Literary Text: Afro-American Folklore in *Their Eyes Were Watching God*," *Callaloo*, 11: 3 (Winter 1988), 627–35.

Benveniste, Emile. *Problems in General Linguistics*. Trans. M. E. Meek. Coral Gables: University of Miami Press, 1971.

Bercovitch, Sacvan. *The Puritan Origins of the American Self*. New Haven: Yale University Press, 1975.

Berger, Peter L. and Thomas Luckmann. *The Social Construction of Reality: A Treatise in the Sociology of Knowledge*. New York: Doubleday, 1966.

Bergson, Henri. *Comedy*. Garden City: Doubleday Anchor, 1956.

Bernstein, Basil. "Aspects of Language and Learning in the Genesis of the Social Process," *Language in Culture and Society*. Ed. Dell Hymes. New York: Harper & Row, 1964, pp. 251–63.

———. *Class, Codes and Control: Theoretical Studies Towards a Sociology of Language.* New York: Schocken Books, 1971.

Berryman, Charles. "Vonnegut's Comic Persona in *Breakfast of Champions*," *Critical Essays on Kurt Vonnegut.* Ed. Robert Merrill. Boston: G. K. Hall, 1990, pp. 162–69.

Bersani, Leo. *A Future for Astynax: Character and Desire in Literature.* Boston: Little, Brown, 1976.

Berthoff, Warner. *The Example of Melville.* Princeton: Princeton University Press, 1962.

———. *A Literature Without Qualities: American Writing Since 1945.* Berkeley: University of California Press 1979.

Bezanson, Walter E. "*Moby-Dick:* Work of Art," *Moby-Dick: Centennial Essays.* Ed. Tyrus Hillway and Luther S. Mansfield. Dallas: Southern Methodist University Press, 1953, pp. 31–58.

Bird, John. " 'These Leather-Face People': Huck and the Moral Act of Lying," *Studies in American Fiction,* 15 (Spring 1987), 71–80.

Booth, Wayne C. *The Company We Keep: An Ethics of Fiction.* Berkeley: University of California Press, 1988.

———. *The Rhetoric of Fiction.* Chicago: University of Chicago Press, 1961.

Bourdieu, Pierre. *Ce que parler veut dire: l'économie des échanges linquistiques.* Paris: Fayard, 1982.

———. "The Economics of Linguistic Exchange," trans. Richard Nice, *Social Science Information,* 16 (1977) 645–68.

Bridgman, Richard. *The Colloquial Style in America.* New York: Oxford University Press, 1966.

Brodhead, Richard H. *Hawthorne, Melville, and the Novel.* Chicago: University of Chicago Press, 1976.

Brown, Gillian. "Getting in the Kitchen with Dinah: Domestic Politics in *Uncle Tom's Cabin*," *American Quarterly,* 36 (Fall 1984), 503–523.

Buck, Lynn. "Vonnegut's World of Comic Futility," *Studies in American Fiction,* 3 (1975), 181–98.

Buell, Lawrence. "The Last Word on 'The Confidence-Man'?" *Illinois Quarterly,* 35 (1972), 15–29.

Burhans, Clinton S., Jr. "Hemingway and Vonnegut: Diminishing Vision in a Dying Age," *Modern Fiction Studies,* 21 (1975), 173–91.

Burke, Kenneth. *Permanence and Change.* New York: New Republic, 1935.

Cantor, Jay. *The Death of Che Guevara.* New York: Knopf, 1983.

Carton, Evan. *The Rhetoric of American Romance: Dialectic and Identity in Emerson, Dickinson, Poe, and Hawthorne.* Baltimore: Johns Hopkins Press, 1985.

Cassirer, Ernst. *The Philosophy of Symbolic Forms, Language.* vol. 1. New Haven: Yale University Press, 1953.

Charvat, William. *The Profession of Authorship in America, 1800–1870: The Papers of William Charvat*. Ed. Matthew J. Bruccoli. Columbus: Ohio State University Press, 1968.

Chase, Stuart. *The Tyranny of Words*. New York: Harcourt, Brace, 1938.

Chatman, Seymour. *The Later Style of Henry James*. New York: Barnes and Noble, 1972.

Clemens, Samuel L. *Adventures of Huckleberry Finn*. Ed. Walter Blair and Victor Fischer. *The Works of Mark Twain*. vol. 8. Berkeley: University of California Press, 1988.

———. *The Autobiography of Mark Twain*. Ed. Charles Neider. New York: Harper & Row, 1959.

———. *Mark Twain's Notebook*. Ed. Albert Bigelow Paine. New York: Harper and Brothers, 1935.

Coindreau, Maurice. "The Faulkner I Knew," *Shenandoah*, 16 (1965), 27–35.

Colacurcio, Michael J. "Footsteps of Ann Hutchinson: The Context of *The Scarlet Letter*," *ELH*, 39 (1972), 459–494.

Coleridge, Samuel Taylor. *Complete Works of Samuel Taylor Coleridge*. Ed. Professor Shedd. 7 vols. New York: Harper and Brothers, 1864.

Cooper, James Fenimore. *The American Democrat*. Ed. George Dekker and Larry Johnston. Baltimore: Penguin, 1969.

———. *The Deerslayer, or The First War-Path. The Writings of James Fenimore Cooper*. Ed. James Franklin Beard. Albany: State University of New York Press, 1987.

———. *Notions of the Americans*. 2 vols. Philadelphia: Carey, Lea and Blanchard, 1841.

———. *The Redskins, or Indian and Injin*. Boston: Houghton Mifflin, 1898.

Cowart, David. "Culture and Anarchy: Vonnegut's Later Career," *Critical Essays on Kurt Vonnegut*. Ed. Robert Merrill. Boston: G. K. Hall, 1990, pp. 170–87.

Cowley, Malcolm. "The Middle American Style: D. Crockett to E. Hemingway," *New York Times Book Review*, July 15, 1945, p. 3.

———. *A Second Flowering*. New York: Viking Press, 1973.

Cox, James M. *Mark Twain: The Fate of Humor*. Princeton: Princeton University Press, 1966.

Crews, Frederick C. *Sins of the Fathers: Hawthorne's Psychological Themes*. New York: Oxford University Press, 1966.

Darnell, Donald. "Cooper's Tragedy of Manners," *Studies in the Novel*, 11 (1979), pp. 406–15.

Davis, David Brion. "The Deerslayer, A Democratic Knight of the Wilderness: Cooper, 1981," *Twelve Original Essays on Great American Novels*. Ed. Charles Shapiro. Detroit: Wayne State University Press, 1958, pp. 1–22.

DeLillo, Don. *End Zone*. Boston: Houghton Mifflin, 1972.

Dillingham, William B. *Melville's Later Novels*. Athens: University of Georgia Press, 1986.

Dimock, Wai-chee. "Debasing Exchange: Edith Wharton's *The House of Mirth*," *PMLA*, 100 (1985), 783–92.

——. *Empire of Liberty: Melville and the Poetics of Individualism*. Princeton: Princeton University Press, 1989.

Donaldson, Scott. "Humor in *The Sun Also Rises*," *New Essays on The Sun Also Rises*. Ed. Linda Wagner-Martin. Cambridge: Cambridge University Press, 1987, pp. 19–41.

Douglas, Ann. *The Feminization of American Culture*. New York: Knopf, 1977.

Dryden, Edgar A. *Melville's Thematics of Form: The Great Art of Telling the Truth*. Baltimore: Johns Hopkins University Press, 1968.

Duncan, Jeffrey L. "The Problem of Language in *Miss Lonelyhearts*," *Iowa Review*, 8 (1977), 116–28.

Eble, Kenneth. "The Craft of Revision: *The Great Gatsby*," *Fitzgerald's The Great Gatsby: The Novel, the Critics, the Background*. Ed. Henry Dan Piper. New York: Charles Scribner's Sons, 1970, pp. 110–117.

Edwards, Jonathan. *A Careful and Strict Inquiry into the Prevailing Notions of the Freedom of the Will*, rpt. in *Works*, 4 vols. New York: Leavitt and Allen, 1843.

Eliot, T. S. *Collected Poems 1909–1962*. New York: Harcourt, Brace, 1968.

——. *To Criticize the Critic and Other Writings*. New York: Farrar, Straus & Giroux, 1965.

Ervin-Tripp, Susan. "Is Sybil There? The Structure of Some American English Directives." *Language and Society*, 5 (1976), 25–66.

Faulkner, William. *As I Lay Dying*. New York: Random House, 1946.

——. *The Hamlet*. New York: Random House, 1956.

——. *The Sound and the Fury*. New York: Random House, 1956.

Featherstone, Mike. "Postmodernism, Cultural Change, and Social Practice," *Postmodernism/Jameson/Critique*. Ed. Douglas Kellner. Washington, D.C.: Maisonneuve Press, 1989, pp. 117–138.

Feidelson, Charles, Jr. "The Scarlet Letter," *Hawthorne Centenary Essays*. Ed. Roy Harvey Pearce. Columbus: Ohio State University Press, 1964, pp. 31–77.

——. *Symbolism and American Literature*. Chicago: University of Chicago Press, 1966.

Felman, Shoshana. *The Literary Speech Act: Don Juan with J. L. Austin, or Seduction in Two Languages*. Trans. Catherine Porter. Ithaca: Cornell University Press, 1983.

Fish, Stanley E. *Is There a Text in This Class? The Authority of Interpretive Communities*. Cambridge, Mass.: Harvard University Press, 1980.

Fisher, Philip. *Hard Facts: Setting and Form in the American Novel.* New York: Oxford University Press, 1985.

Fitzgerald, F. Scott. *The Great Gatsby.* New York: Charles Scribner's Sons, 1925.

Fokkema, Douwe W. *Literary History, Modernism, and Postmodernism.* Amsterdam: John Benjamins, 1984.

Foley, Barbara. "From New Criticism to Deconstruction: The Example of Charles Feidelson's *Symbolism and American Literature*," *American Quarterly*, 36 (1984), 44–64.

Foster, Elizabeth S. Introduction, *The Confidence-Man: His Masquerade.* New York: Hendricks House, 1954.

Foucault, Michel. *L'ordre du discours.* Paris: Gallimard, 1971.

Fowler, Roger. *Language and Control.* London: Routledge and Kegan Paul, 1979.

Franklin, H. Bruce. *The Victim as Criminal and Artist: Literature from the American Prison.* New York: Oxford University Press, 1978.

———. *The Wake of the Gods: Melville's Mythology.* Stanford: Stanford University Press, 1963.

Franklin, Wayne. *The New World of James Fenimore Cooper.* Chicago: University of Chicago Press, 1982.

Gabler-Hover, Janet. *Truth in American Fiction: The Legacy of Rhetorical Idealism.* Athens: University of Georgia Press, 1990.

Gallop, Jane. *The Daughter's Seduction: Feminism and Psychoanalysis.* Ithaca: Cornell University Press, 1982.

Gass, William. "An Interview with William Gass," *Anything Can Happen: Interviews with American Novelists.* Ed. Tom LeClair and Larry McCaffery. Urbana: University of Illinois Press, 1983, pp. 152–75.

Gates, Henry Louis, Jr. *The Signifying Monkey: A Theory of Afro-American Literary Criticism.* New York: Oxford University Press, 1988.

Gerber, John C. "The Relation between Point of View and Style in the Works of Mark Twain," *Style in Prose Fiction.* Ed. Harold C. Martin. New York: Columbia University Press, 1959, pp. 142–71.

Gilman, Richard. *The Confusion of Realms.* New York: Oxford University Press, 1969.

Gilmore, Michael T. *American Romanticism and the Marketplace.* Chicago: University of Chicago Press, 1985.

Godden, Richard. "*The Great Gatsby*: Glamor on the Turn," *Journal of American Studies*, 16 (December, 1982), 343–71.

Goffman, Erving. *Frame Analysis: An Essay on the Organization of Experience.* Cambridge, Mass.: Harvard University Press, 1974.

Gossett, Thomas F. *Uncle Tom's Cabin and American Culture.* Dallas: Southern Methodist University Press, 1985.

Graff, Gerald. *Literature Against Itself: Literary Ideas in Modern Society*. Chicago: University of Chicago Press, 1979.

Greenslade, William. "The Power of Advertising: Chad Newsome and the Meaning of Paris in *The Ambassadors*," *ELH*, 49 (1982), 99–122.

Grice, H. Paul. "Logic and Conversation," *Speech Acts*. Ed. Peter Cole and Jerry L. Morgan. vol. 3 of *Syntax and Semantics*. New York: Academic Press, 1975.

Guerard, Albert J. "Notes on the Rhetoric of Anti-realist Fiction," *TriQuarterly*, 30 (1974), 3–50.

Guetti, James. *The Limits of Metaphor: A Study of Melville, Conrad, and Faulkner*. Ithaca: Cornell University Press, 1967.

Gumperz, John J. *Discourse Strategies*. Cambridge: Cambridge University Press, 1982.

Gura, Philip F. *The Wisdom of Words: Language, Theology, and Literature in the New England Renaissance*. Middletown: Wesleyan University Press, 1981.

Harding, Susan. "Women and Words in a Spanish Village," *Towards an Anthropology of Women*. Ed. Rayna R. Reiter. New York: Monthly Review Press, 1975, pp. 283–308.

Hassan, Ihab. *The Dismemberment of Orpheus: Toward a Postmodern Literature*. New York: Oxford University Press, 1971.

Hawthorne, Nathaniel. *The Centenary Edition of the Works of Nathaniel Hawthorne*. Ed. William Charvat et al. Columbus: Ohio State University Press, 1974.

Hemenway, Robert E. *Zora Neale Hurston: A Literary Biography*. Urbana: University of Illinois Press, 1977.

Hemingway, Ernest. *Death in the Afternoon*. New York: Charles Scribner's Sons, 1932.

———. *A Farewell to Arms*. New York: Charles Scribner's Sons, 1929.

———. *Green Hills of Africa*. New York: Charles Scribner's Sons, 1935.

———. *The Sun Also Rises*. New York: Charles Scribner's Sons, 1970.

Hite, Molly. *Ideas of Order in the Novels of Thomas Pynchon*. Athens, Ohio: Ohio State University Press, 1983.

Holland, Laurence B. "A 'Raft of Trouble': Word and Deed in *Huckleberry Finn*," *American Realism: New Essays*. Ed. Eric J. Sundquist. Baltimore: Johns Hopkins University Press, 1982, pp. 66–81.

Holloway, Karla F. C. *The Character of the Word: The Texts of Zora Neale Hurston*. Westport, Conn.: Greenwood Press, 1987.

Hume, Kathryn. "Kurt Vonnegut and the Myths and Symbols of Meaning," *Texas Studies in Literature and Language*, 24 (1982), 429–47.

Hurston, Zora Neale. *Dust Tracks on a Road*. Philadelphia: Lippincott, 1942.

———. *Mules and Men*. New York: Negro Universities Press, 1935.

———. *Their Eyes Were Watching God.* New York: Harper and Row, 1990.

Hymes, Dell. "Speech and Language: On the Origins and Foundations of Inequality among Speakers," *Daedalus*, 102 (1973), 59–75.

Irigaray, Luce. *Speculum of the Other Woman.* Trans. Gillian C. Gill. Ithaca: Cornell University Press, 1985.

James, Henry. *The Notebooks of Henry James.* Ed. F. O. Matthiessen and Kenneth B. Murdoch. New York: Oxford University Press, 1947.

———. *The Novels and Tales of Henry James.* New York Edition. 24 vols. New York: Charles Scribner's Sons, 1909.

———. *The Question of our Speech and The Lesson of Balzac: Two Lectures.* New York: Haskell House, 1972.

Jameson, Fredric. *Fables of Aggression: Wyndham Lewis, The Modernist as Fascist.* Berkeley: University of California Press, 1979.

———. "Postmodernism and Consumer Society," *The Anti-Aesthetic: Essays on Postmodernist Culture.* Ed. Hal Foster. Port Townsend, Wa: Bay Press, 1983, pp. 111–125.

———. *Postmodernism, or, the Cultural Logic of Late Capitalism.* Durham: Duke University Press, 1991.

Jehlen, Myra. "The Family Militant: Domesticity Versus Slavery in *Uncle Tom's Cabin,*" *Criticism*, 31 (Fall 1989), 383–400.

Johnson, Barbara. *The Critical Difference: Essays in the Contemporary Rhetoric of Reading.* Baltimore: Johns Hopkins University Press, 1980.

Kaplan, Amy. "Edith Wharton's Profession of Authorship," *ELH*, 53 (1986), 433–57.

Karcher, Carolyn L. *Shadow over the Promised Land: Slavery, Race, and Violence in Melville's America.* Baton Rouge: Louisiana State University Press, 1980.

Kavanaugh, James H. "That Hive of Subtlety: 'Benito Cereno' and the Liberal Hero," *Ideology and Classic American Literature.* Ed. Sacvan Bercovitch and Myra Jehlen. Cambridge: Harvard University Press, 1986, pp. 352–83.

Kelly, William P. *Plotting America's Past: Fenimore Cooper and the Leather-stocking Tales.* Carbondale: Southern Illinois University Press, 1983.

Kenner, Hugh. *A Homemade World: The American Modernist Writers.* New York: Knopf, 1975.

Kissane, Leedice. "Dangling Constructions in Herman Melville's 'Bartleby,'" *American Speech*, 36 (1961), 195–200.

Klinkowitz, Jerome. *Donald Barthelme: An Exhibition.* Durham: Duke University Press, 1991.

Knox, George. "James's Rhetoric of 'Quotes,'" *College English*, 17 (1956), 293–97.

Korzybski, Alfred. *Science and Sanity.* 4th ed. Lakeville, Conn.: The International Non-Aristotelian Library, 1958.

Kristeva, Julia. *Desire in Language: A Semiotic Approach to Literature and Art.* Ed. Leon S. Roudiez. Trans. Thomas Gora, Alice Jardine, and Leon S. Roudiez. New York: Columbia University Press, 1980.

Kwant, Remy C. *Phenomenology of Language.* Pittsburgh: Duquesne University Press, 1965.

Labov, William. *Language in the Inner City.* University Park: University of Pennsylvania Press, 1972.

Lacan, Jacques. *Écrits.* Paris: Seuill, 1966.

Lakoff, Robin. *Language and Woman's Place.* New York: Harper, 1975.

Lang, Amy Schrager. "Slavery and Sentimentalism: The Strange Career of Augustine St. Clare," *Women's Studies*, 12 (1986), 31–54.

Langland, Elizabeth. *Society in the Novel.* Chapel Hill: University of North Carolina Press, 1984.

Lanham, Richard A. *The Motives of Eloquence: Literary Rhetoric in the Renaissance.* New Haven: Yale University Press, 1976.

Lawrence, D. H. *Studies in Classic American Literature.* New York: Viking Press, 1964.

Lebowitz, Alan. *Progress into Silence: A Study of Melville's Heroes.* Bloomington: Indiana University Press, 1970.

Leech, Geoffrey N. and Michael H. Short. *Style in Fiction: A Linguistic Introduction to English Fictional Prose.* London: Longman, 1981.

Leverenz, David. *The Language of Puritan Feeling: An Exploration in Literature, Psychology, and Social History.* New Brunswick: Rutgers University Press, 1980.

Lewis, R. W. B. *The American Adam: Innocence, Tragedy and Tradition in the Nineteenth Century.* Chicago: University of Chicago Press, 1955.

Lewis, Roger. "Money, Love, and Aspiration in *The Great Gatsby*," *New Essays on The Great Gatsby.* Ed. Matthew J. Bruccoli. Cambridge: Cambridge University Press, 1985, pp. 41–57.

Locke, John. *An Essay Concerning Human Understanding.* Ed. Peter H. Nidditch. Oxford: Clarendon Press, 1975.

Lodge, David. *The Language of Fiction: Essays in Criticism and Verbal Analysis of the English Novel.* London: Routledge and Kegan Paul, 1966.

———. *The Modes of Modern Writing: Metaphor, Metonymy, and the Typology of Modern Literature.* Ithaca: Cornell University Press, 1977.

Lotman, Yuri with B. A. Uspensky. "On the Semiotic Mechanism of Culture." Trans. George Mehaychuk. *New Literary History*, 9 (1978), 211–32.

Lukács, Georg. *History and Class Consciousness: Studies in Marxist Dialectics.* Trans. Rodney Livingstone. Cambridge, Mass.: M.I.T. Press, 1971.

Lukacs, John. *The Passing of the Modern Age.* New York: Harper & Row, 1970.

Lyotard, Jean François. *The Postmodern Condition: A Report on Knowledge.* Minneapolis: University of Minnesota Press, 1984.

Mailloux, Steven. "Reading *Huckleberry Finn*: The Rhetoric of Performed Ideology," *New Essays on Adventures of Huckleberry Finn*. Ed. Louis J. Budd. Cambridge: Cambridge University Press, 1985, pp. 107–33.

Mallarmé, Stephane. *Selected Prose Poems, Essays, and Letters*. Trans. Bradford Cook. Baltimore: Johns Hopkins University Press, 1956.

Marcuse, Herbert. *One-Dimensional Man: Studies in the Ideology of Advanced Industrial Society*. Boston: Beacon Press, 1964.

Martin, Harold C. "The Development of Style in Nineteenth-Century American Fiction," *Style in Prose Fiction*. Ed. Harold C. Martin. New York: Columbia University Press, 1959, pp. 114–41.

Matthews, John T. *The Play of Faulkner's Language*. Ithaca: Cornell University Press, 1982.

Matthiessen, F. O. *American Renaissance*. New York: Oxford University Press, 1941.

McCall, Dan. *The Silence of Bartleby*. Ithaca: Cornell University Press, 1989.

McHale, Brian. *Postmodernist Fiction*. New York: Methuen, 1987.

McKay, Janet Holmgren. " 'An Art So High': Style in *Adventures of Huckleberry Finn*," New Essays on Adventures of Huckleberry Finn. Ed. Louis J. Budd. Cambridge: Cambridge University Press, 1985, pp. 61–81.

McWilliams, John P. *Political Justice in a Republic: James Fenimore Cooper's America*. Berkeley: University of California Press, 1972.

Melville, Herman. *Billy Budd, Sailor (An Inside Narrative)*. Ed. Harrison Hayford and Merton M. Sealts, Jr. Chicago: University of Chicago Press, 1962.

———. *The Confidence-Man: His Masquerade*. New York: Hendricks House, 1954.

———. *The Letters of Herman Melville*. Ed. Merrell R. Davis and William H. Gilman. New Haven: Yale University Press, 1960.

———. *The Writings of Herman Melville*. Ed. Harrison Hayford, et al. 15 vols. Evanston and Chicago: Northwestern University Press and the Newberry Library, 1988.

Merrill, Robert. "Vonnegut's *Breakfast of Champions*: The Conversion of Heliogabalus," *Critique*, 18 (1977), 99–109.

Messent, Peter. "*Breakfast of Champions*: The Direction of Kurt Vonnegut's Fiction," *Journal of American Studies*, 8 (1974), 101–14.

———. *New Readings of the American Novel: Narrative Theory and Its Application*. New York: St. Martin's, 1990.

Michaels, Walter Benn. *The Gold Standard and the Logic of Naturalism: American Literature at the Turn of the Century*. Berkeley: University of California Press, 1987.

Minter, David L. *The Interpreted Design as a Structural Principle in American Prose*. New Haven: Yale University Press, 1969.

Mitchell, Lee Clark. " 'Nobody but Our Gang Warn't Around': The Authority of Language in *Huckleberry Finn*," *New Essays on Adventures of Huckle-*

berry Finn. Ed. Louis J. Budd. Cambridge: Cambridge University Press, 1985, pp. 83–106.

Moers, Ellen. *Harriet Beecher Stowe and American Literature*. Hartford: Stowe-Day Foundation, 1978.

Molesworth, Charles. *Donald Barthelme's Fiction: The Ironist Saved From Drowning*. Columbia, Mo.: University of Missouri Press, 1982.

O'Barr, William M. and Bowman K. Atkins, " 'Women's Language' or 'Powerless Language' "? *Women and Language in Literature and Society*. Ed. Sally McConnell-Ginet, Ruth Borker, and Nelly Furman. New York: Praeger, 1980, pp. 93–136.

Ogden, C. K. and I. A. Richards. *The Meaning of Meaning*. 4th ed. rev. London: Routledge & Kegan Paul, 1926.

Ostrom, Alan. "Huck Finn and the Modern Ethos," *Centennial Review*, 16 (1972), 162–79.

Page, Norman. *Speech in the English Novel*. London: Longman, 1973.

Palmieri, Frank. "Neither Literally nor as Metaphor: Pynchon's *Crying* and the Structure of Scientific Revolutions," *ELH*, 54 (Winter 1987), 979–99.

Parker, Herschel. "The 'Sequel' in 'Bartleby,' " *Bartleby the Inscrutable*. Ed. M. Thomas Inge. Hamden: Archon, 1979, pp. 159–65.

Pinsker, Sanford. " 'Bartleby the Scrivener': Language as Wall," *College Literature*, 2 (1975), 17–27.

Pops, Martin. *The Melville Archetype*. Kent: Kent State University Press, 1970.

Portelli, Alessandro. *Il testo e la voce: oralità, scrittura e democrazia nella letteratura americana*. Rome: Manifestolibri, 1992.

Pratt, Mary Louise. "Ideology and Speech-Act Theory," *Poetics Today*, 7 (1986), 59–72.

––––––. *Toward a Speech Act Theory of Literary Discourse*. Bloomington: Indiana University Press, 1977.

Przybylowicz, Donna. *Desire and Repression: The Dialectic of Self and Other in the Late Works of Henry James*. University, Ala.: University of Alabama Press, 1986.

Pynchon, Thomas. *The Crying of Lot 49*. Philadelphia: J. B. Lippincott, 1966.

Quirk, Tom. *Melville's Confidence Man: From Knave to Knight*. Columbia: University of Missouri Press, 1982.

Ragussis, Michael. "Family Discourse and Fiction in *The Scarlet Letter*," *ELH*, 49 (Winter 1982), 863–888.

Rans, Geoffrey. *Cooper's Leather-Stocking Novels: A Secular Reading*. Chapel Hill: University of North Carolina Press, 1991.

Rimmon-Kenan, Shlomith. *Narrative Fiction: Contemporary Poetics*. London: Methuen, 1983.

Robbe-Grillet, Alain. *For a New Novel: Essays on Fiction*. Trans. Richard Howard. New York: Grove Press, 1965.

Robinson, Forrest G. *In Bad Faith: The Dynamics of Deception in Mark Twain's America*. Cambridge, Mass.: Harvard University Press, 1986.

Rogin, Michael Paul. *Subversive Genealogy: The Politics and Art of Herman Melville*. Berkeley: University of California Press, 1979.

Rosaldo, Michelle Z. "The Things We Do with Words: Ilongot Speech Acts and Speech Act Theory in Philosophy," *Language in Society*, 11 (1982), 203–37.

Ross, Stephen M. " 'Voice' in Narrative Texts: The Example of *As I Lay Dying*," *PMLA*, 94 (1979), 300–310.

Roth, Philip. *The Anatomy Lesson*. New York: Farrar, Straus & Giroux, 1983.

Rothschild, Herbert, Jr. "The Language of Mesmerism in 'The Quarter-Deck' Scene in *Moby-Dick*," *English Studies*, 53 (1972), 235–38.

Rowe, John Carlos. *Through the Custom-House: Nineteenth-Century American Fiction and Modern Theory*. Baltimore: Johns Hopkins Press, 1982.

Rowe, Joyce A. *Equivocal Endings in Classic American Novels*. Cambridge: Cambridge University Press, 1988.

Salinger, J. D. *The Catcher in the Rye*. New York: Bantam, 1964.

Sandy, Alan F., Jr. "The Voices of Cooper's *The Deerslayer*," *ESQ*, 60 (1970), 5–9.

Saussure, Ferdinand de. *Course in General Linguistics*. Ed. Charles Bally and Albert Sechehaye. Trans. Wade Baskin. New York: McGraw-Hill, 1966.

Scarry, Elaine. *The Body in Pain: The Making and Unmaking of the World*. New York: Oxford University Press, 1985.

Schatt, Stanley. *Kurt Vonnegut, Jr.* Boston: Twayne, 1976.

Schwartz, Nina. "Lovers' Discourse in *The Sun Also Rises*: A Cock and Bull Story," *Criticism*, 26 (Winter 1984), 49–69.

Searle, John R. "A Classification of Illocutionary Acts," *Language in Society*, 5 (1976), 1–23.

———. *Expression and Meaning: Studies in the Theory of Speech Acts*. Cambridge, Mass.: Cambridge University Press, 1979.

———. "Indirect Speech Acts," *Speech Acts. Syntax and Semantics*. Ed. Peter Cole and Jerry L. Morgan. Vol. 3. New York: Academic Press, 1975, pp. 59–82.

———. "The Logical Status of Fictional Discourse," *New Literary History*, 6 (1975), 319–32.

———. *Speech Acts: An Essay in the Philosophy of Language*. Cambridge, Mass.: Cambridge University Press, 1969.

See, Fred. G. *Desire and the Sign: Nineteenth-Century American Fiction*. Baton Rouge: Louisiana State University Press, 1987.

Seelye, John D. *Melville: The Ironic Diagram*. Evanston: Northwestern University Press, 1970.

Sewell, David R. *Mark Twain's Languages: Discourse, Dialogue, and Linguistic Variety*. Berkeley: University of California Press, 1987.

Showalter, Elaine. "The Death of the Lady (Novelist): Wharton's *House of Mirth*," *representations*, 9 (1985), 133–49.

Simpson, David. *The Politics of American English 1776–1850*. New York: Oxford University Press, 1986.

Small, Michael. "Hawthorne's *The Scarlet Letter*: Arthur Dimmesdale's Manipulation of Language," *American Imago*, 37 (1980), 113–23.

Smith, Barbara Herrnstein. *On the Margins of Discourse: The Relation of Literature to Language*. Chicago: University of Chicago Press, 1978.

Smith, David. "Huck, Jim, and American Racial Discourse," *Mark Twain Journal*, 22 (Fall, 1984), pp. 4–12.

Smith, Henry Nash. Introduction. *Adventures of Huckleberry Finn*. Cambridge, Mass.: Houghton Mifflin, 1958.

——— . *Virgin Land: The American West as Symbol and Myth*. Cambridge, Mass.: Harvard University Press, 1951.

Smith, Herbert F. "Melville's Master in Chancery and His Recalcitrant Clerk," *American Quarterly*, 17 (1966), 734–41.

Smith, Philip M. *Language, the Sexes and Society*. Oxford: Basil Blackwell, 1985.

Spencer, Benjamin. *The Quest for Nationality*. Syracuse: Syracuse University Press, 1957.

Spilka, Mark. "The Death of Love in *The Sun Also Rises*," *Hemingway and His Critics: An International Anthology*. Ed. Carlos Baker. New York: Hill and Wang, 1961, pp. 80–92.

Stein, Jean. "The Art of Fiction XII: William Faulkner," *Paris Review*, 12 (1956), 28–53.

Stepto, Robert B. *From Behind the Veil: A Study of Afro-American Narrative*. Urbana: University of Illinois Press, 1979.

Stern, Milton R. *The Golden Moment: The Novels of F. Scott Fitzgerald*. Urbana: University of Illinois Press, 1970.

Stowe, Harriet Beecher. *The Life and Letters of Harriet Beecher Stowe*. Ed. Annie Fields. Boston: Houghton-Mifflin, 1897.

——— . *Oldtown Folks*. Ed. Henry F. May. Cambridge, Mass.: Harvard University Press, 1966.

——— . *Uncle Tom's Cabin or Life Among the Lowly*. New York: Viking Penguin, 1981.

Sundquist, Eric J. "Benito Cereno and New World Slavery," *Reconstructing American Literary History*. Ed. Sacvan Bercovitch. Cambridge, Mass.: Harvard University Press, 1986, pp. 93–122.

——— . "Suspense and Tautology in *Benito Cereno*," *Glyph*, 8 (1981), 103–26.

Sussman, Henry. "The Deconstructor as Politician: Melville's *Confidence-Man*," *Glyph*, 4 (1978), 32–56.

Swingewood, Alan. *The Sociology of Literature*. New York: Schocken, 1972.

Tani, Stefano. *The Doomed Detective.* Carbondale: Southern Illinois University Press, 1984.

Tanner, Tony. *City of Words: American Fiction, 1950–1970.* New York: Harper and Row, 1971.

Thomas, Brook. *Cross-examination of Law and Literature: Cooper, Hawthorne, Stowe, and Melville.* Cambridge: Cambridge University Press, 1987.

Tichi, Cecelia. "Melville's Craft and Theme of Language Debased in *The Confidence-Man,*" *ELH,* 39 (1972), 639–58.

Tocqueville, Alexis de. *Democracy in America.* Ed. J. P. Mayer and Max Lerner. Trans. George Lawrence. New York: Harper & Row, 1966.

Todorov, Tzvetan. *The Poetics of Prose.* Trans. Richard Howard. Ithaca: Cornell University Press, 1977.

Tompkins, Jane. *Sensational Designs: The Cultural Work of American Fiction 1790–1860.* New York: Oxford University Press, 1985.

Trachtenberg, Alan. "The Form of Freedom in *Adventures of Huckleberry Finn,*" *Southern Review,* N. S. 6 (1970), 954–71.

Trilling, Diana. *"The House of Mirth* Revisited," *American Scholar,* 32 (1962–63), 113–26.

Trilling, Lionel. *The Liberal Imagination: Essays on Literature and Society.* New York: Scribner, 1976.

———. "Our Hawthorne," *Hawthorne Centenary Essays.* Ed. Roy Harvey Pearce. Columbus: Ohio State University Press, 1964, pp. 429–58.

Trimpi, Helen P. "Harlequin-Confidence-Man: The Satirical Tradition of Commedia Dell'Arte and Pantomime in Melville's *The Confidence-Man,*" *Texas Studies in Literature and Language,* 16 (1974–75), 147–93.

Uspensky, Boris. *A Poetics of Composition: The Structure of the Artistic Text and Typlogy of a Compositional Form.* Trans. Valentina Zavarin and Susan Wittig. Berkeley: University of California Press, 1973.

Volosinov, V. N. *Marxism and the Philosophy of Language.* Trans. Ladislav Matejka and I. R. Titunik. New York: Seminar Press, 1973.

Vonnegut, Kurt. *Breakfast of Champions.* New York: Delacorte Press, 1973.

———. *Wampeters, Foma and Granfalloons.* New York: Delacorte, 1974.

Warhol, Robyn. "Toward a Theory of the Engaging Narrator: Earnest Interventions in Gaskell, Stowe, and Eliot," *PMLA,* 101 (1986), 811–818.

Washington, Mary Helen. Foreword to Zora Neale Hurston, *Their Eyes Were Watching God.* New York: Harper and Row, 1990, pp. vii–xiv.

———. "'I Love the Way Janie Crawford Left Her Husbands': Zora Neale Hurston's Emergent Female Hero," *Invented Lives: Narratives of Black Women, 1860–1960.* Garden City: Doubleday, 1987, pp. 237–54.

Watkins, Floyd. *The Flesh and the Word: Eliot, Hemingway, Faulkner.* Nashville: Vanderbilt University Press, 1971.

Watt, Ian. "The First Paragraph of *The Ambassadors*: An Explication," *Essays in Criticism*, 10 (1960), 250–74.

———. *The Rise of the Novel: Studies in Defoe, Richardson and Fielding*. Berkeley: University of California Press, 1967.

Way, Brian. *F. Scott Fitzgerald and the Art of Social Fiction*. New York: St. Martin's, 1980.

Weinsheimer, Joel. "Theory of Character: Emma," *Poetics Today*, 1 (1979), 185–211.

West, Nathanael. *The Complete Works of Nathanael West*. New York: Farrar, Straus & Giroux, 1957.

———. "Some Notes on *Miss Lonelyhearts*," *Contempo*, 3 (1933), 1–2.

Wharton, Edith. *The House of Mirth*. New York: Charles Scribner's Sons, 1905.

———. *The Writing of Fiction* (1925). New York: Octagon Books, 1966.

White, Allon. "Bakhtin, Sociolinguistics and Deconstruction," *The Theory of Reading*. Ed. Frank Gloversmith. Sussex: Harvester Press, 1984, pp. 123–46.

Wiener, Norbert. *The Human Use of Human Beings: Cybernetics and Society*. New York: Discus Books, 1954.

Wilson, James C. " 'Bartleby': The Walls of Wall Street," *Arizona Quarterly*, 37 (Winter, 1981), 335–46.

Wilson, Robert Forrest. *Crusader in Crinoline: The Life of Harriet Beecher Stowe*. Philadelphia: Lippincott, 1941.

Wolff, Cynthia Griffin. *A Feast of Words: The Triumph of Edith Wharton*. New York: Oxford University Press, 1977.

Yeazell, Ruth Bernard. *Language and Knowledge in the Late Novels of Henry James*. Chicago: University of Chicago Press, 1976.

Zelnick, Stephen. "Melville's 'Bartleby the Scrivener': A Study in History, Ideology, and Literature," *Marxist Perspectives*, 8 (1979–80), 74–92.

Ziff, Larzar. "The Social Basis of Hemingway's Style," *Poetics*, 7 (1978), 417–23.

Zimmerman, Don H. and Candace West, "Sex Roles, Interruptions and Silences in Conversation," *Language and Sex: Difference and Dominance*. Ed. Barrie Thorne and Nancy Henley. Rowley, Mass.: Newbury House, 1976, pp. 105–25.

Zwark, Christina. "Fathering and Blackface in *Uncle Tom's Cabin*," NOVEL, 22 (Spring 1989), 274–87.

Index